W9-ACZ-068

Chas. S. Keinodz

Will Rogers

WILL

AN AMERICAN HERITAGE BIOGRAPHY

ROGERS
His Life and Times

by Richard M. Ketchum

In co-operation with
the Will Rogers Memorial Commission
and Staff of the Will Rogers Memorial,
Claremore, Oklahoma

Published by American Heritage Publishing Company, Inc., New York
Book trade distribution by McGraw-Hill Company

Contents

Staff for this Book

Editor
Richard M. Ketchum

Managing Editor
Kaari Ward

Art Director
Terrence Gaughan

Picture Editor
Margaretta Barton
Ellen Zeifer, *Assistant*

**American Heritage
Publishing Co., Inc.**

President and publisher
Paul Gottlieb

Editor-in-Chief
Joseph J. Thorndike

Senior Editor, Book Division
Alvin M. Josephy, Jr.

Editorial Art Director
Murray Belsky

General Manager, Book Division
Kenneth W. Leish

Copyright © 1973 by American
Heritage Publishing Co., Inc. a subsidiary of McGraw-Hill, Inc. All
rights reserved. Printed in the
United States of America. No part
of this publication may be reproduced, stored in a retrieval system,
or transmitted, in any form or by
any means, electronic, mechanical,
photocopying, recording, or otherwise, without the prior written permission of the publisher

Library of Congress
Cataloging in Publication Data

Ketchum, Richard M.   1922–
  Will Rogers, his life and times.

  (An American heritage biography)
  1. Rogers, Will, 1879–1935.
I. Title.
PN2287.R74K45   791'.092'4 [B]
73–8713
ISBN 0–07–034411–6
ISBN 0–07–034412–4 (deluxe)

This book was made possible through the
cooperation and assistance of members of
the Rogers family—especially Will Rogers, Jr.,
and James Rogers; and through the active
participation of the staff at the Will Rogers
Memorial in Claremore, Oklahoma.
In particular, the author and the
publisher wish to express their deep appreciation
to Mrs. Paula McSpadden Love,
Curator of the Will Rogers Memorial,
and to Robert W. Love, its Director,
for their unfailing and generous help.
Their knowledge of Will Rogers and their
dedicated collection and preservation of
all the materials bearing on his life has
transformed what might otherwise have
been only a repository into a living memorial
to an extraordinary man.
Grateful thanks are also due to members
of the staff at the Will Rogers State
Historic Park, Pacific Palisades, California.

Preface

No one ever had quite the same hold on the American public that Will Rogers did. Nearly four decades after his death, people still recall the shy grin, the easy manner, the total absence of sham, and above all, the way he had of putting things that went to the very heart of the matter. Mention his name to one of his contemporaries and the response is an immediate smile and, as often as not, the recollection of a Rogers story that had been tucked away with the memories.

He was, in the first place, a direct link to the original Americans—the Indians—and to the frontier that determined so much of the nation's history. And it was somehow fitting that his story should end in the age of flight, when the United States, having fulfilled its continental destiny, was beginning to taste the power and responsibility that come with leadership of the world.

He was also, as has often been said, the most beloved figure of his time. Americans became acquainted with him in a variety of ways—as a performer in vaudeville and the Ziegfeld Follies, in silent and talking pictures, and radio; as the newspaper columnist whose down to earth, spontaneous humor were the first words they turned to and chuckled over each morning. Tens of millions who had never met him personally considered him their friend, having come to realize that he had a way of speaking for them all. He was a kind of gentle, smiling deputy for everyone who was little or had once been little and who still had love for and faith in the basic institutions of the country. And what he somehow succeeded in doing was to bring the affairs of the world into the living rooms of America, as if he were part of the family, making people realize that the goings on of kings and presidents and congressmen were not much different, after all, than those of the folks next door.

With all the fame that came his way, he never really changed. He was exactly what he seemed to be. "I am just an old country boy in a big town trying to get along," he once wrote. "I have been eating pretty regular and the reason I have is, I have stayed an old country boy."

In the end, the news of Will Rogers' sudden death in an airplane crash made the kind of headlines reserved for the world's great, and the sense of loss was as keen abroad as it was in the land of his birth. It was not simply the realization that a friend was gone but, as one of Will's friends said, that "a smile has disappeared from the lips of America."

THE THOMAS GILCREASE INSTITUTE

"My ancestors didn't come on the *Mayflower* but they met the boat."

WOOLAROC MUSEUM

George Lowrey (left), son of a white man and a Cherokee woman, was painted by George Catlin. The chief was with the first detachment of Cherokees to go west over the Trail of Tears (above) in the great removal. The medal on his chest bears a likeness of James Monroe; it was given to him by the President.

We are the sum of so many diverse parts it is not easy to see where the individual truly begins and where the traces of his ancestry and family, his environment, and other forces leave off. Like so many Americans, Will Rogers was a composite of many worlds. He happened to be born in Indian Territory in 1879, at the time when nearly everyone there bore the scar of that shameful episode in United States history known as the great removal. The Trail of Tears, the Cherokees called it—a forced hegira by which the so-called Five Civilized Tribes (Choctaw, Chickasaw, Creek, Seminole, and Cherokee) had been evicted from their ancestral lands in the southeast in the 1830's and compelled to emigrate beyond the Mississippi River to an alien region.

In all of American history there has been nothing quite like it. For two centuries, to be sure, the natives had been pushed steadily westward by the encroachment of white settlers; but not until Andrew Jackson became President did the process become national policy, nor, until then, was it executed on such a massive scale.

To this day no one knows with certainty what the origins of the Cherokee Nation were. It was a numerous and powerful tribe when encountered by Hernando de Soto in 1540, in possession of a vast region in the southern Appalachians, where the people had been living for as long as archaeological evidence can determine. There were probably about twenty-five thousand Cherokees at the time de Soto met them—farmers and hunters who ranged from the western Carolinas and northwest Georgia into northern Alabama, the Cumberland plateau in Tennessee, and along the Ohio River, spilling over into parts of Virginia and Kentucky. The pattern of their life was to settle in

9

a region, farm there until the soil was exhausted (they used no fertilizer), and then move on, subsisting on the corn, beans, and squash raised by women and on the game provided by hunters. As for so many other Indians, intertribal warfare was a game, indulged in for social status and prestige. Physically, the men were taller than most whites of the day; their hair was plucked, except for a lock at the back of the head; and most of them decorated their olive-colored skin with designs made by pricking the flesh and then staining the holes with gunpowder.

In the settlers' book Cherokees were "warlike"—a term frequently used to justify killing or removing Indians; but it might be more accurate to say that the Cherokees had an abiding unwillingness to be pushed around. James Adair, a historian and trader who lived among them for forty years during the eighteenth century, thought the trait so pronounced that it would lead to their eventual annihilation. And they were as proud as they were determined: as an English officer sent by Virginia's Governor Dinwiddie to enlist their support against the French remarked, "They are like the Devil's pigg, they will neither lead nor drive." Continually fighting with their neighbors—whites, and Indians who had been set against them by whites—they boasted at the time that they could, on short notice, put six thousand braves on the warpath.

The white man, characteristically, tried from the outset to convert them to Christianity. It is recorded of one such encounter that the Indians listened politely to the determined missionary and, when he had finished, informed him that they knew very well that "if they were good they would go up; if bad down; that he could tell them no more; that he had long plagued them with what they nowadays understood and they desired him to depart the country."

In 1760, to the surprise of nearly everyone, the proud, independent Cherokees decided to acknowledge the sovereignty of George II, and seven of them, including two chiefs, sailed for England with an interpreter, were received at Windsor Castle, and overnight became the rage of London. What had provoked this move was the Cherokees' realization that His Majesty's representatives in America usually respected treaty obligations, whereas the colonial frontiersmen, restlessly seeking land and hunting grounds, tended to ignore them. A result of the alliance was that the Cherokees remained loyal to the king during the American Revolution, clinging to the status quo. Hoping to hold onto their land against the white intruders, they fought

When in 1760 the Cherokee delegation reached London on their diplomatic errand the presence of these curiously garbed strangers from another world understandably caused a sensation. Sir Joshua Reynolds painted the portrait of Syacust Ukah (right); Frances Parsons did the impressive. likeness of Cunne Shote. shown far right.

BOTH: THE THOMAS GILCREASE INSTITUTE

COLONIAL WILLIAMSBURG COLLECTION

the rebels long after Charles Cornwallis surrendered at York-town—an action that did nothing to endear them to the citizens of the new republic.

From 1730 on, English, Scottish, German, and Irish entrepreneurs were actively moving about the Cherokee Nation, trading with the Indians, marrying Cherokee women and siring half-breed children, and slowly and inexorably turning members of the tribe toward white ways. Occasionally, white women settled down with Cherokee husbands, and by the end of the eighteenth century so much interbreeding had occurred that the fact of being Cherokee was almost more a state of mind than a question of genetics. (Will Rogers' paternal great-grand-father, an Irishman named Robert Rogers, married a woman named Betty Cordrey, whose father was also Irish and whose mother was a full blood of the Cherokee Blind Savannah clan. On the maternal side Will's great-grandsire, John Gunter, a Welsh trader and powder maker, married a full-blooded Cherokee of the Paint clan.)

Inevitably, other whites were pushing in the perimeters of the hunting grounds, until one Indian complained, "We have no place to hunt on." And in 1775 a Cherokee named Dragging·Canoe protested a cession of land to Richard Henderson's Transylvania Company, stating with remarkable prescience that "We had hoped that the white man would not be willing to travel beyond the mountains. . . . Finally the whole country, which the Cherokees and their fathers have so long occupied will be demanded, and [we] will be compelled to seek refuge in some distant wilderness." In 1791 the tribe negotiated a treaty with George Washington affirming "Perpetual peace between the United States and the Cherokee Nation" and forbidding Americans to hunt on Cherokee lands; but never again did they know a President whose policy was to defend the rights of Indians. Despite that agreement, they were shoved out of South Carolina; whites crowded into the area west of the Great Smokies, and in 1794 the new state of Tennessee was established—half of it, including the town of Nashville, on former tribal lands. Some years later President James Monroe expressed the whites' attitude in a message to Congress, saying, "Independent savage communities cannot long exist within the limits of a civilized population." The answer, he added, was that "their independence as communities should cease."

As their ancestral lands diminished in size, the Cherokees became more unified as a people and—considering their in-

"They sent the Indians to Oklahoma. They had a treaty that said, 'You shall have this land as long as grass grows and water flows.' It was not only a good rhyme but looked like a good treaty, and it was till they struck oil. Then the government took it away from us again. They said the treaty refers to 'water and grass; it don't say anything about oil.'"

from Weekly Article
Feb. 5, 1928

12

dependent spirit—came to a truly remarkable decision concerning future relations with the whites. Since none of their dealings with the settlers had had the slightest effect in preserving the integrity of their property, they concluded early in the nineteenth century (before hearing James Monroe on the subject) that they would adopt the white man's ways, accept his missionaries and religion, welcome his teachers and their message, and reorganize their government, patterning it on that of the new United States. It was, in short, a program that meant almost total abandonment of an ancient culture and its replacement with that of the educated, Christian white, all in hopes of convincing the American that they were entitled to his respect and friendship. As a consequence, they came to be known, along with other tribes of the southeastern U.S., as "civilized" Indians. But little good the white man's civilization did them. Adopting nearly all of his ways, they were turned away and frustrated at every turn; assuming nearly all the aspects of what passes for civilization, they continued to be treated as savages.

By 1820 the territorial limits of the Cherokee Nation had shrunk further: it now extended from the Tennessee River to the Little Tennessee, down the Appalachians to the Chattahoochee River, then west past Kenesaw Mountain, and on to the Tennessee River. Even so, it was a substantial area—about the size of the state of Massachusetts—and the Cherokees had their race's characteristic reverence for it and all it contained. Out in the broad savannas and fertile river basins they were practicing agriculture, raising crops and herds of cattle and other livestock, building homes and roads and schools, trading with whites, and governing themselves on a representational basis. Yet beneath these outward signs of conformity to the white man's ways, they retained a passionate, mystical attachment to the earth that had nurtured them and that held the bones of their ancestors. The forests and streams and springs, the mountains and lush valleys, they regarded as friends and providers—not as property—and it was a concept few whites would ever comprehend.

Neither, however, could the Indians comprehend the attitude reflected by one administration after another in Washington. Abiding by their treaties, which gave them permanent tenure of their lands "as long as grass shall grow and waters flow," the Indians soon found that Presidents Adams, Jefferson, Madison, and Monroe—unlike Washington—were no friends of the Cherokees, while Andrew Jackson proved to be the worst

"To tell you the truth, I am not so sweet on old Andy. He is the one that run us Cherokees out of Georgia and North Carolina. . . . Old Andy, every time he couldn't find any one to jump on, would come back and pounce onto us Indians. . . . But old Andy made the White House. . . . The Indians wanted him in there so he could let us alone for awhile."

from Weekly Article
Feb. 5, 1928

13

AMERICAN ANTIQUARIAN SOCIETY

LIBRARY OF CONGRESS

The Cherokee Phoenix, first published in February, 1828, ran articles in English and in Sequoyah's new syllabary. In the drawing above, Sequoyah points to his characters; combined like letters of the alphabet, they formed words (as x p d n c represents the spoken "expediency").

enemy of all. As one Cherokee viewed their deteriorating relationship with the Federal government, "The Indians . . . don't know how to understand their Father, the President. A few years ago he sent them a plough & a hoe—said it was not good for his red children to hunt—they must cultivate the earth. Now he tells them there is good hunting at the Arkansas: if they go there he will give them rifles." Between 1794 and 1819 the United States government forced the Cherokee Nation into twenty-four treaties involving land cessions (it was little wonder that the Indian referred to the surveyor's compass as the white man's "land stealer"), but the worst was yet to come.

Before long the Cherokees added one more accomplishment to a list of achievements, which was extraordinary by any lights: they became literate almost overnight. Some credit for this must go to the presence of missionaries and to the continuing practice of intermarriage with educated whites (a process that filled the Cherokee Nation with Irish names like Dougherty and Adair, Scotch names like Ross, Vann, and McIntosh); but the giant step was taken after 1821 when a Cherokee named Sequoyah, who also called himself George Gist (his father was purportedly Nathaniel Gist, a Virginia trader and friend of George Washington's), devised a highly successful system of phonetics by which an intelligent Cherokee could bridge the gap between illiteracy and literacy within a matter of days.

After Sequoyah had been disabled in the Creek Wars of 1813–14, he devoted his energies to solving a problem he had been turning over in his mind for years. He was impressed with the white man's system of writing and reading, and after studying linguistics, finally hit on the idea of identifying all the basic syllables in the Cherokee language and adopting a symbol for each one. Then all any Cherokee had to do was to learn the characters and sounds they represented in order to write or read his native tongue. Sequoyah's invention became practicable when a missionary obtained a printing press and a font of movable type, and helped the Indians establish a newspaper called the *Cherokee Phoenix*, whose first issue appeared in 1828. By then the Nation had, in addition to its own written language, a republic, a constitution that had been duly ratified, a principal chief or president, a bicameral legislature, a supreme court, and a codified body of laws. It was a society, one might have thought, worthy of acceptance by white Americans. But no one who believed so reckoned with the greed and cupidity the Cherokees were to encounter from nearby states.

In 1828 the Georgia legislature suddenly declared that it had jurisdiction over all Cherokee lands within the state's boundaries, pronounced Cherokee laws null and void, and subsequently conducted a statewide lottery for distributing the Indians' land and homes to white residents. The mood of the time was reflected in a little song popular among Georgians:

> *All I ask in this creation*
> *Is a pretty little wife and a big plantation*
> *Way up yonder in the Cherokee Nation.*

That same year gold was discovered on Cherokee land. Those whites who poured into the region and who were disappointed in their search for the precious metal were consoled by their first glimpse of the magnificent land—deep woods covered with enormous stands of hickory, oak, chestnut, mountain laurel, magnolias, and azaleas; broad, sunlit savannas where corn, cotton, and orchards bloomed; mountain pastures where cattle and horses grazed. The houses were equally tempting; although many were unpretentious, some were on the scale of small plantations. Peacocks strutted about the grounds of Chief John Ross' place, which was said to resemble that of a "well-to-do farmer in the North," and included a "small and well-organized library." John Martin's elegant home at Rock Springs had marble mantels and hand-carved stairways, and Joseph Vann's residence near Springplace was described as a mansion. The whites took one look and began moving in.

These Georgians were abetted by President Andrew Jackson who, in his first message to Congress, announced plans to remove all the southeast Indians to lands west of the Mississippi River. Within two weeks the Georgia legislature passed a series of laws confiscating huge portions of Cherokee land, prohibiting further meetings of the Cherokee council, and authorizing the arrest of any Indian who influenced his tribesmen not to emigrate westward. In May, 1830, Jackson's intention became law. The bill passed by a slim margin, despite opposition by a number of Congressmen, including Vermont's Horace Everett, who called the Indian Removal Bill "all unmingled, unmitigated evil." The evil, he said, "is enormous; the violence is extreme; the breach of public faith deplorable; the inevitable suffering incalculable." (Afterward, Congressman Davy Crockett humorously proposed a bill for the removal of whites from East Tennessee to a place beyond the Mississippi, lest they stand in the way of Georgia's territorial designs.) For the next eight years the Cherokees—along with the Choctaws, Creeks, Chickasaws, and Seminoles—were to experience an ever-increasing pattern of oppression, brutality, double-dealing, and outright theft that finally culminated in their national disaster known as the great removal. In 1833, after the homes of Chief Ross, John Martin, Joseph Vann, and many others were seized and occupied by Georgia lottery winners, some of the Indians decided to pull up stakes and leave while they could still take their belongings with them. But the ultimate deadline for all was set by the U.S. Senate, which by a single vote ratified a treaty on May 23, 1836, setting a date for the final removal of the Cherokees two years later. During that period about 2,000 Cherokees made their way to the lands bordering the Arkansas River, leaving about 15,000 fellow tribesmen behind.

The government's action stirred up a storm of protest all over the country (interestingly, it was along political lines similar to those drawn prior to the Civil War, with the Northern states opposing removal and the Southern ones favoring it). John Quincy Adams, now a representative from Massachusetts, declared the treaty "infamous" and said, "It brings with it eternal disgrace upon the country." And when General John Ellis

Wool was sent in 1838 to enforce the law, he asked to be relieved of his command as soon as possible. If he could, he said, he would "remove every Indian tomorrow beyond the reach of the white men, who, like vultures, are watching, ready to pounce upon their prey and strip them of everything they have." Wool foresaw all too accurately what would occur, and as a chief of the Cherokees predicted in a final, desperate plea to the President, if the regular Army was not sent to protect the Indians, "we shall carry off nothing but the scars of the lash on our backs."

The exodus began on May 23, 1838, according to schedule, supervised by U.S. Army regulars who, to their lasting credit, treated the Indians with kindliness and respect, and by Georgia volunteers, who regarded their mission as one to dispatch the Cherokees as quickly and as ruthlessly as possible, and urged on the laggards at bayonet point. As one regular recalled years afterward, "I fought through the civil war and have seen men shot to pieces and slaughtered by thousands, but the Cherokee removal was the cruelest work I ever knew." The Indians, he said, were dragged from their homes, and few were permitted time to collect their possessions. "Well-furnished houses were left a prey to plunderers, who, like hungry wolves, follow in the train of the captors. These wretches rifle the houses, and strip the helpless, unoffending owners of all they have. . . . Some, who have been allowed to return home, under passport, to inquire after their property, have found their cattle, horses, swine, farming tools and house furniture all gone."

The summer of 1838 saw the worst heat and drought men could remember, and the Cherokees obtained permission from the Army to conduct their own removal in the fall, after the drought abated. But not until October could they depart, and then thirteen thousand of them, proceeding, one observer said, "like the march of an army, regiment after regiment," set out on the thousand-mile trip toward an unknown land. Those who were to travel by water went to Memphis, where they boarded barges and flatboats for the long, confining voyage down the Mississippi and up the Arkansas to Fort Smith and Fort Coffee. Others went by land—northwest to Nashville, and on to the Ohio River, across the Mississippi and down through Missouri, then west through Arkansas toward Fort Gibson, where they were mustered and given rations.

In camps along the way most of them had only tents and blankets to protect them from the severe early winter; at toll gates they were charged outrageous prices; merchants and farmers on the route gouged them mercilessly when they tried to buy food; their line of wagons bogged down in the November rains, chewing up the muddy roads till they were a soupy morass; and every night when they made camp it was reported that they were burying ten or fifteen of their numbers. One man from Maine who saw them confessed he wept like a child when he witnessed their plight; there were old men and women, newborn babies, pregnant women, the halt, the lame, the blind, the idiots, all without shelter or privacy, suffering from dysentery, measles, whooping cough (earlier emigrations had also had to contend with cholera), preyed on by tricksters who got them drunk on whiskey and then cheated them.

It was little wonder that the pitiful migrants were sick in spirit or that eyewitnesses remarked that they wore the look of death. For to make matters worse, none of them knew what lay ahead. "With regard to the West," one Indian wrote, "all is dark as midnight. . . . O that my head were waters and mine eyes a fountain of tears that I might weep day and night for the slain of the daughters of my people." Behind, on the Trail of Tears, were the shallow graves of four thousand Cherokees—nearly one-fourth of the entire Nation—who had perished along the way.

When at last this caravan of heartbreak and misery arrived in Indian Territory, it was to find that its predecessors in the removal—those who had gone to Arkansas and beyond, were now firmly entrenched and regarded themselves as old settlers. They had their own farms, mills, and stores, their own government, and they were not eager to share any of this on an equitable basis with the new arrivals. For a time the two groups came close to civil war, and not until 1846, when the Cherokees were given land in what is now eastern Oklahoma and were reimbursed to some extent for their losses in the southeast, did anything like harmony prevail in the relocated Nation.

Yet somehow the Cherokees survived the shattered wreckage of their past. Patiently, painstakingly, they went about the business of creating a new society, clearing and plowing the land, building schools, churches, and government buildings, and initiating diplomatic relations with the other Civilized Tribes and the neighboring Plains Indians. They had no way of knowing it, of course, but their isolation from the white man was to be no more than temporary.

Inauguration of the last principal chief of the Cherokees, 1843, in Tahlequah

WESTERN HISTORY COLLECTIONS, UNIVERSITY OF OKLAHOMA LIBRARY

BOTH: WILL ROGERS MEMORIAL, CLAREMORE, OKLA.

"My father was one-eighth Cherokee Indian and my mother was a quarter-blood."

The only existing picture of Will's mother, Mary America Rogers, appears at left. "What little humor I have" came from her, he said; "I don't remember her humor but I can remember her love and understanding of me." The photograph above shows his father Clem as a youth.

Among the hundreds of Cherokee families from Georgia who had moved west in anticipation of the removal was Robert Rogers and his wife, Sallie Vann, both of whom bore that blend of blood which led some Americans to refer to the Cherokees as "white Indians." Robert Rogers' father was a white man, his mother was part Indian; Sallie was one-fourth Cherokee and three-quarters Irish; and when the couple set out for Arkansas Territory in the 1830's they carried most of the same dreams and plans that were part of all pioneers' baggage. A big, brusque, dark-skinned man, Rogers settled in 1835 or 1836 in the Going Snake district in what is now Oklahoma; there he built a five-room log house, established a ranch, and prospered almost immediately in the fertile bottom land where he had the use of all the acreage he could maintain for his longhorn cattle and horses. When a child, Clement Vann, was born to the couple in 1839, Robert Rogers had only one more year to live, but it is with his son that the story of Will Rogers properly begins.

Clem grew up on his father's ranch and attended a Baptist mission school and the Cherokee-run Male Seminary at Tahlequah. But he hated classes and did not get along with his stepfather (he was five when his mother married William Musgrove, and Clem not only refused to attend the ceremony but threw rocks at the newlyweds as they drove off on their honeymoon). At the age of seventeen—restless, ambitious, eager to strike out on his own—he left home to find a new life in what was called the Cooweescoowee country, bordering the Verdigris River. His mother and long-suffering stepfather gave him twenty-five longhorn cows, a bull, four horses, supplies for the ranch and trading post he intended to start, and two Negro slaves named Rabb and Huse, who had belonged to his father.

The last Confederate general to surrender at the end of the Civil War was Cherokee leader Stand Watie.
COLLECTION OF MR. & MRS. JOHN MAHONEY

In 1856, the year he arrived with his stake, the Coowee-scoowee district was virgin land, held in common by the Cherokee Nation for use by any of its members. While his two slaves devoted their time to farming, planting corn to feed the livestock, young Clem turned his cattle out on the bluestem grass that stretched unbroken for miles. The story is told that Clem, who was always quick to see and seize an opportunity, camped near a trading post operated by Osage Indians, and before long he was running the store and the Osages were peering in from the outside. He built a two-room log house, his business flourished, and several years later he married a tall, dark-haired girl named Mary America Schrimsher, whom he had met in Tahlequah. A quarter-breed Cherokee—her father was Dutch, her mother half-Welsh and half-Indian—Mary had attended a Cherokee school in Arkansas and may have gone to the Female Seminary at Tahlequah. When she moved to Clem's ranch the only neighbors were a few scattered settlers, itinerant fur traders, and Osage Indians who came to the post to trade or steal; the prairie was a sea of bluestem grass where wild turkeys, quail, and prairie chickens were as "thick as blackbirds," as one old-timer recalled. In the Verdigris bottom land were wild geese, flocks of green parakeets, deer, wolves, and panthers. Life was not easy, but both the ranch and trading post were successful, and for three years it began to look as if Clem's future was secure. Then, as it had so often in the past, the shadow of the white man fell across the Cherokee land.

It was 1861, and the Rogers ranch was only thirty miles from the Kansas border, where Union and Confederate sympathizers were turning the prairies into as dark and bloody a ground as anything the Cherokee Nation had known in the southeast. The Indians were as divided on the subject of the conflict between North and South as they had been over the question of the removal (even the Negro brothers Rabb and Huse, Clem's slaves, fought on opposite sides during the war). A good many of the so-called white Indians—the mixed bloods—owned slaves, as Clem Rogers did, whereas few full bloods had them. John Ross, the principal chief of the Cherokee Nation, hoped to preserve neutrality, but he was increasingly frustrated in this by the belligerence of the mixed bloods, who were led by Stand Watie, and by offers made to the Nation by agents of the Confederacy. Southerners were quick to see that the Indian Territory provided bases for raids into Kansas, gave them a highway into Texas, and could furnish supplies they needed;

and when David L. Hubbard, the Confederacy's commissioner of Indian Affairs, appealed to the Cherokees to support the South, there were few who could deny the logic of his message.

"Go North among the once powerful tribes, " he told them, ". . . and see if you can find Indians living, and enjoying power and property & Liberty, as do your people and the neighboring Tribes from the South. If you can, then say I am a liar and the Northern States have been better to the Indian than the Southern States." And on October 7, 1861, the Cherokee Nation made an alliance with the Confederate States of America. (Even so, numerous tribesmen fought with the Union Army, and the scars of the war lasted for years. As one Cherokee Confederate recalled, "We all carried guns until statehood and hung blankets over our lighted windows at night."

After sending Mary to his mother's home (where she remained for a time before going to her family's place in Tahlequah and finally fleeing for safety with her parents and sisters to Texas), Clem enlisted in the Cherokee Mounted Rifle Regiment. He served as captain under Stand Watie, who became a Confederate brigadier general in 1864 and had the distinction of fighting on for two months after Appomattox—the last Confederate general to surrender. When the war ended, the Federal government contended that the Five Civilized Tribes had forfeited their lands by supporting the Confederacy, but eventually the U.S. took only the western portions of their territory, as a future home for other Indian tribes, and left them the eastern section under previous treaty status. The Indians were required to liberate their former slaves, of course, and it was hoped that the tribes would form a united territorial government that would eventually become a state. One treaty referred to this potential commonwealth as "Oklahoma," from the Choctaw *okla homma*, meaning "red people."

Returning after four years of war, Clem Rogers found that the entire Cherokee Nation was devastated, and that everything he had left behind was gone: his own ranch had been overrun by troops and had grown up to brush, his cattle and horses were confiscated, his slaves freed, and there was no money with which to begin again. After joining Mary and their baby Sallie in Texas, he made his way back toward the old homestead by degrees, stopping for a year with his mother and stepfather in the Choctaw Nation while he raised a crop, moving on to Fort Gibson the following year, where he restored his sister-in-law's home and put in another crop. In 1867 he was still in Fort Gibson, but now he hired a Cherokee boy to farm for him while he went to work for a German named Oliver Lipe who owned a store and a mill, and Clem spent two hard years driving a six-mule freight wagon from Kansas City to Sedalia and on to Fort Gibson, saving enough money, finally, to buy some cattle in partnership with Lipe's son, Major. Now he was ready to return to the Cooweescoowee country.

In 1868 he chose a location for his second ranch, about seven miles east of the original one, in the middle of thousands of untouched acres of rolling prairie covered with tall bluestem grass. This land, according to the traditional practice of the Cherokees, was free to anyone who would occupy and improve it, the only stipulation being that he could not encroach on land claimed by his neighbors. As long as a man occupied the land, in other words, it was his; when he vacated it, anyone had a right to take possession and hold it, paying the original owner only for the improvements, but owning it outright as though he held the title. All things considered, the region Clem Rogers picked out was a rancher's paradise. Rich grazing land abounded (there were, of course, no fences anywhere in the area); the fertile Verdigris River bottom land provided abundant water for livestock and soil that would support wheat, alfalfa, corn, vegetables, fruit, and other produce. The summers were long, the winters mild, the grass as good as any that grew, and it was the best possible place for fattening cattle. It was and is gentle country, where you come up on top of a rise and suddenly see for a distance of twenty miles, and Clem's site was in the "blue mound" region of the Verdigris valley—grazing lands spotted here and there with earthen mounds that seem to have been placed there by accident, with no rhyme or reason to them.

In the fall of 1870 Clem brought Mary to the new ranch, where he had constructed a log house and fenced off several acres for gardens and farm crops, and three years later they began building what was to be their permanent home—a structure of hewn logs, plastered on the inside and weather-boarded on the outside, two stories high, with seven large rooms. Downstairs was the big, square parlor with an open fireplace, the only piano in the Cooweescoowee district, and curtains hung with lace; across the entrance hall was the family bedroom, where their children would be born; and in the rear, in an addition that ran along the north end of the house, were the dining room, kitchen, and a bunkroom for cowboys working on the ranch.

On the second floor were two large bedrooms, which were eventually used by the Rogers daughters. When the house was finally completed in 1875 and painted white, it was an imposing place, considered to be one of the finest homes in the Territory. Facing south, the house stood at the foot of a rocky hill that protected it from north winds. Barns, granaries, other outbuildings, and corrals were situated to the east, and the whole complex looked off toward the Verdigris valley, three-quarters of a mile away, beyond which lay the mesalike hills. North and west were hundreds of miles of bluestem country, the grass waving in the ever-present wind (from the air the ranch would have appeared like an oasis in the great prairie); the nearest towns of any consequence were Coffeyville, Kansas, 40-odd miles to the north, and Fort Gibson, 60 miles south in Indian Territory. There were few roads worth mentioning in any part of this country, and provisions came to the ranch once a month by freight wagon, while mail from the outside world arrived three times a week from Coffeyville by buckboard.

This home place that Clem and Mary America Rogers had created in the unbroken grassland of Indian Territory was a great deal more than the word "home" suggests. Like so many of the first homesteads across frontier America, it quickly became a focal point of the entire region, a gathering place for distant neighbors and passers-by, for this was a time when towns, farmsteads, and campfires were few and far between, when every man needed his neighbor and was needed in turn, when nobody remained a stranger for long.

Mary Rogers seems to have possessed a quality that made the ranch a warm, inviting place that everyone liked to visit. In front of the house, flanking the broad stone walk from the front gate to the porch, a row of cedars was planted, and the picket fence was lined with flowers—jonquils, hyacinths, cockscomb, and bachelor's-buttons. Families moving into the Verdigris valley were all welcome, and Mary—a gay, lighthearted soul with a fine sense of humor and a love of music and dancing—was always asking entire families to spend the night so that they could enjoy an evening of square-dancing and songs with the family and the cowhands. She and Clem were also known for their willingness to help anyone in trouble, and friends remembered how Mary would travel on horseback or in a buggy, day or night, to take food to the sick. By 1878 seven children had been born to Mary and Clem—five girls and two boys—but, as was so often the case in those days, three died in infancy, leaving

Some have **JH** on side. Texas cattle have horizontal bar on left loin. Horses branded **JH** on left hip.

Clem Vann Rogers marked his cattle with the distinctive "CV" brand shown above.
WILL ROGERS MEMORIAL, CLAREMORE, OKLA.

"In those days a Doctor would bring you into the World for two Dollars a visit, and make good money at it. . . . I was named by an Indian Chief, William Penn Adair, he says Mary I want another young Chief named for me, I name him Will Penn Adair Rogers. . . . I just looked at him when he named me and thought by the time I get big enough to be Chief we wont have any more Country than a Jay Bird."

from notes for Will Rogers' autobiography

only Sallie, Robert, Maud, and Mary. On November 4, 1879, the eighth and last child was born, a boy who was christened William Penn Adair Rogers for his father's Civil War comrade in arms and close friend.

At the time Will Rogers was born his father was one of the most successful and prominent men in the Territory. Unlike Will's mother, Clem was gruff and rather forbidding by some accounts, but he was known as a man who could be taken at his word. A shrewd, ambitious, driving businessman, he had staked out his range before the country was surveyed and before township lines were established, and had placed his corners so that the ranch included everything needed for raising cattle — rich grassland, fresh water, cropland, trees that protected the animals from the summer sun, hills that sheltered them in winter. The Rogers range included about sixty thousand acres, forming an enormous V or wedge between the Caney River on the west and the Verdigris on the east. Each side of the V was about 12 miles long, and the open end at the top was about 15 miles from river to river. The Caney and the Verdigris helped to keep his herd from drifting off to east or west, but the northern boundary, near the Kansas border, where Clem's land was adjacent to the grazing land of other ranchers, had to be patrolled continually by line riders — cowboys who were out all year round, turning back cattle that strayed onto a neighbor's land.

The rhythm of ranch life was determined by the manner in which the cattle were collected, fattened, and marketed. Texas was the breeding ground for numberless thousands of longhorns, and at a time when steak sold for 25 cents a pound in New York City a steer on the range could be bought for $1 or $2. The animals that far-sighted cattlemen began driving north after the Civil War were the lean, rangy descendants of cattle brought to America by the Spaniards, and which had escaped from missions in the eighteenth century and had run wild through southern Texas; they were, first and last, virtually untamable. "We have seen some buffaloes that were more civilized," a St. Louis newspaper noted in 1854. It was estimated that five million of these beasts, untended, were ranging the Texas frontier when the Civil War's end released thousands of men who returned home, looking for work and opportunity. And, simultaneously, the North and the Rocky Mountain West were clamoring for beef.

Texas trail bosses like Charles Goodnight and Oliver Loving

TEXT CONTINUED ON PAGE 30

Southwest Cattle Empire

NEW YORK PUBLIC LIBRARY, SPENCER COLLECTION

No artist caught the action of the Western cattle country better than Charles M. Russell, whose sketch this is. The photograph of the roundup was taken near Woodward City, Oklahoma Territory, in 1897.

TEXAS HISTORY CENTER, UNIVERSITY OF TEXAS

COLLECTION OF FANNIE B. MISCH

After the Texas cattle were rounded up, the trail drive began. Above, a herd crosses the Arkansas River near present-day Tulsa. Clem Rogers fattened such steers for market on the native bluestem grass.

KANSAS STATE HISTORICAL SOCIETY

Cowboys relax around a chuck wagon (above) on a trail drive. Below, at left, is a roundup scene about 1900; and below is a town typical of so many that sprang up around railheads in the Territory.

BOTH: WESTERN HISTORY COLLECTIONS, UNIVERSITY OF OKLAHOMA LIBRARY

As soon as a cowboy roped a calf, a member of the branding team moved in to throw it to the ground.

showed the way, and in their footsteps came dozens of other entrepreneurs like Clem Rogers, eager to take advantage of the opportunity represented by bringing a much-needed commodity to a waiting market. Completion of the transcontinental railroad in 1869 opened the way to East and West coasts; investors from England and Scotland were buying up thousands of acres of buffalo grass; the buffalo themselves were being slaughtered by the millions; and big ranches were opening up all the way to the plains of Wyoming and Montana. Equally important, there were new meat-processing plants in Chicago and St. Louis, and new railheads in Kansas.

Ranchers thought the bonanza would go on forever; most Americans believed that the great plains were a semiarid desert where agriculture could not succeed, and the attitude of cattlemen was expressed by one of them, who remarked, "This aint' no country fer little two-by-four farmers. . . . The big thing about the plains is that you don't have to feed stock. It can rustle fer itself . . . [and] the dollars crawl into yer jeans." And so, for a few years, they did.

While two men held the animal (still on the end of the rope), a third cowboy branded it with the hot iron.
BOTH: LIBRARY OF CONGRESS

Clem Rogers bought steers in Texas, drove them to his ranch for a year's fattening on bluestem grass, then trailed them to St. Louis, which was the closest market. At the time of Will's birth he was already handling as many as five thousand head a year this way. After assembling a herd in Texas, it took two or three months to drive it to the Verdigris valley—a trip that was made across miles of open country, over streams swollen with spring rains, and in totally unpredictable weather. Customarily, the cowboys would drive the herd 20 or 30 miles a day at the outset to tire the wild, spooky animals; from then on they were more likely to cover 12 or 15 miles daily. At dawn they would get the cattle to drifting along, grazing as they went; by mid-morning they would push them closer together, getting the lead steers to move faster while the flanks of the herd were nudged inward until the long line of animals—perhaps a thousand or more—was strung out over several miles. At noon the cattle grazed while the cowboys ate at the chuck wagon; then the process began all over again, with the herd moving northward until twilight. With the coming of darkness the men rode slowly

31

around the herd, in ever-decreasing circles, moving the long-horns into a compact mass until they lay down for the night. All through the hours of darkness the cowboys took turns on watch, circling the herd, softly singing to quiet the animals, always on the alert for the sudden noise—a flash of lightning, a clap of thunder, even the snapping of a stick—that would startle the cattle into a stampede.

Fire was the most fearsome, dreaded event on the prairie. Often a sudden thunderstorm would come up, lightning would strike the ground, and—because there was nothing to stop it—would gather into a huge rolling ball of flame and race across the plains for miles until it burst with a deafening explosion. Sometimes in fall or winter a prairie fire would start, and the flames would rush along the dry grass, roaring across the land like an immense tidal wave driven by the wind, raging for days or even weeks, blackening the sod for hundreds of miles, killing animals, destroying houses and barns, and ruining the land for grazing until the following spring.

A cowboy had to be as skilled at his trade as any craftsman, and the horse he rode almost human in his understanding of what was required of him. Clem Rogers loved fine horses, and he purchased or raised some of the best animals in the Territory, keeping as many as a hundred fifty brood mares and retaining choice cow ponies for use in the business. In cutting out a calf from the herd, these ponies would take after it, following every turn it made, putting the rider in the best position for lassoing it; the moment the rope went over the calf's head the pony would slow down, stop, draw the rope tight and keep it taut until the cowboy had the animal tied. On the trail these cow ponies knew how to move quietly and slowly; they could swim rivers and avoid potholes or fences at night; and they were absolutely essential in every aspect of the cattle business—cutting out and catching steers, tying, branding, penning, and shipping them.

On the Rogers ranch three big roundups were held every year. In the spring the new calves were collected for branding with Clem's "CV" mark; in summer there was a beef roundup, when fat steers were herded together for shipment to market; and in the fall all the animals on the range were rounded up and sorted out—those belonging to the Rogers ranch to be taken to winter range, while strays from other herds were returned to their owners. The calf roundup in the spring took from six to eight weeks, and for days on end the cowboys would turn their ponies into the herd, work a cow and her calf out of it, rope the calf, and drag it to the branding fire. One man would grab the animal, throw it to the ground, and hold its head and front leg while a second cowboy hung onto a hind leg and dragged it over to be branded. After the beef roundup in summer, shipments of animals might be made two or three times a week; enough for a drive were collected and then trailed across country to the railhead at Coffeyville, Kansas, with the process repeated until all the animals to be sold had been disposed of. On these drives the distances traveled each day were usually short, to let the animals have plenty of food and water so as to be in prime condition for market.

Under normal circumstances losses were minimal, and a steer for which Clem Rogers had paid a few dollars in Texas would bring $30 or $40 at the northern railhead; so the profits could be—and often were—substantial, since he was marketing between 2,000 and 4,000 head a year. And although he paid his help well for that time and place, the rule of thumb was that the annual cost of labor per animal was only about 75 cents.

By the time Will Rogers was old enough to know what was going on around him, the pattern of life at the ranch was well established, and it was a good one indeed. The 1890 census of Cooweescoowee district sheds some interesting light on the magnitude of Clem Rogers' operation. There were, according to the list, three dwellings, seven other structures, three farms, 300 enclosed acres, 300 acres under cultivation. Improvements were valued at $15,000, and the farm was producing 3,000 bushels of corn, 1,000 bushels of wheat, along with oats, apples, mules, goats, domestic fowls, and—of course—cattle and horses. The farm machinery, some of it rare for the area, was enumerated, and the list concluded with a notation that the family possessions included, aside from the parlor piano, one clock.

As Will's wife wrote many years later, a good many people thought—because he was careless about his speech and dress and manners—that he was "a poor, uneducated cowboy who struggled to the heights from obscure beginnings." It was true that he did not have a college education, she said, but that was only because he would not go to school. And as for his being a poor boy, "the truth is that, as the only surviving son of an indulgent father, Will had everything he wanted. He had spending money and the best string of cow ponies in the country. No boy in the Indian Territory had more than Uncle Clem's boy."

The CV Ranch on the Verdigris

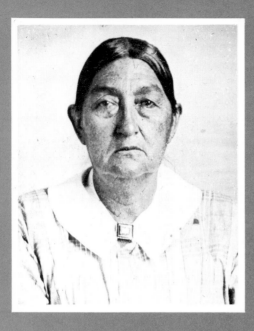

Will Rogers was only a small remove from his Cherokee ancestry, as the photograph of his maternal grandmother at left suggests. The other pictures on these pages, taken at various times, show his father's ranch in the Verdigris valley—the scene of Will's childhood, where he spent most of his first twenty-two years.

Facing south, the house looked out across unbroken miles of prairie.

Will was born in his parents' bedroom—the first floor room on the right, behind the group of children.

After the Civil War, while the large house was being built, Clem Rogers lived in this cabin.

ALL: WILL ROGERS MEMORIAL, CLAREMORE, OKLA.

Only a few hills broke the sweep of the horizon.

BOTH: WILL ROGERS MEMORIAL, CLAREMORE, OKLA.

"Three years in McGuffey's Fourth reader, and I knew more about it than McGuffey did."

The nationwide bicycle craze hit Indian Territory in the nineties, and here (at left) is Willie, a proud owner, demonstrating a stunt. Above, appearing somewhat the worse for wear but still unmistakably Will, is his baby picture.

In nearly every respect, Will Rogers' growing up was about as close to the nostalgic ideal of a nineteenth-century boyhood as it is possible to come by. The hard, lean years of the frontier were passing—for the Rogers family, certainly—and while life was simple it was also immensely rich, full of the joys of a childhood in rural America. From the time he could walk, Willie—as everyone called him—was riding a horse or working a rope in his hand. He was given his first pony at the age of five, and three or four years later took part in his first roundup (carefully watched over by a cowboy his father had assigned to the job of taking care of Will). The long, golden days of youth were spent painstakingly learning to throw a rope under the guidance of Uncle Dan Walker, a Negro cowboy who worked for Clem, or galloping hell-bent across the prairie in pursuit of a coyote or jack rabbit, or riding to the swimming hole, where the boys would pull the saddles off their horses, lead the animals into the water, grab their tails, and float behind them as they swam.

As Spi Trent, a youthful companion of Will's, wrote of those days: "Seems like I can close my eyes and feel that hot sun pouring down on my bare back, can smell the dogwood blossoms and the dainty scent of the wild roses on the brier bushes, can hear . . . the hum and buzz of them big dark blue dragon flies and the way ole Will could outholler all of us, 'Come on, fellers, the last one in is a Ring Tail Hoss!' " There were always plenty of friends to play with—white, Negro, and Indian children—and usually something exciting was going on at the ranch. Neighbors stopped by for a visit, an evening of square-dancing, or a picnic; there were long rides over the range to call on friends; it was even an outing to go for the *New York Times*, which Clem received regularly and which had to be picked up at the nearest post office, twelve miles away.

Willie was too young to remember his older brother Robert,

Two of Will's three sisters, dressed from the same bolt, are May (above), who died in 1909, and Maud, who later married Cap Lane.

WILL ROGERS MEMORIAL, CLAREMORE, OKLA.

who died when Will was two, but the loss made a great difference in the way he was brought up. His mother was forty when Willie was born, and it was clear that there would be no more sons. His parents were indulgent, the little boy was strong-willed ("There's a lot of mule in Willie," his father liked to say), and the result was that he got nearly everything he wanted. From the moment Clem gave him his first pony, his mother worried about him; watching the little sorrel mare rear up on her hind legs when Willie tried to pull himself into the saddle, she would cover her face and call to his father, "Clem, you're going to get my boy killed." But Willie was determined, fearless, and he had the advantage of all Oklahoma youngsters, he said later: "I was born bowlegged so I could sit on a horse."

More than anything else he liked to rope, and he spent hours with Uncle Dan Walker or with anyone else who would show him a fancy loop or a throw he didn't know. When he was older, there were days on a stretch when instead of riding the range as he was supposed to do, he would find a shady place and practice roping endlessly, "cutting curliques," he remembered, "and things in the prairie breeze or lassoing prairie dogs and things not made to be lassoed."

When he was six his oldest sister Sallie married a man named Tom McSpadden, and later that year Willie embarked on his first experience with school—one for which he had very little tolerance or interest, like his father before him. He went to live with the McSpaddens at their farm near Bushyhead, and every morning Sallie would follow him outside, help him tie his dinner pail to the saddle horn, and watch until he rode down to the end of the lane, making certain he was heading for the classroom. Drumgoole School was a small, one-room log cabin, and all the students—most of them Indians—rode horseback or walked for miles to get there. Will used to say that he had just enough white blood in him to make his honesty questionable with all those Cherokees, and he spent most of his time racing with them, on foot or on horseback, growing more and more restless all the time he was indoors, where he hated the routine and the endless drills. When it was apparent that Drumgoole was not going to take, he was sent off to Harrell International Institute in Muskogee, a girls' boarding school which his sister May attended. The Reverend T.F. Brewer, president of the school, also had an eight-year-old son and decided that the two boys could attend classes safely with all the young ladies, but Will said he felt just as Custer did when he was surrounded by Indians. The experience was not successful, and before long the Reverend Brewer was writing to Clem: "I regret to inform you that your son is not doing well in school and would suggest you remove him."

That summer, for the first time in Will's memory, tragedy struck the ranch. His sisters Sallie and Maud had typhoid fever, Willie came down with a bad case of measles, and while he was sick his mother fell ill with what was finally diagnosed as amoebic dysentery. Everything that could be done for her was done; but on May 28, 1890, Mary America Rogers died and was buried on the ranch beside her son Robert and the three infants, in a family cemetery enclosed by an iron fence and lined with twisted cedars and crape myrtle bushes. Willie and his mother were alike in so many ways: her gentle manner, sense of humor, love of music, and her easy way with people were some of the strongest traits the boy inherited. Will's wife said later that he never got over his mother's death; he cried when he told her about it years afterward, and he once wrote of her, "My mother's name was Mary, and if your mother's name was Mary and she was an old-fashioned woman, you don't have to say much for her. Everybody knows already."

That fall—in the same month his father was organizing a posse to chase the Dalton boys, outlaws and rustlers who had stolen some of his horses—Willie was hustled off to yet another school, this time in Tahlequah, and he liked it no better than its predecessors. Restless and wild, he became unkempt and careless in his person and his studies, and his father decided to send him to Willie Halsell College at Vinita, about forty miles from the ranch. The school's catalogue claimed that the community was "noted for its literary taste, sobriety, good morals and culture," but an old-timer who lived there remembered it rather differently. "Vinita was sure one muddy town," he said. "Besides being flat, with little natural moisture drainage, there were no sewers, no curbs, no pavement. When it rained, the moisture stayed until it was dried by sun and wind. Meanwhile every passing vehicle churned the black, sticky mud deeper and deeper." The "college" was really a private boarding academy, roughly the equivalent of a modern junior high school; most of the pupils were boys and girls from around home with whom Will had grown up, and he spent four happy years there. At the commencement exercises, when awards were being made for academic achievement, the Vinita *Indian Chieftain* noted that "The recitation of Willie P. Rogers was rendered so well that

Will's boyhood friend Charlie McClellan, done up to the nines in stiff white collar, pince nez, and long pigtail.
WILL ROGERS MEMORIAL, CLAREMORE, OKLA.

"My little friend . . . do you ever go to see your girl . . . her big sister Mamie is my girl and the little one is yours. I have got the prettiest girl in the country, she is John Gores sister, she lives at Bluejacket about twelve miles from here. Dont you tell any of them fellows from out there. . . ."

Will Rogers to
Charlie McClellan
Mar. 28, 1893

the judge decided he was also entitled to a medal.''

Now his father insisted that he attend Scarritt Collegiate Institute in Neosho, Missouri, and for a time, so far as Clem knew, Will did well there. But at the end of the first term the boy unexpectedly turned up at the ranch. He had been expelled. The difficulty, it turned out, was Will's passion for roping. He had spent every idle moment during the fall practicing with a lariat, but unfortunately he and the headmaster did not see eye to eye on the importance of this particular skill. One rope after another was taken away from him. The real crisis came when a mare owned by the headmaster wandered onto the campus with her colt one day, and Will, on a dare, fashioned a lasso out of some rope which had been used to tie up a trunk and caught the colt. Unfortunately, he didn't have a tight grip on the makeshift lariat; the colt and mare bolted, ran through a tennis court net, jumped a fence, and disappeared. The upshot was that the headmaster decided that though Will might not be able to get along without his rope, the school could certainly manage without him and his antics.

While Will was at Halsell his father remarried and moved to the town of Claremore; his sisters had married and moved away, and were raising families. The life he had known on the ranch was gone, irretrievably, it seemed. He still had friends

What did young boys in Indian Territory do?—play Indian, of course. Here are two of Will's friends, John Brown and Charlie Mc-Clellan (more comfortably dressed than he is on p. 39).

among the cowboys there, but the ranch had become a lonelier place, and people who saw him out on the range noticed that he talked to himself a good deal. Clem was not pleased when Will was sent home from Scarritt and announced to his son that he was sending him to Kemper Military School in Boonville, Missouri. The discipline, he thought, might tame the boy.

When Will showed up to begin what would now be called sophomore year in high school, he cut quite a figure; he had on a cowboy hat, a flannel shirt with a fiery-red bandanna at his throat, a brightly colored vest, and high-heeled boots with red tops and spurs. (As Spi Trent recalled, Will "in his boyhood days was a Regular Dude. He not only liked to be duded up but he liked to look the part he was playing." In this particular instance "He was just puttin' on a little extra performance for the benefit of Kemper and the Honor of the Ranch.")

Along with his luggage, for all the cadets to see, were lariats of various sizes. Will had not only spent countless hours practicing roping, he had also had his eyes opened to another side of the art at the Chicago World's Fair in 1893. He and his father had traveled to Chicago with a trainload of cattle and seen all the wondrous sights at the exposition, including Buffalo Bill's Wild West Show, with its "Congress of Rough Riders of the World"; but the high point of the visit for Will was a perform-

COLLECTION OF MR. & MRS. JOHN FOREMAN McCLELLAN

While at Scarritt, Will invited little Maggie Nay to a party, but her mother said "no"—he ran around with those "wild" boys who were said to take a swig from a bottle on occasion. The rejected suitor, turned seventeen, wrote a soul-searching reply:

A Suitor Scorned

My Dearest Friend if you can not be my Sweetheart

I received the note a little bit ago and was more than glad to hear from you but was sorry to hear my fate. . . . but then if your mother does not want you to go with me why it is all right. I would hate to do anything contrary to her will. I know I drink and am a wild and bad boy and all that bit. Then you know that Marvin is a model boy. He never did anything in his life. He is as good as an *angel*. I am an outcast I suppose, so of course dont do anything that will get you with a *drunkard as I am*. . . .

I was a fool for trying to go with you any way. I might have known you would have not gone with me. . . . I am too far below you to write to *"you"* and then you do not want my picture, you want the one you are going with not I.

Well I suppose you have heard enought of this *Drunkard* that they call Will Rogers, so I will close hoping you all a merry evening as I expect I had better not go as your Mother might object to me and as Jess says that no decent person would speak to me and I know all of you are decent but I am *very* sorry that I can not come. But dont think that I am mad at you in the least and I like you more than I ever did. The truth never hurts me. . . .

Now please dont let any one see this Maggie and I will not let any one see your note.

your would like to be S – – – – –

COURTESY MRS. FRANZ VERKAMP

Innocence personified in a derby, Will poses with two "wild" Scarritt buddies. The unapproachable Maggie is above.

WILL ROGERS MEMORIAL, CLAREMORE, OKLA.

ance given by a group of Mexican vaqueros, led by one Vincente Oropeza, who was billed as "the greatest roper in the world." Oropeza, gloriously attired in an embroidered jacket, buckskin trousers with brass buttons, a red sash, and a hat trimmed with gold braid, went through dozens of spectacular rope tricks, concluding with one in which he wrote his name with his lasso, one letter at a time, in the air. Will, in the phrase of the day, had seen the elephant.

For a time he seems to have enjoyed Kemper, and at the end of his first six months he had an academic average of 79 (with 100 in American History and 85 in Elocution). Military discipline and drill were something of a novelty; besides, he liked the uniform, and when he came back to the ranch for vacations he would show off his new finery to the cowboys. Once he borrowed a rifle from one of the hands and went through the whole manual of arms, but when he grounded the gun authoritatively it went off and the bullet grazed the side of his forehead, leaving a long white scar he wore all his life.

At Kemper, as at all the other schools, Will was bright enough, but the ups and downs of his marks reflected an academic interest that waxed and waned. His best subjects were usually History and Education (he did well in what his classmates called the "talking" subjects); he had a remarkable memory and memorized with no difficulty huge chunks of Lyman's formidable Historical Chart, in which the march of world events was indicated in different colors for different countries and civilizations. Americans—and particularly those who lived on the frontier—were not by nature histrionic people, but the schools put a great deal of emphasis on elocution, for public life was the most honored career, and the law and the ministry the most respected professions (Will's mother wanted him to be a preacher, but Clem remarked sourly that there was not much money in it). In elocution class the students were taught to speak the classic orations—"Friends, Romans, countrymen, lend me your ears," Patrick Henry's "liberty or death" speech, and others—all with textbook gestures that were rigidly standardized, but Will never could resist an opportunity to get a laugh out of his audience, and his gift for timing and for misplaced emphasis often broke up the class. Every school had a boy like that, and at Kemper it reached a point where all Will had to do was stand up to recite, make some subtle gesture or raise an eyebrow, and the whole class would go into hysterics. As one of his fellow students remarked, "He'd torture his face

The very model of a young Kemper cadet—Willie, home on furlough, about the year 1898
WILL ROGERS MEMORIAL, CLAREMORE, OKLA.

43

till it looked like a wrinkled saddle blanket, make funny motions with his hands and roll his eyes and, some way or other, manage to make us laugh. I never saw him get up in front of a class without making them laugh before he sat down."

He played football and baseball, but mostly it was the lariat that kept him occupied; every chance he got he would persuade a classmate to get down on all fours and run and bawl like a calf as he threw a loop over him. Exasperated teachers were always taking ropes away from him, but inevitably he managed to lay hands on another and coil it around his waist, under his shirt, so no one would find it. Between his fascination with the lasso and distaste for cleaning his rifle, Will accumulated an impressive total of demerits, which had to be worked off by solitary marching; but he found he could even turn this to advantage: he would arrange for his penance to be paid off near the kitchen and then ask the cook "if he wouldn't do something for the vanishing American."

As Will described his military career, "I spent two years at Kemper, one in the guardhouse and one in the fourth grade." When spring came the old wanderlust came with it. He had a total of one hundred fifty demerits, which meant as many hours of marching guard, and as he listened to stories his friend Billy Johnston told about the big cattle outfits down in Texas he concluded that he would never see eye to eye with the commandant of Kemper and decided then and there to "quit the entire school business for life." Which he did, at the age of eighteen. The first his father knew about it was when he received a letter from his friend W.P. Ewing in Higgins, Texas, saying that Will was there and what should he do with him?

Clem's suggestion was that Ewing should try to get any work that he could out of the young man, and for several months Will stayed on the ranch before striking out for what looked like greener pastures in Amarillo. All he possessed were the clothes he wore and a few dollars; but he bought a spooky old horse, and rode to Amarillo. There he tried to sign up for service in Colonel Theodore Roosevelt's cavalry regiment of Rough Riders, which was recruiting for the Spanish-American War, and after being turned down because of his youth, looked for other work. Hearing of a trail boss who needed a hand, he arrived in time to listen to another cowboy applying for the position. "And right there," he said, "I saw a fellow talk himself out of a job." The other boy began by telling the trail boss in glowing terms what a good cowhand he was, and by the time he had finished,

44

the man told him, "I'm in need of a hand, all right, but I think you'd suit me too well." Will, having learned the lesson, told the boss, "maby I could do the work. He told me to get on my horse and come out to his camp. Them was the happiest words I ever heard in my life."

He wrangled horses, helped drive a herd up to Kansas, and then returned to Texas, where he rode seven days a week, rounding up cattle, roping and branding calves, as happy as a teen-age boy could be, with a horse and saddle and bedroll of his own, working with seasoned cowhands for $30 a month.

On his first visit home he shipped his saddle by express and traveled himself by freight train until he reached a point about twenty miles from Clem's ranch, where he bought a ticket so he could step off the train first class. But the gesture was wasted; there wasn't a soul at the depot when he arrived. Clem and several others, including Will's friend Jim O'Donnell, were riding through a pasture when they saw someone galloping toward them, and Will's father remarked that it looked like Willie. It was obvious that Will was not certain what Clem was going to say about his running away from school, O'Donnell remembered, "but after shakin' hands with us he started right in tellin' us all about workin' for the big cow outfit in the Panhandle. He didn't get very far, when Uncle Clem says, 'Son, go back to the house and wash your neck and ears and put on a clean shirt.'" (The homecoming also produced a comment from the woman at the ranch who washed Will's clothes: "That child," she complained, "was wearin' overalls for drawers.")

Later Will drifted out to New Mexico, where he worked on other ranches until he was sent to California with a trainload of cattle for the Hearst ranch. After they had been delivered, he and another cowboy went to San Francisco and put up at a small hotel; the next morning when they didn't appear, someone went to their room and discovered that they had been nearly asphyxiated. The boys were used to kerosene lamps back in Indian Territory and before going to bed one of them blew out the gas jets to turn out the lights. At the hospital, Will said, "the main doctor gave me up, but a lot of young medical students, just by practicing on me, happened to light on some nut remedy that no regular doctor would ever think of and I came to. I landed back home in pretty bad shape." His father sent him to Hot Springs to recuperate, and when Will returned to the ranch after another stay in Texas, Clem decided it was time for the boy to settle down.

School Days

For four years Will attended classes at Willie Halsell College.

When Willie first went off to school he boarded at the home of his sister Sallie and her husband Tom McSpadden, above.

Cadet Willie Rogers and a friend pose while playing a desperate game of cards at Kemper School.

ALL: WILL ROGERS MEMORIAL, CLAREMORE, OKLA.

Nothing equaled roping, but Will (first row, second from right) also enjoyed playing football at Kemper.

KEMPER SCHOOL·

MONTHLY REPORT·

Boonville, Mo. *March* 189 7

Grades of *Will Rogers*

for *4th* school month ending with date.

Mental Arithmetic	Astronomy
Practical Arithmetic 82	Geology
Algebra 62	Zoölogy
Geometry	Psychology
Trigonometry	Reading
English Grammar 82	Letter-Writing 82
Rhetoric	Composition 74
English Literature	Book-keeping 48
Latin	Bible 70
Greek	History, U. S.
German	History, General
French	Elocution 84
Geography	Drawing
Physical Geography 80	American Literature
Physiology	Political Economy
Physics	Civil Government
Chemistry	Av. of Lesson Grades 79

DEMERITS for month 50

Seated right, Will with a hard-bitten crew of Kemper comrades; above is his report card, with creditable grades (except in Algebra and Bookkeeping)—and 50 demerits.

BOTH: WILL ROGERS MEMORIAL, CLAREMORE, OKLA.

"We spoiled the best Territory in the World to make a State."

Left, Will, aged about twenty, was quite the blade when he dressed up and rode off on Comanche in search of amusement. Above, in the year 1889, "boomers" await the signal for the run into Oklahoma.

The fourteen years between Will Rogers' birth and his visit to the Chicago World's Fair of 1893 saw immense changes in the old Indian Territory—changes that altered forever the life of the Cherokee Nation, and of the big ranchers like Clem Rogers. The final subjugation of the Plains Indians was going on, the huge cattle drives from Texas were ending, feverish railroad building interlaced all but the most remote places in the West, and millions of acres of land were opening up for settlement. Those days of the open range, when the longhorn cattle roamed the unfenced prairies and the dollars crawled into the ranchers' jeans, were over. In 1862 Congress had passed a Homestead Act drafted by a gentle-faced Pennsylvanian named Galusha Grow, providing that any adult citizen or alien who had filed his first papers could, after paying a $10 fee, claim one hundred sixty acres of the public domain, and—if he stayed there five years—obtain title to it.

Drawn by the ancient magic of free land, thousands upon thousands of small farmers and stockmen moved west, gobbling up acreage, building sod huts and erecting fences on the plains where buffalo and cattle had run unchallenged, applying the same relentless pressure on cattlemen that whites had exerted on Indians. Railroad owners whose lines crossed Indian Territory complained that those lands were closed to settlement (and thus to freight), but they quickly discovered that some of the Civilized Tribes—for their participation on the Confederate side—had forfeited nearly two million acres to the government after the Civil War, and that these "unassigned" lands had not

49

yet been allocated to other tribes. While lobbyists pressed for legal seizure of this enormous domain, land seekers from Kansas, hoping to jump the gun, crossed the border illegally and posted claims. For a while Federal troops drove them back, but finally the government capitulated to the incessant demand, paid the Indians $1.25 an acre for the land in what is now central Oklahoma, and ordered it to be surveyed into hundred-sixty-acre parcels for settlement. It was opened for claims at noon on April 22, 1889.

That morning some twenty thousand people, on horseback, on foot, driving wagons, wheelbarrows, and every imaginable conveyance, lined up at different entry points on three sides of the area and awaited the pistol shot signaling the opening of the verdant prairies to settlement. Some "sooners" had already stolen a march on them, but troops held back most of the homesteaders until the gun was fired, when bedlam broke loose. Within a few hours after the fighting horde of men, animals, and wagons had burst across the line, nearly all of the two million acres had been claimed; tents, shacks, and other structures were being erected all over the once-empty prairie; and by nightfall the new settlement of Oklahoma City had a population of 10,000 and Guthrie nearly 15,000. The following year, when the first U.S. census was taken in the region occupied by the Five Civilized Tribes, it revealed that there were 103,393 whites, 18,636 Negroes, and only 50,055 Indians.

For Clem Rogers 1889 also marked the end of trail driving. During the previous year he had unloaded twenty-two freight carloads of Texas cattle at the yards in Adair, but despite all his efforts to stop the railroad, the steel rails of the Missouri Pacific came through the west side of his ranch that year, dividing the range in two, and on the strength of what he had seen happen after the land rush, he realized that it was only a matter of time until settlers would be swarming into the Verdigris valley. The little town of Oologah came into existence as a whistle stop on the Missouri Pacific line in 1889, six miles southwest of Clem's ranch, and from then on, the area was destined to be farm country instead of cattle country. Clem also foresaw that more was at stake than the open range. Those settlers he disliked so intensely would not only change the countryside into one of small, fenced farms, they would also bring about the end of the Cherokee Nation. Already there was talk that the government was going to throw open Cherokee lands to settlement, after giving each Indian a pro rata share of the tribal lands, and

Clem, seeing what lay ahead, began to alter his operation from one in which longhorns grazed on the open range to one in which shorthorn cattle were fed in fenced pastures.

In 1891 he built the first barbed-wire fence in the Verdigris country, from the river to the right of way of the Missouri Pacific—a distance of about eight miles. Then the railroad fenced its right of way, completely cutting his range in two from north to south, and Clem decided to keep cattle on the eastern side and put the rest of the ranch under cultivation. For some time he had been upgrading his herd, purchasing the first purebred shorthorn bulls in the Territory, adding Herefords later. In addition to cattle and horses, he was also breeding hogs and poultry, and was the first man in the region to introduce wheat on a large scale. Actually, the Cherokee country's fertile, sandy loam, climate, and rainfall proved ideal for farming, and the wheat crops thrived; Clem was planting between 300 and 500 acres of the grain, and in 1895 the Claremore *Progress* observed proudly that "Clem Rogers, the Oologah wheat king, " had harvested 13,000 bushels. He was also growing oats, all sorts of garden vegetables, fruit, berries, grapes; but the two big cash crops were livestock and wheat as long as he kept the ranch. But how long that would be remained to be seen.

West of the Cherokee Nation lay the most extensive and richest of their cattle ranges—some six and a half million acres of grassland south of the Kansas border known as the Cherokee Strip. For years the Cherokees had collected grazing fees from individual cattlemen, but in 1883 they leased the area to the Cherokee Strip Livestock Association under terms of a bill written and introduced in the Cherokee Senate by Clem Vann Rogers. The trouble with the Strip was that it was too rich. As one Cherokee wrote of it to Chief Dennis Bushyhead, ". . . there is no better country in the west than this, you can picture any kind of land and location for homes and find it here. Rich loamy Prairie or timbered bottoms and Black limestone valleys and uplands . . . well watered and timbered, it is a shame that our wealth should be here as it is only to enrich speculating and land stealing whites. . . ."

In 1893, after unremitting pressure by white farmers on Congress, the Cherokee Strip was sold to the United States government for $8,500,000, and the most spectacular land rush of all followed, with a hundred thousand people pouring into the region and stampeding across the waving grasslands to stake out claims. Clem Rogers, now fifty-nine years old, had

TEXT CONTINUED ON PAGE 56

THE THOMAS GILCREASE INSTITUTE

CIRCULAR.

To the Settlers in Oklahoma.

General Merritt, in command of the Military Department of which this Territory constitutes part, wishes all law abiding people to know that the U. S. Troops are here; 1st, for the protection of Government property and the United States Mails; 2nd, to guard the people from lawlessness and disorder.

He desires to impress on the settlers the necessity of conducting their affairs in a quiet and orderly manner, deferring to the Courts the settlement of all controversies and conflicting claims. It is hoped that wise counsels and due respect for the law will prevail without necessity for invoking its power, civil or military, which is ample for all purposes of protection to law-abiding settlers, and for the due control of those who seek to take the law into their own hands.

Headquarters Department of the Missouri,
(In the field,)
April 21, 1889.

For this now-famous photograph of the 1893 rush into the Cherokee Strip the cameraman built a special platform from which to take his picture. (He must have been the only stationary figure within miles.) The circular above, from the 1889 run, explained the presence at the scene of U.S. Army troops.

OKLAHOMA HISTORICAL SOCIETY

Men seeking lots in Guthrie fan out in all directions, carrying their belongings, on April 22, 1889.

Instant cities were the consequence of the 1889 run, as these photographs of Guthrie testify. Lots could be bought from the gentleman above on April 22, and by May 6 the town of Guthrie (right) was already so far along that few signs remained of the virgin prairie land on which it stood.

ABOVE: COLLECTION OF ROBERT CUNNINGHAM

ALL THREE: WESTERN HISTORY COLLECTIONS, UNIVERSITY OF OKLAHOMA LIBRARY

Two rough-and-ready earlycomers, lot staked out and tent set up, are ready for anything.

On the prairies, building materials were scarce, and many a family lived in a "soddy" or hut made from square-cut chunks of sod. This one, located south of Stillwater, was also the local post office.

COLLECTION OF ROBERT CUNNINGHAM

been made an assistant to the Dawes Commission—a group appointed by President Grover Cleveland to persuade the members of the Five Civilized Tribes to give up their tribal form of government and accept individual allotments of land from the government. As part of its efforts, the commission began making up tribal rolls listing all those among whom the land would be divided. The solution was not looked upon with favor by all the Indians, of course; as one Cherokee described their situation, they had no sooner reconstructed their lives and homes after the devastation of the Civil War than "the government took another shot at us and set up the Dawes Commission. . . . We owned all the land as a whole and could farm all we wanted to as long as we didn't infringe on a neighbor's land. We had a good government of our own just like we had back in Georgia, but the white man wanted our land just as they wanted it in Georgia."

In 1894 the Cherokees received the first of five annual payments for the sale of the Cherokee Strip, with each Indian getting $367.50 in cash from the bank in Vinita, which handed out a total of $1,700,000 to the crowd that packed the main street of the little town. Three railroads now crossed the Verdigris country, and every passenger train that came through unloaded dozens of new settlers at town sites along the right of way—in Chelsea, Tulsa, and Claremore; but it was the passage of the Curtis Act in 1898 that finally put an end to Clem's cattle empire. That law forced allotment of all land held in common by the Cherokee Nation to individuals, abolished tribal law, and substituted a new code of U.S. laws for the Indian Territory. Between them, Clem and Will received allotments of 148.77 acres—all that remained to them of the 60,000-acre ranch; and although Clem succeeded in buying up some fractional allotments that bordered the old homestead, the place could no longer be described as anything more than a farm, and a fairly small one at that.

It was clear that thousands more settlers would come in the wake of the Cherokee Run, and Clem Rogers, a complete realist, once again saw opportunity in the offing. He and several friends concluded that Claremore—a rail junction about twenty-four miles northeast of Tulsa—was the most promising town in the area for a bank, and in 1898 Clem sold his cattle, traded his horses, rented his farmland to a man from Illinois, and moved into town. It was to be a permanent move; never again did he live in the old ranch house on the Verdigris.

A curious dichotomy pervaded the lives of people like Clem and, to a lesser extent, Will Rogers—a kind of dual personality forced upon them by the circumstance of an Indian heritage and the relentless encroachment of white civilization into the Territory. At this distance it is difficult to do more than speculate about Clem's feelings on the subject, but there are a few indications as to where he felt he belonged. As Will's son Bill suggests, Clem and Will were both "upwardly mobile, ambitious men, and I am sure they saw nothing wrong in trying to adopt the ways and attitudes that led to success, i.e., the white man's way. Today we might say that they should have paid more attention to the ancient Cherokee culture. But I think that was a concept that did not occur to them."

Clem, we know, was a realist about what was going on in his world. As he warned Chief Bushyhead in 1883—at a time when many Cherokees still believed they could maintain their own government and the old tribal ways—"We are *fast fast* drifting into the ways of the white man." Sensing the advantages of moving in that direction, Clem found no difficulty in being a useful and contented citizen of both worlds; perceiving the inevitability of white dominance, he adapted to the change. He un-

". . . it would be a Godsend to this convention if there wasn't so damned many lawyers here."

from speech by C. V. Rogers
Constitutional Convention
Dec. 20, 1906

derstood the Cherokee language, although he did not speak it, and did all he could "to help the full-bloods in the different capacities in which he worked with them as politician, friend, and neighbor," as his niece Paula McSpadden Love writes. But what was more significant from the standpoint of the way his son was raised and came to see himself, Clem followed the ways of the white man in nearly all respects.

Along with his business acumen, Clem Rogers was one of those men to whom civic service comes naturally: perhaps because of his own limited schooling, he was intensely interested in education; he gave unstintingly of his time to the affairs of the Cherokee Nation and, later, Oklahoma—devoting, in all, forty-four years of his life to politics.

Quite naturally, Will never possessed the same degree of identification his father had with the Cherokees. His upbringing and appearance were those of whites; he left home at a fairly early age; and his later associations were almost entirely with whites. Yet the Indian blood was there, and he became too much of a showman not to realize the appeal an Indian background had for an audience.

When Will returned to the ranch from Texas for the first time in a year, he discovered that his father was living in Claremore and was expecting him to run what was left of the old operation. In January, 1899, Clem restocked it with cattle, gave Will a number of animals of his own, and sent Will's friend Spi Trent to help manage the place. But it was no longer the same boyhood home for Will: all the family furniture had been removed from the house, which was neglected and run down, and Will found that he had nothing in common with the Illinois tenant farmer and his family—there was no longer the excitement of talk centering around horses and cattle, trail drives and roundups, roping and branding. Nor were there the kind of meals mother used to make. The farmer's wife didn't seem to understand that a young, active cowboy likes hot biscuits and cream gravy, navy beans, and canned preserves three times a day. So after an unsettling, unhappy time, Will and Spi moved out and built a twelve-foot-square log cabin of their own a few miles from the ranch house, where they lived as though they were out on the range, with Spi doing the cooking and Will wrangling horses. Their spartan quarters were furnished with a double bed, a cookstove, two lanterns, and two boxes that served as chairs. (To the vast amusement of a Negro named Hayward who had sawed and notched logs and split shingles for

"Doc Denny congratulated Uncle Clem Rogers in such a hearty manner on Christmas Day [over his success in securing a good county] that in 'patting' him on the back he broke one of Uncle Clem's ribs and he is now suffering considerably from it and it is doubtful whether he will be able to attend the meeting of the constitutional convention at Guthrie next week."

from Claremore *Progress*
Jan. 3, 1907

All duded up for an outing, Will and Spi Trent (right) leave the cares of the ranch behind and enjoy the companionship of the two McClellan girls, Mary (left) and Pearl.
WILL ROGERS MEMORIAL, CLAREMORE, OKLA.

their cabin, the boys had forgotten to put in any windows.) But Will was happy. They had navy beans three times a day, Spi recalled, "week days and three times on Sundays and any time you rode in on us you would always find a big ole iron kittle full to overflowin' with 'em. And no invitation needed. Just grab a tin plate and help yourself."

For about a year and a half they lived there, operating the ranch, but with Will always on the lookout for other forms of amusement. He sang tenor in a local quartet and entertained the girls with renditions of the latest songs ("I Ain't Got A Dollar I Can Call My Own" was one of his favorites), attended every dance within riding distance, played baseball on the Oologah team, and roped and rode wild horses with other cowboys on Sundays. Almost inevitably, he bought the first rubber-tired buggy in the area and drove his friends around in it. Everybody knew Will; he was always the center of attention, and, as a contemporary said, "he could think up more devil-

59

This illustration of Will's "dogiron" brand (the iron is shown below) was printed on a letterhead that read "W.P. Rogers, Cattle Dealer."
WILL ROGERS MEMORIAL, CLAREMORE, OKLA.

ment in a minute than an ordinary person could in a month." But for all his pranks, he was more conservative in some ways than most of his friends, since he did not play cards, smoke, or drink. Jim O'Donnell recalled that Will talked all the time and was known as "Rabbit"—a tribute to his big ears and to the fact that he was constantly in motion. He wore a funny-looking hat, different from what other boys had, and "His hair looked like it had been cut with a knife and fork."

What finally put an end to the bachelors roughing it was a pair of unforeseen circumstances: two horses Will had tethered to a log of the house shied, jerked back, and tore off one whole side of the building—and this event conspired happily with the tenant farmer's desire to return to Illinois, so Will moved back to the ranch house, where his sister Mary and her husband had also come to live. He had a growing herd of his own now, all bearing his "dog iron" brand, and busy as he was on the ranch, he found time to participate in some of the roping contests that were coming into vogue then. Will had always enjoyed the excitement of the roundup, particularly cutting out cattle and roping them, and—given the time he had devoted to his lasso—he was now something of an expert at it. "Will was a good roper," an old-timer recalled; "He was the quickest tie man I ever knew. Sometimes he missed a loop, but couldn't be beat tying the legs." Roping was an achievement, a good horse was a necessity, and Will was almost as determined to own every good roping horse he saw as he was to master the art of roping. There were, he once explained, two types of horses for ranch work: "A steer roping horse and a calf roping horse are not the same animal. When you rope a steer, after you catch 'em you throw your slack rope over his rear axle and then run your horse on by (having roped him by the head), the rope going over behind the steer jerking all four feet out from under him. Then while you tie him, the horse is supposed to keep pulling and dragging the steer as he attempts to get up. Now, in calf roping, the minute you catch your calf, the horse stops. You jump off and go throw the calf yourself. The horse is supposed to keep the rope tight, but his head is toward the calf, and he does it by backing up instead of pulling away like a steer. Of course, you can in rare instances have a horse that will work both ways, but most ropers have two different horses. . . ."

Will's favorite was a little yellow pony named Comanche that Clem had bought as a colt and given him to break and train. As Jim O'Donnell, who rode the horse in a number of roping contests and followed rodeos for forty years, said long afterward, "I have seen some wonderful horses, but none like Comanche. . . . He could outrun a steer, so that you had to pull him up before you throwed your rope." He went on to tell about a roping-and-riding contest a group of them attended in Springfield, Missouri. Another cowboy, riding Comanche, roped his steer and threw it in front of the grandstand, but when he jumped off and ran back to tie the animal the steer rolled over, got to its feet, and charged him. Without a moment's hesitation, Comanche turned, pulled the rope tight, and flipped the steer by himself, so that the cowboy did not lose more than three seconds' time. A New Yorker came down from the stands and asked who owned the pony and was told that it belonged to Will. When he located him he offered $500 for the horse (this, at a time when $100 was considered a big price).

Will replied, "A dollar looks as big to me as a wagon wheel, but I don't want to sell him."

Surely, the New York man said, the horse could be bought for some price—"Name it, and I'll ship him back to Long Island."

"Mister," said Will, "I don't know how much money you got, but there is not money enough in that grandstand to buy old Comanche."

Throughout his life, Will could never resist the temptation to buy a good roping horse, and he owned so many good ones it was impossible to keep track of them all. But Comanche always came first.

For all Clem Rogers' hopes that his son would settle down once he had his own herd and the responsibility of running the ranch, Will was finding it humdrum in comparison to the exciting life on the immense open range of Texas and New Mexico. Ranching on the Verdigris was a tame proposition those days, and Will was spending more and more time at the roping contests held in nearby towns. The first time he won a prize was in Claremore on July 4, 1899, and after that he entered the contests whenever and wherever he could, picking up tricks by watching the top competitors he faced. When Roosevelt's Rough Riders held a reunion in Oklahoma City Will was there, mixing with cowhands who had come from Texas, New Mexico, Arizona, Colorado, and Wyoming as well as Indian Territory, and although he won no prize money, he did get to meet Teddy Roosevelt. But as far as Will was concerned, the high point of these days was his trip to St Louis in 1899 for the annual fair, where he participated in a roping-and-riding contest run by "Colonel" Zach Mulhall (the title was strictly honorary). "The winner of each contest," it was announced, "can consider himself the champion of the world, as in gaining those laurels he will find it necessary to compete with the very best riders and ropers in this country, and it is well known that the best riders in the world are Americans." This, Will said later, was the beginning of his show business career.

Mulhall, who was the general stock agent for the Frisco Railroad, had three daughters—one of whom, Lucille, was the first woman to be called a cowgirl. She could rope and tie a steer with any man. After the fair Mulhall organized a cowboy band of about sixty musicians and made a tour of state fairs throughout the Middle West. Since most of those musicians, as Will said, "could not ride in a wagon unless their shirttails was nailed to the floor," Mulhall decided he should take along a few real cowboys for authenticity, and Will and a friend were hired. During a performance Mulhall would make an offer to pick out boys from the band who could ride any outlaw horse or rope and tie a steer in less time than any man in the audience could, and Will and his friend Jim O'Donnell were employed for that purpose. The rest of the time Will sat with the band, pretending to play a trombone on which he couldn't make a sound. In San Antonio, after the steer-roping contest was over, the local people invited the band members to a barbecue and someone asked Will to speak, just as he was "stacking in the grub." It was the first of many after-dinner speeches he was to give and surely one of the shortest.

He got to his feet, blinked, scratched his head, and stammered, "Well, folks, this is a mighty fine dinner, what there is of it."

Later, recalling the laughter that greeted his remarks, he said, "I saw I wasent going so good, so I said, trying to cover up, 'Well, there is plenty of it, such as it is.' "

The speech was a success.

When the tour ended and Will returned home, he realized that if he wasn't entirely content with life on the ranch, neither was his father with the way he was operating it. "I dident exactly run it to suit him," he observed. "I danced all my young life to the music of old country fiddlers and . . . between dances and roping contests, I dident have time for much serious ranching business."

And now he had found another interest to pursue.

WILL ROGERS MEMORIAL, CLAREMORE, OKLA.

C.V. Rogers
of Claremore, I.T.

The First National Bank in Claremore, shown about 1900

Passage of the Curtis Act in 1898, forcing allotment of the Cherokee lands, put an end to the free range, and Clem Rogers sold his stock, rented the land on the Verdigris River to a farmer, and moved into Claremore. After his second wife died, he moved to rooms on the second floor of the bank (left) on Main Street, of which he was vice president. He continued to be active in affairs of the Cherokee Nation, served on the delegation that worked with the Dawes Commission, and was a representative from the district to the Constitutional Convention of the new state of Oklahoma in 1906.

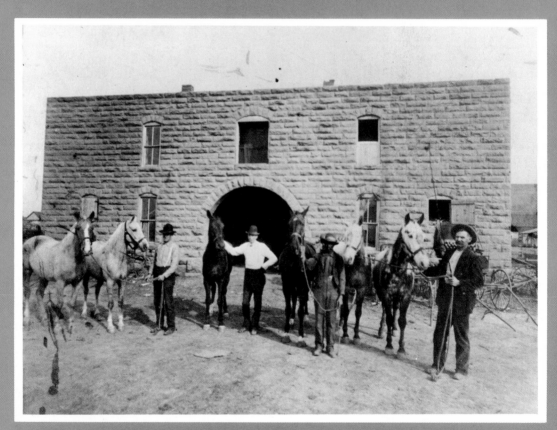

Clem, known as one of the best horsemen in the Territory, owned this solid-looking livery stable in Claremore.

ALL THREE: WILL ROGERS MEMORIAL, CLAREMORE, OKLA.

Representatives of the Dawes Commission traveled by wagon throughout Indian Territory, taking the tribal rolls.

OKLAHOMA HISTORICAL SOCIETY

Clem Rogers (left rear) was a member of the Cherokee delegation that met with the Dawes Commission in 1898–99.

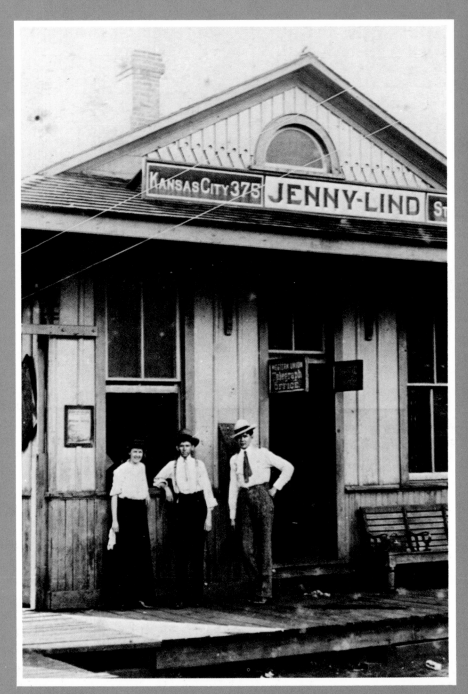

KANSAS CITY 375   JENNY-LIND   Sp

BOTH: WILL ROGERS MEMORIAL, CLAREMORE, OKLA.

"Nobody but an Indian can pronounce Oologah."

At the depot in Jenny Lind, Arkansas, Betty Blake (far left) was mistress-of-all-work. From an early age the daring cyclist (above) practiced the stunts with which he tried to impress her on her initial visit to Indian Territory.

In the fall of 1899 a nineteen-year-old girl named Betty Blake arrived in Oologah to spend some time with her sister and brother-in-law, who was then the station agent for the Missouri Pacific Railroad. She was just recovering from a severe attack of typhoid fever, which had left her thin and with her hair cut as short as a boy's; and her mother in Rogers, Arkansas, thought the change would do her good, even though the social life in Oologah might not be as lively as it was at home. "The only young people in the town," Betty's sister warned, "are the daughters of the hotel keeper, and there is one boy, Will Rogers, who lives out a few miles on a ranch."

Betty was born in the Ozarks in a town that was named Monte Ne by its most illustrious citizen—William Hope ("Coin") Harvey, a thin, hawk-nosed character who devised an elaborate theory concerning silver coinage which he outlined in a book, *Coin's Financial School.* Among other accomplishments, he built a six-mile railroad (whose first passenger was William Jennings Bryan) from Lowell, Arkansas, to Monte Ne, where he had constructed a Roman amphitheatre; imported a Venetian gondola to glide along the waters of the lake; planned an Egyptian pyramid for the summit of Monte Ne's nearest mountain; and in 1932, at the age of eighty-one, he nominated himself for President of the United States from a platform in Monte Ne.

When Betty was three, her father, a miller, died, and her mother supported her brood of six daughters and two sons by becoming a dressmaker in the nearby town of Rogers. She had a second marriage, which did not last, but which produced another daughter, and for all the family's financial worries, the household was a gay, lively one, full of music and fun. If you passed the house on Sunday, a friend recalled, "you'd hear laughter and see young people havin' a good time. Sometimes they'd overflow out into the yard, there was so many of them."

"Coin" Harvey of Monte Ne, Arkansas; the town (also Betty Blake's birthplace), boasted that it had "the only train in America that is met at the station by a gondola."

MISS VERA KEY

As soon as the children were old enough they went to work, and Betty and two of her sisters were clerks in a local store. Vivacious and well-liked, she fancied pretty clothes, and a good deal of her earnings seem to have gone into them. She worked for a while as a filing clerk for one of her brothers, the depot agent for the Iron Mountain Railroad at Jenny Lind, Arkansas, where her duties also included checking all the cars in the yard when he was otherwise occupied. And still another job was setting type for the Rogers *Democrat*, where she was the first person to make a dollar a day as compositor.

By all accounts she was pretty, good company, and much sought after by young men (her first serious beau was Tom Harvey, one of Coin's sons, whose assets included a railroad pass and free access to the gondola), and one of her admirers recalled that he used to call for her in a handcar while she had the railroad job, and that they would travel on it to Fort Smith to see plays at the opera house.

After the excitement of Monte Ne and Rogers, Oologah must have been something of a letdown. The town had, besides the depot and some stock pens, a two-story frame hotel, a livery stable, a church that also served as a school, a handful of frame houses, and plank sidewalks on either side of the main—and only—street. Beyond were the rolling prairies—mile upon unending mile of them, with scarcely a tree in sight. Twice a day passenger trains stopped at the station where Betty's sister and brother-in-law lived and worked, and the Arkansas girl used to sit on the telegraph table in the bay window of the depot watching the townspeople who turned out regularly to meet the trains, wondering if anyone would get off before the cars pulled out again and left the platform deserted and quiet.

One evening a young man stepped off the train from Kansas City and came up to the ticket window. Betty's brother-in-law wasn't around, so she went over to see what the fellow wanted; but as she described the encounter, it was notable only for its brevity. "I looked at him and he looked at me," she wrote later, "and before I could even ask his business, he turned on his heel and was gone without so much as saying a word." When her brother-in-law came in a moment later with the express packages, one of which was a banjo addressed to Will Rogers, she realized who the boy must have been, and that he had been too shy to ask for his parcel. The next morning she saw him again, riding by the window on a little dun-colored pony, his overcoat collar turned up against the cold and a derby hat perched on his head. A few days later she met him; one of the hotelkeeper's daughters, Kate Ellis, who was a good friend of Will's, invited Betty for dinner because he was coming over. He had brought all the new popular songs from Kansas City, and Kate was sure he would sing for them. After dinner—during which, Betty remembered, Will was awkward and very still—they went into the sitting room where he sat in a low rocking chair with a roll of music in his lap and gradually thawed out and began to sing. "He had a high tenor voice," she noted, and sang without accompaniment all the songs he had heard in the big city, including "Hello, My Baby, Hello, My Honey, Hello, My Ragtime Gal." Afterward they popped corn, pulled taffy, and Will gave her the music for the new songs, asking her to learn to play them on the piano. He would be back, he said.

The two met often that fall. A few days later, to impress the new girl in town, Will rode a horse up and down in front of the depot, showing off his horsemanship; next he appeared on a bicycle for the same purpose. There were visits to farms and ranches all over the neighborhood (the Vinita *Indian Chieftain* noted that "nutting parties, gypsy teas and possum hunts were all the go" that season), and many more evenings of music, with Betty playing the piano or banjo while Will sang, before she had to leave for Arkansas just before Christmas. Shortly after the first of the year, 1900, she received her first letter from him, addressed "My Dear Friend." He knew she was having a great time, he wrote, "after being out among the 'Wild Tribe' " so long—well, he had not been at home three nights in a month himself, and had "taken in every Ball in the Territory and everything else I hear of." He reported on Kate Ellis ("still as pretty as ever") and her sister Lil ("just the *cutest* girl I know and I am as silly about her as ever"), asked her to return as soon as she could, and concluded, "Hoping you will take pity on this poor heartbroken cow pealer and having him rejoicing over these bald prairies on receipt of a few words from you." He was, he said, her "True Friend and Injun Cowboy, W.P. Rogers, Oologah, I.T."

In the middle of March another letter came, datelined "Headquarters, Dogiron Ranch," addressed to "My Dear Betty." It was self-conscious, full of jealous references to the good times she was doubtless having in Arkansas with the "smoothe" young men there, who must offer quite a contrast to the broken-hearted, ignorant Cherokee cowboy, and it was unmistakably a love letter, which he asked her to burn. She didn't

The effervescent, fun-loving Blake girls of Rogers, Arkansas, strike a pose for a local photographer. From top to bottom are Cora, Anna, Waite, Theda, Betty, Virginia, and Zulecki (who was the only child of a second marriage).
WILL ROGERS MEMORIAL COMMISSION

69

burn it, but neither did she reply. The next time the two met was several months later in Springfield, Missouri, where Will was performing with Mulhall's troupe; he put on a wildly exuberant show when he discovered she was in the audience, which led to much teasing by Betty's friends. They saw each other again in the fall, at an Arkansas fair, and Will—lonely, shy, and fiercely proud of his Indian blood—realized that her companions would give her a difficult time over her uncivilized friend. That night there was a dance, and Betty kept looking for Will, but she had only a glimpse of him standing alone outside the hall, watching her dance by. It was the last time she saw him for two years, during which there were no more letters from the Injun Cowboy.

Will had the wanderlust again. Managing a relatively small herd of cattle in fenced pastures held very little appeal for a young man who had grown up on a huge ranch; what he was really longing for were the old days that his father had known in the early years of the Indian Territory, but unhappily that was all gone for good. Will's dreams happened to coincide with a lot of talk circulating through the West about ranching in Argentina; down there, it was said, were endless pampas in a country free of farmers and barbed wire, where a man could ride all day and never see a plowed field or a fence. As Will's nephew Herb McSpadden put it, Will "wasn't used to getting off his pony every few minutes to open a gate, or to working cattle into a fence corner," and by now he realized that to be a successful rancher in Oklahoma he would have to become a farmer.

He made up his mind that Argentina was the place for him, and late in 1901 he went to see his father to announce his decision to leave. Apparently the two had some sharp words: Clem wanted his son to stay on the ranch and take on more responsibility; but responsibility was exactly what Will didn't want. He was determined to ride his own horse, as Clem always had, and after agreeing to sign up for a twenty-year life insurance policy as a token of his responsible nature, he departed. Generously, Clem bought back for $3,000 the herd he had given Will; Will sold off his other steers and said goodbye to the old family ranch for what was in truth the last time. As it turned out, he would never again live in the Verdigris valley, but as he headed out into the world from the land of his birth he took with him the most enduring influences on his life: his Indian heritage, all the Oklahoma roots that ran so deep, and a warm spot in his heart for Betty Blake, the visiting girl from Arkansas.

"My Dear Betty . . .

The social milieu in Rogers, Arkansas, on a Sunday after-noon; an admirer is threatening Betty's curls (left center).

For me to attempt to express my delight for your sweet letter would be utterly impossible so will just put it mild and say I was *very very* much pleased. I was also surprised for I thought you had forgotten your Cowboy (for I am yours as far as I am concerned) . . . I am not 'smoothe' like boys you have for sweethearts. But I know you have not one that will think any more of you than I do although I know they may profess to. Now Betty I know you will think me a Big Fool (which I am) but please consider that you are the one that has done it. But I know you did not mean to and I ought not to have got so broken up over you. But I could not help it so if you do not see fit to answer this please do not say a word about it to any one for the sake of a broken hearted Cherokee Cowboy. . . .

Hoping you will consider what I have told you in my undignified way and if not to please never say anything about it and burn this up.

I am yours with love,
Will Rogers"

A demure Betty Blake, age eighteen

BOTH: WILL ROGERS MEMORIAL COMMISSION

Social Life in the Territory

There was little activity or traffic on Claremore's main street at midday.

WILL ROGERS MEMORIAL, CLAREMORE, OKLA.

At the time of Betty Blake's first visit to Indian Territory the joys of young people her age were simple ones, their fun homemade, and events regarded as humdrum by later generations apt to be special occasions because they were so rare. On these pages are scenes of that charming and long-gone day near the turn of the nineteenth century.

When the railroad first came to Tahlequah it was a lark for the Seminary girls to walk the new-laid ties.

COLLECTION OF LEE AND MARY ELIZABETH GOOD

In these pastoral surroundings members of the Pocahontas Club were photographed during a summer outing.

COLLECTION OF MR. & MRS. JOHN FOREMAN MCCLELLAN

Draped with flags, a wagon crammed with young folks stands in readiness for a 1901 parade in Claremore.

NORTHEASTERN STATE COLLEGE LIBRARY

BOTH: WILL ROGERS MEMORIAL, CLAREMORE, OKLA.

"I cant tell you where to write for I dont know where I will be."

TEXAS JACK'S CIRCUS.
THE
CHEROKEE KID
THE WORLD'S
CHAMPION LASSOER.
He will perform the following feats with the Lasso!

Throwing the Rope with his Foot

THE MOST WONDERFUL FEAT KNOWN.

As a genuine representative of the Wild West, Will became a headliner in remote parts of the world. It is hard to say which pleased him more: featured billing in South Africa or the fiery red velvet suit (at left) acquired in New Zealand.

There was a certain irony to the picture: two footloose young men leaving what was still known as Indian Territory, their eyes starry with the vision of a faraway rancher's paradise where life would be rugged and uncivilized. Will had no difficulty persuading a kindred soul named Dick Parris to accompany him. Although neither had the slightest idea how to get to Argentina, they did know it was off to the south, so they went first to New Orleans, which seemed a logical place to find a ship going in the desired direction. There they learned that no vessels sailed directly to Buenos Aires; they would have to go to New York. But there the story was the same—no ships for the Argentine. Probably they should go to England, someone suggested, since ships from Liverpool occasionally sailed for Buenos Aires.

After taking in the sights of New York the two embarked on the S.S. *Philadelphia* in March, 1902, bound for England. It was the first of many ocean voyages for Will, on each of which he would be deathly seasick; by the time they reached the British Isles he had about decided to become a naturalized citizen unless someone built a bridge back to the States. Once on land, he was full of good humor again. He wrote his sisters about going through customs, where they searched his baggage for tobacco and spirits: "I didn't chew," he said, "and my spirits had all left me on that boat." He and Dick were in a hotel room "almost papered with pictures of Queen Victoria, who certainly had a stand in with the photographer," and he was having difficulties common to all Americans—figuring out the English money, getting used to the food, and understanding the language as spoken there (everyone talked so fast, Will said, that he finally "flagged" a man he had asked for directions, saying he was "perfectly willing to pay him for his over time" if he

When the innocents from Indian Territory arrived in London in 1902, the city was decked with flags and bunting in preparation for the coronation of Edward VII.
RADIO TIMES HULTON

would only speak more slowly).

The time the two young men spent in London coincided with the preparations for Edward VII's coronation, which Will referred to as the "big blow-out." They even caught a glimpse of "his big Nibs at a distance. Don't think he recognized us, though." The entire city was in a state of excitement and confusion in anticipation of the event, but the two Americans found their way to Parliament, London Bridge, the Tower, to several theatres (the English, Will stated, were "not up to the Americans in tragedy or comedy"), and to Westminster Abbey, to gaze at the monuments to the great. "I knew very few of the men personally," he said.

Then, in company with two hundred Spanish and Portuguese emigrants ("There seems to be every kind of woolie in the world on this boat," he remarked; "I can't understand a soul but Dick"), they set sail by slow freighter, finally reaching Buenos Aires during the first week in May. After all they had been led to expect, their first brush with the cattle business in Argentina came as a huge disappointment. In one of the early letters he wrote his father from South America, Will observed that he had been into the interior and had discovered that, while it was marvelous cattle and farm country, "it is no place to make money unless you have $10,000 to invest," and for those without that kind of capital there were hundreds of men competing for every job. He was trying to learn Spanish ("I think I can say 6 words—did know 7 and forgot one"); but because of the language barrier, his unfamiliarity with the country, his distaste for the local food, and the wages offered ($5 to $8 a month), Will soon concluded that Argentina was not for him. After two weeks Dick was so homesick that he decided to leave. Will's bankroll was about to give out after three months of travel, much of it first class, and on the theory that Clem might be sending him some money, Will bought his buddy a ticket home and spent most of what he had left on presents for his father and sisters, which he sent with Dick. There were broad hints in Will's letters to his father that money would be welcome; but none was forthcoming.

In mid-June Will decided that there was no further point of staying in Argentina, and he wrote his father to say he might be starting home at any time. In a letter to the Claremore *Progress*, filled with information about the country, the customs, the methods of riding and handling cattle (Will was fascinated with the saddles, stirrups, and rawhide ropes used by the gauchos), his parting words of advice were "for all you people to fight shy of this part of the globe. You never know a country until you leave it, so stay where you are." By this time he had checked out of his hotel and was sleeping in the park. Unable to speak more than a few words of Spanish, homesick, his money gone (he claimed to be living "in perfect ease, picking up a few unthought of facts but no loose change"), he may or may not have realized that his father was letting him work things out his own way, but he did know that he had to have work immediately if he was going to eat. Early one morning he wandered down to the city's stock pens and watched some workers trying to round up mules in a corral. The mules were uncooperative, the men not adept, and Will, sitting on the fence watching the animals run around, couldn't resist throwing a loop over the head of one mule, catching it on the first try. The boss was impressed and offered Will the equivalent of 25 cents for each mule he roped, and he spent the entire day at it, taking no time out for lunch or dinner. Later he heard about a job tending cattle on a boat sailing for Africa. Will wasn't enthusiastic about the work or the destination, but since things couldn't get much worse than they already were, he decided to take it.

With their bolos, gauchos could "rope a steer further than I could hit him with a rock," Will discovered.
COURTESY OAS PHOTOS

Before leaving Buenos Aires he wrote a letter to his father, the tone of which seemed to indicate either that there had been some friction between them or that Will's conscience was troubling him. Whatever the case, he wanted to straighten matters out. He had heard or sensed that Clem's friends thought he was squandering his father's money, and this bothered him. He wrote, in part:

I have spent a world of money in my time, but I am satisfied as some one else has got the good of some of it . . . if you will only give me credit for just spending my own as I think I have I will be as happy as if I had a million. . . . I am more than willing to admit that you have done everything in the world for me and tried to make something more than I am out of me (which is not your fault) but as to our financial dealings I think I paid you all up and everyone else.

I only write these things so we may better understand each other. I cannot help it because my nature is not like other people to make money, and I don't want you all to think I am no good simply because I don't keep my money. I have less . . . than lots of you and I daresay I enjoy life better than any of you, and that is my policy. I have always delt honestly with every one and think the world and all of you and all the folks and will be among you all soon as happy as any one in the world, as then I can work and show the people that I only spend what I make. . . . Don't think about me for I am the happiest one in the lot, and will get along all OK. Address my mail to me at Capetown in care of the American Consul, South Africa. . . ."

It was an expression of a philosophy that was to remain with him all his life. Money, as such, had little importance for Will; it was never anything more than the means to enjoyment for himself and others. Meanwhile, in typical fashion, he was on his way to the next stop. Implicit in the letter, as in so many others he wrote to his father over a long period, was the powerful familial tie that exerted such a strong pull on him. If there were occasional disagreements between the headstrong young man and the positive-minded parent, they were no more than might be expected between two generations of the same blood. What comes through the lines of all Will's effervescent, newsy letters is the deep admiration and respect he had for his father, along with a half-defensive hope that the older man would not be disappointed in him because of what he was doing.

During the twenty-five agonizing days it took the *Kelvinside* to run from Buenos Aires to Durban, South Africa, Will served as night watchman on the cattle deck since, as he said, he was too

Groping for a comparison, Will wrote his sisters that Buenos Aires (above) and other Argentine cities "are built something on the order of San Antionia, Texas."
PHOTOWORLD

sick to do anything else and there was no way they could fire him. What he called a "menagerie ship" was hauling 750 mules, 300 cows, 700 sheep, 300 work horses and 50 thoroughbred horses, 40 Shetland ponies, and feed and water for them—a cargo belonging to an Englishman with the unlikely name of Mr. Piccione—to South Africa, where Piccione raised and raced thoroughbred horses. The Englishman had offered him work, which was the only way he could get into South Africa, and he arrived in time to see the aftermath of the Boer War. Many British troops were still in evidence, but Will's sympathies were all for the Boers, whom he thought fine people, peaceful, law-abiding, and friendly. For two months he worked on Piccione's estate (the stables were "veritable palaces," Will said, "being heated by steam and lighted by electricity"), feeding and exercising the horses, helping the veterinarian and the blacksmith, and learning to jump well enough so that Piccione made him his steeplechase jockey. Interestingly, Will said that the Englishman was the only man he ever saw who could "holler louder and more at a person than Papa." But once again he was discovering that there was no place quite like home. He ad-

Pretoria, the capital of the Transvaal, had not changed much in the fifteen years between the time this picture was taken and when Will visited the town in 1903.
INFORMATION OFFICE OF SOUTH AFRICA

vised his friends in Claremore "to fight shy of this country," where all the common labor was done by kaffirs or Negroes— wild-looking people with "rings, chains, and all kinds of old scrap in their ears and nose" and some with horns tied to their heads. They were always singing, he noticed, traveled at a run, and were "as crazy as snakes."

By November's end Will was on the move again. He wrote his father that he was going to drive a bunch of mules two hundred fifty miles from Durban to Ladysmith. His beloved saddle and outfit had been lost or stolen; but, he proudly added, he had enough money to send $140 to pay for that insurance policy that signified responsibility. He didn't need any money for himself; he was going to work in a day or two. In familiar style, he was putting off going home; he told his father not to look for him for three months or so. He expected to return in the spring, and he begged Clem not to let anyone touch old Comanche while he was away. As it turned out, he was correct about his arrival in Indian Territory in the spring, but he was just a year off on the date.

Ladysmith, in Northern Natal province, was a curious sort of place for Will Rogers' show-business career to begin; but fate has a way of bringing people together in unpredictable ways with unpredictable results. The town was named for the wife of the British colonial governor, Sir Harry Smith; she was a Spanish woman he had rescued during the Peninsular War. Between 1899 and 1900 it had been the site of a protracted siege of British troops by the Boers under Petrus Joubert. But Will's encounter with fate had nothing to do with Boers or Ladysmith, but with an import from America: Texas Jack's Wild West Show. It was playing in the town when Will arrived with his herd of mules, and it was like a breath of fresh air from home for the young man.

The American cowboy and frontiersman were legends in their own time—at home and abroad—and the so-called Wild West shows were bringing riding and shooting exhibitions, roping demonstrations, and mock battles between cowboys and Indians to thrilled audiences throughout the United States, Europe, Australia, and to towns like Ladysmith in South Africa. The most famous and successful of the shows was Buffalo Bill's "Wild West and Congress of Rough Riders of the World," featuring "Colonel" William Cody himself—former army scout and buffalo hunter—with flowing yellow hair and mustache, dressed in buckskins and high boots, riding a magnificent white horse. Cody, with the famous Annie Oakley, put on exhibitions of fancy shooting, Chief Sitting Bull was on the payroll, and the extravaganza had even been put on for an approving Queen Victoria. At least two of Will's neighbors had joined up with Buffalo Bill, and when they came back from their tour in 1899 the Vinita *Indian Chieftain* was full of eye-popping statistics about the show. It had been on the road for 200 days, given 341 performances in 132 towns and 24 states. But what was more impressive was the magnitude of the operation: 529 employees; 325 riding horses and 119 head of baggage stock to draw 35 wagons, 2 water tanks, 2 engines for producing electric light, 4 buggies, 2 fieldpieces with caissons, and 1 gatling gun (by 1899 the mock battles were getting bigger and bigger). To haul the show around the country required 16 flatcars, 15 stock cars, and 8 sleeping cars, along with seats enough for 13,000 spectators.

If Buffalo Bill's show was the top, Texas Jack's was a long way down the line, but in 1902 it looked good to Will, and he went to see if Texas Jack was really an American and from Texas, and if

"The conveyance in towns," Will wrote of the Zulu rickshaws, *"is a two-wheel doings that a large guy with horns hitches himself in."*
PHOTOWORLD

With Texas Jack in South Africa

At right is the dashing impresario of Texas Jack's Wild West Show, whose entire cast is assembled below. It included Jack's wife, a cowboy band, various riders and trick ropers, a zebra and monkeys, clowns, Mr. Ajax the "Flexible Marvel," and one Harry Ward, who doubled in brass as a "trapeze artiste" and heavyweight lifter. Certain artistic liberties were inevitable: for pitched battles the parts of redskins were played by Zulus and Asiatic Indians. Will Rogers (at center, under 8) was billed as The Cherokee Kid.

BOTH: WILL ROGERS MEMORIAL, CLAREMORE, OKLA.

he had any news of Will's friends. Jack was not only authentic, but immediately wanted to know how good Will was at roping and riding. Like the cowboy he had heard applying for a job in Texas some time ago, Will told Jack a little more than was necessary. He wasn't much of a rider, he said, but he could do a few rope tricks, and proceeded to show Texas Jack one of his best, the Big Crinoline, which was a classic of rope-spinning and a sure-fire crowd pleaser. Starting with a small loop, the roper twirls the line around his body, gradually letting out more and more rope until the entire length—as much as 30 to 60 feet—is part of a huge circle spinning around the man. As it turned out, Texas Jack had been offering £50 to anyone who could do that trick and in five years hadn't had a taker; then Will had to execute it before he knew about the offer. Jack gave him a job then and there, and as an employee Will wasn't allowed to compete for the prize.

There were about 35 or 40 people and 30 horses in the show, and the usual schedule was to stay in a town for two or three days before moving on to the next one. As Will was careful to inform his father, it was not "a wild mob" like the circuses at home. Texas Jack, who billed himself as the "World's Greatest Sharpshooter" was, Will said, a much better shot than Buffalo Bill, a fine rider, and never touched tobacco or liquor. He liked Will and encouraged him to keep experimenting with his rope tricks. And as the young man wrote half-apologetically to Clem, "Of course the business is not the best business, but so long as there is good money in it and it is honest, there is no objection to it." He was certain that he would learn things from Texas Jack "that will enable me to make my living in the world without making it by day labor." Jack had hired him as a trick roper, but he was also riding a bucking horse and performing in "blood curdling scenes of western life in America," in which he sometimes took the part of an Indian, sometimes a Negro, and did the cakewalk and sang "coon songs," as the genre frequently sung by black-face comedians was called. On the program he was billed as "The Cherokee Kid—the Man Who Can Lasso the Tail off a Blowfly," and Will had some cards printed to hand out to admirers:

THE CHEROKEE KID
Fancy Lasso Artist and Rough Rider
TEXAS JACK'S WILD WEST CIRCUS

With all the practice and experimenting with new tricks, he

To the tune of "Any Old Place I Can Hang My Hat is Home, Sweet Home to Me":

I've traveled round this world
a bit,
I've been from coast to coast,
Had every kind of food to eat,
From beans to quail on toast.
There's not a land discovered yet,
But's good enough for me,
So when I'm asked where I live,
I answer, on the I.T.
        Chorus
I aint got no regular place
That I can call my home
I can't go back to America,
She's far across the foam.
Walking, there's nothing doing,
Passage aint free,
So any place I can hang my
panama
Is home, sweet home to me.

Will Rogers to "Dear Home Folks" from South Africa
Nov. 17, 1902

83

was getting to be quite a fancy roper indeed, and at matinees, which were always crowded with children, Will was the center of attraction. Texas Jack always gave a medal to the boy who could throw a lasso best, and Will was constantly trailed by groups of youngsters who wanted him to show them what to do so they could win a medal. South Africa may have had plenty of enthusiasm for trick ropers, but it did not have the kind of rope needed for his act, and several letters to Clem include appeals for "about 100 feet of the best kind of hard twist rope. . . . Any of the boys will show you what I used to use. Pretty small but hard twist. I can't get a thing here that we use." He was also writing to Sallie, asking her to send him some "coon songs." ("Just Because She Made Dem Goo-Goo Eyes," which came out in 1900, was typical, and Will loved to sing, as Betty Blake had discovered on her visit to Oologah.)

He was homesick, he admitted in a letter to the folks in Indian Territory, but he had found his favorite saddle, bridle, "leggins," and spurs, and had been raised from $20 to $25 a week, less his meals, which cost about 75 cents each, and he was continuing to learn from Texas Jack, whom he later called "one of the smartest showmen I ever met." Apparently, Jack first gave Will the idea of a stage act involving a pony, and he certainly taught him the tricks of the trade: as Will was to say, "He could do a bum act with a rope that an ordinary man couldn't get away with, and make the audience think it was great, so I used to study him by the hour and from him I learned the great secret of the show business—*learned when to get off.* It's the fellow that knows when to quit that the audience wants more of." It was, all in all, an immensely valuable experience, but by the fall of 1903 Will had had his fill of South Africa, home was calling, and he decided to be on his way—on his way, that is, via a small detour.

He thought he might as well head for the U.S. by first completing a trip around the world. Texas Jack hated to see him go, but he gave Will as glowing a recommendation as a young, ambitious performer could ask for. Written on stationery embellished with a full-length picture of Jack, the "World's Greatest Sharpshooter," it read:

I have the very great pleasure in recommending Mr. W. P. Rogers (The Cherokee Kid) to circus proprietors. He has performed with me during my present South African tour and I consider him to be the champion trick rough rider and lasso thrower of the world. He is

"Dear Willie—

. . . Little Charley McClellan died in Tennessee where he was going to school just before Christmas. They brought him home & buried him here at Claremore Cemetary. People commence to take their allotments on the first of January. I havent taken mine yet. I got my & your no. They are about 3434 & 5. Willie if you don't come home this fall you will have to send me a Power of Attorney to take your allotment for you. . . . Me, you, & Spi will take the old home place. . . .

Your Pa, C. V. Rogers Feb. 9, 1903"

sober, industrious, hard working at all times and is always to be relied upon. I shall be very pleased to give him an engagement at any time should he wish to return.

Will renewed his acquaintance with the miseries of ocean travel—the trip lasted twenty-five days, across the Indian Ocean to New Zealand and then to Australia—and his first letters to the family revealed that he planned to be home not later than December 1. However, he had decided that he would just see a little of the country as long as he was there. As usual, he was intrigued by all the sights: Australia, the greatest sheep-raising country in the world; aborigines who could throw a boomerang so that "it will shave your hat off going and your head off coming back"; kangaroos as common as jack rabbits. And, inevitably, his letters were filled with observations about the different methods of handling cattle and the types of saddles in use. He also regarded Australians as the most conceited people on the face of the globe.

Then he announced yet another change of plans. His tour of Australia had consumed all the money he had saved with Texas Jack, so he had taken a job with the Wirth Brothers circus in New Zealand, performing a roping and trick-riding act, which proved a great success. The Auckland *Herald* went out of its way to compliment his "highly original exhibition" which "fairly dazzled the crowd. He seems to be able to lasso anything from the asset of a professional bankrupt or a wildly galloping steed to the business end of a flash of lightning. It was certainly the best performance of the sort ever seen here. The Cherokee Kid is a gentleman with a large American accent and a splendid skill. . . ."

For the second year in a row Will spent Christmas thousands of miles from home, but he vowed it would be the last one. He had heard that St. Louis was planning a world's fair in the summer of 1904, and he would be there for the opening, he assured the family. After eight months with the Wirth show he had earned enough money to book third-class passage from New Zealand to San Francisco, and from there he rode a freight train home. During his two-year absence he had traveled fifty thousand miles (many of them while seasick). As he summed it all up: "I started out first class, dropped to second class, and come home third class. But when I was companion to those cows on that perfumed voyage to Africa it might be called no class at all."

". . . I was always proud in America to own that I am a Cherokee, and I find on leaving them that I am equally as proud to own that I am an American, for if there is any nation earning a rep. abroad it is America. I have had arguments with every nationality of man under the sun in regard to the merits of our people and country . . . all these big fish stories are traced to the Americans, and you have got to uphold the rep.

I am as ever your loving son. William Sydney, Australia"

Will Rogers to family Sept. 28, 1903

WILL ROGERS MEMORIAL, CLAREMORE, OKLA.

"It is either stage and make a good living or no show business at all for me."

In one of the few likenesses that suggests his Indian blood, Will poses on his favorite horse, Comanche, at the 1904 St. Louis World's Fair. Above is a special issue of Campbell's Journal, *dedicated to the Fair.*

MISSOURI HISTORICAL SOCIETY

When at last the prodigal returned, the news was duly noted in the pages of the Vinita *Daily Chieftain* for April 12, 1904: "Will Rogers of Talala was here today enroute home from a trip to southern Africa." He had seen a lot of the world but had hardly made his fortune, people observed. Yet he had acquired something else, according to Spi Trent, "a kind of sure-footedness . . . which comes to a feller who has learned to paddle his own canoe."

Theodore Roosevelt, whom Will had met when the colonel and his Rough Riders held a reunion in Oklahoma City, was President of the United States now, and many other changes had taken place during Will's absence. In Claremore business was booming. An oil strike at Red Fork, near Sapulpa, had caused another of those rushes for which Indian Territory was already famous, described by a local newspaper as "a never ending stream of wildly excited men" flocking to the scene. "Each train brings new recruits to the throng that now overcrowds the town, and swarm through the streets of the tent city. . . . Farms have been abandoned in the mad rush by men who have been stampeded by the greatly exaggerated stories sent out from here." Up in Vinita they had what they called home-manufactured ice now, in place of what used to be cut from ponds and rivers in winter, and the first automobile had arrived in town on September 20, 1902, to a chorus of wry comments. "Stockades are being built around a number of Muskogee residences in anticipation of a possible uprising among the bronco element," an editorial writer noted, and a petition was circulated requesting an ordinance to prohibit the running of motor cars on the public streets.

Clem Rogers was serving his final term as senator from the Cooweescoowee district and was as busy as ever in the affairs of the Cherokee Nation, which, as he had foreseen, was about to vanish forever. In fact, the last regularly elected National Council of the Cherokees was serving its final term of office. Clem, as usual, was looking to the future, and for the next half-decade he would devote his great energy, strong opinions, and ability to the movement for Oklahoma statehood. (He was one of fifty-five delegates elected from Indian Territory to the constitutional convention that assembled in 1906, and that year the district he represented was named Rogers County for him. This work finally culminated in the proclamation by Theodore Roosevelt on November 16, 1907, declaring Oklahoma a state.)

But to Clem's son Will none of these developments was half as exciting as what was going on in St. Louis, Missouri, two weeks after his return. It seemed as if everyone in the country was singing "Meet me in St. Loo-ey, Loo-ey, meet me at the Fair!"; and anyone who could scrape up the cash was planning to visit the exposition celebrating (one year late) the one-hundredth anniversary of the Louisiana Purchase. In an era before packaged entertainment, the love of a show was still strong, and the coming of one still enough of a rarity that people would make extraordinary efforts to attend it. The mood of America was still

No effort was spared to make the centennial of the Louisiana Purchase the most lavish affair of its kind. At left is the ornate Hall of Festivals, flanked by cascades and a lagoon. Opposite, horses on parade on the Pike, or midway, prior to the opening of a horse show.
BOTH: MISSOURI HISTORICAL SOCIETY

one of youth and freshness, and there existed a feeling of wonder and awe regarding the new day science and industry would bring. As Edgar Lee Masters described it, the country "seemed a land of liberty and happiness, approaching an era of enlightenment and wisdom." Thomas Jefferson had purchased a vast, almost unpopulated wilderness in 1803, and what the nation was celebrating just now was the miracle that had transformed it, within the span of a century, into thirteen states peopled by twelve and a half million Americans. That commemoration was to take the form of the largest world's fair ever held. London's Crystal Palace exhibition had occupied 20 acres, the Columbian Exposition in Chicago in 1893 over 600 acres, but this would cover a 1,400-acre tract. Fifteen new buildings, laid out in the shape of a fan, featured the Palace of Electricity and the Palace of Machinery (in which the eye-catching attraction was 100 automobiles, one of which had made the trip all the way from New York under its own power). There would be extensive foreign exhibits—replicas of Robert Burns' birthplace and the Grand Trianon of Versailles, of a typical Swedish farmhouse, an English garden, and grass-thatched huts from America's newest territorial acquisition, the Philippine Islands.

Sculpture and statuary by Augustus Saint-Gaudens and Daniel Chester French were to be set off by a six-acre rose garden, a colossal floral clock, and numerous waterfalls and miniature lagoons. (The necessity for having clear water in these cascades and pools had not been lost on the Fair's promoters: it was said with much justice that St. Louisans could not see their feet in a bathtub, and Mark Twain—commenting on the "batter" that passed for water in those parts—claimed that a tumbler of it held an acre of land in solution. But, happily, chemical coagulants and a system of newly installed reservoirs had cleared up the water by the time the gates opened on May 1, 1904.)

A roar went up from two hundred thousand throats when, in response to an electrical signal from the White House in Washington, ten thousand colored flags were simultaneously unfurled, those fountains and waterfalls unloosed their cascades of chemically clarified water, the world's largest electrical pipe organ burst into song, and John Philip Sousa's mighty band struck up the Fair's official song, "Hymn of the West." (By closing day, seven months later, when Sousa led his musicians in "Auld Lang Syne," some twenty million Americans had seen and marveled at the Louisiana Purchase Exposition.)

Beyond the Fair's array of exhibits stretched a long, wide street or midway called the Pike, where venders swarmed (it was claimed that the ice cream cone, the hot dog, and iced tea were introduced for the first time on the Pike that summer), and where the amusement concessions were also clustered. These included a 264-foot Ferris wheel, which had been the sensation of the Chicago Exposition, the Temple of Mirth, the Jungle of Mirrors, Hagenbeck's Wild Animal Show, and, predictably, a Wild West show.

Almost as soon as he returned from his global junket, Will was summoned by his old employer, Colonel Zach Mulhall, who was assembling a group of riders for the Wild West Show. Will was home for only a week before he left for the Mulhall ranch near Guthrie to discuss plans. Spi Trent always thought the Colonel exerted a good influence on Will, and certainly the whole Mulhall family was immensely fond of him. By this time Mulhall's daughter Lucille had made quite a name for herself as a performing cowgirl: she won a diamond medal at Fort Worth, where she ran off with top honors roping and tying a steer; she broke the record for roping and tying at McAlester, in Indian Territory; and she was an increasingly popular attraction at fairs and contests throughout the West. The cowboys

Every day gawkers witnessed exotic scenes like this one, at Cairo-on-the-Pike.
MISSOURI HISTORICAL SOCIETY

Mulhall had sent for were drifting in every day, and one of them was a young man from Pennsylvania named Tom Mix, who had been a bartender before beginning work on a ranch. For nearly a week Will stayed with them, working away at his rope tricks and nearly driving Mrs. Mulhall to distraction by endlessly picking on the piano a tune called "I May be Crazy, But I Ain't No Fool."

Some indication of how frenetic and confused Will's activities were that summer and fall may be gleaned from the numerous letters to his family that survive, indicating how he was shuttling from one thing to another, busily engaged in several pursuits simultaneously, or at least in some overlapping fashion. The chronology tends to become blurred, but what is certain, at least, is that he worked at the Fair for Mulhall, and later for two men named Cummins and Tompkins; that he performed with his friend Theo McSpadden at the Standard Theatre, a burlesque house in St. Louis, where the two put on a trick roping act; that he got a job in vaudeville that took him to Chicago for several weeks; that he had in mind working up an act in which he would rope a horse on stage if only he could find the right pony with which to do it; that he traveled back and forth between St. Louis and Indian Territory frequently—on at least one occasion to sell his father a horse and buggy in order to raise some money (he wanted $350 in cash, and "this is your chance for he is cheap at that," Will told Clem, but the old man had been trading for horses before Willie was born, and the negotiations went on for a month or so before the deal was settled); and that he renewed his friendship with Betty Blake.

When he arrived at the Fair Will found that the Mulhall troupe of cowboys was to be combined with the Cummins Indians in a spectacular show involving some six or seven hundred horsemen. They had only been performing for about a month when Mulhall and the head stable man got into a fight; after an evening performance they met on the Pike, and Mulhall pulled a gun and started shooting. The Colonel's shots only grazed his opponent but wounded seriously a young boy who was watching the battle, as well as a cowboy who was trying to break it up, and Zach was hustled off to jail and held without bail. (When the news reached Vinita, the *Daily Chieftain* editorialized indignantly that "The world knows all it need to know of the wild and lawless spirit that was indiginous in this country a generation ago," and observed that the Wild West show had "run its course, at least, on this continent.") In the aftermath of

Having one's photograph taken in a Japanese rickshaw was one of the things to do.
MISSOURI HISTORICAL SOCIETY

the shooting some of Mulhall's disgruntled cowboys pulled out and went home, but Will joined Cummins and his Indians on the midway and at some point performed in a small Wild West show Charles Tompkins was running inside the fairground. Years later Tompkins recalled Will's almost fanatical devotion to practicing rope tricks. Every morning at daylight, while the other cowboys were lying in bed waiting for the breakfast call, he would be down in the arena with his lariats, experimenting with new throws, perfecting old ones. As Tompkins remarked, he often heard showmen claim that they had taught Will what he knew about roping, but that just wasn't so: "No one taught Will anything. He got it the hard way, by hard work."

Betty Blake, unaware that the "Injun Cowboy" was even back in the States, had come to St. Louis to visit one of her sisters and take in the Fair. As she was walking through one of the exhibits on a Sunday morning she overheard a girl remark that Will Rogers was performing in the Wild West Show. Betty sent him a note, and back came a reply, addressed "Dear Old Pal," asking her to come to the afternoon performance and send for him; she could see the show and then they would have dinner and spend the evening together. Her sister and a friend gave her the usual hard time over her cowboy acquaintance, and since she "was not particularly thrilled about Will's profession" anyway, as she later confessed, she approached the arena with some misgiving. When Will appeared her worst fears were realized. He was wearing a skin-tight red velvet suit, trimmed with gold braid, and Betty was so embarrassed she didn't even hear the applause for his act. After the performance there was a long wait for Will to join them (he was chasing the manager all over the fairground to collect his back pay), and when he showed up, breathless and apologetic, he explained the spectacular suit. In Australia, where he had occasionally been billed as "The Mexican Rope Artist," Mrs. Wirth, the circus owner's wife, had made him the velvet costume on the apparent theory that a Mexican rope artist would wear a colorful get-up (Will had never quite forgotten the sensational Vincente Oropeza, either). Normally, Will wore chaps, a colored shirt, and a handkerchief around his neck when he appeared, but he wanted to look his best for Betty. (He never wore the red suit again after seeing her reaction.) The couple had dinner together, strolled all evening along the Pike, went to the Irish Village where a tenor named John McCormack was singing for the first time in America, and said goodnight. The following morning Betty

One man termed the Fair "an astonishing pattern of elaborate and universal chaos."
MISSOURI HISTORICAL SOCIETY

received a contrite note from Will: he was sorry to miss seeing her again, but he had received a telegram from his father and was leaving for Claremore that day on business.

When she next heard from him it was late October and he was in Chicago. During that summer in St. Louis, on free Saturday afternoons, Will had taken a job at the Standard Theatre, where he and Theo McSpadden put on an act Zach Mulhall had once suggested to him—a roping turn on the stage. Someone in the audience liked it well enough to write to the owner of a Chicago theatre chain, and the next thing Will knew he was offered a week's engagement there for $30. Knowing nothing of vaudeville customs, Will sent no photographs or publicity material to Chicago ahead of his arrival, and when he got there discovered that his act had been canceled (when no advance material came the management assumed that he was not coming either). So for days he hung around booking offices or went to the theatre, and one afternoon as he was buying a ticket for a show, he heard the house manager say he needed an act. Will informed the man that he had one and was told that he was hired, provided he could collect his gear and be at the theatre in time for the curtain. He opened that afternoon and played for the rest of the week, and during one show he was going through the rope tricks he had perfected with Texas Jack when a dog from an animal act ran onto the stage; without thinking, Will tossed a loop over the animal and hauled him in. The laughter and loud applause this produced made him realize that people wanted to see him actually catch something. And that in turn reminded him of Texas Jack's notion that an act involving a pony would be a hit on the stage. What quickly evolved in Will's mind was something that had never been done before in a theatre—roping a running horse—and he was sure he could bring it off if he could obtain the right animal. The right one, he knew, was a beautiful little bay pony, with a black mane and tail, that Mrs. Mulhall had offered to sell him for $100.

Will didn't like Chicago much, he told Betty, and he was thinking of coming back to St. Louis to earn enough money to buy the horse he needed. Then he launched into a subject that was very much in his thoughts: he had seen her only long enough to learn that she was not yet married, but he wanted to know if she was "contracted for" or if she had "a steady fellow." In that case, "please put me down and out in the 1st round. But if not then please file my application." According to form, he said, both of them "should have matrimonied long ago. It

The Tyrolean Alps Restaurant, set amid peaks, catered to the Fair's hungry.
MISSOURI HISTORICAL SOCIETY

wouldent do for this young gang to look at our *teeth*, you know."
He had not had a girl since he left on his world tour, he told her
—he had been too busy making a living, and when he returned
home had felt out of place and behind the times, so many of his
friends were married or engaged. But, he went on, "I could just
love a girl about your caliber. See you know I was always kinder
headstrong about you anyway. But I always thought that a
cowboy dident quite come up to your Ideal."

Apparently Betty took offense at the remark about her age
and unmarried status, for early November found Will back in
St. Louis, writing his apologies, assuring her that it was a joke
"meaning we both should of married *each other* or somebody by
now." He had made good in Chicago, but hadn't been able to
convince anyone about the horse act, so he was going home for
Christmas. As evidence of his seriousness of purpose, he wrote
her something quite reminiscent of the letter he had sent Clem
from South America. "I havent been a bad fellow," he said,
"and never did anything bad only just foolish and a spendthrift
and blew in a little fortune all my own, not a cent of my Father,
as people might think, only mine. But at that I have done some
good. I spent it on other people." Now that he was making his
own way he didn't want to stay in the Territory, since people
would only think he was living off his father. As one more
promise of his financial future he added, "I will own the old
home place and farm and am even with the world and am so
happy or can be but thats why I dont stay at home."

After winning a blue ribbon at a performance for visiting
cattlemen during the final days of the Fair, he returned to
Claremore just before Thanksgiving, and was begging Betty
to write him a long letter (the last one, he said, was so chilly he
had had to wear his overcoat while reading it) and to join him
there for Christmas. He had, he said, a nice little rope for her.

Meantime, he was rehearsing with the pony, Teddy—
named for Theodore Roosevelt—which he had bought from
Mrs. Mulhall. He had staked out a plot of ground as big as a
stage and was going over and over his new routine until he had
it down pat. By spring he thought he was ready to try out the act
in New York, and once again Colonel Mulhall figured in his
plans. Zach had been sentenced to three years in jail for the St.
Louis shooting, but appealed and was acquitted after a second
trial, and early in April, 1905, he loaded his horses and equipment aboard a train and headed east to perform with the Wild
West Show in New York. Will sent Teddy and his roping horse

Comanche with Mulhall while he and Jim Minnick, a Texas friend, traveled east by way of the nation's capital, where they called at the White House.

On April 27, 1905, Will Rogers made his New York debut in Madison Square Garden with the Mulhall ropers and riders, a troupe that included Lucille, Tom Mix, and a number of Will's cronies. The Colonel was a natural showman who loved the spectacular but could not abide phonies, and Will liked to recall that every one of his cowboys was the genuine article. Will was making $20 a week as the featured roper in the show, and within two weeks after they opened he got one of the big breaks of his career.

According to a New York *Herald* clipping he sent to his family, Lucille Mulhall was roping to the music of the Seventh Regiment band when a big, eight-hundred-pound steer, with horns that spread five feet, ran into the ring and suddenly started for the stands. Lucille and some of the cowboys tried to head it off, but the steer leaped the bars into the seats and, while the crowd panicked, loped up the stairs all the way to the balcony, where it disappeared behind the box seats. Hot on its heels were the cowboys, and, as the *Herald* article described it, "The Indian Will Rogers . . . headed the steer off" and got his rope around its horns. "Alone and afoot, he was no match for the brute's strength, but he swerved it down the steps on the Twenty-seventh street side, where it jumped again into the ring" and was roped by the men in the arena and led away. According to the account (which ran a subhead, "Indian Cowpuncher's Quickness Prevents Harm"), the Seventh Regiment band fled during the excitement, occupants of seats on one whole side of the Garden stampeded for cover, with women screaming and men shouting, and Colonel Mulhall had been heard yelling to Lucille to "follow that baby up the stairs and bring him back or else stay there" herself.

In a letter to the editor of the Claremore *Progress*, to whom he also mailed the clipping, Will announced proudly that he "made the biggest hit here I ever dreamed of in my Roping Act and finished my good luck by catching the wild steer that went clear up into the dress circles of the garden among the people." No man to miss an opportunity, he set out to capitalize on the publicity with theatrical managers, for he had already concluded that the days of the big Wild West shows were numbered, and he had decided to break into what was then the most exciting and glamorous aspect of show business—vaudeville.

TWO COWBOYS WILL TRY TO TAKE BIG PRIZE

Minnick and Rogers on Way to New York to Enter Broncho Riding Contest.

J. H. Minnick, of Seymour, Tex., and Will Rogers, of Claremore, I. T., two of the most celebrated cowboys of the Southwest, passed through Washington ....erday on their way to New York, where they will enter the $1,000 prize broncho riding contest in Madison Square Garden on Monday night.

Mr. Minnick was here during the inauguration, and is remembered as the cowboy in the red shirt who did such wonderful tricks with his pony and rope on the Avenue as the parade passed by. His friend and comrade, Will Rogers, is perhaps the finest ropeman in the world, doing a number of fancy tricks with a rope which few cowboys ever attempted.

This morning the two Westerners, attired in their cowboy boots and hats, went to the White House, and did some of their choice tricks for the entertainment of the children of the President. Rogers showed the children how a cowboy jumps the rope.

Rogers is one of the few cowboys who can use two lassoes at once, and he has attained more success at this feat than any man living. He can catch a rider with one rope and the horse with the other.

The two companions will try to capture the $1,000 prize in New York Monday. They will come back through Washington, and say that they will be here when President Roosevelt arrives. It is their intention to give a special performance for his benefit.

Here, Goldie St. Clair, known as the World's Champion Bucking-Horse Rider, hangs on with aplomb. In 1910 she appeared in a stage act produced by Will.

Hitting the Tanbark Trail

There were two versions of the Wild West show—that uniquely American institution that recreated the old West for spellbound audiences all over the world. One was the blood-and-thunder spectacle of cowboys, Indians, mock gunbattles, and the inevitable attack on a stagecoach racing across the arena. The other was the form of entertainment that eventually became the rodeo. Assembled by entrepreneurs like Colonel Zach Mulhall, the likes of Will Rogers, Tom Mix, Lucille Mulhall, and others hit the trail in pursuit of fame and fortune (see clipping opposite from a Washington paper). For Will, the lightning struck in New York's Madison Square Garden (below) when he roped a crazed steer that had run into the stands. In this photograph, he identified himself with an "X" and marked with an "O" the spot where he finally brought down the steer.

ALL: WILL ROGERS MEMORIAL, CLAREMORE, OKLA.

O where I roped the steer

PHOTO BY HAAS

One of the best of the cowboy-
and-Indian shows was that
put on by the Miller Brothers'
101 Ranch, as a sideline to
its ranching and experimental
farming activities near Ponca
City, Oklahoma. The photographs here and on the next
two pages were taken before
1910 by Emil Lenders, a
Philadelphia artist, as studies
for his paintings, and they
bring back the action and excitement of the extravaganzas
that thrilled American audiences after the real Wild West
had vanished into oblivion.

BOTH: WESTERN HISTORY COLLECTIONS
UNIVERSITY OF OKLAHOMA LIBRARY

The 1909 program for the 101 Ranch Wild West Show listed such varied fare as real Osage and Pawnee Indians, Prince Lucca and the Cossacks, the Deadwood stagecoach, and a re-enactment of the Pat Hennessy massacre. At left are a pair of Mexican roping artists; at right, a bevy of cowgirls enters the ring; and below comes the denouement of the stagecoach attack, complete with prop mountains and Indian tepees.

ALL: WESTERN HISTORY COLLECTIONS, UNIVERSITY OF OKLAHOMA LIBRARY

BOTH: WILL ROGERS MEMORIAL, CLAREMORE, OKLA.

"All other performers think I have the greatest act in the business."

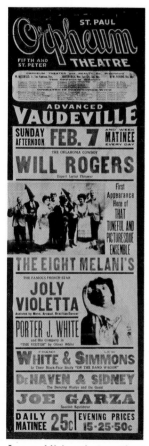

In a publicity photograph at left, a dapper Will poses with his rope. By the time he hit St. Paul, Minnesota, his name headed the list of acts (above).

Something like what came to be called vaudeville had flourished for a good many years in England, where it was generally known as "variety" entertainment. In this country vaudeville's past was rather checkered, its evolution a coming together of some peculiarly American forms of entertainment, including the sort of programs that might be seen in either stationary or mobile form. Among the former lot were museums—notably the institution founded by Charles Willson Peale for the display of natural history objects and paintings by him and his sons, which was such a success in the early nineteenth century and which was later absorbed into Phineas T. Barnum's more famous establishment on Ann Street in New York City.

By the 1890's small-time imitators of Barnum were legion: "dime museums" and "store shows" had "professors" who conducted paying customers on a goggle-eyed tour of midgets, dog-faced boys, pickled human embryos, sword swallowers, and other assorted freaks. And for those Americans who neither lived near a big city nor were likely to visit one, hundreds of promoters were taking entertainment to the hinterlands. The traveling circus of the eighteenth century had expanded into a two- or three-ring affair and now included something called a "circus concert"—an extra-admission program held after the regular performance. It featured numerous variety acts and the inevitable tableaux of "living statuary," in which men and women, covered with white paste or fluid and wearing white wigs, posed heroically before a black curtain.

By far the most popular form of traveling entertainment between 1840 and 1880 was the minstrel show, and its line of stock jokes, "coon" songs, and sentimental ballads became familiar to virtually every American. Many features of the min-

103

strel show eventually found their way into vaudeville: blackface comedians, soft-shoe numbers, female impersonators, and the "olio," or mixture, which was a potpourri of specialty numbers, dances, vocal and instrumental music, and speeches, followed by a grand finale in which the entire cast participated.

Still another highly mobile form of entertainment was the medicine wagon, which had been a feature of the American landscape for many years. Quack doctors and medicine men hired entertainers to drive their wagons, on the theory that a man who could sing, juggle, or pose as a cigar store Indian could attract the attention of a crowd which would then be ripe for the "doctor's" spiel and the purchase of health-giving elixir or patent medicine. And the wagon made it possible to get out of town fast when circumstances required a hasty retreat.

Toward the end of the century traction companies sniffed the profits to be made by attracting trolley and interurban passengers to the end of the line, and "car parks" came into being —amusement areas with ponds, rowboats, roller coasters, and live entertainment, where a family on an outing might be exposed to anything from ballet and opera to animal acts and acrobats.

So vaudeville had many antecedents, but if any one particular establishment may be said to have put this form of entertainment on the tracks, it was the Gaiety Museum, which opened for business in a deserted candy store in Boston, Massachusetts, in 1883. Operated by a richly mustachioed former circus performer named Benjamin Franklin Keith—who had tired of bouncing around the countryside in wagons loaded with freaks—it initially boasted a one-and-one-half-pound midget named Baby Alice and a stuffed mermaid. To this thin leaven were later added a tattooed man, a three-headed songstress, a chicken with a human face, and a pair of comedians, Joe Weber and Lew Fields. Before long, Keith was giving the customers continuous performances, hiring talented artists of the day and bringing good clean acts to the city of Boston, which had a well-known preference for that type of show. In 1885 Keith and a mild-appearing, ruthless chap named Edward F. Albee, who was occasionally described by members of the trade as Keith's "Richelieu," were presenting the sensationally popular operettas by William Gilbert and Arthur Sullivan, and their success in this venture enabled them to acquire the real estate which soon became the largest chain of theatres in the world the Keith chain boasted houses in nearly every American city with a population of one hundred thousand.

As might be supposed, within this mélange of vehicles there were shows for men only and more seemly ones for mixed audiences, but as theatrical headliners moved into "big-time" vaudeville and what was called "class entertainment," there was a tendency for all of the acts to be laundered. Keith's bias against smut was not confined to Boston—he didn't want it anywhere; and when Tony Pastor made a success of the first family vaudeville performances at his Bowery Opera House in New York, producing shows that even children could attend, there was a rush on the part of other theatre owners to clean up their bills.

At the time Will Rogers decided to make a career for himself in vaudeville, Keith and Albee, in addition to their extensive properties, had a virtual monopoly on the booking of acts for theatres through their United Booking Office. But if they dominated the business of vaudeville, a man named Willie Hammerstein ruled what has often been called its heart.

Hammerstein's father, Oscar, had come to America from

CULVER PICTURES

Willie Hammerstein; Hammerstein's Victoria Theatre and Roof Garden in New York looked like a paradise to an aspiring vaudeville actor.

BROWN BROTHERS

Berlin, gone into cigar making, and had somehow become the nation's impresario of grand opera, in which role he built a dozen theatres. Grandest of them all was the Victoria Music Hall, at the corner of Broadway and 42nd Street in New York, where, for the 50-cent admission price, one could take advantage of the theatre, music hall, smoking room, billiard room, lounge, Oriental café, and roof garden—the last being Willie Hammerstein's special domain as long as his father was alive. Years later Will Rogers remembered the Victoria as "the greatest Vaudeville theatre of that and all time," and stated that "we have never produced another showman like Willie Hammerstein." Willie's special contribution to vaudeville was the "freak" act, and he frequently had a bizarre celebrity waiting in the wings to surprise and titillate the customers—it might be a woman who had shot her husband or lover, a man with a seventeen-foot beard, a wrestler, champion bicycle rider, or polar explorer. No one knew what to expect next. He hired a pair called the Cherry Sisters, booked them as "America's Worst Act," and hung a net in front of the stage to ward off vegetables and fruit thrown at them by the audience. He gave New York Gertrude Hoffman, who for twenty-two sensational weeks performed Salome's dance of the seven veils. He brought the French apache dance craze to America for the first time. Nor was he above perpetrating a hoax on the public: there was Shekla, the Court Magician to the Shah of Persia (who was actually a Hindu Willie had seen performing in a London music hall) and Abdul Kadar, Court Artist of the Turkish Sultan, who appeared with his three veiled wives. (Like Shekla, Abdul was not quite what he seemed; in fact, he was a German named Adolph Schneider and the "wives" were his wife, daughter, and sister-in-law, who avoided talking to inquisitive reporters by falling to their knees and repeating the name of Allah whenever they were asked a question.) When the Victoria opened its doors in 1898 big-time vaudeville was just coming into its own, the whole country was singing and whistling tunes from the new shows, and under Willie Hammerstein's talented and often inspired management his theatre pulled in customers for seventeen years, grossing more than $20 million before it finally shut down in 1915.

Hammerstein's theatre was the big time, but by 1910 there were some two thousand theatres in the small towns of America, offering what was naturally known to the trade as "small-time" vaudeville to audiences that were basically easygoing, friendly,

Cherry Sisters
BROWN BROTHERS

and simply out for a good time—which meant that they expected pratfalls, wheezy jokes, and plenty of folksy humor. Whatever talents the itinerant performers might have had on stage, these show people added a bit of mystery and spice to any town they visited, as they drifted in and out of railroad depots with worn trunks plastered with stickers from faraway places and gave the natives the chance to ogle their sporty traveling clothes, flashy jewelry, and exotic women. But the surface veneer of glamour concealed a life of very real hardship and difficulty. The touring actor had to travel constantly, in all kinds of weather and often at strange hours in order to make a split-week engagement. Enduring long, dirty, jolting train rides, second-rate hotels, and unappetizing lunchrooms, he also had to spend many hours in the company of people he might dislike heartily, tolerate the frequent outbursts of temper and temperament, the whims of rival acts and uncooperative stage-hands, and above all, survive the tyranny of the theatre man-

Gertrude Hoffman as Salome
CULVER PICTURES

ager, who often cared little about performers and everything about box office receipts. An act's position on a playbill told a good deal about what the manager thought of it, and his bias was usually set during the first performance; depending on how the audience received an act, the manager would put it in what he considered its appropriate spot, or he might throw it out altogether.

This somewhat arbitrary placement also had a lot to do with determining salaries. An opening act—often a silent, or "dumb," one performed by jugglers, acrobats, or animals to warm up the audience while the people were settling into their seats—received a top wage of $150 a week on the small-time circuit. The second act, often a song-and-dance routine performed by a couple, might draw down $25 more; the number three act as much as $300; and the next-to-closing (which was the main attraction on the bill), $350. If the last happened to be

*A pensive Will, in traveling
suit and gold watch chain*
WILL ROGERS MEMORIAL, CLAREMORE, OKLA.

also a headliner—which was not often the case in the tank towns—he would get even more money, of course.

For a long time the public seemed to want the same routine from an act whenever they saw it—the same hoary jokes, the same baggy pants, or whatever the trademark might be—and many bits went absolutely unaltered for years. (The comedian George Jessel recalled that the Avon Comedy Four played a sketch called "The New Teacher" without variation from 1908 until 1935, and a theatre historian noted that Moore and Littlefield's skit, "Change Your Act or Go Back to the Woods," was not changed for twenty-five years.) But about the time that Will Rogers was trying to make his way into vaudeville, audiences generally were beginning to demand something new and different.

The story of how Will broke into his new trade has all the elements of the classic show-business saga that was seen again and again in plays and movies: the stage-struck rube arrives in the big city, receives some publicity as a result of performing a heroic feat (in this case, roping a nervous, half-crazed steer that had run amuck in Madison Square Garden), but is turned down by unfeeling booking agents who can't imagine that his act is any good (and who certainly don't believe he can rope a horse on stage). Finally, nearing the point of desperation, he overhears one of them telephoning Keith's Union Square Theatre and saying, "Put this nut and his pony on at one of your supper shows and just get rid of them." The rube not only gets the job, but to everyone's surprise (including his own), his act goes over, and he heads for fame and his name in lights.

Will didn't know enough to realize it, but the supper show for which he was engaged during the week of June 12, 1905, was the toughest possible way to break into vaudeville, and one that old-timers avoided like the plague. It was scheduled between 6 and 8 in the evening when, as Will wrote later, "nobody that had a home or somewhere to eat would be in a theatre." His first appearance was announced by a sign bearing the singularly unprovocative message, "Extra Act." Whether the audience felt sorry for him or whether they took pity on his pony, as Will supposed, the fact was that the act was a hit, the tough supper-show crowd liked it, and the following week he moved up to Hammerstein's roof at the Victoria—"the swellest Vaudeville place in America," he told his sisters, with whom he shared his concern about having to take the pony up to the roof on an elevator each night.

Even inveterate theatregoers admitted that Will's routine was quite a novelty. "Will P. Rogers, the sensational lariat thrower, is making his first appearance at the Paradise Roof, and has proved a sensation in every way," the New York *Herald* reviewer observed, noting that his "charming specialty [is] well out of the ordinary run." As the orchestra played a medley of tunes—inevitably, "Pony Boy" and some cowboy songs—Will made a spectacular entrance on Teddy, who wore specially made felt-bottom boots, buckled like galoshes, to keep him from slipping on the stage. Will would slide off the pony, give him a slap on the rump and send him into the wings, and then begin his rope tricks, which he performed silently in rhythm to the soft orchestra music. His was a "dumb" act, with no patter, and he used a variety of ropes—selecting a different length or weight according to the demands of the throw. (He had every conceivable size, and Tom Mix, who had shared a room with him at the Putnam Hotel, said: "Every time I came in I stumbled over his ropes on the floor. Sometimes, when I got up at night, I would step on one and think I'd landed on a snake.")

Will's roping act is virtually impossible to describe, and the way to appreciate the complexity and artistry it combined is to see the various tricks in one of his early silent films, *The Ropin' Fool*, in which he did fifty-three of them, ranging from the simple to the nearly impossible. What comes across in this film, as it did to the vaudeville crowds to which Will was playing, is a combination of almost unbelievable timing, skill, and amazing grace, along with an ability to figure out a series of actions that produce, at times, enormously complex results. There were a number of so-called small-loop routines which could be done in a relatively confined space and which lent themselves well to the stage. He usually began with the simplest of them— the flat spin—in which he twirled the rope in front or to the side, parallel to the stage. From this he might go into the merry-go-round, in which the rope, constantly spinning, is passed from the right hand, under one leg, to the other hand behind the body, where the right hand picks it up again. One of Will's variations on this trick was to have a flat spin going with two ropes—one in each hand—pass the two ropes around the sides of his body, exchange them to the other hand behind his back, and keep them going, around and around. Or he would jump in and out of a spinning rope, or run along, putting one foot into the loop and out of it as he moved across the stage.

One of his specialties was the juggle, or bounce, in which the

"The old Station [in Kansas City] was really just a Valise, or Grip, Exchange. I popped through there one time jumping to Seattle, Washington, to do my little Act on the Orpheum Circuit. Well, do you remember in those days every man that traveled any farther than from the House to the Barn thought he had to have an Alligator Bag, with big warts on the side of it, that would rub Bunions on the side of your Legs if you carried it over a block. That and a Diamond Ring were the first things you were supposed to buy. . . .

"So I had just worked long enough to have both. One Toothbrush, a Couple of shirts, and five Ropes, were nestling in this Crocodile bound inclosure. . . . I had to buy a Ticket, and in those days it took an Agent longer to make out a Ticket to Seattle than it did to go there. . . . Well the Afternoon I spent buying my Ticket, I forgot to keep one foot solidly implanted on my deceased Crocodile. Some lover of Animals kindly annexed by prosperous Trade Mark, and when I turned around the one year's savings I had invested in Hides was just passing over the Kaw River. . . .

"Coming back, I played Butte, and lost the Diamond Ring. So it took two thieves to at least try and give me the appearance of a Gentleman. Now when I see a Man wearing either a Diamond Ring, or an Alligator Valise, I offer up thanks to the two men who robbed me."

from Weekly Article
June 1, 1924

The Ropin' Fool

The five sequences on these pages, which run from top to bottom, are from the film The Ropin' Fool, as is the still above, showing Will roping a mouse with a string. From left to right, he is shown: (1) throwing a huge loop out in front of an oncoming horse and rider and, as the horse runs through, making a difficult catch; (2) skipping through a loop and lassoing horse; (3) throwing a figure eight, which loops around the animal's head and its legs; (4) catching a rider going away from him, as he lets out the entire rope; (5) making a three-rope catch—one loop snares the rider, one the horse's neck, one the body.

ALL: WILL ROGERS MEMORIAL, CLAREMORE, OKLA.

spinning loop travels up and down like a jumping jack, high over the roper's head and down to his feet, and up again. He could jump in and out of two loops simultaneously, or do the Texas skip, dancing back and forth through a large, vertically spun loop (this was his favorite conditioning exercise, and he performed it almost daily to keep in shape). Since he was using ropes that ranged from seven to 90 feet in length, there was an almost infinite variety of tricks he could perform (in *The Ropin' Fool* he lassoes a mouse with a length of string), and another favorite with which he often climaxed his act was to have an usher take one end of a 90-foot rope up the aisle as far as it would reach while Will, standing at the footlights, held onto the other end to show the audience how long it was. Then he would haul it in, coiling it as he brought it back, and after mounting Teddy, would begin twirling a small loop, vertical at first, then lifting it over his head as it increased in size until all 90 feet were out in the Big Crinoline (which had earned him the job with Texas Jack), the glistening white rope spinning in a huge, beautiful circle far out over the heads of the audience. Slowly, Teddy would back up, and suddenly Will would let the rope fall to the stage with a loud thud, give a high-pitched cowboy whoop, and trot offstage into the wings.

As Betty later described that portion of the act in which Will roped Teddy and Buck McKee, who was working with him, "There were many catches—throwing two ropes at once, catching the man with one loop and the horse with the other; a three-rope catch, a nose catch, a figure eight, and a tail catch so difficult that Will never ceased practicing on it. Another variation was to rope Buck, and then throw a half hitch around his hands, another over his head, another around his body, and so on until he was completely tied and helpless." What she mentions lightly as "a figure eight" was in reality one of the most difficult catches; in it, the spinning loop made a figure eight, one half of which caught the rider while the other half went around the horse's head.

After watching Will throw two ropes at once, catching the horse and rider separately, an actor suggested that it might be more effective if he told the crowd what he was going to do before he did it. One night, with no advance preparation, Will stopped the orchestra and announced to the house that he wanted to explain his "next little stunt." "I am going to throw about two of these ropes at once," he said, "catching the horse with one and the rider with the other." He paused, grinned,

"Give them to the kids," he instructed his sisters when he sent them samples of the new cards he had had printed.
WILL ROGERS MEMORIAL, CLAREMORE, OKLA.

and said, "I don't have any idea I'll get it, but here goes."
More than anything he said, his Western accent, his delivery,
and the way he underplayed the statement tickled the audience, and to Will's embarrassment they started laughing. He
came offstage angry and humiliated when he had finished his
turn, and although other performers tried to persuade him that
laughs were good for his act, he was so serious about his roping
that he could not get over the idea that people might be laughing at what he was doing. Although the idea of working some
jokes into his act was a long time in coming, there were other occasions when he learned that a little talk could be helpful. On
one of those evenings when nothing was going right and he was
unable to get any of his tricks to work just the way he wanted, he
grew embarrassed and flustered, the audience was increasingly
restless, and suddenly he began to talk. "Swinging a rope is all
right," he said, "when your neck ain't in it. Then it's hell." And
there were a few chuckles. "Out West where I come from," he
went on, "they won't let me play with this rope. They think I
might hurt myself." By then he had the audience with him;
they forgot the tricks he had missed and began enjoying Will
himself. But it was some time before he did any more talking
than necessary to announce different tricks.

A little theatrical notebook Will began keeping in the sum-

Will ropes the cast for the finale at Keith's in 1905.
WILL ROGERS MEMORIAL, CLAREMORE, OKLA.

113

"Polly vue Francaise
Wee Wee yah, yah. I don't
know a dam word anybody's
saying. But, Pal of Mine,
I sho do know than I am in
Paree and, old hand, she is
certainly the Goods. . . . Stage
Women ain't one two 11 [?] with
these for paint and make up. Oh,
how they do strut. You see some
very well groomed women and
offul pretty dresses but the Men,
they just seem to be a disgrace
to appear in them get ups with
the women. Why they haven't
the 1st idea of dress. There is
absolutely no fashions. They just
curl their mustache and put on
all they have got. Why any mutt
in America has them skinned
a mile.
"And how they do sit and
drink at Cafes with the tables
right out on the sidewalk. They
seem to have nothing else to do."

Will Rogers to Betty Blake
Paris, Mar. 26, 1906

mer of 1905 shows how much in demand he was. After a week each at Keith's and Hammerstein's in New York, he traveled to Philadelphia and Boston before returning to Manhattan for an engagement at Proctor's and a triumphal five weeks at Hammerstein's roof garden. (The location of a theatre, the performer's popularity, and the inexorable laws of supply and demand all had a bearing on what he was paid. Will started at $75 a week in New York on June 12, 1905; later that month he was paid $140 a week in Boston and Philadelphia; and in August he got $250 for a week in Brooklyn.) Through the fall and winter he was on the road constantly, with no time off, and not until March, 1906, was there a break in the two-a-day routine. For the week of March 5, the notebook reads: "Home, on a visit"; and then, "Sailed Mar 17 from N.Y. on S.S. *Philadelphia* for Paris and Berlin." Early in April, less than a year after he had roped the steer in Madison Square Garden and been noticed for the first time by the New York public, Will Rogers was playing the most important theatre in Europe—the Winter Garten in Berlin—where he had a highly successful four weeks (while exercising his pony in the park he met the Kaiser, who was "a dandy good fellow" who saluted every morning as he galloped by); then he went on to London's leading music hall, the Palace, for five weeks at more money than he had ever earned, and was invited to perform at the Ranelagh Club (he later learned that Edward VII had been in the audience).

In mid-July of 1906 Will was home in Indian Territory for the first time in over a year, and his family and friends were glad to see that theatrical success hadn't changed him. His sister Maud invited Betty Blake to join them in Chelsea, and her visit was almost a repetition of the one she had made in the fall of 1899—a steady round of parties, dinners, horseback rides, and evenings of singing around the piano. Although Betty enjoyed her first real visit with Will's sisters, she found Will himself strangely elusive and distant. He paid no particular attention to her, never saw her alone, and she recalled that she was "a baffled young lady when I left for home." What made it so mystifying was that he had been corresponding constantly with her for over a year, sending books, bundles of music, gloves, and—on one occasion—"6 pairs of Female Hosiery." A flood of telegrams, post cards, and letters had descended on Rogers, Arkansas, from every part of the country he had been touring (the salutations had changed from "Dear Old Pal" to "Dearest Betty" and then "My Own Sweetheart"), and nearly all contained the message that he was "the most persistent lover you ever saw," that he wanted her to marry him and "see the world as the *wife* of Rogers the Lariet Expert." For Christmas in 1905 he had sent a lace handkerchief he had bought in South America, accompanied with a message calculated to melt a heart of stone. He prized it very highly, he said, and hoped she would do the same, since "The old Indian Lady I bought from then gave me this asking if I was married. I said no. She said then give it to the wife when you do marry. I have kept it. Carried it all through Africa at times when I didn't have a cent and was actually hungry, to Australia most of the time in an envelope in my pocket, then back home and on all my travels. I did intend always to do as the old woman said but I guess there's nothing doing for me. I will just give it to you as I kinder pride it and you might do the same."

Betty had been back in Rogers, Arkansas, for a week when Will stopped by to see her. He was on his way to New York and had the idea "that we should get married at once." He was earning $200 a week, he was fully booked for the coming fall and winter, and as far as he was concerned, the future looked bright indeed. But Betty had other ideas: like most Americans, she didn't regard show business as a steady or particularly worthy profession. All she knew of it had been gleaned from watching second-rate traveling shows that played Rogers from time to time, and she didn't fancy herself trouping around the country with Will. He couldn't understand her attitude and they seem to have had an unhappy parting. Why did she have to be so bullheaded, he asked. He had not been "worth a *dam*" since she refused him and she was "the *direct* and unwilling cause of it."

As impulsive about his career as he was about marriage, Will suddenly decided to head for England with a Wild West act of his own, and in the spring of 1907 he sailed with Buck McKee and two other cowboys and a number of horses. But the show, which had apparently been put together with no real planning, was a flop, and Will had to take his regular act—Buck and Teddy—on a tour outside London in order to make enough money to send the rest of the troupe back to the States. In June he was home, doing the old routine: two weeks in Philadelphia, two weeks at the Nixon Theatre in Pittsburgh; out on the circuit for a year and a half, playing most of the principal cities in the U.S. and Canada, with interruptions only for a visit to Oklahoma when his father was ill. And the correspondence

"Papa send me about 35 ft of small light hard twisted rope like the boys use there to rope with. . . . Light hard twist to throw not to twirl, also two good red or big check flannel shirts size 15-1/2 and one of those pretty striped Osage Blankets . . . send them so I will get them Sunday Week Oct 8th in Toledo."
Will Rogers to C.V. Rogers
Cleveland, Sept. 27, 1905

"Why papa when you write you
must always put the name of the
Theatre on or I wont get it for
these are big cities. . . .
"I got a rope from Lee Barrett
[owner of a general store in
Vinita, Oklahoma] but it is
no good to me. I aint roping
steers on the stage. Its big
enough for a well rope . . .
I want little hard twist
throwing rope."
Will Rogers to C.V. Rogers
Toledo, Oct. 12, 1905

with Betty Blake went on continuously, Will ever hopeful, Betty ever warm and friendly, but not ready to give in to his plans. Inevitably, there were misunderstandings.

He didn't understand when she didn't write; he kept asking for *long* letters, and when she apologized for the brevity of a note, saying that the house was full of company, he replied that that was an old excuse. "Get a new line of stuff or either don't plan so big." He was "rotten jealous" of Tom Harvey, who was still courting Betty, and quarrels arose from something Will had said, or from an effort on his part to be funny or to make her jealous. Will admitted, "I ain't treating you right." Betty wanted to know more about the girl he said he was taking out; Will—almost fatally honest—made the mistake of sending her a letter from the woman; Betty countered with a description of her own involvement with a promising lawyer ("What all did he promise you, and you him?" Will wanted to know); Will said he had gotten even by falling in love "with an *Actorine* and *gone plum nutty*." Back came a response from Betty, expressing gratitude that she had found out about him and his ways before it was too late, adding that she didn't care for his "unpleasant insinuations" about the boys who were taking her out. Will was contrite, he apologized, and told her she was the only girl in the world as far as he was concerned.

When Will went home to see his father he visited Betty in Arkansas and spoke several times of quitting show business and returning to the old ranch life. As early as the fall of 1905 he had indicated a restiveness about what he was doing: "This is nice work but I am not in love with it only for the money." But he had second thoughts: "It beats that old *farm and ranch* and *store* thing." The panic of 1907 hit ranching as well as the vaudeville business, and Will decided he would do well to stick to his present occupation, though traveling around the country was becoming tiresome, even to him. Nevertheless, Betty remarked, "I felt that at last he was coming around to my way of thinking."

Will's little notebook tells the story of his activities. He was at Poli's theatre in Wilkes-Barre, Pennsylvania, the week of October 26, 1908. The next week was open (a rarity for him, even in bad times), and on November 9 he was heading home. He stopped off in Rogers, Arkansas, en route, and as Betty remembered, "announced flatly that he was going to take me back to New York with him." There followed a notebook entry in big block letters for the week of November 23: GETTING MARRIED.

Courtship by Mail

For nine years Will had been writing Betty Blake from all over the globe, and by 1908 the stream of cards and letters became a flood. Before Christmas in 1906, a letter reached Rogers, Arkansas, announcing that a package was on its way: "Kid I sent you a little Xmas remembrance in the shape of a coat and a muff. Now I don't know if it will fit you and that it is just right. But I hope it will suit you and prove serviceable for there is such a skin game in buying fur it may prove a lemon. But it is the only thing I could think of that would do you any good and that I thought would please you." If the picture above is any indication, the recipient did not regard it as a "lemon."

WILL ROGERS MEMORIAL, CLAREMORE, OKLA.

Knowing that Betty (right) was having a good time at home kept Will in a continual state of anxiety.

"I look happy but I wasnt," wrote the eternally miserable sailor of this Atlantic Ocean crossing.

Will didn't even sit next to Betty (left, on seat) at the July, 1906, house party. Standing, rear, is Dick Parris.

Rochester. N.Y.
Montreal. Canada
Hamilton. "
Toronto. Can
Worcester. Mass.
Brooklyn. N.Y.
Springfield. Mass.
Hartford. Conn.
New Haven.
after set night
go home
home
"
"
"
Bridgeport. Conn.

vel.
Winnipeg. Canada
Duluth. Minn. "
yellowstone Park.
Butte. Montana
Spokane. Wash
Seattle. "

July	6	Orpheum. Vancouver. B.C.
	13	Grand. Tacoma. Wash.
	20	Grand. Portland. Ore.
	27	TRAVEL
August	3	Grand. Sacremento. Cal
	10	National. San Francisco "
	17	Bell. Oakland. Cal.
	24	Wigwam. San Francisco. Ca
	31	TRAVEL
Sept.	7	Temple - Detroit. Mich
	14	Cooks O.H. Rochester. N.Y.
	21	Grand. O.H. Pittsburg. Pa.
	28	Armory - Binghampton N.Y.
Octob.	5	Grand O.H. Syracuse "
	12	Proctor Theatre. Montreal Can
	19	Grand. Auburn. N.Y.
	26	Poli's. Wilkbarre. Pa.
Nov	2	OPEN
	9	Travel HOME.
	16	Home
	23	GETTING. MARRIED.
	30	Proctors. Newark. N.J.
Dec.	7	Open
	14	Colonial- New york
	21	Travel Home.
	28	American. St Louis Mo

29

Will's engagement book shows almost solid bookings in 1908 until November 23rd, when the big event was recorded.

ALL: WILL ROGERS MEMORIAL, CLAREMORE, OKLA.

BOTH: WILL ROGERS MEMORIAL, CLAREMORE, OKLA.

"The day I roped Betty, I did the star performance of my life."

Mrs. Amelia J. Blake
announces the marriage of her daughter
Betty
to
Mr. William P. A. Rogers
Wednesday, November the twenty-fifth
nineteen hundred and eight
Rogers, Arkansas

Will could not decide which of his many friends should receive the wedding announcement (above). A year later the happy couple and a friend were photographed in Portland, Oregon, while he was on a vaudeville tour.

The wedding day was set for November 25, 1908, at Betty's home in Arkansas, and in the interim Will mailed letter after letter to his fiancée, filled with questions or opinions concerning every aspect of the event. Realizing that she had some anxiety about breaking the news to her family and friends, he offered his sympathy (he would have no difficulty with his own folks, he said—"they all like and love you" and were unquestionably relieved that he did not "grab on to some old show girl or bum"). She was not to worry about the arrival of her trousseau; he wanted *her*, not her clothes. He was mailing some family jewelry and an engagement ring—not as large as he wanted, he admitted, but a pure white, perfect stone and "not some big yellow thing." As for the names of his friends she had requested so that announcements could be sent, there were so many that he was afraid of leaving out someone whose feelings would be hurt, he couldn't remember the names of half his relatives, so she was to forget the whole thing. He gave her explicit instructions about packing, so that she wouldn't have to open her trunk until they reached New York. And meantime, he wondered, should he and his family walk from the station to her house on the morning of the wedding? They would arrive by train, and he urged that there be "*no dressing up,*" since he would have on his dark traveling suit and his sisters would be wearing nothing fancy.

The ceremony was to take place immediately after the Rogers' train got in at 11:30 A.M., and since the Blake house was only a few blocks from the station, Betty's brother was assigned

Form No. 1.

THE WESTERN UNION TELEGRAPH COMPANY.

INCORPORATED

23,000 OFFICES IN AMERICA.   CABLE SERVICE TO ALL THE WORLD.

This Company TRANSMITS and DELIVERS messages only on conditions limiting its liability, which have been assented to by the sender of the following message.
Errors can be guarded against only by repeating a message back to the sending station for comparison, and the Company will not hold itself liable for errors or delays
in transmission or delivery of Unrepeated Messages, beyond the amount of tolls paid thereon, nor in any case where the claim is not presented in writing within sixty days
after the message is filed with the Company for transmission.
This is an UNREPEATED MESSAGE, and is delivered by request of the sender, under the conditions named above.

ROBERT C. CLOWRY, President and General Manager.

NUMBER	SENT BY	REC'D BY	CHECK

RECEIVED at _____ 853 am _____ 11-3 _____ 190_

Dated _____

To _____

The bridegroom's state of nerves is apparent in these two telegrams—one sent twelve minutes after the other to correct the number of the train on which he and his family would arrive.
WILL ROGERS MEMORIAL, CLAREMORE, OKLA.

to collect the groom and his family in the buggy. Betty heard the train whistle and watched from her bedroom window as he left, but a few minutes later he was back with an empty carriage; he came upstairs with a woebegone look on his face to say that Will and his family were not on the train, and only when he saw that she was about to burst into tears did he add that the train had two sections that day and that the wedding party was aboard the second one. The wedding was a small affair, with only the two families present, and afterward Betty—in a dark blue broadcloth suit which had arrived in time from Marshall Field's store in Chicago—drove off with her new husband in a carriage through muddy, deeply rutted streets and discovered that the whole town had gathered on the station platform to send them off. Covered with rice and embarrassment, the newlyweds boarded a local and endured the stares of other passengers until they reached a division point, fifty miles away, where Will had reserved a stateroom on the through train to St. Louis.

They had only a few days to themselves, since Will opened the following week at Proctor's in Newark, but he told her they would have a real honeymoon while he toured the Orpheum circuit. Once the tour ended, he had promised, they would settle down on the farm in Oklahoma. This information had been imparted to Betty's home-town paper, which included in the wedding story the fact that the couple would make their home there the following spring.

In St. Louis they went to see the Carlisle Indians play foot-

Form No. 1.

THE WESTERN UNION TELEGRAPH COMPANY.

INCORPORATED

23,000 OFFICES IN AMERICA.   CABLE SERVICE TO ALL THE WORLD.

This Company TRANSMITS and DELIVERS messages only on conditions limiting its liability, which have been assented to by the sender of the following message.
Errors can be guarded against only by repeating a message back to the sending station for comparison, and the Company will not hold itself liable for errors or delays
in transmission or delivery of Unrepeated Messages, beyond the amount of tolls paid thereon, nor in any case where the claim is not presented in writing within sixty days
after the message is filed with the Company for transmission.
This is an UNREPEATED MESSAGE, and is delivered by request of the sender, under the conditions named above.
ROBERT C. CLOWRY, President and General Manager.

NUMBER	SENT BY	REC'D BY		CHECK

RECEIVED at 9 05 am 11-13 190

Dated

To Mrs Betty Blake

I mean no 5 instead of

Bill

ball, had Thanksgiving dinner and champagne served in their
room at the Planters Hotel, and attended *What Every Woman
Knows*, starring Maude Adams, but left early since Betty was
suffering from her first experience with champagne. (Will told
her later he didn't know what kind of a girl he had married
when he saw her swallow so much of it, but had concluded that
champagne drinking must be an "old Arkansas custom.")

In Newark Betty watched Will for the first time on a stage,
and she was not especially impressed or interested. The only
talking he did was to announce different rope tricks, and she
had seen most of those many times over. But his working hours
were ideal for honeymooners; he arrived at the theatre just in
time to go on, and since Buck McKee had his ropes laid out, all
Will had to do was slip on a dark-blue flannel shirt and leather
chaps and walk onto the stage. Because he had a horse in his act,
he almost always went on last, performed for 15 or 20 minutes,
and then left the theatre to be with Betty. Even though he was
doing two a day, which meant matinee and evening performances, they had time to sightsee, attend other theatres, visit with
friends who were in town, or go to a restaurant where Will
could eat his favorite chili. To his disgust (since he had to wear
his "Montgomery Ward" or wedding suit) they also went
several times to the opera. Betty had said she wanted to see
Grant's Tomb and hear Caruso sing, and as Will later described one of their opera evenings, "Caruso was the fellow who
had played the part of a clown but I could not think of a funny
thing that he did; I hate to say it but I enjoyed Grant's Tomb

more cause I stayed outside while my wife went in."

Although it sounds like a busman's holiday, their tour of the Orpheum circuit turned out to be a real honeymoon; Betty had seen little of the country before, and Will wanted to rediscover it all with her. But as she was learning, he was a difficult person to keep up with: "He hated to lose a moment of his life; he wanted to do everything right now. And he nearly ran me ragged." When she objected to a plan Will had concocted for the morning and suggested that they put it off until the afternoon, he would say "no," they should do it now—"then we'll have the afternoon free for something else." Wandering about, taking in the sights, picnicking in the countryside, riding horseback in the city parks—it was a relaxed, carefree life, and Betty began thinking that show business was not so bad after all. Finally the tour ended, but before they had to face up to the question of returning to Claremore an offer came for Will to play the Percy Williams theatres in the East at a much higher salary than he had been getting, and Betty agreed that he should accept. She was, she conceded, "growing reconciled to show business." For one thing, Will was receiving more notice in the newspapers and in public, and after the Williams tour he decided—despite his experience in England the last time he had tried something of the sort—to put together an ambitious show of his own.

He hired Goldie St. Clair, who had just won the women's bucking-horse championship at Cheyenne; Florence LaDue, a fancy roper; Arlene Palmer, a "girl Cossack" who had been with the Buffalo Bill show; and Hazel Moran, who performed a rope dance; and with these and other trick riders he opened what was to be a very short-lived venture. The arrangements for such a large, unwieldy act were hideously complicated and expensive, and Will realized that he would have to fold the company or go broke. But the episode, while disappointing, had one redeeming feature: it was during this tour that Will decided to change his own act, and that decision was probably the most important one in his theatrical career.

They were playing in Philadelphia and Will was standing at one side of the stage, watching the girls and their performances and making wry comments to the audience. Betty was in the wings, and remembered that Goldie St. Clair was on—a young, pretty girl with long blonde hair that hung down her back in a braid; her bucking-horse act was the final one on the program. While Betty stood there waiting for the curtain to come down, the theatre manager joined her, stood beside her for a moment, and said, "Tell me, Mrs. Rogers, why does Will carry all those horses and people around with him? I would rather have Will Rogers alone than that whole bunch put together."

That decided it. Will would break up the troupe and go back to where he had started in vaudeville—just himself and his rope. From an intense, serious lariat artist he had developed into a humorous talker who also spun a rope, and that was to be the pattern from now on. The worst of the decision was saying goodbye to Buck and Teddy, who, though they represented a considerable expense, had been an intimate part of Will's life for the past six years. But with their departure, theatre audiences began seeing an entirely different Will Rogers, doing what he did best.

It was the way he said something—his delivery and superb timing—that got the laughs for the most part, rather than any particular jokes he told. He had a way of looking at the rope, concentrating very hard on its motions, that made almost any remark he made seem impromptu (as indeed it usually was) and fresh. The lariat would spin smoothly, a gleaming white circle above the footlights, and Will would remark, half to him-

Below is a scene from The Red Mill, *one of Fred Stone's biggest hits, in which he appears second from left.*

CULVER PICTURES

"Fred Stone . . . got as far as the Fourth Reader, while I only reached the Third. So that is why I think we always hit it off together so well, neither was liable to use a word which the other couldn't understand."

from Weekly Article
Mar. 11, 1923

self, "Worked that pretty good." Or he might confide to the audience, "Well, I made my joke and the trick come out even." If he missed a throw, which he rarely did, he might comment, "I've only got jokes enough for one miss. I've either got to practice roping or learn more jokes." He found that it paid to miss a trick occasionally on purpose. It was a fairly easy trick in which he jumped with both feet inside a spinning loop, and once he missed and broke the loop. As he was gathering in the lasso to make another try at it, he turned and drawled, "Well, got all my feet through but one." As Betty wrote, "Laughs didn't have to happen twice to Will," and he began missing that trick regularly in order to use the line.

The gum chewing, which became his trademark, was made part of the act by accident. Will was a great baseball fan; whenever he could get away from the theatre he would head for a ball park and shag flies with the local team. On evenings or rainy afternoons ballplayers often came to the show, and from them Will picked up the habit of chewing gum. One day he arrived at the theatre barely in time for the matinee performance and was still chewing a wad of gum when he came onstage. When the audience began laughing Will remembered the gum, walked back and stuck it onto the proscenium arch, and the crowd roared. From then on he often used the business of parking his chewing gum after he missed a rope trick; then he would do the trick perfectly, collect the gum, and resume chewing.

Another modification in the act came about as a result of his friendship with Fred Stone, the actor. Will admired Stone even before they met; in fact, *The Red Mill*, in which the latter played the lead, was the first musical Will took Betty to see in New York. Often the two men found that they were playing the same city, and they formed the habit of meeting early in the morning at the theatre and practicing together, with Will teaching Stone rope tricks while Fred coached him on dance routines. ("Rogers is a surprise when he starts dancing," *Variety* commented after he added it to his act, "and gets away with it big.") The two had a lot in common: both were outdoorsmen who had lived adventuresome lives; both were wholly absorbed in their profession; and neither could tolerate idleness in any form. The Rogers and Stone families spent much time together over the years, and the men, being hyperactive, fidgety types, would customarily rise from the dinner table between courses and start twirling ropes while they continued their conversation. When the meal was over they would pick up the ropes again and, without ever stopping talking, throw loops over a chair at the end of the room.

Most of the Rogers' friends at this time were theatre people: the Chic Sales, Louise Dresser and her husband Jack Gardner, DeWolfe Hopper, and W.C. Fields, among others. Fields, who had achieved a billing as "the greatest juggler on earth" while still a young vaudeville performer, first met Will in a Capetown saloon, not long after the latter arrived there with the boatload of cattle from South America, and they ran into each other again after Will joined Texas Jack's Wild West Show. During the course of a long friendship, Will had the greatest affection for Fields—a feeling that Fields reciprocated, as his biographer Robert Lewis Taylor writes, "with his usual periodic reservations and suspicions." Years after their vaudeville days Fields was ill in a sanitarium in Pasadena, California, and, as Taylor tells the story, Will went to visit him, only to learn that the great comic was supposedly too sick to receive callers. Will thanked the receptionist and departed, walked several hundred yards along the sanitarium wall, climbed a tree, and dropped down inside the grounds to make his way from bush to bush until he reached Field's bedroom window. They had a lively reunion, to which Fields' teen-age nurse was an awe-stricken witness, and when Will left she helped Fields to a couch and said, "Isn't he a *wonderful* man? I just love that voice."

"The son of a bitch is a fake," Fields snarled in his adenoidal rasp. "I'll bet a hundred dollars he talks just like anybody else when he gets home."

Now that Will was doing a single again he was better off financially; although he was making the same money as before, he had fewer expenses and fewer problems. Betty enjoyed their relatively easy life, they were constantly together, and Clem's pride in his son's achievements grew steadily, although for a long while he was baffled that Willie could make so much money in fields so completely different from those familiar to him. "Two hundred and fifty dollars a week," he would say. "Looks like something is wrong somewhere." But the tune changed when he took Sallie and Maud to Washington in 1907, where Will was on the bill for a week at Chase's Opera House. Clem—mellower now and pleased with his son—attended every performance and late in the week looked out over the audience from his box seat and began counting the house. Age had not dimmed the business instinct. "I tell you, girls," he said when they got back to the hotel, "that manager sure is

Advice to young ropers:

"Using about three or four feet of your rope you want to spin a small loop—not too small, till you get so you can keep it going good then you increase the size of it by letting it slide through your hand and increase your speed at the same time. Now one thing to remember— always let the rope turn in your hand—dont hold it tight, hold it and let it turn so the kinks can twist out of the other end. Thats the whole secret of the thing."

Will Rogers to *The Farm Journal*

*"My dear father Rogers—
I have about all my baby clothes
made—I am expecting the
youngster about the fifteenth of
October—Billy wants a boy
of course, but I do not care which
it is—If it is a boy I am going
to name it after Billy—I would
name it for you but there are
so many Clems in the family I'm
afraid they would get mixed up."*

Betty Rogers to C. V. Rogers
Aug. 21, 1911

making a lot of money off Willie."

Clem would stand in the lobby after each show, listening to what the people had to say, and if someone spoke about Will he would introduce himself and ask the person if he would like to meet his boy. When Will emerged from the stage door there was usually a line of men and women waiting to be introduced by his father.

Unhappily, just when Clem and his son were beginning to be closer to each other than they had been for years, it turned out that there would be no more such occasions. On October 20, 1911, Betty gave birth to a son, named William Vann for Will and Clem, and about a week later a package arrived from Clem containing some stockings and a pair of beaded Indian moccasins for the baby. On its heels came a telegram informing them that Will's father had died in his sleep on October 29.

Will never forgot that he was Clem Rogers' son. In 1924 he wrote that he was going home for a few days' visit to Claremore, where people still spoke of him as "Willie, Uncle Clem Rogers' boy who wouldn't go to school but just kept running around the Country throwing a Rope, till I think he finally got in one of them Shows." And years later Betty remarked that although Will had had enough fame to turn anyone's head and had a speaking acquaintance with some of the most important men in the world, he was always able to stand off and appraise himself and remember who he was. "I suspect that Will's modesty had its origin in a tremendous respect for his father," she wrote, "and a knowledge that, at least in early manhood, he was a disappointment to his family." There was a hint of this in the story Will liked to tell about several of his father's cronies who came to see him perform in New York. When they got back to Oklahoma another old-timer asked what Willie was doing. "Oh," said one, "just acting the fool like he used to do around here."

For several years after his father's death Will's career seemed to be stuck on a plateau, and he began to wonder if he had gone as far as he could with the type of act he had. He was hoping to break into something different when, in the spring of 1912, he opened in his first musical show, *The Wall Street Girl*, starring the popular Blanche Ring. But the opening night was marred by tragedy; Will came on stage, stopped the performance, and announced that the *Titanic*, on her maiden voyage, had struck an iceberg and gone down at sea. Although the show had a respectable New York run, the opening night seemed to cast a pall from which it never fully recovered. Will went on tour with it and then returned to vaudeville; he was playing Houston, Texas, when Betty gave birth to their second child, a daughter named Mary.

Will and Betty sailed for Europe in the spring of 1914, leaving the children with Theda and Mrs. Blake, and in London he enjoyed an unexpected success when he took a part in a musical called *The Merry-Go-Round*, in which Nora Bayes played the lead. But Europe was headed for war, he left the show, and by the time they arrived in New York, hostilities had begun. It was back to vaudeville and to a lot more of the same old routine. Show business generally was in the doldrums that year. In addition to the war, there was just too much competition: New York City had 36 legitimate theatres, seating 54,000 people; more than a dozen vaudeville houses, 50 combination vaudeville-motion picture theatres, and numerous movie houses. The only sure-fire show that season was, as usual, the Ziegfeld Follies, the last word in extravaganzas, loaded with beautiful girls and headline acts. But Will Rogers was not yet a headliner, his salary seemed to be fixed, and he was seriously concerned about his future when he sought Fred Stone's advice. Stone had come up by way of vaudeville (from which he had been blackballed for leading an unsuccessful actors' revolt against the intolerable

Blanche Ring stands beside Will above and in the photograph of the grand finale of Wall Street Girl *(below), her first musical. She introduced such songs as "Rings on Her Fingers" and "In the Good Old Summertime."*

BOTH: WILL ROGERS MEMORIAL, CLAREMORE, OKLA.

working conditions dictated by Keith and Albee), and was now one of the top drawing cards in the legitimate theatre. "Stay in New York," he urged Will, on the theory that what Will needed was a part in a show and would never get one as long as he was off trouping in vaudeville. So the Rogers family rented a house for the summer in Amityville, Long Island, and Will continued to play vaudeville houses around New York. There were times when he could not get other bookings and would appear at small suburban theatres under an assumed name for $75 a week. It was not just a question of staying near New York, he had a growing family, a new Overland touring car, and a stable of horses to support.

Their third child, James Blake, was born in the summer of 1915—a time that was also memorable for the arrival of a small, coal-black pony that Will called "the greatest pony for grownups or children anyone ever saw. I don't know why we called him Dopey," he said. "I guess it was because he was always so gentle and just the least bit lazy. Anyhow we meant no disrespect to him." Will had spotted Dopey in Connecticut, liked him, and brought him home, where he became more family institution than pet. He entered the house, walked up and down stairs, and when the children started riding (it was a tradition that they have their first lesson on their second birthday), the little black horse was the animal they rode. "He helped raise the children," according to Will. "During his lifetime he never did a wrong thing to throw one of them off, or a

For his first trip aloft Will was transported piggyback through the surf at Atlantic City and deposited in the Curtiss plane. (He can be seen at left in front of the wing.) The natty pilot was E. K. Jaquith; the proud grin Will's.

BOTH: WILL ROGERS MEMORIAL
CLAREMORE, OKLA.

wrong thing after they had fallen off. He couldent pick 'em up, but he would stand there and look at 'em with a disgusted look for being so clumsy as to fall off.''

The uncertainty surrounding Will's career was made no easier by his attitude toward money. As Betty put it, he had "a haphazard way with money that was sometimes frightening.'' He could *almost* never resist a salesman, he could *never* resist buying a horse he wanted, and he assumed that every man was honest unless proved otherwise. He liked to buy furs for Betty, and he purchased two large diamond scarf pins and a huge yellow diamond for himself—ready currency for a touring actor who found himself stranded without funds. Will's diamond ring was in and out of hockshops frequently, and after America entered World War I he decided to sell it and invest the proceeds in Liberty bonds. Since diamond prices were depressed, he turned to a Philadelphia acquaintance who knew a man who had a friend who might be interested in the ring. Will turned the ring over to the man with the friend, not bothering to obtain a receipt, and several months passed with no word of the diamond or money. "Don't worry,'' Will told Betty, "he's all right.'' (It seemed that he was interested in race-horses.) But as the weeks went by even Will began to wonder. Then an envelope arrived. There was no note in it—just a check for $1,000.

Because he was so relaxed about money, Will was often overcharged, but his attitude toward this was typical: "I would

rather be the one to pay too much," he would say, "than to be the man that charged too much." Similarly with panhandlers; as Spi Trent described it, Will wanted to be able to go to sleep at night and not have to worry that somebody was going hungry because he had a suspicious nature. He carried his pay checks around in a pocket—often eight or ten of them at a time—until he needed money. Then he would cash them. He never kept accounts or business records; as Betty said, he seemed to know instinctively which obligations had to be met and how much money he had in the bank at any time. (Later, when he was making films, someone asked who his accountant was. "Haven't got any bookkeeper or any bookkeeping," Will replied. "We just put a check in the bank and draw on it until it's gone.")

In the summer of 1915 Will took his first airplane ride—an experience that led to a lifelong enthusiasm. He and Betty had gone to Atlantic City to watch some stunt flyers, and on the last day of their visit Will decided to go up in a "flying boat" Glenn Curtiss had made. Another man carried him piggyback out to the plane, and as the aircraft lifted off the water Betty saw him wave to her (as he was to do so many times in the years to come). She could tell that he was "nervous but vastly pleased."

For almost the first time in memory, Will was spending most of the summer at home with the family, and it was a nearly idyllic one—marred only by a head injury he suffered while taking diving lessons from Fred Stone's brother-in-law, Rex Beach. Somehow this affected his right arm, and for several weeks he was unable to do any roping, but even this had a salutary effect: in order to conceal his injury from theatre managers he added more talking to his act and learned to throw many rope tricks left-handed. And there was minor progress as far as his career was concerned: he was asked at the last minute to lend a hand on opening night with the musical *Hands Up*, and the producer—realizing what a hit his act was—kept him on for a few more weeks; and in the fall he played in a review called *Town Topics* briefly, until the show folded. As far as vaudeville went, he had finally hit the top. He was the featured attraction for two weeks at the Palace, which had opened in 1913 and was now the number one vaudeville house in the country.

Late that fall Will heard from a song lyricist and producer named Gene Buck, who offered him a two-week engagement in the Midnight Frolic, a late-night show on the roof of the New Amsterdam Theatre. As it turned out, this probably had more to do with determining his future than any date he ever played.

Family Life
in Forest Hills

*While Will waited for opportunity to knock
in New York the family lived on Long Island,
where the pictures on pages 134–35 were
taken. Forest Hills was but a twenty-minute
subway trip from Broadway; Will's horses
were stabled near the house; and by the time
he began playing in the Follies the three
children were old enough to rope and ride
with him (they were taught to sit a horse
at the age of two). As Betty described this
happy period in their lives, "we were having the best time we had had up to then."*

*Here come the Rogers riders: Bill on Chapel,
Jim on Dopey, Will, and Mary on Dodo.*
WILL ROGERS MEMORIAL, CLAREMORE, OKLA.

Will, Jr.—son of the Old West at an early age.

"ANDREW" IS JUST ABOUT
TO IMPOSE A LIBRARY
ON SOME POOR TOWN

The note on this snapshot of Jimmie (alias Mr. Carnegie) in the family album is in Will's hand.

ALL: WILL ROGERS MEMORIAL, CLAREMORE, OKLA.

The old master has one loop around Jim (left) and another around Mary while young Bill tries a hand at it.

At left, Betty and the children take a spin in the pony cart on Long Island. Above, Betty dries her hair.

BROWN BROTHERS

"He brought beauty
into the entertainment world."

Born in 1869, Florenz Ziegfeld started his show-business career as a promoter at the Chicago World's Fair of 1893; he produced his first Follies in 1907. At left is the New Amsterdam Theatre, showcase for the Follies and Midnight Frolic.
CULVER PICTURES

More important by far than the Midnight Frolic was the fact that it was the property of Florenz Ziegfeld, Jr., who also produced the most famous show in America—the Ziegfeld Follies. The idea of hiring Will came from Ziegfeld's right-hand man, Gene Buck, who saw in the cowboy comedian a new type of entertainer who would be a switch on the familiar and ubiquitous "Dutch" and black-face comics. Ziegfeld's own attitude toward comedians and similar performers was one of utter disdain: he put up with them only because they occupied the stage and filled in time while his beloved girls were changing for their next number. He was a man virtually devoid of humor who could sit expressionless while a funny man broke up the rest of the audience; as W.C. Fields described him, "Ziegfeld was a weird combination of the great showman and the little child. He really did not like comedians and tolerated them only because of the public. His forte was beautiful girls and costumes with elaborate settings."

The Frolic, as Will described it, was "the first midnight show": it began on the stroke of twelve and there were between fifty and seventy-five in the cast, including "the most beautiful girls of any show Ziegfeld ever put on." The loveliest ones, Will said, wouldn't work at a matinee—they never got up that early —so they were put into the Frolic, which was "for folks with lots of money and plenty of insomnia," who came to see the big, garish musical numbers. The Frolic was the fashionable place to be in the early morning hours.

When he started out at the Frolic, Will did pretty much what he had been doing for the past several years—punctuating his rope tricks with jokes that had to do with the show, the girls, Ziegfeld himself, the other acts, and so on. And on almost any

Two pages from Will's small pocket notebook, in which he wrote down ideas for gags for his Follies turn

WILL ROGERS MEMORIAL, CLAREMORE, OKLA.

other stage he could have gotten away with that, but not at the Frolic; there were many repeat customers, and as he quickly discovered, "a man won't laugh at the same joke more than once." His was an unusual act even for the Frolic, and the crowds liked him from the beginning, but Ziegfeld, sitting out front glum-faced, observing Gene Buck's protégé, turned to his assistant and commented flatly, "I don't like him."

Buck argued that the act was going over with the customers, so Ziegfeld agreed to watch it again another night. He did, and said, "I want you to let him go. He doesn't fit in." For some days this by-play went on, Ziegfeld insisting each time that the roper be fired, and finally Buck went to give Will the bad news. But Will had an announcement to give him first.

"I want fifty dollars a week more," he blurted out. "I've got to have the money." Besides, he said, he had a new idea for the act. "My wife says I ought to talk about what I read in the papers. She says I'm always readin' the papers, so why not pass along what I read?"

Reluctantly, Buck told him to try it, left the question of the raise hanging fire, and neglected to say that Ziegfeld was going to let him go, since he knew that the producer would be out of town for a week. As it happened, Will's notion of commenting on the news coincided with the famous effort of the industrialist Henry Ford to stop World War I. Ford had chartered a vessel, the *Oscar II*, loaded it with pacificists, idealists, and feminists, and set sail for Scandinavia, where he hoped to halt the fighting through neutral mediation. As Will came onstage one night, groping for something to warm up his audience, he remarked, "If Mr. Ford had taken this bunch of girls, in this show, and let 'em wear the same costumes they wear here, and marched them down between the trenches, believe me, the boys would have been out before Christmas." The outburst of laughter convinced him that all he needed was a new gag for each show about Ford's peace ship, which would work as long as Ford and the ship were in the news.

When Ziegfeld returned he asked Buck how his cowboy friend had reacted to the news that he was fired. "I haven't let him go," Buck admitted, and to Ziegfeld's question "Whose show is this?" Buck asked the producer to come that night and watch Rogers. Ziegfeld did, and though he was no more impressed than before with the cowboy's act, he had to concede that the customers loved it.

"We'll keep him another week," he said.

138

One more week led to another, and another; Will got his raise; and as Henry Ford vanished from the front pages he cast about for new sources of material. "So I started to reading about Congress," said Will, "and believe me, I found they are funnier three hundred and sixty-five days a year than anything I ever heard of." He would devour the newspapers for hours at a time, trying to work out a humorous angle to the day's news, for he had discovered that people would laugh more readily at what had happened that day than they would at a stereotyped joke written by a gag writer. "A joke don't have to be near as funny if it's up to date," he observed. "So that's how I learned that my own stuff, serving only strictly fresh-laid jokes, as you might say, goes better than anything else." He found, too, if what he said was based on fact—exaggerated slightly in the telling—the audience liked it even better. And he concluded, about this time, that he didn't really care for the jokes that got the biggest laughs—jokes that were "generally as broad as a house and require no thought at all." What he preferred was the sly, subtle line that made people think and prompted those in the audience to nudge their friends and say, "He's right about that, you know." As Will told an interviewer, "I would rather have you do that than to have you laugh—and then forget the next minute what it was you laughed at."

He had come a long way from the serious, single-minded technician who made the customers marvel at his dexterity with the rope. Now he was talking with his audiences—talking across the footlights, to be sure, but taking them into his confidence as if they were all together in someone's living room, conversing and laughing about the events of the day. He had progressed, too, beyond telling a stock line of jokes between rope tricks. Where audiences once had admired his roping and chuckled at his comments, now they were laughing with Will, who seemed more like an amiable friend than a performer. What made it much easier for him to get across the feeling of intimacy and informality was the fact that the Midnight Frolic was more of a nightclub than a theatre. He was not the type of comedian who tells a funny story; he liked to think on his feet, keeping things fluid and spontaneous, capitalizing on the day's news or even on something that occurred while he was out on the stage talking and spinning his rope. In vaudeville the old test of a joke's newness was to see if the orchestra laughed, and when Will was on, the musicians were as amused as the paying customers, since he almost never said the same thing twice. The

"This theatre [Midnight Frolic] is for the wealthy society people and as it is on the order of a cafeteria the tickets are $2.00 apiece, aside from what you eat. Suffice to say I ate nothing but occupied every minute of my time in looking. However, your Uncle Willie would order a lemonade for both your Aunt Maud and I. His act here is practically the same as at the other theatre but the little girl with whom he dances here wears the cutest white wooly chaps and my how she enjoys her part! The Grand Finale consists in the whole company coming in a very jolly sort of way and your Uncle Willie roped one of the chorus girls and quickly tied her to a wire which was just above their heads.... She turned to a gentleman sitting near and asked him to untie her. He gallantly did so and was roped in his turn and forcibly pulled along with the chorus. The house went wild...."

Sallie McSpadden
to her children
Nov. 13, 1915

extemporaneity of his performance also meant that it constantly varied in length—much more so than acts that were rehearsed over and over; one night he might be on stage for eight minutes, the next twelve. But however long his turn ran, it was always one of the shortest in the theatre; Will never forgot the secret he learned from Texas Jack: get off while the audience still wants more.

Will's one-week engagement stretched out for months; he was still in the Frolic in the spring of 1916 when Ziegfeld—again as a result of Gene Buck's prodding—asked him to join the cast of the Follies. Will's refusal must have come as a surprise to the producer, but there were reasons for it: neither Will nor Betty thought the salary Ziegfeld offered him was adequate, particularly since a Follies job meant that he would have to go on the road again, for no matter how good business was in New York, Ziegfeld had a traditional schedule for his annual show—spring and summer in New York, Thanksgiving in Pittsburgh, Christmas in Chicago, with a new edition of the Follies going into rehearsal soon afterward. Will was enjoying a sane home life for the first time in years; the family had a house in Forest Hills, kept horses in a nearby stable, and he and Betty devoted a lot of time to the children or went riding in the country. As Betty told it, she talked Will out of going with the Follies mainly because they had decided he should get the salary he wanted even if he had to wait for it.

They attended the opening of the 1916 Follies with Betty's old beau, Tom Harvey, and his wife, expecting to have the time of their lives, but while the show was extravagant and spectacular, it was also deadly dull. Through the long evening Will kept whispering to Betty, nudging her and saying, "See, Blake, what did I tell you? This was my one big chance." Or, "Boy, I wish I could have got my crack at it." It was apparent that Will's homespun act would have been a standout amid all that glitter, and when they left the theatre they were sunk—Betty blaming herself for the mistake, both feeling that Will had lost an opportunity that might not come again.

Several days later Mr. Ziegfeld called (a great many Follies actors referred to him as Flo or Ziggy, but to Will he was always Mr. Ziegfeld). The show was not good, he said, it lacked humor, and he wanted Will to join it at once. By now Will was so eager to break into the Follies that he didn't even discuss salary. He would go on that night, he said, with no announcement whatever. TEXT CONTINUED ON PAGE 146

The Most Beautiful Girls in the World

Gorgeous costumes were one of the hallmarks of a Ziegfeld production. Above is the 1925 theatre playbill.

WILL ROGERS MEMORIAL, CLAREMORE, OKLA.

BOTH: CULVER PICTURES

Ziegfeld's idea of a perfect production was a stage, dazzlingly set and lit, ornamented with beautiful girls—clad partially, or in outrageously resplendent costumes, or not at all. None of this is apparent in the photograph of a Follies rehearsal above, but when the curtain rose at the New Amsterdam there were gasps from the audience at the showman's latest, lavish "glorification of the American girl," exemplified at top and opposite. It was said that the only reason Ziegfeld hired comedians was to fill the time void while his girls changed costumes. "He brought beauty into the entertainment world," Will said at the time he died; but he also gave the country some of its outstanding comedians: W. C. Fields, Eddie Cantor, Ed Wynn, Fanny Brice, Bert Williams, and many others.

The Ziegfeld girls' costumes were often as out-landish as they were sumptuous, as may be seen at the four corners of these pages. Ziegfeld's

WILL ROGERS MEMORIAL, CLAREMORE, OKLA.

*taste kept the level of the shows within accepted
bounds and nudity, when displayed as above,
was usually in the chaste form of a "tableau."*

CULVER PICTURES

Will often appeared to be a grinning puritan in a sea of pulchritude, and his manner made him an unfailing foil for beauty in any guise.
BROWN BROTHERS

It was, Betty reported, "the very proudest moment of our lives. When Will went on stage that night, the audience broke into applause. Never had he gone over so well." He made a second appearance, spinning his rope and commenting on personalities and events, and immediately after the curtain rang down went upstairs to the roof to do his turn in the Frolic. As Betty wrote, "his magic stayed with him," and after the two shows they stayed up, eating sandwiches and drinking beer, waiting for the early editions of the morning papers. "All of them," she said, "gave Will excellent notices—the best, most important he had ever received."

Two shows a night and two matinees a week kept him on his toes, particularly since the Follies and Frolic were in the same theatre and Follies patrons would drift up to the roof to eat, drink, and be entertained some more. This meant that Will had to have an entirely different act twice every night. He had acquired the habit of opening with the same phrase, "Well, all I know is what I read in the papers," and going on from there.

Since New York jokes did not go especially well with the Follies audiences, which consisted mostly of out-of-town businessmen, he tended to use more local material in the Frolic. But timeliness was the secret of his act, and he pored over the noon editions of afternoon papers for his matinee performance; read stories from the final and home editions for the Follies; and extracted material from the bulldog edition for the midnight show. "I buy more newspaper extras than any man in the world," he claimed, "because I've made up my mind no joke can get over after it is six hours old." All his comments were brief—usually no more than three or four lines; in the time that most monologuists told eight or ten stories, Will averaged forty or more. The nature and brevity of his stuff was such that one critic referred to him as the "columnist of the theatre."

He also formed the habit of joking with guests who came back again and again to see the Frolic, which in turn led to introducing prominent personalities from the audience—a technique he then adopted for the Follies. Ushers would keep an eye out for celebrities and send notes to Will's dressing room indicating the

From left to right, the array of comic headliners in this 1918 Follies skit included W. C. Fields, Will Rogers, Eddie Cantor, and Harry Kelly, vying for Lillian Lorraine's affections.

CULVER PICTURES

"You read a lot of highbrow articles on America and its humor. . . . Now the guys who write those dont have to get out and . . . make a living trying to make an audience laugh. Now I have traveled for four years with the Follies, the biggest stage show on the road, and all I had to do was to tell the audience new things to make them laugh each night.

"My little stunt consisted of talking on what I had read in the papers every day. Well, when the war commence to get serious for us I thought here is where you will have to change your style of act, you cant keep on kidding people, and other people told me the same thing: 'You will have to be pretty careful what you say.' It only showed how little we understood the American public."

from notes for Will Rogers'
*What People Laughed at
During the War*

location of their seats; or Ziegfeld would tell him when friends of his were in the house; or sometimes Will, peering over the footlights, would spot a friend or someone known to the audience (the house lights were always kept on when he talked, and the actress Else Janis, whom he once roped and pulled up on stage, said he must have had eyes in the back of his neck). Since he said whatever came into his head, it was an act that captivated everyone. One night he swung his rope out over the crowd and lassoed Fred Stone, who was seated on the aisle about three rows from the front. Despite his protests, Will hauled him up on stage, made him perform one of his own rope tricks, meantime leaning against the proscenium arch and visiting with him, asking about Mrs. Stone and the children. It was the kind of unexpected treat that proved irresistible.

One of Will's old Texas friends, about whom he often spoke to theatrical friends, was Clay McGonigle. Clay had a special, unprintable nickname for Will, and before one performance a note was delivered to Rogers' dressing room, saying, "I'm in town and will be out in front watching the show." The salutation was the nickname, it was signed Clay McGonigle, and Will was delighted. Throughout the performance he addressed remarks to his old buddy, reminisced about the old days, and scanned the audience trying to locate him, hoping for a familiar cowboy yelp in response. There was no sign of Clay, but Will persisted, to the mystification of all others present. After the performance he dropped into W.C. Fields' dressing room long enough to remark how strange it was that old Clay hadn't showed up, and then he went off to look for him, spending a good part of the night checking into bars and railroad stations. Not for some time did a friend tip him off to the fact that Fields had sent the note.

During his years with the Follies Will always occupied the same dressing room—a tiny, cell-like, third-floor room with one window and no carpet, which had a primitive dressing table, a row of hooks along one wall where he tossed his clothes, and a few straight chairs. As a surprise for Will, his wife and a friend once fixed up the room, hanging curtains to hide the hooks, adding a couch, a rug, and some comfortable chairs. But the improvements did not last long; Will was accustomed to a lot worse in the theatres he had played around the world, he didn't want his dressing room "fancied up," and out went the new décor.

What had drawn people to the Follies ever since the first one

opened in 1907 was, of course, the combination of beautiful
showgirls, the fantastic costumes and sets, and the sprinkling of
high-priced talent—performers like W.C. Fields, Bert Williams, Fanny Brice, Ann Pennington, Eddie Cantor, and dozens of
other headliners. When rehearsals began in the winter, Will
and Betty often sat together in the darkened house while Ziegfeld and his assistants worked out the various spectacular numbers. Will always enjoyed kidding about the girls—most of
whom worked hard, since every stage-struck hopeful dreamed
of being picked for the Follies (in 1914, when playboy Tommy
Manville's current wife sued him for divorce and a $150,000
settlement, it came as no surprise that she was a Follies girl).
"We have a hard time keeping our girls together," Will once
remarked on tour; "every time we get to a new town some of
them marry millionaires, but in a few weeks they catch up with
the show again."

When it was Will's turn to rehearse he generally kidded
amiably about the show and the performers or remarked on in-
cidents that had occurred during the tryouts, but it was not, in
fact, a rehearsal for him. His act was always as fresh to members
of the cast as it was to the audience, with the result that the cast
usually collected in the wings to hear him every night.

By the time Will joined Ziegfeld, the Follies was an established American institution. "A funny thing about the Follies," Will wrote, "people never spoke about in comparison to
any other show. It was always, 'It's better than the last year's,
or it's not so good as last year's.' The Follies always stood
alone." It was true: Ziegfeld was his own greatest competition.
So when the time came for Will to decide whether or not he
would go on tour it was extremely difficult to say "no," but he
was determined not to leave New York unless he got a substantial raise. Ziegfeld came to his dressing room one day to talk
things over and overwhelmed Will with an offer of a two-year
contract at $600 a week the first year and $750 the second—far
more than he had considered asking. Then the producer
suggested that he stop by his office the next day and sign a contract, but Will said, "I don't like contracts. You can trust me
and I know I can trust you."

Ziegfeld thought it over, called in Charles Dillingham, another producer who happened to be backstage, to witness their
verbal agreement, and the deal was made. Will was to work for
Ziegfeld for ten years without a contract; when he left for
Hollywood at the end of that period, the producer gave him a

Fanny Brice

CULVER PICTURES

watch with the engraved inscription, "To Will Rogers, in appreciation of a real fellow, whose word is his bond."

In numerous other ways Ziegfeld looked after Will. The Follies cast traveled in a special train, and the producer arranged for two of Will's horses, with a cowboy friend in charge of them, to go along in the scenery car so that Will could ride each morning and practice roping on horseback.

Of all the road trips Will made he was proudest of the occasions on which he played for President Woodrow Wilson. The first was in Baltimore, at a benefit performance called the Friar's Frolic, in 1916, shortly before the United States entered the war. Just before the opening the cast heard that President and Mrs. Wilson were coming from Washington to see the show, and Will immediately developed a bad case of stage fright. He had planned to devote most of his act to the country's state of unpreparedness and to the diplomatic notes going back and forth between Wilson and various European powers, and while he had no qualms about talking this way at the New Amsterdam Theatre to the general public, telling it to the President of the United States was another matter altogether, especially since Will knew that everyone in the theatre would be watching the Wilsons' box, waiting for the reaction. The closer it came to curtain time, the more nervous he grew. George Cohan, Willie Collier, and others, sensing the dilemma, came by to pat him on the back and reassure him, saying, "He's just a human being; go on out and do your stuff." But when the moment came Will felt like a condemned man ascending the gallows and had to be shoved out on the stage. He stood there for a moment, grinning sheepishly, rubbing his head, and remarked to everyone's delight, "I'm kinder nervous here tonight."

Writing about the experience later, he said, "Now that is not an especially bright remark . . . but it was so apparent to the audience that I was speaking the truth that they all laughed heartily at it." Then he began easing into the material he had planned to use. "I shouldn't be nervous," he added, "for this is really my second Presidential appearance. The first time was when Bryan spoke in our town once, and I was to follow his speech and do my little Roping Act." Glancing at the Presidential box and seeing Wilson laugh, he went on, "As I say, I was to follow him, but he spoke so long that it was so dark when he finished they couldn't see my roping." Then a pause: "I wonder what ever became of him."

A few jokes about "Pancho" Villa, whom General John J.

CULVER PICTURES

Bert Williams

CULVER PICTURES

Pershing was chasing in Mexico, followed: "I see where they have captured Villa. Yes, they got him in the morning Editions and the Afternoon ones let him get away." The Republicans, he said, "are kicking on our Mexican policies. They claim we are paying for a war and not getting it."

Now he turned to the country's lack of military preparedness —a subject on which Wilson was being criticized daily. "There is some talk of getting a Machine Gun if we can borrow one. The one we have now they are using to train our Army with in Plattsburg. If we go to war we will just about have to go to the trouble of getting another Gun." When Will saw that the President was leading the laughter, he added a pointed remark about the exchange of diplomatic notes between the U.S. and Germany, which Wilson afterward repeated to friends, saying it was the best joke told on him during the war. "President Wilson is getting along fine now to what he was a few months ago. Do you realize, people, that at one time in our negotiations with Germany that he was 5 Notes behind?"

Chic Sale

Will later called this the proudest and most successful night he had ever had—made more memorable by the fact that the President came backstage during intermission and shook hands with everyone in the cast.

U.S. entry into the war put no stop to Will's jokes about it. On the contrary, he found that Americans "laughed better during the war than any other time, and the more serious the situation the better they laughed if you happened to hit the right angle to it." At thirty-eight, with a wife and three children, he was exempt from the draft, but attempted to compensate for that in various ways, appearing at benefits and other fund-raising occasions and playing for returned veterans. To the president of the American Red Cross he wrote in May of 1917 to say that he had tried honestly to estimate what he might contribute personally. "While not a wealthy man," he noted, "I earn a very good salary," and pledged a donation of 10 per cent of his next year's income—or $5,200—to the organization; he would continue to give $100 a week for the duration of the war.

He was telling Follies audiences that Germany couldn't understand how the United States could get trained men to Europe so quickly; what the enemy didn't comprehend, he said, was that "in our training manual there's nothing about retreating. When you only have to teach an army to go one way, you can do it in half the time." One of his most successful routines was his advice on how to obtain a commission in order to

Ann Pennington
CULVER PICTURES

fight the war in Washington: all it required was a visit to your Senator. After receiving the commission, a clerk at the uniform store could tell you what insignia to wear and which end of the puttees should go on top. Military training would include dancing lessons, to avoid catching your spurs in a girl's dress, but the hazards to be faced were legion: ten men had been wounded in one day getting in and out of taxicabs, "two choked through their collars being too tight . . . 61 hurt through typewriters choking up . . . 500 prostrated when they heard the war was over and they would have to go back to work."

Nor was he neglecting other sacred cows on the home front. During the early days of the war the New York, New Haven & Hartford Railroad had had a number of wrecks, in one of which fifty people were killed, and that night Will commented, "I see where the NYNH&H have started in on their spring drive." The following day an irate officer of the road sent word to Ziegfeld that his comedian should eliminate any reference to the company, so Will obliged by reporting that "one of our railroads" had started its big spring drive. "You see," he added with a smile, "I did not mention the name of any railroad in that," and the official who had tried to censor his material ought to be pleased: "I did not say a word about the NYNH&H." That was one railroad, he had observed, where "You see friends bidding each other goodbye at their depots just as though they are going to war."

With the signing of the Armistice, which "read like a second mortgage" while the peace terms "read like a foreclosure," Will commented that it had taken eighty thousand words to tell Germany what we thought of them. Now that American troops in large numbers were returning home, there was criticism that they were not being brought back fast enough, and the reason, Will explained, was "so they can get the mail that was sent to them during the war." To those veterans who had already arrived triumphantly in the States he remarked, "If they had divided up all the money they spent on parades for you boys, you wouldent have to be looking for a job," and as an afterthought he wondered, "If they really wanted to honor the boys, why dident they let them sit in the stands and have the people march by?"

By this time his jokes were being quoted so frequently that he collected a number of them, added others, and in 1919 published two books which achieved a modest success. The first was *Rogers-isms: The Cowboy Philosopher on the Peace Conference*, on the dust jacket of which he had written, "I made this book short so you could finish it before the next war." That volume was followed quickly by *Rogers-isms: The Cowboy Philosopher on Prohibition.* "You wont find the Country any drier than this Book," the cover proclaimed, and inside was an assortment of gags which had enlivened his Follies and Frolic routines. "It will take some men two years solid rehersing to learn how to order a soft drink without blushing," he predicted; soda fountains would have to go to the extra expense of adding foot rails; and among the coming generation there would be people who "can name 12 different Phosphates that couldent name 2 Presidents." He perceived a few good things about Prohibition, though: if it would just stop some men trying to repeat stories they had heard, it would not be in vain, and it had already been "the cause of more road improvement between dry and wet towns than any other thing," since "Bad roads have broke more bottles of booze than the authorities." Until the Volstead Act had run its course, it would remain one of his favorite targets.

With the publication of these slim books, Will made his first venture onto the literary scene. But it was short-lived. He had discovered another medium representing new opportunities during the summer of 1918.

Nothing tickled a big butter-and-egg man from Chicago so much as to go backstage at the Follies and have his photograph taken with Will Rogers, the famous comedian.
WILL ROGERS MEMORIAL, CLAREMORE, OKLA.

CULVER PICTURES

"... anybody can open a Theatre. It's keeping it open that is the hard thing."

The public birth of motion pictures occurred at Koster & Bial Music Hall (above) in 1896. Twenty-two years later Will Rogers appeared in his first film, Laughing Bill Hyde, *a six-reeler by the novelist Rex Beach, from which the scene at left is taken.*

BROWN BROTHERS

"Film art," the critic Erwin Panofsky wrote in 1934, "is the only art the development of which men now living have witnessed from the very beginning." Although Will Rogers and thousands of his fellow countrymen had been exposed in some fashion to the novelty known as moving pictures, neither he nor most others were aware that those first primitive films would one day be called an art form, nor could they guess that this magical new medium would, during the next three or four decades, transform the entertainment world and transfix a majority of Americans (not to mention the inhabitants of the rest of the globe).

So far as the general public was aware, the excitement started at the Koster & Bial Music Hall west of Broadway in New York (now the site of R.H. Macy & Company), one evening in April, 1896. Koster & Bial's variety house normally catered to a middle-class clientele, but on this particular occasion Manhattan's upper crust turned out, dressed to the nines, to see a demonstration of the latest invention by the electrical genius, Thomas Alva Edison. The program included the usual vaudeville fare—an English music hall performer, a Russian clown, acrobatic dancers, a pair of French singers, and a sketch called "London Life"—all of which the crowd regarded as tedious; as the evening wore on, the audience became increasingly impatient to see the last item on the bill before intermission: "Thomas A. Edison's Latest Marvel, THE VITASCOPE."

At last the moment arrived. A twenty-foot white screen descended in front of the stage, lights were extinguished, a curious mechanical object in the center of the balcony began to buzz and wheeze, and a brilliant light filled the screen. Suddenly the figures of two women appeared and were seen to smile, pirouette daintily around their parasols, and dance; they vanished, and in their place an angry, surging wave crashed toward the audience. Thomas Armat, the Vitascope operator, recalled afterward that the realism of the surf "started a panicky commotion" in the front seats as the water appeared to cascade over them, and later the spectators went wild and cheered when a showgirl named Annabelle performed "The Butterfly Dance" on the screen. In short, an audience of sophisticated, mature New Yorkers was thrilled, delighted, and behaved like a flock of children. The theatrical producer Charles Frohman was there and sensed at once the significance of what he had seen. "That settles scenery," he told a reporter after the show. "Now that art can make us believe that we see actual, living nature, the dead things of the stage must go."

In truth, the "invention" demonstrated that night was not Edison's own, but a projector developed by Armat and a man named Jenkins that Armat had turned over to Edison to manufacture because of the prestige of his name. Armat, it should be noted, was not the only man to devise such a machine; on the contrary, the notion of making pictures move on a screen dated back to the 1850's and earlier, when a shutter was added to the venerable magic lantern to make a series of drawings look like a figure in motion. The principle—then and now —of creating an illusion of motion was based on a phenomenon known as "the persistence of vision," by which the optic nerve "remembers" a still image for a fraction of a second. The trick was to flash a sequence of images on the screen at a speed of sixteen frames per second, faster than the eye could catch. Various experimenters—among them the American Eadweard Muybridge, who had something he called a Zoopraxiscope to display animals in motion in the 1880's—had produced workable motion-picture projectors. (It is possible that Will and his father may have seen Muybridge's pictures in 1893 at the Chicago World's Fair, where he exhibited them in the Zoopraxographical Hall.)

Oddly enough, Edison was only mildly interested in Armat's projector; he had a bigger fish of his own to fry—something called the Kinetoscope. Out at his laboratory, where the principle of "collective invention" was practiced, an imaginative employee named William K.L. Dickson had been given the assignment of making moving pictures to accompany the playing of Edison's beloved gramophone. After seeing the potential of George Eastman's new Kodak film, Dickson soon confronted his boss with a machine that produced a talking picture on a screen. Although there is some uncertainty about the date, it appears that this may have taken place as early as 1889—nearly four decades before the first talking picture, *The Jazz Singer*, electrified the country; but for various reasons the idea of combining sound and pictures was shelved temporarily, and Dickson plunged ahead with his work on the Kinetoscope, which Edison began marketing in 1894.

This is what came to be known as a peepshow—a machine activated by placing a coin in a slot so that one person could watch about fifty feet of film. By the hundreds these upright viewers were installed in rows in the "phonograph parlors" in towns and cities across the land where customers were already congregating to listen to Edison's gramophone. At the time Edison's associates tried to interest him in a film projector, the Kinetoscope business was booming, and he replied, "No, if we make this screen machine that you are asking for, it will spoil everything. We are making these peepshow machines and selling a lot of them at a good profit. If we put out a screen machine there will be use for maybe about ten of them in the whole United States. With that many screen machines you could show the pictures to everybody in the country—and then it would be done. Let's not kill the goose that lays the golden egg."

Not surprisingly, the first institution to see the possibilities of the motion-picture projector was vaudeville, and from 1896 to 1900 many houses showed films to supplement their live stage entertainment. But the pictures, which consisted, by and large, of movement for movement's sake—photographs of natural phenomena like Niagara Falls, of trains and fire engines in motion, parades, and an occasional news scene (William McKinley's 1896 Presidential campaign being one of the first)—began to pall, the novelty faded, and by the turn of the century most of the vaudeville houses that retained their projectors were showing movies as "chasers," to clear the theatre before the next show. Yet while middle-class audiences in the vaudeville houses wearied of such fare, workers and thousands of new immigrants from Europe delighted in the noisy, garish penny arcades, where they could listen to Sousa's marches or operatic arias on the gramophone or peer into a hand-cranked Kinetoscope and watch the bewitching pictures move. Operators of these establishments were quick to sniff the money that could be made by turning the arcades into picture theatres and increasing the potential size and turnover of their audiences, and they began buying projectors and demanding new films to show on them. Before long these makeshift, back-room theatres became the most popular form of entertainment for America's lower class. Enchanted by the wonder of motion on a screen, caught up in the excitement generated by a crowd of people watching something together, thousands of illiterate folk found escape from dreary lives and surroundings at a price they could afford. Movies provided not merely entertainment—a dramatic chase, a courtship, a comic confrontation between Happy Hooligan the tramp and a prim, respectable banker; they supplied a wealth of palatable information to men and women largely ignorant of their adopted homeland and its customs. While the upper levels of society saw all this as nonsense and cheap claptrap, shrewder souls perceived in the growing popularity of films the basis for profit and the makings of a new industry.

In Chicago two entrepreneurs named George K. Spoor and Aronson formed a company called Essanay and began to capitalize on the excitement inevitably produced by chase scenes. Logically enough, they transferred elements of the Wild West show to the screen, and Aronson (who changed his name to G.M. Anderson and achieved fame as "Broncho Billy") was soon grinding out horse operas at the rate of one a week. William Selig, another Chicagoan, got in touch with Will Rogers' old friend Tom Mix, hired him, and thereby gave the American boy one of his first screen idols.

The theatre that provided a name for all the others was Pittsburgh's Nickelodeon, a converted store, which opened in 1905 with a showing of the first important Western, *The Great Train Robbery* (made in New Jersey by another Edison employee, Edwin S. Porter). That film set the pattern for hundreds more to follow: beginning with a scene in which two badmen slug a stationmaster, it moves quickly to a murder in the baggage car of a train, the dynamiting of a strongbox, a horseback chase, and a gunfight between the good and bad guys. With the coming of a true narrative to the screen—not just isolated, unconnected episodes—the nickelodeon boom was on. By 1907 there were three thousand of them, by 1910, ten thousand—all with uncomfortable seats, the pungent odor of human sweat, Cracker Jack, and popcorn, and, as the upper crust complained, vermin. They were usually run as a family affair, with mother and daughter selling nickel tickets, father taking them, son operating the projector and the magic lantern (whose slides advised the audience, "One moment, please, while we change

This New York nickelodeon, complete with wistful tots, was a typical store-front operation. By 1913 there were twenty thousand film theatres of all types in the United States.
BROWN BROTHERS

159

Just off the train from the East, Will arrives in Culver City to make his first film.
WILL ROGERS MEMORIAL, CLAREMORE, OKLA.

"I arrived . . . in Beverly Hills just in time to keep Real Estate men from plotting off and selling my front yard. "You buy lots in Los Angeles with the same frequency you would newspapers in other towns. After buying it, you put it back in the hands of the Agents again, for don't think you are going to get away with that lot. It has to be sold three or four times that day. Why, every lot out here has its own Agent."

from Weekly Article
Aug. 1, 1923

reels," or cautioned the ladies, "Kindly remove your hats"), while other children peddled refreshments.

As the demand for films grew, so did the need for stories capable of being transmitted to film, for improved production and distribution facilities, and for a growing number of actors, editors, cameramen, and directors—all the appurtenances of a burgeoning industry. Those nickelodeon operators knew the audiences and their limitations, and what they asked for established certain traditions that were followed for years in silent films. Certain visual clichés emerged: characters who could be recognized on sight as the poor but noble Working Girl, the Villain, the Family Man (who was inevitably tempted by the Vamp); scenes printed in blue or green to denote nighttime; the checkered tablecloth to symbolize a working-class home; gestures and facial expressions that virtually shouted hatred, horror, love, nobility. And yet another characteristic of these early silents was increasingly evident. Although the nickelodeons were shunned like the plague by most of the well-to-do, those citizens began to perceive—at a time when the muckraker's voice was heard across the land—that similar themes were being pushed in the picture houses. The titles alone made that quite clear: *The Girl Strike Leader, Capital vs. Labor, Lily of the Tenements, The Grafters,* and (after the sensational shooting of the architect Stanford White by millionaire Harry Thaw at Madison Square Garden in 1906) *The Great Thaw Trial.* Such films, it was said by the Chicago *Tribune,* had an "influence wholly vicious" and ministered "to the lowest passions of children." As the *Christian Leader* maintained, "A set of revolutionists training for the overthrow of the government could find no surer means than these exhibitions." After the Thaw film was shown in New York, Mayor George McClellan closed down all nickelodeons in the city.

By this time the movie business was big enough to have its own monopoly, the Motion Picture Patents Company. It was created in 1909 to protect the equipment and processes of its members in such a way that no films could be photographed, processed, or exhibited without its consent (inevitably, there had been a good deal of pirating and copying of films by shrewd nickelodeon operators). The trust decided that something must be done about matters and moved quickly to establish a National Board of Censorship to pass on the content and respectability of its pictures.

While it lasted, the motion-picture monopoly was a formidable antagonist for independent producers who persisted in going it alone. Spies employed by the trust raided unlicensed theatres; "illicit" projectors and films were destroyed; hired men posing as extras found work with the independents, and smashed cameras and raided their darkrooms. By the time the monopoly was broken up as a result of a suit under the Sherman Anti-Trust Law, the East Coast had become too hazardous for the independents. William Selig had taken his company to Los Angeles, which was near enough to the Mexican border to enable him to escape subpoenas and save his cameras, and he and others who followed discovered that nature made it possible to

produce movies there in an entirely new manner. The essence of it was virtual year-round sunshine; this meant that interiors could be photographed outdoors without need for electric lights. Moreover, California offered every type of landscape— mountain, desert, fields, sea, lakes, islands—and much of it unoccupied. These were the factors that brought to Los Angeles, in 1910, the man who was to initiate or influence most of the changes that were soon to take place in the motion-picture industry.

The era of silents was the heyday of the director. After all, in the beginning only two technicians were required: one to direct the action; the other to record it on film, the cameraman. The

As clean-cut lead Dustin Farnam (in white shirt) and The Squaw Man *company went on location, little did they dream to what heights the putteed director Cecil B. De-Mille (seated on the running board) would eventually soar.*
CULVER PICTURES

161

A bear for reality, D. W. Griffith shot Way Down East *during one of the most fearsome winters the Connecticut Valley had known.*

CULVER PICTURES

successful director had to be an organizer, a conceiver, an artist, and something of a tyrant, and he had to possess the facility for visualizing a story that theretofore had been told only in words. In David Wark Griffith, a sensitive, intelligent Southerner who was the son of a Confederate officer, the motion-picture industry found the director who gave it an entirely new direction and made the American public take films seriously. Griffith had played in traveling stock companies, sold stories to the Edison company, and acted under Edwin Porter before turning to directing himself; then, within a remarkably short period, he turned out more than four hundred one- and two-reel pictures, filled with innovations of all sorts. He moved the camera about frequently, making it a roving eye instead of a static piece of equipment; he originated such techniques as the long-shot, the vignette, the close-up, the fade-in and fade-out, and the angle shot; he developed modern methods of lighting and was the first to try night photography; he became famous for the "Griffith last-minute rescue"; and he was one of the first men to insist that the public would accept pictures that ran longer than one reel, or fourteen minutes. Creating his scenes as he went along, he used actors and actresses like chessmen, his wife remarked. (One of Griffith's discoveries was a young, golden-haired girl named Gladys Smith, whom he made famous as "Little Mary"; before long the company was receiving the first fan letters—twenty or more a day—asking for her name, which was later revealed to be Mary Pickford.)

In the fall of 1914 Griffith began work independently on a film based on a novel called *The Clansman*, by Thomas Dixon, a melodrama about the Reconstruction period, depicting the Ku Klux Klan as chivalrous heroes. He visualized it in terms unheard-of in the industry—twelve reels, which would take six months to film, at a cost of $100,000. Released in February, 1915, as *The Clansman*, it aroused immediate and intense excitement—so much so that Dixon suggested that the title be changed to *The Birth of a Nation*. It was shown at the White House to President Wilson, the Cabinet, and their families; it was hailed by the press, denounced in Boston, and became an overnight sensation wherever it played. It provoked race riots in several cities, and the public came in droves to see a film capable of producing such passions. For almost the first time, the intelligentsia began to admit that the cinema could no longer be ignored. (Will took his sisters Sallie and Maud to see it in New York, and Sallie wrote her children to say that it was the finest picture show ever made.)

At the same time the public began to take motion pictures seriously, certain directors were soliciting the opposite reaction from the audience. A former actor named Mack Sennett, who had worked with D.W. Griffith and absorbed many of his ideas, was directing comedies and discovered, quite by accident, that if the film was cranked through the camera at a very slow speed it resulted in speeding up the action on the screen with effects that were often hiliarious. Sennett's one- and two-reelers poked fun at all the conventions of the day, revealing the hypocrisy and absurdity of those fetishes by which American society set such store: the successful businessman suffered an ignominious pratfall or received a custard pie in the face; the innocent American girl was portrayed as a beautiful, dumb bathing beauty who had eyes only for the bankroll of a grossly unattractive man; the romantic lover was seen as cross-eyed Ben Turpin or Fatty Arbuckle; America's dedication to the theory that time is money was caricatured in wildly funny chaotic chases demonstrating that speed achieves nothing; imbecilic Keystone Kops revealed the underlying contempt of the country for its law enforcement officers; and Sennett's cynical view of the almighty automobile took shape in the impossible adventures of the Model T, which inevitably came to an explosive, smoky demise.

The film critic James Agee realized that Sennett and the gifted comedians he employed had developed an immense vocabulary of clichés that required the accomplishments of an acrobat, a dancer, a clown, and a mime. There were, he went on to say, four gradations of laughter—the titter, the yowl, the belly laugh, and the boffo—and "An ideally good gag, perfectly constructed and played, would bring the victim up this ladder of laughs by cruelly controlled degrees to the top rung, and would then proceed to wobble, shake, wave, and brandish the ladder until he groaned for mercy. Then, after the shortest possible time out for recuperation, he would feel the first wicked tickling of the comedian's whip once more and start up a new ladder." Buster Keaton, Harry Langdon, and Charlie Chaplin (whom Sennett called the greatest artist who ever lived) all worked for Sennett, and while their comedies were ignored by many respectable citizens, millions of other Americans were crowding into theatres to see them, loving their wild innocence, spontaneity, and vitality, and rocking the picture houses with steady, deafening laughter.

"Old Hollywood is just like a desert water hole in Africa. Hang around long enough and every kind of animal in the world will drift in for refreshments."

from Daily Telegram
Nov. 11, 1931

Mack Sennett gave the world bathing suited beauty and Ben Turpin's comic incompetence.
CULVER PICTURES

By the time Will Rogers began to take a personal interest in motion pictures, the medium was already two decades old and had made the transition from a novelty to big business. The first ten years was the period when episodes from daily life, brief news films, and comic or melodramatic one-reelers were shown in peepshows and then in store theatres; the next period culminated in *The Birth of a Nation*, the rise of the feature film, and the building of palatial new theatres especially for the showing of motion pictures. During this latter decade the movies discovered Hollywood.

About the time the Vitascope was unveiled at Koster & Bial's, a Los Angeles couple named Mr. and Mrs. H.H. Wilcox purchased one hundred twenty acres of land northwest of that city, subdivided the property into lots, and named the development Hollywood. D. W. Griffith, like William Selig and others, had come to California to escape the winters back East, and in 1910 he began filming a picture in Hollywood. Residents of the community were dismayed by what now happened to their town; soon actors and actresses were everywhere; and as other companies followed Griffith, streets were roped off to stage parades or gun battles or automobile accidents; once-quiet hotels were filled with painted women, noisy cavalrymen, Indians, and cowboys; vacant land was gobbled up and turned into studios and movie lots.

In 1913 three partners arrived from the East, rented a barn near the corner of Sunset Boulevard and Vine Street, and began filming a motion-picture version of the stage play *The Squaw Man*. The three were Cecil B. DeMille, a former actor and playwright; Jesse L. Lasky, a vaudeville producer; and Lasky's brother-in-law, Samuel Goldfish, who was born in the Warsaw ghetto, made his way to England and the United States, and went into glove making before joining Lasky and DeMille to produce and distribute pictures.

In quick order DeMille made three successful movies, and the company was on its way. In those days everything about the making of a picture was highly informal: everyone on the set, including the actors, did what was asked of him, from switching props to standing in as an extra to working out gags. What scripts there were, were rudimentary, not much more than a three- or four-page synopsis of a plot line to be improvised on. (Anita Loos, who later wrote *Gentlemen Prefer Blondes*, began sending scripts to Griffith when she was fourteen; he paid her $15 or $25 apiece for them and didn't discover until he met her two years later that she was a child, four feet nine inches tall, with pigtails.) While this completely unstructured, casual approach was all very well for slapstick comedies, where visual gags were often concocted on the spur of the moment by the comedians themselves or the director, novels and plays that were translated into movies usually lost something in the process. The action tended to be static, the characterization suffered, and something clearly had to be done. A pioneer in the effort to improve the quality of scenario writing was Samuel Goldfish, who was about to call himself Goldwyn, and—having formed his own company—he announced that he had hired a group of novelists, to whom he gave the resounding name of Eminent Authors. Among them were Mary Roberts Rinehart, Rupert Hughes, Gertrude Atherton, Gouverneur Morris, and Rex Beach. Since the cinematic output of these luminaries ("the greatest American novelists of today," Goldwyn called them) was generally considered to be a flop, it would have little importance here except for the fact that Rex Beach's wife was the sister of Fred Stone's wife and a friend of Will Rogers.

Beach had sold Goldwyn one of his books, *Laughing Bill Hyde*, and the producer was trying to find an actor to play the lead. It was at the time Will and his family were renting Fred Stone's house in Amityville, Long Island, for the summer while Fred was on the West Coast making a picture, and Rex Beach's wife came to see them with an idea. Over lunch she suddenly announced that Will was the ideal person to play Bill Hyde, and almost before Will had time to think about it she communicated this inspiration to her husband. Samuel Goldwyn came to see Will, told him that the picture could be shot in the Fort Lee, New Jersey, studios during the summer when the Follies was not playing, and Will—despite some hesitation about his ability to play a part and to perform without an audience—agreed to do it.

When it appeared, in September, 1918, the *New York Times* greeted it enthusiastically: "Those inclined to believe that all of the magnetic Rogers personality is in his conversation will realize their mistake if they see this picture. The real Will Rogers is on the reels. Whether Rogers can act or whether he can do anything before the camera except be himself, is not the question."

Goldwyn was pleased with the box-office receipts, and while Will was on tour with the Follies the producer caught up with him in Cleveland and offered him a two-year contract to make

The antics of filmdom's Keystone Kops could only be described as uninhibited anarchy.

CULVER PICTURES

pictures in Hollywood. By then Will was drawing a good salary from Ziegfeld, but Goldwyn offered him double the amount for the first year and triple for the second. According to Betty, they were attracted as much by the prospect of moving to California and having a home of their own as they were by the generous salary terms. There was a fourth child now—Freddie, named for Fred Stone—and in the spring of 1919 Will headed alone for the Coast to look for a house that would accommodate the family as well as their dogs and horses.

Goldwyn solved the latter problem by offering a building

United Artist's "Big Four"—Fairbanks, Pickford, Chaplin, and Griffith
CULVER PICTURES

and a fenced area on the studio lot for the horses, where the children could also ride; Will located a house on Van Ness Avenue; and when Betty and the children joined him, he met them at the station in a big black Cadillac driven by a chauffeur. His first picture under the contract with Goldwyn was *Almost a Husband*, in which he played opposite Peggy Wood, and he was on location when the three boys, Bill, Jimmy, and Freddie, came down with diphtheria. No antitoxin was available in Hollywood, and Will drove all night with some he had found elsewhere, but he was too late to save the baby's life. That tragedy spoiled the house for them, and they decided to buy another in Beverly Hills, where they would live for nearly ten years. They had decided to make California home, and the new property was spacious enough so that they could have a stable, a tanbark riding ring, a swimming pool, and two log cabins for the children —all enclosed by an eight-foot-high brick wall, which Will went to some trouble to get permission to erect and which looked, when completed, like a prison enclosure. Ivy, he and Betty concluded, would camouflage the stark appearance, and a landscape gardener was called in to plant the vines. But when Will returned from the studio that day, expecting to see ivy-covered walls, he was indignant: there were only hundreds of tiny slips stuck in the ground. Impatient as always, he called the landscape man and informed him that he wanted things done the way they were handled on the movie set—if a tree was needed, they got a full-grown tree, not one that would have to grow while they waited. "When I want ivy," he stated, "I want ivy I can see." And ivy he could see was put in—plants with long shoots already grown out. Will was happy, Betty noted; but the cost was "shocking."

Will was not only acting in his pictures, he also had a hand in the scripts and wrote the titles that were used as descriptive clues and as dialogue. He couldn't take himself very seriously as an actor and liked to tell about a letter he had received, which said, "I understand you have never used a double in your pictures—now that I have seen you I wonder why you don't." He missed the presence of an audience, but he thoroughly enjoyed the work; he could go to bed early, arise early, and spend much of his time outdoors. There was no night work to speak of, and occasionally there were weeks of free time between pictures, although Will cannot have been idle much of the time. In addition to the pictures for Goldwyn, he was making a series of weekly shorts for Pathe, takeoffs on "The Literary Digest Topics of the Day," called "The Illiterate Digest," in which his comments on the headlines were flashed on the screen along with pictures of him. All in all, he concluded, it was "the grandest show business I know anything about, and the only place an actor can act and at the same time sit down in front and clap for himself."

One of his favorite pictures was *Jubilo*, based on a short story written by Ben Ames Williams for the *Saturday Evening Post* and adapted by one of the Eminent Authors, who had evidently botched the job so badly that Will refused to proceed with the picture. Instead of using the new script, he suggested that they go back to the original and shoot the picture directly from the

"The way to judge a good Comedy is by how long it will last and have people talk about it. Now Congress has turned out some that have lived for years and people are still laughing about them. . . . [In Hollywood] girls win a little State Popularity Contest that is conducted by some Newspaper; then they are put into the Movies to entertain 110 million people who they never saw or know anything about. Now that's the same way with the Capitol Comedy Company of Washington. They win a State Popularity Contest backed by a Newspaper and are sent to Washington to turn out Laws for 110 million people they never saw."

from Weekly Article
Feb. 18, 1923

lines in the magazine. "It was the only story ever made that was filmed as it was written," he claimed. But, in the meantime, Goldwyn had decided to change the title, and Will telegraphed him in New York on October 7, 1919:

THOUGHT I WAS SUPPOSED TO BE A COMEDIAN BUT WHEN YOU SUGGEST CHANGING THE TITLE OF JUBILO YOU ARE FUNNIER THAN I EVER WAS. I DONT SEE HOW LORIMER OF THE POST EVER LET IT BE PUBLISHED UNDER THAT TITLE. THAT SONG IS BETTER KNOWN THROUGH THE SOUTH BY OLDER PEOPLE THAN GERALDINE FARRAR'S HUSBAND. WE HAVE USED IT ALL THROUGH BUSINESS IN THE PICTURE BUT OF COURSE WE CAN CHANGE THAT TO "EVERYBODY SHIMMIE NOW." SUPPOSED IF YOU HAD PRODUCED THE MIRACLE MAN YOU WOULD HAVE CALLED IT A QUEER OLD GUY. BUT IF YOU REALLY WANT A TITLE FOR THIS SECOND PICTURE I WOULD SUGGEST JUBILO. ALSO THE FOLLOWING:

>A POOR BUT HONEST TRAMP
>
>HE LIES BUT HE DONT MEAN IT
>
>A FARMERS VIRTIOUS DAUGHTER
>
>THE GREAT TRAIN ROBBERY MYSTERY
>
>A SPOTTED HORSE BUT HE IS ONLY PAINTED
>
>THE HUNGRY TRAMP'S REVENGE
>
>THE VAGABOND WITH A HEART AS BIG AS HIS APPETITE
>
>HE LOSES IN THE FIRST REEL BUT WINS IN THE LAST
>
>THE OLD MAN LEFT BUT THE TRAMP PROTECTED HER

WHAT WOULD YOU HAVE CALLED THE BIRTH OF A NATION?

WILL ROGERS

CULVER PICTURES

Grim William S. Hart (above) was one of the sacred cows of the silver screen that Will took off (opposite) in his Uncensored Movies.

By the time his contract expired, Will had made twelve pictures for Goldwyn (six in 1920 alone), in which he mostly played romantic parts. In *Doubling for Romeo* he was a bashful cowboy in love with the heroine; in *Cupid, the Cowpuncher* he was a cowboy so eager to marry off his friends that they called him Cupid (naturally, he fell in love and won the girl). In four of them his leading lady was Irene Rich, a bit player, who was given a part because of her friendship with Will and Betty. The films were pleasant, amusing, and reasonably successful, but the expiration of Will's contract in 1921 came at a time when the industry was in the convulsive throes of reorganization; Goldwyn left the studio; and Will was suddenly on his own, without a contract.

Some of the leading actors and actresses in Hollywood had recently broken with the producers in order to establish their own independent companies (in 1919, when Griffith, Mary Pickford, Douglas Fairbanks, and Charlie Chaplin formed United Artists, word circulated through the movie colony that the lunatics had taken over the asylum), and Will, following their lead, decided to go it alone and write, produce, and direct his own films—starring himself. He and Betty read innumerable books and scenarios, Will mortgaged the house to raise capital, and made a distribution arrangement with Pathe under which that company would release the pictures, refund Will's investment, and pay him a royalty.

In this manner he produced three movies—*Fruits of Faith*, *The Ropin' Fool*, and *One Day in 365*, the last of which was the story of one day at home with his wife and children. *The Ropin' Fool* was and is a delight, a highly amusing film for which Will wrote the titles and which showed him at his best, performing over fifty of his remarkable rope tricks. ("I don't think you might consider it Art," he said, "but there is 30 years of hard practice in it.") And *Fruits of Faith*, according to the *New York Times*, was a charming picture; unpretentious and with a slender storyline, but full of genuine entertainment made human and humorous by the skill of Will Rogers. But none was a financial success, the Pathe agreement went sour, and the Rogers family was on the brink of bankruptcy. Everything Will owned—life insurance, Liberty bonds, savings, real estate—was tied up in those pictures, and finally he had to borrow money on the films themselves, depositing them at the bank as security. He was beginning to understand how Hollywood operated: "If the loan is made for a Moving Picture," he wrote, "the President of the bank wants to write the story for you. The Directors want to know who the Leading Lady is, and if they could, they would keep her as collateral."

WILL ROGERS MEMORIAL, CLAREMORE, OKLA.

Knowing there was work for him in New York, back he went to play in the Follies. What Betty remembered about that year were the countless train trips she made across the country to be with him, leaving her sister Theda to stay with the children. As for Will, she said "he worked as hard . . . as he ever did in his life, and without a break or vacation of any kind. He hated to be away from the children, and he missed his favorite ponies, but when he came home the following summer to accept a new movie contract, much of his indebtedness had been paid."

That was accomplished in large part because of his boundless energy. He had embarked on two new professions, in both of which he succeeded simply by being himself.

FPG

Hollywood:
Action and Romance
In the Golden Silents

Lured to California by Samuel Goldwyn in 1919, Will appeared in a number of romantic spoofs; as in Doubling for Romeo *(left). Off and on until 1927 he was acting in silents, including a series of weekly shorts called* The Illiterate Digest *and comedies for Hal Roach. For a while he produced his own pictures, among them* One Day in 365, *starring himself, Betty, and their children (below). Opposite, he relaxes on the studio lot.*

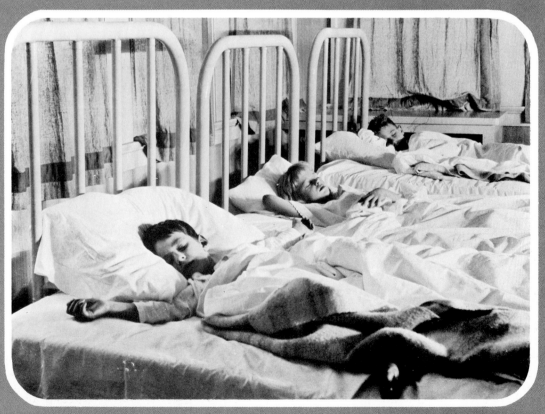

MUSEUM OF MODERN ART, FILM STILLS ARCHIVE.

Will wrote Two Wagons Both Covered—*a takeoff on* The Covered Wagon
—*and played the parts of guides Bill Bunian (above) and Joe Jackson (below).*

BOTH: MUSEUM OF MODERN ART, FILM STILLS ARCHIVE

Wariness of romantic attachment was a typical Rogers attitude, as in Cupid the Cowpuncher *(above); below, Will is shown shooting a scene for* Jubilo *in 1919.*

BOTH: MUSEUM OF MODERN ART, FILM STILLS ARCHIVE AND SAMUEL GOLDWYN PRODUCTIONS

BROWN BROTHERS

"Well, all I know is just what I read in the papers."

From 1922 until 1935 Will's articles appeared in the New York Times, *in whose offices the photograph at left was taken in 1925. Above is Will (with Betty at the piano) during a radio broadcast over Pittsburgh's station KDKA.*

WILL ROGERS MEMORIAL, CLAREMORE, OKLA.

During the course of a long, full career—on the stage, in silent and talking pictures, radio, and journalism—Will's best character part, as so many reviewers pointed out in connection with his films, was playing himself. That is what he did to perfection in the two activities in which he now engaged: after-dinner speaking and writing a syndicated newspaper column.

Before going to the Coast in 1919 Will had made after-dinner speeches, mostly for theatrical friends at the Lambs and Friars clubs in New York, and a few for which he was hired as an entertainer. Now, to recoup the money lost in Hollywood, he acquired an agent who began scheduling luncheon and dinner appearances at the rate of three or four a week all over Manhattan, usually for a fee of $1,000. As a banquet speaker Will relied on the techniques that were so popular with Follies audiences. His act was completely personal. He never told the stock jokes —the Pat-and-Mike routines—on which so many comedians relied; almost everything he used was based on firsthand experience or observation. As he put it, his gags had to be based on facts. "No matter how much I may exaggerate it, it must have a certain amount of truth. . . . Now rumor travels faster, but it don't stay put as long as truth."

Surprisingly, considering the years he had spent on the stage, he suffered from stage fright before every performance. "I am always nervous," he once admitted, "I never saw an audience that I ever faced with any confidence." The first few minutes in front of a crowd were agonizing for Will; he would fumble around nervously, half-muttering his lines, trying to get warmed up and into his stride, and he never did learn to hide the symptoms of discomfort. Friends often told Betty how embarrassed they felt for him and asked why he put himself through such torture.

One of his worst experiences in 1922—the year he began making after-dinner speeches on a regular basis—was at a charity performance at Sherry's restaurant. He was playing to a group of New York society women, and for the first time he could remember, his act fell completely flat; nothing seemed to go over with the ladies. While he was suffering he happened to see William Randolph Hearst and a party of friends at one of the tables. Hearst, who had known Will for years, was roaring with laughter, but Will realized that it was not at the jokes: "He was laughing at me out there dying." The difficulty, Will recognized later, was that "those old dowagers and those young debutantes had no more read a paper than I had Shakespeare." It simply never occurred to him that he would encounter people who didn't follow the news, who wouldn't understand his jokes about what was going on in the world. It was his belief, he once said, that the smartest all-around man in the country was the fellow who had thirty minutes on a streetcar every morning and evening to read the newspaper.

The reception he got the next evening after the fiasco at Sherry's made up for it, though. He put on a performance for the inmates at Sing Sing prison, told them the same jokes that had flopped at the charity affair, and after the show he said, "I was sorry Ziegfeld wasn't there, as I would have got a raise in salary if he had heard how my act went. I don't care what I talked about, they knew all about it." On occasions like this he customarily spoke for about 15 or 20 minutes, but at Sing Sing he went on for an hour and a quarter and wound up the evening by offering to take all twelve hundred men down to New York to see the Follies. The difference between this audience and the one of the night before was that the prisoners read everything they could lay their hands on.

For a year Will spoke at banquets held by automobile manufacturers, automobile accessory manufacturers, automobile dealers; he addressed hat and dress makers, leather and shoe men, corset makers, newspaper women, rug merchants, the Ohio Society of New York, the city's Board of Aldermen. Every conceivable type of organization was listed in his engagement book, and each—to its delight—got the typical Will Rogers treatment.

Instead of the usual formalities employed by after-dinner speakers, he began by startling or insulting his audience. He told the automobile dealers that they were "old time Horse trading Gyps with white collars on." He addressed a group of advertising men as the "Robbing Hoods of America"; he advised the Association of Woolen Men to stay indoors in case of rain or there would be "about 500 men choked to death by their own suits." He called a convention of leather and shoe men "brigands and pasteboard highbinders." He surprised the corset manufacturers by telling them how essential their industry was: "Just imagine, if you can, if the flesh of this country were allowed to wander around promiscuously! Why, there ain't no telling where it would wind up. . . . The same problem confronts you that does the people that run the subways in New York City. You both have to get so many pounds of flesh into a given radius. The subway does it by having strong men to push and shove until they can just close the door with only the last man's foot out. But you corset manufacturers arrive at the same thing by a series of strings." (The front lace, he understood, "can be operated without a confederate," while the others required "accomplices.")

Introducing Al Smith, the governor of New York, to the Newspaper Women's Club, he reminded them that Al got his start as a barefoot newspaper boy on the East Side. "In those days," Will remarked, "there were two professions open to the youth of New York City. One was newsboy and the other, bootblack. Al chose the newsboy as there was no work attached to it. Newsboys all turned out to be politicians and the bootblacks all turned out to be bankers." Speculating on the possibility that the governor had his eye on the White House, Will offered the Democrats some advice: he didn't think they should enter a candidate in the 1924 Presidential election; they ought to let it go by default. "There is only one way to get even with Harding now and that is to leave him in there another term. Besides, the Democrats come nearer getting what they want when they have a Republican President than they do with one of their own."

A roomful of astonished bankers heard that borrowing money on easy terms was a one-way ticket to the poorhouse. "If you think it ain't a sucker game," Will asked, "why is a banker the richest man in town?" He wished that Congress would pass a bill forbidding any person to borrow from another, even if that put all bankers out of business. And as for their future, "I don't care what you do. Go to work, if there is any job any of you could earn a living at. Banking and after-dinner speaking are two of the most non-essential industries we have in this country.

"I have just come in from the train where I was seeing my wife off for what I think is her eighth trip back West since last June. The children are in school in California. You see, when I promised Mr. Ziegfeld to come in the Follies and assist him in Glorifying the American Girl, from what I thought I knew of American Girls I didn't know it would take over three months to get her properly Glorified."

from Weekly Article
Apr. 15, 1923

I am ready to reform if you are." Not that there weren't some pleasant, congenial fellows in banking, of course. There was J.P. Morgan, whom Will called "the Ali Baba of this gang," who had to manipulate the finances of the world in addition to those of his own country; there was Otto Kahn; and Charlie Schwab, who had "the greatest personality of any man in America. Of course Charlie don't hardly come under the heading of banker. He only owns just the ones in Pennsylvania." The problem, Will said, was that these men didn't realize what a menace they were. "As far as being good fellows, personally, I have heard old timers talk down home in the Indian Territory and they say the James and Dalton boys were the most congenial men of their day, too."

He explained to an international gathering of police chiefs why he had been invited to address them: "Although I have never caught a crook, neither have you, so we have a mutual feeling." The president of the organization had told him that they "had the fingerprint of every crook there is. Now all you got to do is find the fingers."

Representatives of the U.S. Chambers of Commerce met in New York in May, 1923, and Will called them the modern male equivalent of the old ladies' sewing circles "that knew everybody's business and were into everything." He also observed, "The minute a fellow gets into the Chamber of Commerce he quits mowing his own lawn."

In April of 1923 Will was once again seeing Betty off to California—he wasn't sure, but he thought it was her eighth trip since the previous June. He remarked that every time she heard a locomotive whistle she grabbed her hat, stuffed a kimono into her suitcase, and started running; and when they went out to dinner in New York, she would ask, "How many cars ahead is the diner?" But as much as he liked to make jokes about it, their life must have been almost unbelievably hectic. Will was still playing in the Follies while carrying on his killing after-dinner speaking schedule; and in December, 1922, he had started writing a weekly column which was syndicated to newspapers. By mid-June of 1923, after a year and a half on the banquet circuit, he had had enough: "I have spoken at so many banquets that when I get home I will feel disappointed if my wife or one of the children don't get up at dinner and say, 'We have with us this evening a man who, I am sure, needs no introduction.'" And he had "talked more and said less in the last year in New York than any man outside of Public Life."

He had also developed a technique for surviving the continuous diet of fruit cocktail, consommé, fish, broiled chicken, and ice cream. Before attending a banquet in New York he would stop in at a chili joint on Broadway and 47th Street to fortify himself with enchiladas and a few bowls of chili. That way he could refuse anything that was offered at the dinner (he was usually too nervous to eat, anyway) and could sit through almost any speech that preceded his own.

One talk Will gave during that frenetic year led to the offer to write a newspaper column. He had been asked to speak in support of Ogden Mills' candidacy for re-election to Congress and appeared at a rally in New York's Town Hall on October 26, 1922. Had the candidate or his backers known what he would say, it is somewhat doubtful if they would have requested his assistance, for what they got was a typical Rogers performance—one of the most remarkable campaign speeches a political audience ever heard. Will walked slowly out onto the stage, grinned, and told them that he didn't want his speech to go over; if it did he was afraid it might lead him into politics, and up to now he had tried to live honestly. He admitted that he did not know his candidate's opponent, but assumed he must be a scoundrel and a tool of the special interests. But the truth was that he didn't know and hadn't met his *own* candidate: that was the reason he was "more apt to say something good of him than any one else." Most people, he thought, took up politics through necessity or as a last resort, but Mills (whom he kept referring to as "this guy") was wealthy before he went into politics—"not as wealthy as now, but rich." Unfortunately, Mills was handicapped by being educated at Harvard, but he was the only candidate who owned his own silk hat and the only politician other than Henry Cabot Lodge who could get past the front door of a Fifth Avenue residence without delivering something. Mills' platform, Will announced, was a living wage for bootleggers and free medical examinations for those who drank the stuff they sold. (Mills, Will recalled, sat through the talk without the suggestion of a smile, not knowing "whether I was for him or against him.")

Now this was the kind of talk Will was accustomed to give every night in the Follies, but as a political address it was highly unusual. (Mills was re-elected either because of or in spite of Will's support.) His speech was reported fully in the *New York Times*, where it was read and appreciated by the founder-proprietor of the McNaught Newspaper Syndicate, a man

Representative Ogden Mills was "endorsed" by Will in his bid for re-election to Congress in 1922 (and he won).
UPI

179

named V. V. McNitt. He wrote Will asking if they could meet to discuss the possibility of his writing a newspaper column, but he received no immediate reply.

McNitt's interest coincided with some conversations Will was having with the New York *Herald* about a weekly article built around a cowboy character called Powder River Powell, who rode into town for a weekly shave and talked with his barber, Soapy. The *Herald* editors didn't care much for the idea (a sample Will showed them did not appear to be the Will Rogers they wanted), and neither, when he heard about it, did McNitt. Through a mutual friend, the cartoonist Rube Goldberg, McNitt and his partner Charles V. McAdam arranged to meet Will and suggested that the *New York Times* might be interested in a weekly column, provided it was the sort of thing Will did so well in his Follies act. In other words, Will should try to get onto paper the type of comments he made on stage, and above all he should be himself—not Powder River Powell or any other fictitious character.

By now Will had already done some writing for publication, beginning with the appearance of his letters from South America and Africa in the Claremore newspaper. His little books of jokes about the peace conference and Prohibition had appeared in 1919, and that same year, en route to California, he had written an amusing political commentary for the Kansas City *Star*. (The *Star*'s theatre critic had sat up until 3 A.M. over chili and onion sandwiches, listening to Will tell one story after another, and begged him to put them on paper.) In 1920 he wrote a series of articles for the Los Angeles *Record* about the Republican and Democratic conventions that year; although he attended neither (he was on location for the film *Cupid, the Cowpuncher*), he reported on them as if he were present. It was the first of many occasions on which he would comment on the quadrennial phenomenon which, he said later, has everything beaten "for stupidity, lack of judgment, nonsensicality, unexcitement, uselessness, and childishness." As might be expected, the convention articles resembled his Follies routine and were little more than a collection of short gags.

That, in essence, was the kind of material that the McNaught people and the *Times* wanted, and Will agreed to write a column for them. As Charles McAdam tells the story, there never was a contract; he and McNitt shook hands with Will and agreed to pay him $500 a week. (Sometime later Will came into the McNaught offices and mentioned that a rival syndicate had

"If the people had had anything to do with the nominations, personally, instead of it being done by a half dozen men in the back rooms of some hotel, why America would be a democracy."

from Weekly Article
Nov. 2, 1924

180

offered him $800 a week, to which McAdam replied that they would give him $1,000. Will told McAdam he was nuts, but that he loved him for it.) Charles Driscoll, an editor at McNaught, was responsible for coping with the awesome spelling, punctuation, and grammar Will sent in, and one of his first admonitions to the new columnist was to refrain from using the word "ain't." That produced the response, "I know a lot of people who don't say 'ain't,' ain't eating."

On December 24, 1922, the first column appeared in the *Times*, and a week later the initial one was syndicated by McNaught—beginning a series that would continue for nearly thirteen years and become a familiar feature of America's Sunday newspapers, for the times were ripe for what Will Rogers had to say about the country and the world at large.

The nation had embarked, in 1920, on the "noble experiment" of Prohibition, which turned out to be virtually impossible to enforce. Warren Harding, whose principal distinguishing characteristic was his looks, was President, and in carrying out his pledge to return the United States to "normalcy" was treating it to some of the most platitudinous remarks ever uttered by a Chief Executive. The "Red Scare" that followed the Bolshevik revolution in Russia had led in 1919 and 1920 to mass arrests of American political and labor agitators by Attorney General A. Mitchell Palmer, but it still lingered in the public memory; and in 1923 there were exposés of other, equally sinister threats. The Ku Klux Klan, whose membership was said to be five million, was terrorizing minority groups in the North and Midwest as well as the South, and there were ugly, persistent rumors of scandals within the Harding administration.

President Warren G. Harding in a characteristic pose: cigar, golf club, and baby.
OHIO HISTORICAL SOCIETY

There were also reports that Harding, unlike his predecessor in the White House, did not care for Will Rogers' brand of humor—particularly the way Will poked fun at the nation's most sacred cow, Warren Gamaliel Harding himself. The trouble dated to the time Will had been in Washington on tour with the Ziegfeld Frolic, a musical that featured a burlesque on the Washington Conference for the Limitation of Armaments. Will had written the skit and played the part of Secretary of State Charles Evans Hughes; but since the Harding administration considered the conference one of its finest achievements, the only politicians to rejoice over the show were Democrats.

Will paid a call on Harding at the White House, and during their conversation the President was genial, friendly, and expressed interest in seeing the show; but the next day one of his aides came to Will's dressing room and asked him not to make so many cracks about the President's golf game. The newspapers, he added, were making too much of it. Will agreed, although he was surprised at the request, and eliminated several golf jokes from the conference sketch and changed his monologue. A few nights later the cast heard that President and Mrs. Harding planned to attend the theatre and assumed that they would come to the Frolic, since the only other show in town was one put on by a road company that had already been touring for two seasons. When the curtain rose, however, it was immediately apparent that the President and his party had gone elsewhere.

Disappointed and angry, Will came out for a curtain call and remarked to the audience, "I have cracked quite a few jokes on public men here, both Republicans and Democrats. I hope I have not given offense. In fact, I don't believe any big man will take offense." The next day the newspapers made a lot of the incident, and Will was contrite and embarrassed, although he felt that Harding's advisers, not the President, were responsible for the incident. Later, when he was playing in the Follies, he heard that Harding wouldn't come to the show and concluded that it was "on account of the humorous relations between the White House and myself being rather strained."

In April, 1923, those relations were strained further by a column Will wrote in the form of an open letter addressed to "Mr. Warren Gamaliel Harding, President of these United States and Viceroy of the District of Columbia, Chevy Chase Golf Club, Washington, D.C." In it, Will applied for the job as ambassador to the Court of St. James's, citing as his accomplishments speechmaking (which he said was 90 per cent of the work), his motion-picture experience (he would never be caught in the background during the photographing of a big event), and his appearance in knee breeches ("we haven't had a decent looking leg over there in years"). While this was all bland enough, Harding may have been stung by the last line of the letter: "Now, as to Salary, I will do just the same as the rest of the Politicians—accept a small Salary as pin money, AND TAKE A CHANCE ON WHAT I CAN GET."

It was rumored that things were not as they should be in the administration, but as yet few Americans were aware that Harding was a distraught and desperate man—betrayed by venal cronies he had put into positions of responsibility. Unable

"Mr. Harding has had quite a little sick spell lately from which he is recovering. I sorter think it's those doctors these presidents have. They are promoted from a horse-and-buggy trade in the country to an admiral in the U.S. navy, or a major general in the U.S. army so quickly that I really believe they have to give so much time trying to learn to salute and to getting their uniforms on proper side forward that they haven't really had time to devote to our President's health."

from Weekly Article
Feb. 4, 1923

to endure his duties or face up to the sordid scandals that were soon to be revealed—disasters that led to suicides, imprisonment, and disgrace—he departed on a trip for Alaska. ("It must be getting near Election time," Will commented; "he has commenced taking up all the Babies and kissing them. . . . Mothers, when you see your Baby picked up by someone nowadays it is either one of two men. It's a kidnapper or a Politician.")

Returning from the trip, Harding died, and was spared the agony of all that came afterward. On August 19, 1923, when Will wrote a tribute to the dead President, there was no way he could know that Harding's widow and a trusted assistant were at that very moment consigning case after case of the Chief Executive's papers to the flames—a task they continued for weeks, to "preserve his memory." Will recalled for readers his first meeting with Harding: he had told him not to think he was being hard on him when he made jokes, because he had told funnier stories about the Democrats. It wasn't fair to kid them now, while they were down, but "the minute they get their head above water again, I will take a whack at them." And years later Will wrote that Harding was, in his opinion, the most human of any recent President. "If he had a weakness, it was in trusting his friends, and the man that don't do that, then there is something the matter with him. . . . Betrayed by friendship is not a bad memorial to leave."

Will's weekly observations on the passing scene included thoughts on politics and politicians, Prohibition, big businessmen, the Ku Klux Klan, the problems of life in New York City, the Constitution, international conferences, and diplomats, and it was his habit initially to turn from one subject to another in quick succession, as excerpts from his early syndicated columns suggest.

As the column gradually evolved, it became less staccato and contained longer anecdotes and fewer punchy gags. Usually, Will's typewritten manuscripts ran to about a page and a half or two pages, single-spaced, and he realized, before long, that this length allowed him to be discursive so that he could ramble on with a story when he wanted to do so. Occasionally, he would devote an entire article to a single person or theme, or he might use the column to advocate a cause he believed in deeply. Yet while the format changed over the years, the tone of voice and the personality behind it did not. The column remained a gently amusing, common-sense, down-to-earth approach to most of the important issues that confronted the people of the world, and to the problems, large and small, that bedeviled the American citizen.

Hardly a week went by without an entertaining story or joke about prominent men and women: kings and queens, presidents and prime ministers, Congressmen, sports heroes, big businessmen, channel swimmers, movie stars—no one escaped. But no matter how Will might disagree with their principles or their politics, he never resorted to malice. There was something about the way he could turn a phrase that removed the sting from his criticism. Even when he was poking fun at a man, he often seemed to be saying something else or to be looking in another direction, as when he remarked that Calvin Coolidge was "the first President to discover that what the American people want is to be left alone."

What he said, or what he might say, was nevertheless a matter of continuing concern to Betty, who was often embarrassed by the informality of his approach to important people. She worried that he would go too far or that someone would take offense. After Will's speech in behalf of Ogden Mills, for instance, she despaired over his lack of tact and even discussed her views with Father Francis Duffy, the famous chaplain of New York's 165th infantry regiment.

"Leave that boy alone," Father Duffy advised her. "He knows what he's doing. He's doing a good job, and don't you try to change him."

It was probably inevitable that life with Will had, as she put it, an "explosive" quality, because neither she nor anyone else ever quite knew what he was going to say or do. The Rogers' two sons, long after their parents' death, remembered vividly the "civilizing" effect their mother had on their father. As Will, Jr., observed, his father came out of the world of Wild West shows, rodeos, the circus, and vaudeville—all "harum-scarum" activities that were not held in universal esteem—and it was Betty who "tamed him" and led him in a more respectable direction. Jim Rogers had much the same thought: he regarded his mother as a balance wheel, a stabilizing influence on his father. "She was also the most severe critic of humor I ever saw," he added, "and she was a censor. When Dad would come out with something a little raw, she would tell him, 'You just can't say that!' "

If Will was outspokenly critical in his column, he frequently picked on a group—lawyers, for example, or diplomats, or

Americans in general—rather than singling out any individual for reproach. In 1924, when Henry Ford announced that he was not a candidate for President, saying that 90 per cent of the American people were satisfied with things as they were, Will took the country to task. "Ninety percent of the people in this Country are not satisfied," he stated. "Its just got so that 90 percent of the People in this Country Don't Give a Damn. Politics ain't worrying this Country one Tenth as much as Parking Space. . . . There is millions of people in this Country that know the Color of Mary Pickford's hair, but think the Presidential office is hereditary. So Mr. Ford should not mistake apparent prosperity for satisfaction. There is more Mortgages in this country than there is Votes. This Country right now is operating on a Dollar down and a Dollar a Week. It ain't Taxes that is hurting this Country; it's Interest."

Fifty years later the weekly articles hold up astonishingly well. Topical as much of it is, the humor is still fresh, and within the commentary on the contemporary scene are nuggets of enduring wisdom and rare understanding. His comment about James Cox, the unsuccessful candidate for the Presidency in 1920, is characteristic: "I don't know of any quicker way in the World to be forgotten in this Country than to be defeated for President. A man can leave the Country and people will always remember that he went some place. But if he is defeated for President they can't remember that he ever did anything."

Gradually, Will formed the habit of opening his column with the line which began his Follies act: "Well, all I know is just what I read in the papers." All over the country Americans were becoming accustomed to turning every Sunday to those weekly asides on the news which were so distinctively Will Rogers. His exposure to the public was not only continuous, it was ubiquitous; he was appearing annually in the Follies and performing at frequent benefits; Americans were reading his weekly column, they heard him on the radio (he made his first broadcast over Pittsburgh's pioneer radio station KDKA); and in 1923 he returned to Hollywood, at a salary of $3,000 a week, to make twelve comedies for producer Hal Roach. The films were successful enough as far as Roach was concerned, but they were not especially gratifying from Will's point of view. The problem, essentially, was that silent pictures lacked the dimension of conversation, the vital aspect of his stage act. So when the contract with Roach expired a year later, in 1924, Will headed East again.

BATTING FOR LLOYD GEORGE—By WILL ROGERS

Copyright, 1922, by The New York Times Company.

I WANT to apologize and set the many readers of THE TIMES straight as to why I am blossoming out as a weekly infliction on you all.

It seems THE TIMES had Lloyd George signed up for a pack of his Memoirs. Well, after the late election Lloyd couldn't seem to remember anything, so they sent for me to fill in the space where he would have had his junk.

You see, they wanted me in the first place, but George came along and offered to work cheaper, and also to give his to charity. That benevolence on his part was of course before England gave him his two weeks' notice.

Now I am also not to be outdone by an ex-Prime Minister donating my receipts from my Prolific Tongue to a needy charity. The total share of this goes to the civilization of three young heathens, Rogers by name, and part Cherokee Indians by breeding.

Now, by wasting seven minutes, if you are a good reader—and ten to twelve if you read slow—on me every Sunday, you are really doing a charitable act yourself by preventing these three miniature bandits from growing up in ignorance. So please help a man with not only one little Megan, but three little Megans.

A great many people may think that this is the first venture of such a conservative paper as THE TIMES in using something of a semi-humorous nature, but that is by no means the case. I am following the Kaiser, who rewrote his life after it was too late. I realize what a tough job I have, succeeding a man who to be funny only had to relate the facts.

Please don't consider these as my memoirs. I am not passing out of the picture, as men generally are who write those things. I want to warn you of a few pitfalls into which our poorly paid but highly costing politicians are driving us daily.

We pay an awful lot of dough in the course of a year to try to get our country run in such shape that a certain per cent. of our citizens can keep out of the poorhouse. The shape we are in now, over and above all the taxes we pay, allows us to hang on to about 8 per cent. of our gross earnings.

Now, that's entirely too rich we are getting—too prosperous. So they are talking of lending Europe about a billion and a half more. I knew there would be something stirring when Morgan visited Washington last week.

He goes down once every year and lays out the following year's program.

Europe owes us now about eleven billions. Lending them another billion and a half would make it just even 12.50. You see it is so much easier to figure the interest on 12.50 than on 11. Of course the interest ain't going to be paid, but it's got to be figured.

The Government could charge it off on their income tax to publicity. I only hope one thing, and that is, if we make the loan, Europe will appreciate this one.

The Allied Debt Conference broke up last week in London.

It's getting harder every day for Nations to pay each other unless one of them has some money.

They called that an Economic Conference, and, as we didn't attend, it was. Why don't somebody lend Germany the money so they can pay France what France owes England, so England can pay us the money to lend Germany to pay France?

It only needs somebody to start it.

Senator Borah opened up and told the U S what he thought of this loan. For speaking right out in church he is the Clemenceau of America.

They are bringing over Ambassador Harvey. He don't know anything about it; over there he has been too busy learning speeches. If they don't have a Concert on the Ship coming over, his trip will be spoiled.

I see they have been holding another Peace Conference in some burg called Lausanne. They are having those things now just like Chatauquas—you jump from one to the other.

This one must have been somewhere near Italy, as that is the stopping place of the Ambassador that we sent there. He didn't go officially, as we don't belong to the League of Nations (we only finance it). Well, this fellow Child, as I say, he went as a kind of Uninstructed Delegate. He got into the game, but his efforts were more like a cheer leader at a football game. They heard him, but he had no direct effect on the game.

It seems that the Allies (that is, those of them that are speaking to each other) wanted Turkey to promise to protect the minor nations within her territory. Now this Turkey is a pretty foxy nation; she's got her mind on something besides wives and cigarettes.

Turkey says: "We'll agree to give minor nations the same protection that you all give yours."

Well, that was not exactly what the Allies wanted, but they took it as a compromise and hope at some future time to get *full* protection for them.

[*Mr. Will Rogers promises further contributions to* THE NEW YORK TIMES, *if he can tame his typewriter.*]

LASSOED !

A CHRISTMAS TREAT BROUGHT
TO YOUR NEAREST THEATRE

MARY

MOTION PICTURES

WORLD'S PREMIER

NAZIMOVA

in a Picturization of

OSCAR WILDE'S

Famous Poetic Drama

SALOME

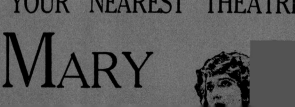

Will Rogers says . . .

Some of the most memorable Rogers lines appeared in the weekly article he began writing in 1922 and continued until the day of his death. (The first one was published in the New York Times' entertainment section on December 24, 1922, and is reproduced on the facing page.) In these and other writings and broadcasts he often returned to a particular theme, and it has seemed appropriate to assemble certain of his comments on the passing scene under topical headings, as on pages 188–89 and elsewhere in the book.

WILL ROGERS MEMORIAL, CLAREMORE, OKLA., GIFT OF PROJECT 20

We are great talkers but we are mighty poor conferers. We have a unique record—we never lost a war and we never won a conference in our lives. Without any degree of egotism we can say, with our tremendous resources, we can lick any nation in the world single-handed, yet we can't confer with Costa Rica and come home with our shirts on.

Half of the unemployed in this country are people that's goin' or comin' from a conference somewhere. Somebody could scare up an egg layin' contest in Czechoslovakia and if America could find out where it was, we would send more delegates and lay less eggs than any nation in the whole hen house.

. . . there is a mess of conferences going on. But they are just like the poor and the Democrats, they will always be with us.

I have always noticed that any time a man can't come and settle with you without bringing his lawyer, why, look out for him.

. . . any time we can attend a conference and come out as good as we went in, why we are ahead. A conference is a place where countries meet and find out each other's short comings and form new dislikes for the next conference.

Will we ever quit sending delegations off to conferences? We just wait for a Conference to get in wrong with somebody. There should be a heavy export duty on "good will" groups and delegates to Conferences. We have had so many Conferences that we are even sore at each other here at home.

Everyone . . . says "something must be done," and it looks like it will be us.

We get nothing at a conference only the trip. It looks like depression would hurt the conference business but it don't. They can always dig up enough to go and get in wrong.

The world has just conferred itself into bankruptcy. A conference is just an admission that you want somebody to join you in your troubles. The world can't improve till it gets so poor that it can't send delegates to a conference. Then it will begin to improve by depending on itself.

There is one line of bunk that this country falls for, and always has. "We are looking to America for leadership during the conference: She has a great moral responsibility." and we like a big simp, just eat it up. Our delegates swell out their chests, and really believe that the world is just hanging by a thread and the American delegates control that thread. Why, they didn't discover us till 1492 and the world had had 1492 wars. 1492 peace and economic conferences, all before we was ever heard of.

Why not have a permanent commission, appointed by the year and they just go from one to another of the conferences? Get men that love to travel, and don't take international affairs too serious, just go for the trip and the laughs. I'll consider heading that delegation.

I have always said that a conference was held for one reason only, to give everybody a chance to get sore at everybody else. Sometimes it takes two or more conferences to scare up a war, but generally one will do it. I'll bet there was never a war between two nations that had never conferred first.

was very good in conference."

It is certainly gratifying to read about one conference that got somewhere. The Navajo Indians held a conference and decided that they could get along without the services of about 25 white office holders that had been appointed to help look after them. The Indians said they were doing it to save the white man money. Who said the Indians didn't have any humor?

———

There is nothing as sad, forlorn, and forgotten, in the world as a delegation returning from a conference. We have forgot now who we sent over.

———

There is no better place in the world to find out the shortcomings of each other than a conference.

———

The best omen of international good will is that conferences are getting shorter. Now if they will do away with 'em entirely there will be no war.

The biggest one ever held was at Versailles after the war, and all the others held since then was to fix something that was done wrong at that one. The biggest disarmament conference was at Washington in 1922, and all the other disarmament ones have been held to try and fix what was done wrong at that one, so the ideal thing is, don't hold the original conference, then you won't have to hold any more to fix anything. The same bunch of delegates go to all of 'em anyhow, so, just put 'em on a government pension, let 'em put on their high hats, take movies of 'em, and play like they was at a conference.

———

Every time there is a big conference, they always have a war to go with it.

———

You can't hope to gain ground at a conference. You only try to remedy the damage done at the last one. . . . Generally our delegates arrive at a conference with a band and leave incognito.

AT THE DISARMAMENT CONFERENCE
The Honorable Chairman: Now, Gentlemen, is it the sense of the conference that poison gas should kill non-combatants without suffering, or cause them to suffer without killing them?

"... you have to have a serious streak in you or you can't see the funny side of the other fellow."

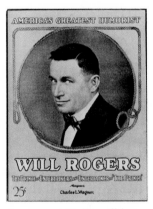

In 1925, billed as "America's Greatest Humorist" by manager Charles L. Wagner, Will hit the lecture circuit. Whenever possible, Betty accompanied him; at left they are about to board a B&O train for his next stop.

BOTH: WILL ROGERS MEMORIAL
CLAREMORE, OKLA.

It was 1924, a Presidential election year, and since Will had no set act in mind for the Follies, he informed his readers that he would stop off in Washington en route to New York to pick up some new jokes. "Congress," he explained, "has been writing my material for years."

Actually, most of the politicking was going on outside the capital, and before tryouts began for Ziegfeld's annual extravaganza Will headed for Cleveland, where the Republicans were holding what he called the "Coolidge Follies—a one-star show." This was the first national political convention he attended (he went as a commentator for the McNaught Syndicate), and he was disappointed. It was altogether too tame and circumspect; Coolidge, who had succeeded Harding upon the President's death, "could have been nominated by post card," and Will thought the only likelihood of excitement was if a delegate misplaced the key to his hotel room.

As far as he was concerned, the sole memorable moment was a lunch he had with William Jennings Bryan, which he described as "the thrill of my entire life." The old Democratic war-horse was a correspondent at the time, covering the Republican convention for Will's syndicate, and when they first met in the press box—"the only two aliens in the entire hall"—Bryan turned to Will and said, "You write a humorous column, don't you?"

Will admitted that he did.

"Well," Bryan remarked, "I write a serious article, and if I think of anything comical or funny, I will give it to you."

"I thanked him," said Will, "and told him, 'If I happen to think of anything of a serious nature, I will give it to you.' When he said he wrote seriously and I said I wrote humorously, I

"Personally I don't think [a public opinion poll] demonstrates but one thing: that is that there are more Republicans that can write than there are Democrats."

from Weekly Article
Oct. 26, 1924

thought afterwards: 'We may both be wrong.' "

After seeing Coolidge nominated on the first ballot at Cleveland, Will left for Atlantic City for rehearsals and then went to New York, where the Follies opened on June 23, the same day the Democratic convention began at Madison Square Garden. Typically, Will was involved in both shows.

He had agreed to cover this convention for McNaught, too, and for a flat fee, which proved a costly mistake. The meeting lasted from June 24 to July 9, during which time the names of 60 candidates were placed in nomination for President (as everyone who had a radio heard, Alabama unceasingly cast 24 votes for Oscar Underwood). Finally, on the 103rd ballot, John W. Davis was chosen as the nominee, and William Jennings Bryan's brother Charles was later nominated for Vice President.

As the convention dragged on endlessly, Will found himself objecting to certain time-honored rituals. Day after day, he said, the people in the hall heard the identical speech given by one man after another, each extolling the virtues of "the man I am going to name." Young Franklin D. Roosevelt had an opportunity, Will thought, to make a nominating speech that would have lived through the ages—if only he had had the sense to say, " 'Delegates, I put in nomination Alfred Smith; try and find out something against him' "; but no, he had to talk "what we have heard for four days—'corruption, honesty in government, and the man I am about to name.' " In nominating a man Will wondered why it should be necessary to spend two hours telling what he had done. "If he has not done anything that the people already know about, he has no business being a candidate; and if he has they already know it. If a man had had sense enough to have gotten on that platform and said, 'Delegates, I present to you for President Mr. John Smith' . . . and then sit down, there would have been the wildest excitement in that hall you ever saw and his candidate would have probably been elected on the spot, just as a relief and a rebuke to those terrible orators."

By July 2, the ninth tedious day of the convention, Will decided to place his own candidate in nomination, and wrote a speech in his behalf. The man he was about to name, he said, never saw Wall Street, was not a member of the Klan, and had no connection with oil. He belonged to the creed whose voters were in the majority, and he was the only man who would win in 1924. His name, Will stated, was Calvin Coolidge.

Will never passed up an opportunity to meet a celebrity, and a high point of the Republican convention in 1924 was talking with William Jennings Bryan, who was then working as a correspondent.

UPI

By July 4 Will was recommending once more that the Democrats let the election go by default. The next day, to his astonishment, two Arizona delegates, with half a vote each, cast them for Will Rogers. (He had never heard of the men before, he said, but he had heard of Arizona.) On July 9 the by-line of thirteen-year-old Will Rogers, Jr., appeared on the column, which stated, "Papa called us all in last night and made his last will and testament. . . . He put in the will that I being the oldest was to take up his life's work, that of reporting the Democratic National Convention." Finally, on July 9, the miracle happened, John W. Davis was nominated; and Will could remind readers that he had predicted Davis' nomination (a visit with Davis had convinced him on July 1 that he was "a political dark horse turning white.")

In one of his weekly articles during the convention, Will remarked that if Mrs. Davis got into the White House, no titled European visitor would ever embarrass her, since she knew all the rules of etiquette. "She will never tip her Soup plate even if she can't get it all," said Will—a remark that led to a delightful exchange of articles with Percy Hammond, the New York drama critic, who made the mistake of chiding Will about his ignorance of table manners.

When the results of the Presidential election were in, Will remarked that they were "just as big a surprise as the announcement that Xmas was coming in December." Whatever he may have felt about Coolidge's victory, he could rejoice in the return of one of his favorite targets to the White House. The first time Will had mentioned Coolidge in his weekly column was a few weeks after Harding's death, when he discussed in some detail Coolidge's "failure" as the new President. "From what I read about what people want him to do he seems to be about the most colossal flop of any President we ever had," Will began, and then enumerated all the problems Coolidge had failed to solve during his several weeks in office: he had not produced rain for the farmers, he had not come out against boll weevils, he had not raised the price of wheat, he had not made France pay its war debt, he had done nothing for capital or labor, and he had not taken a stand on what size baseball bat Babe Ruth should use. About the only way Coolidge could make up for all these failures, Will suggested, was by not calling Congress back into session. If he did that, he would go down in history as another Lincoln.

Later that year, commenting on Coolidge's message to Congress, Will said that the only thing he could find to criticize was the President's delivery. "But when you figure that the Gentleman hasn't used his voice for months, why, any little defects in delivery can readily be overlooked." In 1925, when there was talk that certain American bankers were recommending that the United States forgive France's war debt, Will discovered that he and Coolidge were on the same side of the issue. "That Boy ain't going to let any French Wine go to his head and cancel any Debts. In fact one of the most characteristic things I ever heard about Mr. Coolidge was how a party of men had talked to him for an hour to get his opinion on these Foreign Debts and finally he said just six words: 'They Hired The Money, Didn't They?' That's all he said: 'They hired the money, didn't they?' Now where but Vermont would you ever hear the word 'hired'?

Backstage at the New Amsterdam Theatre in 1924, while Will was in the Follies

FPG

A Little Lesson in Etiquette

In 1924, Will predicted in a column that Mrs. John W. Davis, the wife of the Democratic candidate for President, would know how to behave at formal White House dinners. She knew enough, he said, not to tip her soup plate. Percy Hammond, a New York drama critic, took Will to task, with this result:

Percy Hammond: "For years I have been tipping my Soup plate, but never until Mr. Rogers instructed me, did I know that I was performing a Social error. Consultation with the polished and urbane head waiters of the Middle West, where I spent my boyhood, taught me, I believed, to eat Soup. One wonders if Mr. Rogers has given as much thought to soup as he has to the Lariat. Perhaps he does not know, being recently from Oklahoma, that in many prominent eastern Dining rooms one may tip one's Soup plate, without losing his social standing. I regard Mr. Rogers' interference as prairie, impudent, and unofficial. . . ."

Will Rogers: ". . . Percy, I thought you were a Theatrical Critic. Now I find you are only a Soup Critic. . . . I am just an old country boy in a big town trying to get along. I have been eating Pretty regular, and the reason I have been is because I have stayed an old country boy. . . . You say I came recently from Oklahoma, while You come from the Middle West and 'by consultation with the Head Waiters have learned the proper way to eat soup.' . . . You say you learned to eat Soup from a Head Waiter in the Middle West. Well, I admit my ignorance again; I never saw a head waiter eat Soup. Down in Oklahoma where I come from, we wouldn't let a head waiter eat at our Table, even if we had a head waiter, which we haven't. If I remember right I think it was my Mother taught me what little she knew of how I should eat, because if we had had to wait until we sent and got a head waiter to show us, we would have all starved to death. . . .

"As bad as you plate tippers want all you can get, you don't want it in your lap. Custom makes manners, and while I know that it is permissible to tip plates, I still say that it is not a universal custom. Manners are nothing more than common sense, and a person has no more right to try and get every drop of soup out of his plate than he has to take a piece of bread and try and harvest all the Gravy in his plate. If you are that hungry, they ought to feed you out of a Nose Bag. . . .

"So, Perc, you string with the High Brows, but I am going to stick to the Low Brows, because I know I am at home with them. For remember, if it was not for us Low Brows, you high brows would have no one to discuss. . . . You must remember, Perc, that the question of the World today is, not how to *eat* soup, but how to *get* soup to eat."

Will Rogers' Illiterate Digest, 1924

If you have ever dealt with a Vermonter you know they are not giving away any 11 Billion Dollars. Even for 11 Dollars they would go to war with you."

During the next four years there were frequent mentions of Calvin Coolidge in the weekly column—most of them sympathetic in tone. It was no accident that Will liked, admired, and was amused by the thirtieth President: both men came from a plain, rural background, both had a simplicity of expression, a subtle, dry wit, and both frequently employed exaggeration or understatement to make their points. In retrospect, it is interesting to see how different Will Rogers' picture of Coolidge was from that presented by many editors, journalists, and critics of the period (Boston Brahmin Henry Cabot Lodge described him scornfully as the type of man "who lives in a two-story house"), and by later historians, who regarded the man either as an enigma or as a "fumbling sphinx." Will happened to think that Coolidge was basically a man of sound judgment who knew when to say or do anything and who realized that "over half the things just needed leaving alone."

The 1924 edition of Ziegfeld's Follies was the last one for Will, and there is a strong hint in Betty Rogers' biography of her husband that he felt tricked by the producer. He was not especially enthusiastic about the show to begin with. After eight years of playing in the Follies, he had had enough, and only when Ziegfeld promised that he could quit after the New York run did Will reluctantly agree to join the cast once again. The understanding was that as soon as the show went on the road, as it always did, Will would leave; but this time Ziegfeld altered his traditional schedule. He kept the show in New York for over a year and held Will to his word, much to the latter's annoyance.

When the show closed, he returned to California. Except for the occasion in 1928 when he filled in for his friend Fred Stone in the musical *Three Cheers*, it was Will's last Broadway season after nearly two decades on the New York stage.

During this period he made occasional radio appearances, but he was never entirely at ease behind a microphone, especially in a studio, where no audience was present. As an extemporizer, laughter and applause stimulated him, and many of his best lines were spontaneous, impromptu reactions to the mood of a crowd. "That little microphone that you are talking into," he wrote, "its not going to laugh, so you don't

Will pulled a switch on ancient John D. Rockefeller by handing the multimillionaire golfer a new, shiny dime.
WIDE WORLD

know . . . whether to wait for your laugh, or just go right on." In a theatre the audience had a certain personality, and he could gauge the effect of certain jokes, but with radio he was up against "every known specie in the world." Radio, he decided, was made to order for a singer or for someone making a speech, "but to have to line up there and try to get some laughs, I want to tell you its the toughest test a Comedian has."

Not long after he finished at the Follies he began playing to another kind of audience and, according to Betty, he got more satisfaction out of this experience than anything else he did in the 1920's. Will himself did not think of becoming a lecturer; the idea was proposed to him by Charles L. Wagner, who was, at the time, probably the best-known lecture manager in this country and who thought of Will as a natural for this type of work. Wagner offered to arrange a tour in which Will—backed up by a male quartet, the de Reszke Singers—would deliver sixty or more lectures between October 1 and November 30, 1925, for a fee of $1,000 each plus travel expenses. After December 1 he was to receive $1,500 per appearance, which meant that it was possible for him to earn the same amount of money in 11 weeks that he had been making in the Follies for 26 weeks' work. (His income-tax return covering the year 1924 showed total earnings of $157,428.00, of which $83,000 came from the Follies, nearly $47,000 from the movies, and $26,000 from weekly articles, and it says something for the relatively easygoing attitude of that day's Internal Revenue Service that all of the last amount was claimed as a deduction for salary paid to Betty Rogers. The following year his total earnings were up to $235,000, of which the Ziegfeld Follies—in which he had not wanted to perform—accounted for $115,000 and the lecture tour $75,000.)

Before he set out, Will was elated. "A man only learns by two things," he said, "one is reading and the other is association with smarter people. I don't like to read and one can't find the associates in New York. I am going out among the people whom New Yorkers call Rubes. But these people . . . are the people that just look at New Yorkers and laugh."

The venture began on a sour note. Wagner had booked Will into Elmira, New York, for his opening, on the theory that citizens in Mark Twain's old home town would appreciate a humorous lecture, but Will was not the sophisticated Twain and the hall Wagner had selected was a church. Will's assortment of jokes from his Follies routine fell flat, the audience was as cold and unresponsive as the surroundings, and about half-way through his act he realized that he had lost them. Nothing he tried worked, and the evening seemed endless.

The next few bookings went much the same way, and Will was increasingly dejected, feeling that he should never have allowed himself to get into such a fix. Then Wagner received a letter from a woman who said that Will's Follies jokes didn't amuse her and why didn't he spend more time discussing the important topics. Will took the hint, dropped the gags about Follies girls and wealthy men, and soon devoted his entire lecture to such subjects as Congress, international conferences, the war debt, and other timely items. This was the turning point.

From October, 1925, to mid-April of the following year, he gave one hundred fifty-one lectures—speaking to women's clubs and social groups in theatres, school auditoriums, concert halls, lodge rooms, churches—in places he hadn't seen since the old vaudeville days. If the community had "a railroad and a Town Hall," he promised, "we will be there sooner or later." And meanwhile he was having the time of his life.

On arrival in a town that was unfamiliar to him he would go to the newspaper office to collect what he called "the dope." He inquired about traffic problems, the city council, the police force, the bond issue. "What about the mayor?" he would ask, "what's he doin' now?" He would write names and snippets of information on the back of an old envelope, stuff it into his pocket, and just before going on stage, read his notes to be certain he had the names right. Once he was on, he never looked at them again.

He liked to work material of this nature into the opening of his lecture and might include a few remarks about himself to warm up the audience. "If a smart man was going around the country doing this," he would say, "it would be a lecture. If a politician was doing it, it would be a message." Then he would branch off into a discussion of state politics and finally go into the topical remarks about national and international affairs that were his stock in trade.

Notes and typewritten sheets, headed "Lecture Routine," survive to indicate the type of material Will was using at this time. ("I don't make jokes," he would say, "I just watch the Government and report the facts and I have never found it necessary to exaggerate.") He might throw in a remark about evening clothes, which he never wore: "More people should work for their dinner instead of dressing for it."

He spoke about the *Shenandoah* and *Los Angeles*, the two dirigibles. The trouble with them, he would say, was that one couldn't go up until they took the helium gas out of the other; we had two dirigibles but only one set of air.

He had heard that we wanted to raise the guns on our battleships, but were prevented from doing so because of treaty commitments with England and Japan. All we asked, he said, was to be able to point the guns in the general direction of the enemy; the way they were pointing now, if the boat rocked we would shoot ourselves.

America, he liked to say, had never lost a war or won a conference.

He would move on to discuss such topics as New York's subways, rumrunners, college football, and Coolidge. Florida, motion pictures, and Congress might come next. Often there was something of a personal nature to pass along. A Congressman had read part of one of Will's articles into the *Congressional Record*, at which another legislator jumped to his feet and objected to the remarks of "a professional joke maker" being included in that august journal. As Will saw it, Congressmen were the real comedians. "Every time they make a law it's a joke and every time they make a joke it's a law."

In 1925 Brigadier General William Mitchell went on trial in Washington, D.C. A distinguished officer, he was the country's leading exponent of air power and had already demonstrated the military potential of the airplane by sinking target battleships with aerial bombs. To the defense establishment's further dismay, he advocated a unified command of the armed forces, and he provoked his own court martial by accusing the Army and Navy brass of "incompetency, criminal negligence, and almost treasonal administration of national defense." On one of Will's visits to Washington Billy Mitchell had taken him up for a flight over the city on what proved to be Mitchell's last day as a general officer; the court martial found him guilty, reduced his rank, and suspended him for five years without pay or allowances.

After describing his flight with Mitchell, and telling how frightened he was, Will added that it had been an honor to fly with him on his last trip as brigadier general. "And if it's any honor to you, Colonel Mitchell," he added, "you've been up with me on my last flight." Actually, Will loved flying, and no man was more of an enthusiast for it in the early days. And he realized the truth of Billy Mitchell's predictions. "The next war

In 1924 the editors of *Vanity Fair* nominated Will Rogers to their "Hall of Fame" with this comment:

"Because in all his comedy he breathes the essential spirit of America; because he has brought the lariat and the lasso into the highest society in America; because he is a well-loved figure in movies; because the Ziegfeld Follies have long successfully revolved around him; but chiefly because as an author and political observer he is as shrewd, satirical and clever as they make them."

"Photographers were there to get our picture. I could just see the picture with this label under it: 'Last Photograph Taken of the Deceased.' . . . But I never let on. I remembered how nice the papers always speak of a man who goes to the gallows with a smile on his face, and how they laud his nerve. . . . Here I was thousands of feet up in the air when you can't even get me to ride a tall horse. I had always figured that if the Lord had intended a man to do any flying he would have sprouted something out of his back besides just shoulder blades."

from Weekly Article
May 10, 1925

is going to be in the air," Will promised. "Nobody is going to shoot anything at you, they're just going to drop it on you."

Unlike the traditional lecture fare, these performances were so informal and casual it was virtually impossible for an audience not to warm to Will immediately, and he could play on his listeners the way a talented musician performs on an instrument. "You're doing fine," he would say when they roared with laughter; "We'll get out early tonight. It takes twice as long to get out when you have to explain the jokes."

With his sense of timing he could string several jokes together, each funnier than the one that preceded it, and then, just when people least expected it, top them all. Frequently, an audience kept him talking until he was exhausted and sat down on the edge of the stage with his feet hanging into the orchestra pit. He would grin at them and say, "I'm tired. Now, you folks go on out of here and go home—if you've got a home."

A nephew, Bruce Quisenberry, who worked with Will for three seasons as manager of his company, remembered with a sense of awe his incredible energy. He never seemed to mind the killing pace of his schedule; he never even seemed to be tired. He never worried, never asked to see the books or requested an accounting, and never disappointed an audience. Once, a

Wearing what he called a "one-piece suicide suit," Will flew with Brigadier General Billy Mitchell, the controversial advocate of air power.
LIBRARY OF CONGRESS

packed house of Texans kept him talking well past the appointed closing time, and when the performance ended, people crowded onto the platform and into the aisles to give him a standing ovation, with the result that Will and his nephew missed the train they had planned to catch to Wichita, Kansas. He called the station agent, asked if he could hire a private train, and when told that it would cost him $1,100, said, "Tell 'em to saddle her up." And off they steamed, arriving in time to make the Kansas date. On another occasion he was driving through Arkansas, hurrying to a benefit performance, and came to a little town where 20 or 30 children were standing on the sidewalk holding a sign that read, "Welcome Will Rogers." Will told the driver to stop, explaining, "They may have been here all morning"; and despite the fact that it made him late for the benefit, he got out one of his ropes and did a few tricks for the children.

Although he was already lecturing as often as six nights a week, and writing his weekly article, he had agreed to prepare a daily column for McNaught called "The Worst Story I Heard Today." This consisted of a joke which he attributed to a friend or some prominent person; but it was not Will Rogers at his best, and he knew it, and soon tired of the feature. The formula simply was not right for him, and after a time he gave it up.

In the spring of 1926, at the conclusion of his first lecture tour, Will was asked by George Horace Lorimer, editor of the *Saturday Evening Post*, to write a series of articles for the magazine. The *Post* had run a feature called "Letters of a Self-Made Merchant to his Son," which was a big success, and Lorimer wanted Will to go to Europe and write a series called "Letters of a Self-Made Diplomat to His President." Will agreed, and at the end of April he and Will, Jr., sailed on the *Leviathan*, shortly after he informed *Post* readers of his "assignment from President Coolidge." His first open letter to Calvin Coolidge, published in the *Post*, explained that he had not bothered to call at the White House while he was in Washington; their understanding about his mission was "so antiseptic that I knew there was no use in talking over personally what I am to accomplish." He had, however, called on Vice President Charles G. Dawes, who was "asking very anxiously after your health. I had to disappoint him by telling him you were never better in your life. [Dawes] said the worry of the Presidential office had been too much for many of our Presidents. I told him I had never known a Vermonter to do any tremendous amount of worrying on $75,000 a year."

He had had some difficulty obtaining a passport, he told the President, a little mixup over the fact that he had no birth certificate: "You see, in the early days of the Indian Territory where I was born there was no such thing as birth certificates. You being there was certificate enough. We generally took for granted if you were there you must have at some time been born. . . . Having a certificate of being born was like wearing a raincoat in the water over a bathing suit."

In England, as the self-appointed Ambassador to the President, he managed to meet nearly everyone of any consequence —including the Prince of Wales, Lady Astor, Sir James M. Barrie, Sir Thomas Lipton, Sir Harry Lauder, and George Bernard Shaw. Then he and young Will were off to Paris by plane, and once he recovered from his initial nervousness about flying he realized that this was the way he wanted to get around from now on. That old restlessness never left him, and airplane travel precisely suited his passion to be on the move, to get from one place to another the quickest possible way. Traveling around the Continent, he visited the Preliminary Conference on Disarmament in Geneva; he met the king of Spain and was entertained by the American ambassador in Berlin; he had an inter-

Occasionally the Jokes Were Not Appreciated by All Those Present

Before Will spoke at the 1926 barbeque of the Old Trail Drivers' Association in San Antonio, a smiling Mrs. R.R. Russell of the Ladies Auxiliary pinned a membership button on him (above). The other two pictures were taken after he said, "You Old Trail Drivers . . . did all right. You'd start out down here with nothing, and after stealing our cattle in the Indian Nation, you'd wind up in Abilene with 2,000 head or more." Mrs. Russell was not amused: "My husband was no cattle thief," she retorted. "Don't insinuate that he was." Somehow Will managed to mollify the lady, and the prudent photographer never printed the pictures, which did not come to light until thirty years after the encounter.

ALL: SMITHERS COLLECTION, HUMANITIES RESEARCH CENTER, UNIVERSITY OF TEXAS

view with Mussolini, the Fascist dictator of Italy; and went to Russia, hoping (without success) to talk with Trotsky.

Perhaps nothing illustrates the man's sheer animal energy so well as his activities during the summer of 1926. Most husbands find it tiring enough to take a wife and children on a rigorous sightseeing trip through Europe. Will not only did that in his usual whirlwind fashion (Betty, with Mary and Jim, joined him in June, and Will was determined that they should see everything); but he combined the tour with appointments to interview prominent people. Beyond this, he found time for a dizzying number of other projects. He was, of course, writing articles regularly for the *Post*—enough to make a fair-sized book when they were all complete. The material from his Russian trip became another book—*There's Not a Bathing Suit in Russia*. He returned to London and made a motion picture called *Tip Toes* with Dorothy Gish. He made twelve travelogues, for which he also wrote the humorous lines that appeared on the screen. He played in a musical review produced by Charles Cochran, whom Will called "the British Ziegfeld." He continued to write his regular weekly article for American newspapers. He made a radio appearance. He went to Dublin to play a benefit for the families of victims of a theatre fire. And on July 29 he sent a cable to the *New York Times* which resulted in his writing a series of daily telegrams that would occupy a portion of his immense energy for the next nine years, becoming the best-known thing he ever did and making the name of Will Rogers a household word throughout the United States.

What prompted the cablegram was Lady Astor's imminent visit to New York. Will and Betty had lunched with her one day, and after she sailed for the States he wired Adolph Ochs, the publisher of the *Times:* "Nancy Astor, which is the nom de plume of Lady Astor, is arriving on your side about now. Please ask my friend Jimmy Walker to have New York take good care of her. She is the only one over here who don't throw rocks at American tourists. Yours, Will Rogers."

Ochs printed the message in a box on the front page of the second section and wired Will, requesting more of the same. So for the rest of his stay in Europe—with the exception of five days when he was on a mountain-climbing expedition in Switzerland—Will sent the short items to the *Times*. He had no particular thought of continuing the series when he returned to the States, but after he arrived he discovered that Ochs, his friend Larry Winship, editor of the Boston *Globe*, and numerous

Lady Astor
WIDE WORLD

In London, as everywhere else his travels took him, Will paused to strike up a conversation and make a new friend on a street corner.

FPG

readers were clamoring for more, and he decided to oblige.

Before long the McNaught Syndicate handled the daily telegrams as a regular feature, under the by-line "Will Rogers Says," and eventually they were featured in more than five hundred newspapers in the United States with forty million readers. As Betty wrote, "When he really got into the swing of the thing, these daily pieces became his favorite medium. In later years his schedule was often overcrowded, and he would have been glad to drop the weekly article, but doing a daily wire, though it might sometimes be difficult, was never drudgery."

From October 16, 1926, until the day of his death Will filed his telegram every day, six days a week, no matter where he was or what he was doing. Bruce Quisenberry who went with him

Will Gets an Autograph

"The boy handed him some photographs. [Mussolini sat] right down to his desk and started in autographing one to me. Not only that, but put my name on it—after asking what it was—'Signor Rogers, Compliments, Mussolini.' It was of a horse—and him accompanying him—making a jump. . . . I then told him that I certainly appreciated it, but that it was so far away that it dident show his face up. He set right down and picked out another one, a close-up of him and the horse. He autographed it, but dident put my name on it, as he dident want to ask what it was again."

from Will Rogers' *Letters of a Self-Made Diplomat to His President*

WILL ROGERS MEMORIAL, CLAREMORE, OKLA.

on lecture tours, came to recognize the signs that accompanied the creation of this article: "Getting his newspaper dispatch off was always a dramatic event. It had to be filed by half-past one. He would watch the time, then at the last possible moment, he would put his portable on his knees, stare into space for a few moments, then begin to peck. His hands—so amazingly skillful with a rope—were all thumbs when he tackled a typewriter. *Peck-peck-peck!* Sometimes he would stop, turn up the page and scowl at it for a minute. Then peck-peck-peck! If, by some chance, he finished early, he would read it to us—the singers and me—and ask what we thought. If we didn't get the point readily, he might slip the sheet back into the typewriter and start pecking again. When the telegram was finally ready, I would hop off at the first stop and file it. Sometimes I would have to run like mad to catch the train. When I would finally get on he would say, 'I'll bet we lose you some day.' "

Written under every conceivable circumstance, while he was on location for a movie, in a hospital bed, or traveling about the world by steamship, airplane, automobile, or train, this concise expression of Will Rogers' philosophy greeted and cheered the American reading public every day for almost nine years. At the time he began it, he was known as a popular comedian, but as the daily telegram continued, Americans began to think that he was a good deal more than that; what he had to say, they realized, was an authentic reflection of what most of them were thinking. Through this medium, more than any other, he emerged as a philosopher as well as a humorist and became, in the end, a national institution.

Throughout that summer of 1926 Will gave Americans a view of Europe unlike anything they had read since Mark Twain's *Innocents Abroad* appeared in 1879. Interspersed with all the open letters to the President were special cablegrams, addressed to "CALCOOL Whitewashhouse," and signed "WILLROG," summarizing what Americans thought about Europe but had never seen expressed in quite the same manner.

England, he said, "has the best Statesmen and the Rottenest coffee of any country in the world." From Italy he reported that San Francisco Bay would make the bay of Naples look like the Chicago drainage canal, and if Miami "ever cleaned those gin bottles out of that harbor of theirs would lay it all over the Mediteranian." Rome, he discovered "has no more culture than Minneapolis or Long Beach, California. They live there in Rome amongst what used to be called Culture, but that don't mean a thing. Men in Washington you know yourself, Calvin, live where Washington and Jefferson and Hamilton lived, but as far as the good it does them, they just as well have the Capitol down at Claremore, Oklahoma—and, by the way, I doubt if Claremore would take it; there is a Town that has never had a setback. So, you see, Association has nothing to do with culture."

All over Europe he saw American tourists forming a half-circle around a guide who "tells them what he has read in their guide books. They listen and mark it off and move on over to another picture." Sightseeing was no pleasure, he decided; it was a business.

Until he got there he didn't know that "Rome had Senators. Now I know why it declined." And if you took everything out of Rome that was supposedly done by Michelangelo ("the Charley Russell of the old paintbrush"—although "Charley never has had to resort to painting the inside of roofs of buildings. Charley will set down and paint, but he won't lay down on his back and paint"), Rome would be as bare of art as Los Angeles. Those old Romans, he said, "loved blood. What money is to an American, blood was to a Roman. A Roman was never so happy as when he saw somebody bleeding. That was his sense of humor, just like ours is. . . . Where we like to see you lose your hat, they loved to see you leave a right arm and a left leg in the possession of a Tiger."

In Nice ("pronounced neece, not nice; they have no word for nice in French") he learned that Europeans just didn't comprehend America's democratic way of life; "They can't understand a race of people as big as we are paying any attention to just a Senator." A short visit to the casinos of Monaco gave him an idea he passed on to the President: "If Monaco can support their entire little Country in luxury and yachts and no taxes . . . what could we do by having this right in Washington, where everybody could come and play without the inconvenience of a passport?" He had discovered that "People don't mind spending their money if they know it's not going for taxes."

Having talked to everyone he could buttonhole, he had learned that all Europeans felt the same way about disarmament and the League of Nations and the World Court: "They feel like England and France runs the whole thing and they don't want anything to do with it." Not only that, he concluded, there wasn't one European country "got any use for the other one, and you can't blame 'em for looking out after themselves. Say, you give them as much ocean on each side of them as we have, and then on the other two ends a Mexico and a Canada, they might start talking some disarming with you too. There is a lot of things talk good in a speech, but you come to working it out when you are up against hundreds of years of previous wars and hatreds, they don't pan out."

At last he was on his way home with the "last surviving American tourists," but there were a few more cables to CAL-COOL: everybody on the ship, he reported, "is having a hard time packing, trying to make bottles look like soiled clothing," and the final cable read, "Back home and broke. WILLROG."

When he landed in New York Will actually did send the President a telegram and was invited to the White House to make his "report." Other than what appeared in his weekly article, there is no record of what they discussed, but Will informed his readers later that he had had fish hash for dinner (which was just about "the most economy in food"). His summation of the summer's experience was that America "don't stand as good as a Horse Thief" in Europe; "The only way we would be worse with them was to help them out in another war."

When his collection of letters appeared in book form in October, 1926, published as *Letters of a Self-Made Diplomat to His President*, a *New York Times* reviewer commented, "there has rarely been an American humorist whose words produced less empty laughter or more sober thought.... Perhaps Will Rogers has done more to educate the American public in world affairs than all the professors who have been elucidating the continental chaos since the Treaty of Versailles." And Franklin D. Roosevelt remarked later that "the first time I fully realized Will Rogers' exceptional and deep understanding of political and social problems was when he came home from his European trip in 1926. While I had discussed European matters with many others, both American and foreign, Will Rogers' analysis of affairs abroad was not only more interesting but proved to be more accurate than any other I had heard."

Will was now forty-seven years old and had entered upon the most productive and creative phase of his life. With the possible exception of films, he had succeeded magnificently at everything he had tried and was known not only in the United States but in most countries of the Western world. The man who used to sign himself the "Injun Cowboy" had come a long way.

Will Rogers says:
"If there is a safer mode of

Hurrah for our aviators that broke the continuous flight record. Fifty-one hours! . . . No automobile ever went fifty hours without stopping or refueling or meeting a train at a grade crossing or something, yet we spend a billion dollars on good roads for them. Why not a subsidy to commercial aviation? Congress is waiting two more wars to see if they are practical. This had better make us think. Fifty hours—they can send 'em here from any nation in Europe.

When we nearly lose the next war, as we probably will, we can lay it onto one thing and that will be the jealousy of the army and navy toward aviation. They have belittled it ever since it started and will keep on doing it till they have something dropped on them from one, and even then will say it wasn't a success.

Didn't we invent aeroplanes and then think after we had invented them that that was all you was supposed to do with them?

European nations might not have our foresight for amassing the dollar, but they know what altitude of the elements the next war will be held in.

I see where Mr. Coolidge says "Lindbergh's feat grows on him." I wonder if we should really be honest with ourselves, wouldn't we admit over here that the way France has appreciated the feat and honored him had something to do with waking us up to its real importance. You know they appreciate good aviation and know it when they see it.

I always told you we have the aviators. Just give them the planes. I have flown in the past

year with at least a dozen boys whom I wouldn't be afraid to start to Siberia with.

Don't get the idea because three of our planes flew to Europe and made it that we are ahead in aviation. It's not how far can three men fly, but what have you got for the other hundred and ten million to fly in; and where are they to land when they come down?

Every paper is raving about legislation to stop ocean flying because thirteen people have been lost, just a fair Sunday's average in auto deaths. From ten to fifteen is just about the number that are always in a bus when it meets a train at a grade crossing, yet you never see an editorial about relief from that. You may not die as spectacularly in a machine as you would if you dropped in the ocean, but you are just as dead.

While you are talking about progressing aviation, don't overlook . . . . Western Air Express. One year and a half ago they started with only twenty pounds of mail. Today, in here packed around me, is 550 pounds.

. . . what pilots those air mail babies are. Lindbergh came from a great school.

It looks like the only way you can get any publicity on your death is to be killed in a plane. It's no novelty to be killed in an auto any more.

Left Chicago last night at 10 o'clock in a snowstorm and flew to Omaha. These mail babies go through. They can get through weather that most people couldn't find their way from the house to the garage with a well-lighted course. Good planes and good pilots!

ransportation I have never found it."

Just read the Smithsonian Institution's explanation about the Wright flying machine. They say the trustees decided Langley's machine could have flown first but didn't. I could have flown first but didn't. I could have flown to France ahead of Lindbergh but I just neglected doing it. I had a lot of other things on my mind at the time.

———

Say, you luncheon clubs, stop eating and singing songs long enough to get you some paint and a brush and go out and put the name of your town on the biggest roofed building you got. It would be a tremendous aid to aviators. Lots of towns can't afford an airport, but any of you can do this. You Kiwanis's or Rotary's could do it some day and not miss over half of some speech.

———

When will the newspapers commence giving aviation an even break? There were eight people killed all over America in planes Sunday and it's headlined in every newspaper today. If there was a single State that didn't get that many in automobiles yesterday it was simply because it fell below its average.

———

Just flew in from Santa Barbara and found a real, legitimate use for my polo field. We landed on it.

———

There has been and will be lots of fine pilots lost in developing aviation to such a point that it will be safe for a lot of folks less useful to the world than these fine young fellows are.

———

If flying is dangerous pass a law and stop it. But don't divide your nation between a class

that should fly and one that shouldn't. Aviation is not a fad, it's a necessity and will be our mode of travel long after all the people who are too valuable to fly have met their desired deaths by the roadsides on Sunday afternoons.

———

There is one sure fire recipe for a pilot in a strange town, that don't know where the field is located. Locate a high tension line. There is almost sure to be a field there. If not, follow it till it comes to an intersection of three or more lines and there will be located the city's municipal field.

———

Claremore, Okla., is just waiting for a high-tension line so they can go ahead with locating an airport.

———

I don't think people have realized yet the most important thing these ocean flights have brought out, and that is the quicker transporting of our marines to other people's wars. . . . . our slogan will be now: Have your civil wars wherever and as far away as you want, but on the opening day we will be there.

———

Army flew in here with 150 planes and General Fechet wanted to lead me into every one of them and show me what they were really doing. Friday night we went over the city with some bombers, and where I stood was the place for four thousand pounds of high explosives. Millions of lights under you and hundreds of thousands of defenseless people.

———

They went to London to make cheaper battleships, and not a word was said about restricting the things that you are going to be killed with in the next war.

UNDERWOOD & UNDERWOOD

"... if your time is worth anything, travel by air. If not, you might just as well walk."

With a delegation of Oklahomans (left), Will appeared before a House Committee on flood control in 1928, urging action to prevent such disasters in the future. Above, a citizen of Mounds, Illinois, fords the knee-deep water covering Main Street.
UPI

That summer of 1926 was a fair sample of what Will Rogers' life was to be like from then on. "He was always nervous and in a hurry to get anything done he had to do," his friend Spi Trent said, and the tendencies were exaggerated by involvement in a multitude of activities that made incessant demands on his energies. In earlier years he had concentrated on one thing at a time—vaudeville, the Follies, films—before moving on to something else. Now, as if driven by some inner demon, he was actively pursuing half a dozen careers simultaneously, without pause. Each day was a new adventure, launched with a spur-of-the-moment decision to go somewhere and see something he might otherwise miss. It was almost as though he were on a permanent quest, certain that he could find what he sought if only he kept moving after it. "We are here just for a spell and then pass on," he once wrote. "So get a few laughs and do the best you can. Live your life so that whenever you lose, you are ahead." There were no vacations, in the usual sense of the word, for Will. "It's always a bird that never does anything that enjoys a vacation," he observed. "There's nothing in the world as hard as playing when you don't want to."

Although some of this bustle can be laid to temperament—that old restlessness that had been with him since he was a young boy—the continuous need for material for his newspaper articles also played a part. Never satisfied with secondhand information, he wanted to see things for himself, to witness what was going on and to talk with the people involved, and whenever the mood took him he hopped on an airplane and was off. "I got one little old soft red grip," he said, "that if I just tell it when I am leaving it will pack itself. A few white shirts with the collars attached, and a little batch of underwear and sox that you can replenish at any store anywhere. All I take is my typewriter and the little red bag, one extra suit in it. It's always packed the same, no matter if I'm going to New York or to Singapore."

In a day when comedians and columnists rely on gag writers and researchers for much of their material, it is difficult to fathom how Will Rogers could have written everything himself, but that is precisely what he did. Much of it was composed hurriedly and carelessly, but it was all his own, and considering the circumstances under which it came to life, the overall quality is astonishingly high. His wife noted that he took considerable pains with his daily telegrams, "fussing and worrying to get them right," and close associates remembered that Will often read an article to them to get their reaction; if it did not produce the desired response he would work it over until it did. But the weekly articles were often dashed off carelessly, with the result that some of the later ones, as Betty remarked, were very bad indeed. He wanted to drop the articles in later years (he hoped to confine his newspaper work to the daily telegram, his favorite format); nevertheless, the feature remained so popular that the McNaught people talked him out of quitting it.

Arthur Brisbane, the columnist and a friend of Will's, suggested that he use a dictaphone, since talking came so easily to him; but once the machine started running he lost all sense of what he was going to say, gave up, and went back to "wrestling" with the typewriter, as Betty described it, "hitting the wrong keys, strewing commas all over the place, and using capitals almost at random." Will's copy was enough to give an editor fits. He never retyped anything, never made a carbon, didn't bother to correct spelling, grammar, or punctuation. Yet in the same way that his easy, relaxed manner took the bite out of certain remarks he made about people, the singular spelling, grammar, and construction of his written work had a curious softening effect. As a writer, he was suspicious of new words: "Old words is like old friends," he would say, "you know 'em the minute you see 'em." When he did revise an article he worked with a soft pencil on the original draft (which was usually typed on a Western Union telegraph blank), but frequently he didn't even read his articles over. "When I write 'em I am through with 'em," he admitted. "I am not being paid reading wages."

No one conducted his affairs more casually; if ever a man's office could be said to be in his hat, Will's was. Even when he

"I generally give the Party in Power, whether Republican or Democrat, the more digs because they are generally doing the Country the most damage, and besides I don't think it is fair to jump too much on the fellow who is down. He is not working, he is only living in hopes of getting back in on the graft in another four years."

from Weekly Article
Nov. 11, 1924

finally did rent space in an office building in Beverly Hills, it was no more than a place for mail to be received and sorted— and there, to sift through fan letters and replies to his newspaper articles, Mrs. Daisy Tyler was ensconced. A public stenographer whom Betty had hired to help with the daily accumulation of letters and post cards, she recalled that during the eight years she worked for Will he probably never dictated more than eight letters. She would select the mail she thought would interest him, take it to his home, and on weekends he would type the answers himself, never making a carbon copy. As she described the procedure, he never distinguished between important and unimportant people; he answered the subject rather than the person, and as often as not he would fire off a telegram in response.

The frantic pace at which Will was moving in 1926 is suggested by the fact that he set off on his second lecture tour the day after he visited Calvin Coolidge at the White House, following the frenetic summer in Europe. He was enlivening the talks now with fresh material from his travels on the Continent, and both his lectures and the daily telegrams reflected the increasingly jaundiced view he took of the international situation. Wherever he looked, the United States seemed to be interfering in the affairs of other nations: "Our gunboats are all in the Chinese war, our marines have landed in Nicaragua, [Secretary of State] Kellogg is sending daily ultimatums to Mexico and Coolidge is dedicating memorials to eternal peace. Who is the next country wants their affairs regulated? . . . If Nicaragua would just come out like a man and fight us, we wouldn't have to be hunting away off over in China for a war." He concocted a few patriotic slogans for the Central American adventure: "Join the navy and help America find Nicaragua." "Stop Nicaragua while there is still time."

When he embarked on the lecture circuit Betty returned to California to enroll the two younger children in school, and Will, Jr., the oldest, was sent to Culver Military Academy. On his fifteenth birthday young Bill received a letter written by his father in Spartanburg, South Carolina. Will was planning to be home for Christmas, he said, and would see his son then. Meanwhile, he was heading for Oklahoma and had, as usual, a new project in mind. He was going to buy some more land and "fix up the old ranch place"—stocking it with more cattle, some sheep, and two hundred and fifty goats. "We are going into the goat raising business," he announced.

Regarding the defeat of James Cox as Presidential candidate:

"Shrewdness in Public life all over the World is always honored, while honesty in Public Men is generally attributed to Dumbness and is seldom rewarded."

from Weekly Article Nov. 30, 1924

The ranch Will had inherited had deteriorated sadly during his long absence, and after renting the land to a succession of tenant farmers he finally decided in 1919 to do something about it himself. His sister Sallie's son, Herb McSpadden, came out of the Army that year, and Will asked him to look after the place. According to Herb, it was "terribly run down, fences and buildings in a state of collapse, pasture land overgrazed, farm land in bad shape, road into the place nearly impassable," and for eight years Herb did little more than act as caretaker. Then Will gave him the task of improving the ranch and putting it back into operation as a going concern.

On Will's part there was more sentiment than business sense involved in this venture, as he himself realized. Urging President Coolidge to support a farm relief program, he had once suggested in an article: "Put him on a farm with the understanding he has to make his own living off it, and I bet he will give the farmers relief next year. I offer mine for the experiment, and if he makes a go of it he is not a President, he is a magician." One important consideration in Will's decision to restore the Oklahoma ranch was that his roots—along with the family and friends he cared for deeply—were there and were never far from his thoughts. "I'm just an old country boy in a Big Town tryin' to get along," he said. "I been eatin' pretty regular, and the reason I have been is because I've stayed an old country boy."

In May, 1925, he had made a sad journey to the town of Chelsea for the funeral of his sister Maud Lane, following which he wrote one of his few entirely serious weekly articles. "I am out in Oklahoma, among my People, my Cherokee people, who don't expect a laugh for everything I say. . . . I have today witnessed a Funeral that for real sorrow and real affection I don't think will ever be surpassed anywhere. They came on foot, in Buggies, Horseback, Wagons, Cars and Train, and there wasent a Soul that come that she hadent helped or favored at one time or another. Some uninformed Newspapers printed: 'Mrs. C.L. Lane, sister of the famous Comedian, Will Rogers.' It's the other way around. I am the brother of Mrs. C.L. Lane, 'The Friend of Humanity.' And all the honors that I could ever in my wildest dreams hope to reach would never equal the honor paid on a little Western Prairie hilltop, among her people, to Maud Lane. If they will love me like that at the finish, my life will not have been in vain."

They were a close family, the old ties ran deep, and as Will's niece Paula McSpadden Love wrote, the greatest excitement in the lives of relatives in Oklahoma was to hear that Uncle Willie was coming home, which he often did when crossing the country. If Betty was with him she would play the piano after dinner while Will sang the latest musical hits in his high tenor voice; he impersonated other actors, told jokes and stories, and showed the home folks some of his new routines. Between visits, Paula recalls, there was a steady flow of "letters, clippings, rare and distinctive gifts, the latest sheet music and always a wealth of postal cards from all over the country and many foreign lands."

At the time Will decided to enlarge and refurbish the ranch, he owned a total of 1,610 acres and rented another 4,000, and he stocked it with several hundred sheep, goats, hogs, and between 350 and 450 steers. "Anything done on that place," Herb McSpadden said, "was with the thought of restoring it. If we made any money on it, it was put right back into the place." When Will was coming to visit, he would "telegraph my mother at Chelsea to get me word, and she'd phone Oologah and some one would drive out to tell us." If the newspaper reporters got word that Will was arriving, Herb said, so many visitors would show up that "you couldn't set a sack afire and smoke them off of him." What Will liked to do best was to get on a pony and ride around the ranch or rope some goats, after which Herb's wife would cook him a pot of beans with ham hocks. He could always get good beans in Oklahoma, Will would say, and "That's what makes a good Cow outfit, is good beans. Just give me some beans and I will follow you off." His nieces, wrote Irene McSpadden Milam, were taught "to cook navy beans as he liked them, with plenty of soup. Then there would be home cured ham, hickory smoked, cured just the same as it was on the old ranch, and cream gravy with hot biscuits." And in the springtime there would be tiny wild onions, scrambled with eggs.

Yet as much as he loved Oklahoma, the home place, and the informality of life there, his commitments and interests simply would not permit him to return for any extended period (as it turned out, he never again lived at the ranch near Oologah). As a substitute for what he felt he was missing, he began turning over in his mind the possibility of selling the Beverly Hills house and building on land he had acquired in the Santa Monica Mountains. The reasons he outlined in a letter to Will, Jr., say a good deal about his nature: "There is no more fun at home now," he wrote. "Everything is finished. I am anxious to get to work on something new."

That was easier said than done. Just before Christmas of 1926 the daily telegram began to be signed "Hon. Will Rogers." The publicity-minded folk of Beverly Hills, thinking that they had no mayor, decided to appoint Will to the office, and on December 21, when he returned home for the holidays, the local residents turned out en masse—movie actors, a corps of motor-cycle police, two brass bands, and people carrying banners and placards reading "The Kiddies' Pal," "The Dogs' Best Friend"—to see Will presented with a five-foot scroll honoring him as mayor. "They say I'll be a comedy mayor," he said in his acceptance speech. "Well, I won't be the only one. I never saw a mayor yet that wasn't comical. As to my administration, I won't say I'll be exactly honest, but I'll agree to split 50-50 with you and give the town an even break. I'm for the common people, and as Beverly Hills has no common people I won't have to pass out any favors."

Fortunately for Will's other interests, the mayoral term was brief. As the self-styled "moving Mayor of a fast moving town"

UNDERWOOD & UNDERWOOD

Beverly Hills turned out en masse to greet its "mayor." To His Honor's left are William S. Hart (in cap), Will Jr. (in military school uniform), Jim, and Betty Rogers (holding a bouquet). Below, Will inspects the community's natty police force.

WILL ROGERS MEMORIAL, CLAREMORE, OKLA.

Above is the long winding drive to the Santa Monica ranch, in a picture taken before construction was started on the house. At right is the family polo team—Mary, Will, Will, Jr., and Jim— suited up and ready for a game.

BOTH: WILL ROGERS MEMORIAL, CLAREMORE, OKLA.

put it, "The State Legislature of California passed a law saying that no one not a politician could hold office." It seemed that in sixth-class cities, like Beverly Hills, the president of the board of trustees was constitutionally the mayor, so Mayor Rogers was deposed. "I ain't the first mayor that's been kicked out," he wrote. "If I'd knowed Beverly Hills was a sixth-class town I wouldn't made the race."

He began to concentrate with a vengeance on the Santa Monica place. He had purchased 150 acres, which he eventually increased to 300—nothing to compare in size with the Oklahoma property, but enough so that he referred to it as a ranch. (It did not really merit the name, he admitted, "but we call it that. It sounds big and don't really do any harm.") There were no paved roads in the vicinity, the land was brushy and steep, laced with canyons, and the only open space in the sea of greasewood and sagebrush was a small clearing made by a truck gardener. This lay on a mesa that was accessible only by means of a virtually impassable road, but the view was worth all the trouble of reaching it—in the days before smog one could see off in the distance Santa Monica Bay, the Pacific Ocean, and Catalina Island.

Things started to hum: Will hired men to clear away the brush with mule teams and build a corral and stables, then the ground was leveled for a polo field. When he was away from California, which he was a good part of the time, his letters to the family were full of instructions about what was to be done. To Jim, who was then only eleven years old, he wrote: "I wish you would look after some things down there at the Ranch for me. Get 'em to build the back part on the big barn. . . . Get those Logs put around the outside of the east hill. Then if they have time move the old Stables, and fix up a Bunk House out of part of the old one. Now see what luck you can have on this. . . . I want one of those Polo Racks with a Saddle on it out in the Riding ring to hit a ball off of, like Tommy Hitchcock had on Long Island. There is nothing to do only put a high carpenter's bench Horse there with a Saddle on."

He had been introduced to polo years earlier, while the family was living in Amityville, Long Island. Jim Minnick, who rode with him in the Mulhall Wild West Show and was then training and selling polo ponies in New Jersey, taught Will the game, which he played with the reckless abandon that characterized his rodeo work. On Long Island, Minnick, the cowboy-artist Ed Borein, the actors Leo Carillo and Fred Stone, and the dancer Vernon Castle often teamed up with Will. "The people who watched us play our Sunday games," he remarked, "soon learned that in a spill, if the falling rider hit on his feet, it was Fred Stone. If he hit on his head, it was me. We were both equally safe." After the move to California there was more time for polo, and he taught all three children the game; the four Rogerses made a family team until, as Will said sadly, "Mary went social on us."

In the spring of 1927, during his lecture tour, one of the worst floods in history laid waste the Mississippi valley. Hundreds were dead, hundreds of thousands were homeless, the damage ran into millions of dollars; but the Federal government showed a curious reluctance to do anything about the plight of the sufferers. The business of America is business, Calvin Coolidge had said, and the administration was convinced that private relief agencies could handle the immense task of feeding and clothing the destitute. Will thought otherwise: the Red Cross was appealing for $5 million, but for the million people who had been victimized, "That would be only five dollars a head. Five dollars ain't much good to you, even if the water's just up to your ankles." And as for Congress' promise to do something for the victims, "I don't want to discourage the Valley but I would advise them to put more confidence in a boat builder. . . . One

Will and Cowboy, between chukkers of a polo game; in the background are the stables.
WILL ROGERS MEMORIAL, CLAREMORE, OKLA.

rowboat will do more for you in a flood than all the Senators in Washington talking about you."

He plunged into action. In daily and weekly articles he plugged away at the need for assistance and donations. "Look at the thousands and thousands of Negroes that never did have much, but now its washed away," he wrote. "You don't want to forget that water is just as high up on them as it is if they were white. The Lord so constituted everybody that no matter what color you are you require about the same amount of nourishment." He wired Florenz Ziegfeld to say that he would put on a benefit for flood victims if Ziegfeld would donate the theatre, and Will and the tenor John McCormack raised nearly $18,000 for the Red Cross. Another performance in New Orleans produced $48,000, and Will kept hammering away at his newspaper readers to open their pocketbooks. He was tired of reading about towns that had met their quotas; there was no quota—"If you were hungry and some one gave you a sandwich would you have your quota?" If a disaster of this magnitude had hit the East, he observed, "they would raise fifty millions in a day. Come on, let's help them, even if they are not Armenians. They can't help it because of their nationality."

On May 21, 1927, the daily telegram expressed what was on the mind of every American. "No attempt at jokes today," it read. "An old slim tall bashful, smiling, American boy is somewhere out over the middle of the Atlantic ocean, where no lone human being has ever ventured before." But not even Charles A. Lindbergh's solo flight across the Atlantic took Will's mind entirely off the flood victims. What would be better to celebrate the pilot's safe arrival, he asked, than another donation for people "that are not even fortunate enough to be flying over water, but have to stand huddled up on the banks and look into it as it washes away their life's work?"

From that day on Will was one of Lindbergh's most ardent fans: according to him, the aviator was the greatest American since Theodore Roosevelt, and he hoped his countrymen would have sense enough to leave him alone and not make a sideshow out of him. Almost half a century after the event, it is difficult to describe the worldwide outpouring of joy, excitement, and admiration that resulted from Lindbergh's twenty-seven-hour flight from New York to Paris in *The Spirit of St. Louis*. There are those who still recall it as the most thrilling moment of their lives, yet there had been other great flights, other modest, attractive, and brave young fliers. What somehow caught the

As an all-out polo enthusiast, the hard-riding Will broke two ribs in this spill (the horse rolled over on him).
WILL ROGERS MEMORIAL, CLAREMORE, OKLA.

223

With typewriter and a bag of food for the trip, Will prepares to board airmail plane.
WILL ROGERS MEMORIAL, CLAREMORE, OKLA.

imagination of people all over the world was the American's exceptional integrity and courage, his indifference to the usual hallmarks of success. As U.S. Ambassador to France Myron Herrick described the remarkable adventure: "He started with no purpose but to arrive. He remained with no desire but to serve. He sought nothing; he was offered all."

Lindbergh, Will Rogers said, was our biggest national asset and ought to be allowed to spend his time promoting aviation instead of making an "exhibition out of himself"—a message few Americans would heed. The flier not only fulfilled Will's concept of a hero, he was also a member of a fraternity Will had come to admire enormously: the barnstorming pilots of the twenties who were practicing a gospel Will was preaching constantly, the practicality and the promise of aviation.

After World War I—the first conflict in which aircraft played a real role—aviation had fallen on evil days in the United States. There was almost no demand for planes, military airfields were deactivated, and the psychological aftermath of war produced a widespread public attitude that associated the once-glamorous airplane with death and violence. Only a few adventurous young would have any part of it, and they were flying surplus DH-4's and Curtiss Jennies, hopping from county fair to carnival to give exhibitions of wing walking, stunting, and parachute leaping. These fellows had to be skilled mechanics and first-rate pilots, and for a time they were very nearly the only nonmilitary aviators around.

In Europe, by contrast, commercial aviation had caught hold of the public imagination, and Will saw in 1926 how far the Germans, French, and British had progressed while America lagged behind. One reason for this was that European governments were subsidizing commercial lines, which could not hope to cover their operating costs through passenger revenues, while the U.S. government was loath to become involved in anything that smacked of Federal control over private enterprise. What eventually changed this attitude was the decision of the U.S. Post Office to fly the mail.

After establishing air-mail service from Washington to New York, the Post Office made plans for a route from New York to Chicago, but almost at once the hazards of crossing the Allegheny Mountains proved too much. On what was called the "graveyard run" because of prevalent storms, the absence of navigational aids, and inferior, open cockpit, rebuilt warplanes, 32 of the first 40 pilots hired by the Post Office Department were killed before the operation was turned over to commercial pilots. In 1925 legislation providing for the encouragement of commercial aviation was passed by Congress, and the Post Office requested bids for various feeder routes. Since there was more profit to be made from carrying mail than from transporting passengers, few lines made any effort to attract the latter, and only after 1926, when the landmark Air Commerce Act was passed, did the new Bureau of Aeronautics begin licensing American planes and pilots and setting up standards for aircraft, landing fields, navigational aids, and the other requisites of aviation. So it was little wonder that Will's was a relatively lonely voice in advocating the public acceptance of flying. In 1924, commenting on the twentieth anniversary of the Wright brothers' first flight, he remarked that in 1904 people wouldn't believe that a man could fly, "and Congress don't believe it yet." While France was launching its 54th air squadron, he said, our air service "is waiting for Congress to make an appropriation to have the Valves ground and Carbon removed from the Engines."

Three years later, in 1927, after making those commercial flights in Europe, he began taking planes whenever and wherever he could, and from this time on his daily telegrams reflect a constant preoccupation with air travel. Not that it was easy to arrange in those days. The only way he could fly to some of the out-of-the-way places he was visiting was on a plane carrying the U.S. mail. His son Will, Jr., remembers that his father would come into his bedroom at the Beverly Hills house at 2 A.M. and shake him awake. "Come on, boy. Get up. I got to go to the airport," he would say, and they would drive through the darkness to a landing field on the edge of Los Angeles, where Will would pull on a fleece-lined leather flying suit, a helmet, and goggles, and then get on the scales. "They didn't put stamps on him," Bill says, "but he paid for his own weight as if he were a package." As soon as Will climbed into the forward cockpit of the open plane the ground crew would pile sacks of mail around him and on top of him. Usually, it was still dark when the plane taxied onto the runway and warmed up at the end of the field; then it would roar down the strip, and young Bill, driving home in the car, would see it climb into the dawn sky as daylight was breaking in the east.

One pilot Will flew with was Dewey Noyes, who had a mail route between Cleveland and Pittsburgh in 1927 and 1928. Dewey's wife Blanche, as a young bride, sometimes rode with her husband, sitting on a pile of mail sacks, and in 1928 she learned to fly herself. Several years later she received word that Will Rogers was in Chicago and wanted to get to Cleveland in a hurry, and she flew west through a snowstorm to pick him up. By the time she arrived, the storm was so bad she didn't believe it was possible to return to Cleveland, but Will reassured her.

"Oh now, little girl, you can make it all right. If I don't get to Cleveland, my column won't be any good, because my column is written and in, dated 'Cleveland.'"

Finally, Blanche agreed to try it, "but what I went through!" As she recalled it, "God was flying the ship, I wasn't."

Eventually, Will flew with most of the outstanding aviators of the time, and although he occasionally made a pretense of concern, it was clear that he had little, if any, fear of flying. Charles Jones, who took him up several times, remembered the day Will was to fly with Captain Frank Hawks in a Navy plane and was given a big, heavy flying suit and a parachute. He blustered about the chute, Jones said, and finally asked how to work it. Why, he wanted to know, was the ring that pulled the ripcord way over on the left side, in such an awkward position? The answer was that most men, in an emergency, reach for their heart, and that was why the ring had been put there. "If I have to reach for mine," Will replied, "I'll grab myself by the neck and choke myself to death."

As Hawks himself said, Will "never paid any attention to the weather or the flying procedure while he was in the air. He read most of the time. . . . He placed all his confidence in me, figured that I knew my business, and would always get him to his destination." Flying was simply one of his great enthusiasms, and he never lost his love for it, perhaps because he was fearless. As Spi Trent once observed, "Dying was always kind of a joke to Will, he was always so well and strong, and he used to make a lot of cracks about it."

He would be in several plane crashes; but in the early summer of 1927 Will had his first close brush with death, and it had nothing to do with airplanes. He was in Bluefield, West Virginia, lecturing, when he began to suffer intensely from what he said was nothing more than a bellyache. "Ordinarily when a pain hits you in the stomach in Bluefield, West Virginia," he said, "you would take it for gunshot wounds," but this was different. He had a recurrence of the symptoms a few weeks later, while visiting the ranch in Oklahoma, and when he arrived in Beverly Hills Betty called in the family physician, Dr. Percy White, who diagnosed the problem as gallstones. Will would have to have an operation, he said, and advised that a specialist be consulted. As Will told the story, the doctor then "phoned for what seemed like a friend, but who afterwards turned out to be an accomplice." This man, a surgeon named Dr. Clarence Moore, was "the most famous machete wielder on the Western Coast," and when White asked what he advised, he said he should operate. ("Imagine asking a surgeon what he advises!" Will commented. "It would be like asking Coolidge, 'Do you advise economy?' ")

What bothered Will was that he had promised to speak at a banquet that night to raise money for Occidental College, and he prided himself on never disappointing an audience. It was finally arranged that his friend William S. Hart, the cowboy hero of the silent films, would take his place, and Hart and Betty both spoke at the dinner. Although Will was seriously ill following the operation, he managed not to miss a single one of his daily columns (he wrote no weekly article, however, between June 19 and July 17); just before he was wheeled away to the operating room, he dictated the daily wire ("I am in the California Hospital, where they are going to relieve me of surplus gall, much to the politicians' delight. . . . Never had an operation, so let the stones fall where they may"). On Sundays his wire did not appear, so he could skip Saturday, but on the next day he dictated his Monday message, just six words long: "Relax—lie perfectly still, just relax."

For a few days his condition was grave, and his sister Sallie came from Oklahoma to be with him. "I wouldn't have minded the whole thing so much," he informed his readers, "but they wouldn't let me have any chili or chili con carne as you amateur eaters call it. I sure do love my chili. If I could have just bogged down to a few bowls of good old greasy chili, I would have been well in a week. But I got the next best thing that I wanted, and that was some real cornbread. . . . I had to have my sister . . . show 'em how that should be made."

With an uncanny ability to put experience to good use, Will not only wrote about the operation in his daily and weekly articles (later using the story on the lecture circuit), but published several articles about it in the *Saturday Evening Post*, which were brought out later as a book, *Ether and Me, or "Just Relax."*

For a while he was down—but not out. Betty complained that "It was impossible for him not to be building something, starting something, or doing something. The nurses at the hospital had to watch him constantly to keep him from getting out of bed." While he was still hospitalized, hundreds of telegrams poured in from well-wishers, including President Coolidge, and as Will remarked, "People couldn't have been any nicer to me if I had died."

On his first day at home, "convalescing," he thought up the idea of offering $500 to the winner of a "non-stop flight" by Ford car from Claremore, Oklahoma, to Beverly Hills, California. The idea went into his daily article, and to his astonishment what had been intended as a joke produced a stream of Fords traveling between the two towns. Ten days later he was writing, "Say, stop that Ford-Claremore-Beverly Hills flight. They are coming in here from Oklahoma so thick we can't see the movie stars. Every time I hear a noise outside I know it is another Ford car. . . . I will be more careful with my jokes after this. It's costing me more to joke than I get for them. So if there are any more Fords coming please turn back. Imploringly." The next day he said, with finality, "The pay season on Oklahoma Fords entering Beverly Hills is closed, sine die, positively."

While he was still at home Calvin Coolidge, vacationing in the Black Hills, issued his famous statement about the 1928 election: "I do not choose to run." As Will saw it, this was "the best-worded acceptance of a nomination ever uttered by a candidate. He spent a long time in the dictionary looking for that word 'choose,' instead of 'I will not.' "

Back on his feet again, he began shooting what was to be his last silent film, *The Texas Steer*, in which he played the part of a Texas rancher who was elected to Congress. (When someone asked if he had read the script he replied, "Nope, what's the fun of making pictures if you know how they're goin' to come out?") When the company arrived in Washington, D.C., to film some political scenes against the backdrop of the Capitol, the National Press Club put on a reception for Will, invited most of the city's notable figures, and appointed him "congressman-at-large for the United States of America." Will was pleased with the reception and the speech in his honor, but said it was "the poorest appointment I ever got."

He went on to say, "I certainly regret the disgrace that's been thrust on me here tonight. I . . . have lived, or tried to live my life so that I would never become a Congressman."

While the Press Club's title was bestowed in fun, the next one Will received was intended seriously. He was invited to become the nation's "unofficial ambassador to Mexico."

Secretary of Commerce Herbert Hoover looks on as the National Press Club president presents a scroll to the new "congressman-at-large."
UPI

Back Home
In Oklahoma

*His native soil never lost its allure for Will
Rogers, who stopped off to visit the old Okla-
homa ranch house (above). whenever possible.
The photograph below—of Will asleep on the
ground, watched over by his vaudeville pony
Teddy—was taken near Claremore about 1912.*

BOTH: WILL ROGERS MEMORIAL, CLAREMORE, OKLA.

Although any moving target was fair game for Will, roping goats on the ranch became a particular passion.

MUSEUM OF MODERN ART

By 1926, when Will chinned with Aunt Juliette Schrimsher, Oologah's main street (right) had changed hardly at all since his youthful days.

BOTH: WILL ROGERS MEMORIAL, CLAREMORE, OKLA.

At Vinita's Old Settlers' Day in 1934 Will suggested the annual rodeo, which later was named for him.

WILL ROGERS MEMORIAL, CLAREMORE, OKLA.

Will Rogers says: "Coolidge…either nobody thinks he will do, or he won't

UNDERWOOD & UNDERWOOD

Mr. Coolidge attended his daily rodeo and the Sioux Indians made him big chief of their tribe. He said he didn't choose to be chief again, but he was drafted.

does one of two things: he does what do nothing. Generally the latter."

WIDE WORLD

UPI

I never liked him in that yachting cap.

Calvin sho' does look good in those cowboy clothes.

BROWN BROTHERS

And that old Mother Hubbard apron that they had him pitching hay in, for the pictures up in Vermont that time, was terrible. But those chaps will sure bring out the dude rancher vote. If he keeps on taking on all these mannish ways, why it looks like the old mechanical horse is liable to be for sale.

LIFE

Amusement — *Personalit..*
News — *Sport*

15 *Cents* — *November* 2 192.

WESTERN UNION

12019

PATRONS ARE REQUESTED TO FAVOR THE COMPANY BY CRITICISM AND SUGGESTION CONCERNING ITS SERVICE

SIGNS

DL = Day Letter
NM = Night Message
NL = Night Letter
LCO = Deferred Cable
CLT = Cable Letter
WLT = Week-End Letter

CLASS OF SERVICE

This is a full-rate Telegram or Cablegram unless its deferred character is indicated by a suitable sign above or preceding the address.

NEWCOMB CARLTON, PRESIDENT — J. C. WILLEVER, FIRST VICE-PRESIDENT

The filing time as shown in the date line on full-rate telegrams and day letters, and the time of receipt at destination as shown on all messages, is STANDARD TIME.

Received at 621 Madison Ave., New York

L1N FNI 28

NEWYORK NY 1025A NOV 1 1928

LIFE
598 MADISON AVE
SEND FOLLOWING WIRE TO WINNER COLON HEARTIEST CONGRATULATIONS ON
YOUR GREAT VICTORY STOP YOU WILL BE A FINE PRESIDENT STOP AS FOR
ME I WOULD RATHER BE RIGHT
WILL ROGERS
1030A

THE QUICKEST, SUREST AND SAFEST WAY TO S

**VOTE FOR ROGERS
VOTE FOR SMITH
VOTE FOR HOOVER
BUT — VOTE!**

"I'd rather be right than Republican."

In 1927 Will made a good-will visit to Mexico, as did Lindbergh (above, arriving in The Spirit of St. Louis*). After Will "ran" unsuccessfully for President in 1928 he sent the wire (left) to the winner.*
UPI

Relations between the United States and Mexico had never been serene. Following the war between the two countries in the 1840's, Mexico had given up the territory that now comprises the states of Arizona, Nevada, California, and Utah, parts of New Mexico, Colorado, and Wyoming, as well as its claims to Texas north of the Rio Grande. All in all, it was an acquisition of land by the United States second only to the Louisiana Purchase, and Mexicans had neither forgotten nor forgiven.

In 1916 President Wilson sent General John J. Pershing and a punitive expedition to Mexico to pursue the rebel "Pancho" Villa, whose guerrillas had been responsible for the deaths of Americans on both sides of the border; and a year later Americans were incensed by publication of the so-called Zimmermann Telegram. The German Foreign Secretary, Alfred Zimmermann, sent a message in code to the German minister in Mexico stating that if war between Germany and the U.S. broke out the diplomat should propose an alliance with Mexico by which the latter country would reconquer its lost territory in New Mexico, Texas, and Arizona.

Commercial interests in this country had pursued a policy of "dollar diplomacy" south of the border for years, and by the mid-twenties there was even talk in mining and oil circles of annexing Mexico—an attitude that had the tacit support of the American embassy there. By 1927, when President Coolidge named his Amherst College classmate Dwight Morrow as ambassador, relations could scarcely have been worse. Morrow was a partner in J.P. Morgan & Co., and there were those—including Will Rogers and a good many Mexicans—who looked on the appointment as a mixed blessing.

Will had a genuine affection and sympathy for the Mexicans, many of whom he had met in roping contests and rodeos, and he had decided views about the U.S. policy toward that country. "Up to now," he had written, "our calling card to Mexico or Central America had been a gunboat or violets shaped like Marines"; yet we couldn't understand why they didn't like us, since "we always had their goodwill and oil and coffee and minerals at heart. . . . So when the punitive smoke had cleared away we couldent figure out why they dident appreciate the fact that they had been shot in the most cordial manner possible, that we were only doing it for their own good. . . . We couldent realize their attitude in not falling on our necks and blessing us for giving them the assistance of our superior knowledge of government." Mexico, he concluded, "has got her problems and we are most of them."

Although he had some reservations about Morrow's potential effectiveness, Will was glad to see him "get into Mexico intact." As for his being a Morgan partner, maybe that would work to his advantage. Ever since Andrew Mellon, the Pittsburgh financier, had become Secretary of the Treasury, it had "kinder encouraged these rich men to get out and try and do something for their country. . . . If millionaires in the country would just go to work, why we wouldent need any immigration for years."

Early in November Will and Betty took some time off and roamed through the Southwest, sightseeing. According to Will, it was the first time in his life he had nothing to do and nowhere to go, and he decided to spend it as a tourist. Then he headed east for the long-awaited unveiling of Henry Ford's new automobile. After selling more than fifteen million Model T's since the first one appeared in 1909, Ford was switching to the so-called Model A, and Will proclaimed the news: "Here is what you have been waiting for for years; get ready, everybody. HE HAS CHANGED THE RADIATOR!" He flew in one of the new Ford trimotor transport planes and then returned to the West Coast to celebrate Thanksgiving, which he described as a holiday "started by the Pilgrims, who would give thanks every time they killed an Indian and took more of his land." What we had to give thanks for in 1927, he added, was what the Republicans had given the country: a war in Nicaragua and China and a rehearsal for one in Mexico, two floods, a coal strike, and pictures of the Black Hills, where Coolidge spent his vacation. At the end of the month his readers learned that he was going to

As one of Henry Ford's biggest boosters, Will was given the first Model A car.
WILL ROGERS MEMORIAL, CLAREMORE, OKLA.

make a trip to Mexico.

Shortly after Ambassador Morrow arrived at his post he had an inspiration: to invite Will Rogers and Charles A. Lindbergh to visit the country on a goodwill mission. Already, Morrow had gotten off on the right foot with the Mexican man in the street by touring the country for several weeks with President Plutarco Calles. (Many wealthy Mexicans who regarded Calles as a revolutionary criticized Morrow, who, in turn, told them bluntly, "I came here accredited to this Government to the men who are at present running it, and not to the aristocracy.") Will showed up in time to join the two men aboard the heavily guarded Presidential train.

On the second day of the trip he was late for dinner, and a member of Calles' party who found him talking with the troops suggested that it was impolitic to keep the President waiting. "You tell President Calles," Will said, "that I've been in Mexico only a few days and I have found out that it's better down here to stand in right with the soldiers than with the President." One American who was on the train recalled that Will "was all over the place making jokes, very impertinent, making fun of everybody and getting away with it." One reason he succeeded so well was that Calles' interpreter was an American named Jim Smithers, who had a gift for reproducing Will's comments in Spanish.

Will's candor endeared him immediately to Calles, as did his love of close harmony singing, which he and Morrow performed to the accompaniment of the Presidential guitar. He attended a bullfight (to the amusement of the crowd he buried his head in his arms to avoid seeing horses gored by the bull), he played polo, flew over the crater he called "Popocatepillar," and was guest of honor at a banquet given by Morrow and attended by Calles—the first time a Mexican President had ever visited the American embassy.

As his contribution to the goodwill mission, Lindbergh had agreed to fly nonstop from Washington to Mexico City, but lost his way somewhere over Mexico. While he flew over the countryside trying to locate the airfield, two hundred thousand people, including President Calles and his cabinet officers, waited patiently for eight hours and then gave him as tumultuous a welcome as he had received in Paris. As Will described it, "In France and America they like to tore up the plane to carry off souvenirs. Here hundreds took it up on their own shoulders and carried it to the hangar. Here instead of being bombarded with ticker tape the streets were two inches thick with flowers." He and Morrow were resigning as ambassadors, he said; Lindbergh was taking over. Seemingly, the only person in the country who didn't care about seeing the aviator was Dwight Morrow's twenty-year-old daughter Anne, who had just arrived for the Christmas holidays and considered Lindbergh no more than a newspaper hero—the baseball player type, and "not at all 'intellectual' and not of my world at all." She was certainly not going to worship Lindy ("that *odious* name," she called it); but when she met him at the embassy she found him much more poised than she had expected—tall, slim, a boy in evening dress, with a refined face that was unlike the grinning Lindy pictures she had seen. (A year later she was writing to a friend to say, "Apparently I am going to marry Charles Lindbergh.")

Mrs. Morrow worried about the effect Lindbergh's arrival might have on Will Rogers' popularity. Will was scheduled to

Will hated Mexico's bullfights (too many horses were hurt), but he thoroughly enjoyed a roping and riding exhibition at Rancho de Charros, with Morrow (left) and Lindbergh (third from right).

WILL ROGERS MEMORIAL, CLAREMORE, OKLA.

speak at a dinner that very evening, and she felt both sorry and nervous for him. But Will was more than equal to the occasion. "From the first sentence he held the whole room in the hollow of his hand," she recalled. "I had entirely underestimated his power and his understanding of an audience. He shocked, flattered, cajoled, teased, tormented and enchanted the guests." Like audiences everywhere, when they were exposed to the typical Will Rogers performance they loved it. "I didn't come here to tell you that we look on you as brothers," he began. "Nope, not at all. We look on you as a lot of bandits. And you look on us as one big bandit."

Then he offered some views on diplomacy: "A diplomat tells you what he don't believe himself, and the man he's tellin' it to don't believe him, so it balances. Diplomats meet and eat, then rush out and wire their Government they've completely fooled the other fella." But Morrow, he said, was different: he recognized that the only way for people to get along was to be honest and tell each other what they think and get to understand one another. "He knows we don't hate you and that you don't hate us." But just so the ambassador did not escape unscathed, Will gestured to his wife: "There at the head table is Mrs. Morrow," he said. "She's the only one who ought to be there. She got a degree at Smith. Then one day she went slumming to Amherst and got herself a husband."

From the point of view of Morrow and of relations between Mexico and the United States, Will's visit was a triumph, and he carried away a lasting attachment for the ambassador, whom he described as "Wall Street's sole contribution to public life."

The meetings with Lindbergh in Mexico served only to whet Will's appetite for flying. He had been introduced to the flyer even before the Mexico trip, when Lindbergh came to California in September to be welcomed in Los Angeles and to visit the Ryan factory in San Diego, where *The Spirit of St. Louis* was built. Will and Betty went to San Diego, where there was the inevitable dinner, with one speaker after another heaping praise on the "Lone Eagle." Then Will got to his feet. All those other orators, Will told the aviator, had been talking about his wonderful record, "but they ain't mentioned the one record that will remain unsurpassed and go unbroken down through the ages. This is that you are the only man who ever took a ham sandwich to Paris."

The next day Betty and Will flew with Lindbergh in a Ford

plane, with Will in the copilot's seat discussing aviation and asking innumerable questions.

"How can you tell where to land when you don't know which way the wind is blowing?" was one of them, to which Lindbergh replied by pointing to a clothesline on which laundry was flapping in the breeze.

"That tells me," he said.

"Suppose it ain't Monday?" Will asked.

"I just wait till it is," Lindbergh responded.

Will flew part of the way home from Mexico to be with his family for Christmas, and on December 29 he was in the air again, this time courtesy of the U.S. Navy. He took his first flight in a plane catapulted from the battleship *Pennsylvania.* "Just watch your head," he advised, "and see that you don't leave it behind you." And to President Coolidge he said, "Keep after this air stuff, Calvin. Let's get all the planes we can, do all the commercial aviation we can to keep the boys in training, and get our navy fleet the biggest there is."

The "Lone Eagle" and the cowboy-philosopher first made their acquaintance when Lindbergh visited San Diego, California, in September, 1927.

WILL ROGERS MEMORIAL, CLAREMORE, OKLA.

The year 1928 had barely begun when Will was involved in the most ambitious radio program ever put on—a nationwide hookup connecting forty-five stations at the then unheard of cost of $1,000 a minute. Fred and Dorothy Stone in Chicago, Al Jolson in New Orleans, and Paul Whiteman's orchestra in New York were all introduced by the master of ceremonies, Will Rogers, speaking from his home in Beverly Hills, and the program was no sooner under way than Will announced that he had a surprise for the millions of listeners.

"I want to introduce a friend of mine who is here and wishes to speak to you," he said, and then, pursing his lips and imitating the high-pitched Vermont twang of Calvin Coolidge, he delivered his version of the President's State of the Union message. The President had recently returned from a western trip intended to mollify hard-pressed farmers, and the speech began with reassurances to them.

"Farmers, I am proud to report that the country as a whole is prosperous. I don't mean by that that the whole country is prosperous, but as a hole it is prosperous. That is, it is prosperous for a hole. A hole is not supposed to be prosperous and you are certainly in a hole. There is not a whole lot of doubt about that."

He turned to other subjects. Secretary of the Treasury Andrew Mellon, he observed, "has saved some money for the country and done very well for himself. . . . He is the only treasurer that has saved faster than Congress could divide it up. . . . Congress is here now though to grab what he had got. . . . Just a few words on the public issues of the day. . . . They won't seat two Republican senators. . . . The Democrats dident mind them buying their seats but it was the price they paid. . . . On our Foreign Debts, I am sorry to state that they are just as Foreign as ever, if not more so. . . . Prohibition, prohibition is going down about as well as usual. . . ."

He was a good mimic, and to his dismay a surprising number of people across the country actually believed that Coolidge was talking. He immediately sent the President a note explaining that the thing had been meant in fun, and back from the White House came a letter in Coolidge's hand telling Will not to give it a moment's thought: "I thought the matter of rather small consequence myself, though the office was informed from several sources that I had been on the air." The exchange merely confirmed Will's views about poking fun at important figures: "You can always joke good naturedly a big man, but be

Will waves from a Navy plane as it is hoisted aboard. the battleship Pennsylvania.
WILL ROGERS MEMORIAL, CLAREMORE, OKLA.

sure he is a big man before you joke about him."

It was another Presidential election year, and politics, naturally, were beginning to dominate the news. As Will left for the Democrats' Jackson Day dinner in Washington, D.C., it occurred to him that if the country could just settle on a candidate it could do away with both political conventions. "There is nothing as useless as a delegate to a political convention," he said, "unless it is the man that he is a delegate for." Where the conventions would be held was still an open question, but he assumed that the Democrats would have to draft some town, since none had applied for the honor, and he just hoped Claremore "don't draw it. We are just getting on our feet good there now." When he heard that Houston, Texas, had been selected he was delighted. "I certainly did what I was sent here to do; I kept it out of Oklahoma."

The Jackson Day dinner brought back old memories about what the Cherokees had suffered at Old Hickory's hands, and, Will remarked, "I am not so sweet on old Andy. He is the one that run us Cherokees out of Georgia and North Carolina. I ate the dinner on him, but I didn't enjoy it. I thought I was eating for Stonewall." After hearing all the speeches he concluded that "Democrats can just naturally stand more oratory than any other race," but since they "save up four years stuff to tell about the Republicans . . . it's sure worth the money."

After a brief visit to the Pan-American conference in Havana, he left at once on another lecture tour, and on the platform and in newspaper columns emphasized his growing concern about the nation's economic health. What he said came across in the familiar Rogers' style, couched in good-humored remarks, but there was no mistaking his worry over the situation. His trips around the country had convinced him that the good times Americans were enjoying were only on the surface. The attitude of most people was, "We'll show the world we are prosperous, even if we have to go broke to do it." One of the chief culprits, he believed, was the New York Stock Exchange, where "They stand and yell and sell something they haven't got, and buy something they will never get." Another was the almost universal reliance on borrowed money—a habit he tried to avoid in his personal affairs and wished the Federal government would shun. "We don't have to worry about anything," he remarked with some irony. "No nation in the history of the world was ever sitting as pretty. If we want anything all we have to do is go and buy it on credit. So that leaves us without any economic problem whatever, except perhaps some day to have to pay for them. But we are certainly not thinking about that this early. Yours for more credit and longer payments.''

His belief that America's well-being was largely illusory was a theme that recurred again and again, even when he seemed to be talking about something else. "Somebody is always quoting figures to prove that the country is prosperous," he observed, "but the only real bona fide indication of it was in the paper today: 'Divorces in Reno have increased over 105 per cent in the last year.' Now, that's prosperity, for you can't be broke and get a divorce. That's why the poor have to live with each other. . . . I maintain that it should cost as much to get married as to get divorced. Make it look like marriage is worth as much as divorce, even if it ain't.''

Summer brought the two national conventions, the political "follies" toward which his attitude was so ambivalent. He had no use for them and enjoyed them at the same time; he could savor all the color and flavor they produced while laughing at the foolishness. It was his conviction that there would not be an original thought uttered during the entire affair and that "no other Country in the world would understand or know for what reason it was being held. But we like it, and its distinctly ours. Its the one place where our public men can do foolish things and due to the surroundings they kinder look plausable at the time. It takes weeks after one is over to really start to appreciate the finer comedy points of one. . . . But when we get home and take one of these conventions apart and just see what was really inside it, why then is when our sense of humor asserts itself. But its too late to do anything about it then, so we just smile and wait four years, and here they are back again.''

All that the noise and excitement and tomfoolery amounted to in the end was that "Those that are in are trying to stay in, and those that are out are trying to get in.''

Two weeks before the Republican convention began, Will made his own debut as a Presidential candidate. The humor magazine *Life* announced that it was sponsoring a new political movement, the Anti-Bunk party, with Will Rogers as its nominee. This was the brain child of Robert E. Sherwood, editor of the periodical, and Fred Cooper, the art director, and it had a genesis of sorts in the campaign of 1924, when Will was nominated by two Arizona delegates to the Democratic convention and received a scattering of write-in votes during the election.

As Sherwood told the story, he went to see Will at the Astor Hotel in New York and talked him into the scheme. Will gave the Anti-Bunk party its name and agreed to write several hundred words each week, describing its program. "We had one hell of a time getting copy out of him," Sherwood said. "When he did get it in it was very sketchy and never nearly enough of it to fill the necessary space. So I filled it out, imitating Will's style as best I could." This was Sherwood's first experience as a ghostwriter for a Presidential candidate, a job he undertook more seriously for Franklin D. Roosevelt in the 1932 campaign and later.

In the issue announcing his candidacy, Will stated that *Life*'s offer had struck him like "a bolt from the Blue" and had left him dazed, but "If I stay dazed, I ought to make a splendid candidate." His acceptance was based on one pledge: "If elected I absolutely and positively agree to resign [and] that's offering the Country more than any Candidate ever offered it in the history of its entire existence." From then until the election in November, the opening editorial pages of the magazine were devoted to a speech purportedly written by Will, followed by Anti-Bunk bulletins composed by Sherwood.

No candidate for the Vice Presidency was chosen, although Lindbergh was considered and rejected on the grounds that he had done too much for the nation "to be rewarded with a sentence of four years in the United States Senate." When it came to the platform, the Anti-Bunk candidate promised that "whatever the other fellow don't do, we will." There were no commitments. "We want the wet vote, and we want the dry vote," Will stated. "We are honest about it . . . so our Plank will run something about as follows: 'Wine for the rich, beer for the poor, and moonshine liquor for the prohibitionist.' "

Thousands of buttons were distributed, showing a picture of Will with the slogan, "He chews to run." As Sherwood said, this was the first Presidential candidate who was intentionally funny, and his Cherokee blood made him an authentic pre-*Mayflower* American. There would be no party leaders ("that's what hurts our two big Political Parties worse than getting caught"); no slogans ("slogans have been more harmful to the country than Luncheon Clubs, Sand Fleas, Detours and Conventions"); no "baby kissing, passing out of cigars, laying cornerstones, dodging issues"; and the candidate would not disguise himself as a farmer, "with a rake in one hand and a sap bucket in the other."

"So much money is being spent on the campaigns that I doubt if either man, as good as they are, are worth what it will cost to elect them."

from Daily Telegram
Oct. 8, 1928

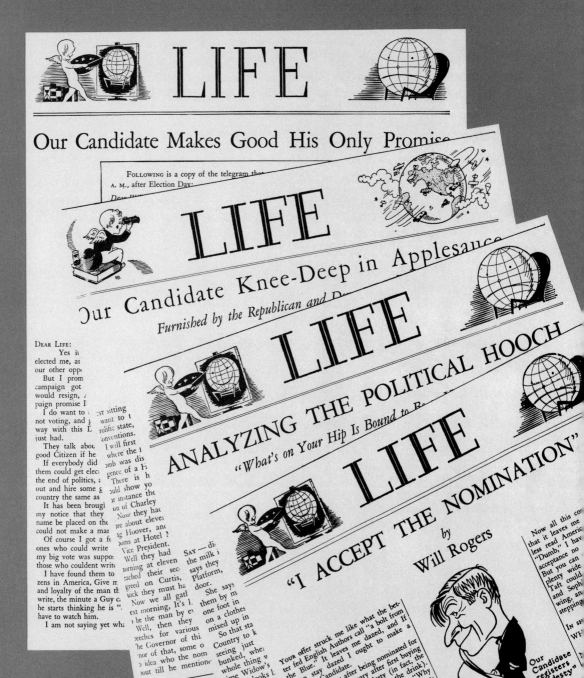

"ELECT ROGERS AND HE WILL RESIGN" *was Will's initial pledge as the Anti-Bunk candidate. His platform appeared in the humor magazine* Life: "WHATEVER THE OTHER FELLOW DON'T DO, WE WILL."

While the voters were absorbing all this, Will was en route to Kansas City, where the Republicans were gathering "to await word from Mr. Mellon as to who will be nominated." During the flight from the Coast his plane broke a wheel while landing and flipped over, which caused Will to comment that he was "the first candidate to land on his head, and being a candidate, it didn't hurt the head." On Sunday he made the rounds of Kansas City's churches, but saw not one candidate or convention delegate in any of them. "Still, this fall, in the campaign, you will hear them get up and shout 'Our religion is the bulwark of our great and glorious country . . . our Church is our salvation.' Well, our Churches are our salvation, but some of these babies won't be among those rescued."

Will said the convention opened with a fervent prayer that Al Smith would not be nominated, and he thought that "If the Lord

Three eminent journalists relax at the Republican convention in Kansas City: Will, columnist David Lawrence, and Emporia's William Allen White.

UNDERWOOD & UNDERWOOD

can see his way clear to bless the Republican Party the way it's been carrying on, then the rest of us ought to even get it without asking for it." If you could believe the keynote speech—an impromptu address that the speaker had been working on for six months—the Republicans were responsible for radios, telephones, baths, automobiles, savings accounts, Prohibition enforcement, workmen's housing, and a living wage for Senators, whereas the Democrats had brought on "War, pestilence, debts, Disease, Bo weevil, Gold teeth, need of Farm relief, suspenders, floods, [and] famines." At one point Will thought the speaker referred to "Our Saviour," but it turned out that he was talking about Coolidge, and the way he rated the world's three greatest men was Coolidge, the Lord, and Lincoln, in that order. When he spoke about money and told how many billions had been saved by the administration, "his voice reached a crescendo"; when he talked about expenditures he spoke in an undertone.

After Herbert Hoover was nominated for President, Will was tickled to see that Charles Curtis was picked for the second spot on the ticket. Curtis was a Kaw Indian, and it was "the first time we have ever got a break—the only American that has ever run for that high office. . . . Come on Injun," he pleaded, "if you are elected let's run the white people out of this country." Soon afterward, Will was in Houston for the Democratic convention, and someone suggested that he run for Vice President on the Democratic ticket, since he was a Cherokee. "Vote for Rogers," he said, "and scalp the Kaws."

Houston was as hot as a Texas city can be at the end of June, and it occurred to Will that if the convention delegates were not helping democracy they were certainly perspiring for it. He listened to Franklin Roosevelt, "a fine and wonderful man who has devoted his life to nominating Al Smith . . . do his act from memory. Franklin Roosevelt could have gotten far in the Democratic party himself. But he has this act all perfected, and dont like to go to the trouble of learning something else. So he just seems satisfied going through life nominating Al Smith."

When it was all over, he considered that the party had nominated its best possible ticket: Governor Alfred E. Smith of New York and Senator Joseph Robinson of Arkansas. The principal issues were Prohibition and Smith's Catholicism, and Will had something to say about each. Smith favored the repeal of Prohibition and Robinson opposed repeal, which meant that the Democrats had straddled the issue, but Will thought that

"The Literary Digest is taking a poll to see how many people there are in the United States who are interested in politics that can write their name. Up to now there has been about a third more Republicans that can write than Democrats."

from Daily Telegram
Oct. 18, 1928

"The only thing I got against Al was his seconders. If so many hadn't seconded him he would have been home a week ago. If his seconders all vote for him he will walk in."

from Daily Telegram
June 28, 1928

247

would be a problem. "They got a wet head and a dry tail. Its better to have your feet wet than your head."

On the subject of Smith's religion he had a characteristically down-to-earth approach. "What do we care about a mans Religion, we dont want to be saved spiritually we want to be dragged out of the hole financially. He has been three times Governor of New York. The Jews elected him. Now if they can trust him to run the biggest state in the world where they own 90 percent of it and trust a Catholic over a Protestant why we shouldnt mind . . . what do we care about a Presidents religion. They dont do any business on Sunday anyway. Its week days we want to use him. Its one relief to find somebody mentioned for President who we do know what their religion is before they get in. There is not 2 out of 10 that can tell me what religion Coolidge is."

In a sense, Hoover's nomination at Kansas City had come as a surprise to Will. During 1927 and the early months of 1928 he remained convinced that Coolidge would run again, and he was one of the few who believed that the Vermonter meant something less than refusal when he said, "I do not choose to run." He had even made a $5,000 bet with publisher William Randolph Hearst that Coolidge would be the Republican nominee—probably as the result of a draft. As Will put it before the convention, the delegates would have to decide whether that word "choose" meant "yes, no, maybe, I can't tell yet, who knows, search me, probably, or perhaps," but he was certain it meant "will," provided enough pressure was exerted by the party.

After Hoover's nomination, Will suggested that Coolidge pay half of his bet with Hearst, since "he layed down on me," but his enthusiasm for the retiring President died hard. As late as October 24 he was still saying of Hoover and Smith that "Coolidge could start tomorrow and beat both of them."

He liked and admired both Presidential candidates, but he wanted everyone to know that neither was likely to be himself during the campaign, since they would be putting on the usual election year show for the public. That was one thing about Coolidge, he said, you couldn't tell when he was acting and when he wasn't. "He was like a ukelele. You can't tell when somebody is playing one or just monkeying with it."

What disturbed him most during the campaign was the way the two parties tried to influence voters on the issue of prosperity. "How a speaker can convince a man that he is pros-

"When the editorial writers get all through analyzing all the various reasons for Smith's defeat—religion, prohibition, Tammany, brown hats, prosperity, wisecracks . . . and all the rest of them— maybe one of them will accidentally hit on the real reason, A Democrat."

from Daily Telegram
Nov. 9, 1928

perous when he is broke, or that he is not prosperous when he is doing well, is beyond me. If a voter can't feel in his pockets and see if he is doing well without having some total stranger tell him, then this Government shouldn't be in the hands of the people. We might as well have candidates argue with us that we have a pain in our stomach."

As the campaign drew to a close, Will was disgusted with the whole thing, and just before election day he wrote, "Well, the promising season ends next Tuesday, and at about 8 o'clock that same night the 'Alibi' season opens and lasts for the next four years. . . . This campaign ends Tuesday, but it will take two generations to sweep up the dirt." Listing all the statements and promises the two candidates had made, he concluded that he would come out for himself, but since his name had been left off the ballot "owing to jealousy, and me not paying my entrance fees," he suggested that people vote for Norman Thomas, the Socialist candidate. "In case he gets in," he added, "we will split it, I will run the Government and he can do the fishing." Speaking more seriously, he predicted that Hoover was a shooin—had been, in fact, since the G.O.P. convention in June. Smith's problem was that he was a Democrat.

The day after Hoover's election the daily telegram appeared in the form of a want ad. "FOR SALE," it read: "Would like to sell, trade, dispose of or give away to right parties franchise of what is humorously known as Democratic Party. . . . If in right hands and only used in times when it had an 'issue' or when the Republican Party had split, think it could be made to pay, but present owners have absolutely no business with it. Under present management they have killed off more good men than grade crossings have."

As the year came to a close he was depressed by the state of the Democratic party, but more so by the state of the nation. In an unusually bittersweet column that is Will Rogers at his best, he told his readers why:

The nation never looked like it was facing a worse Winter. Birds, geese, Democrats and all perishable animals are already huddled up in three or four States down South. We are at peace with the world because the world is waiting to get another gun and get it loaded. Wall Street is in good shape, but Eighth Avenue never was as bad off. The farmers are going into the Winter with pretty good radios, but not much feed for their stock.

Yours,
Will Rogers

BOTH: CULVER PICTURES

"If you have missed anybody . . . and have no idea where they are, they are right here in Beverly Hills trying to get into the talkies."

After he and Betty arrived in Los Angeles (left) in June, 1929, Will began work on his first talking picture, They Had to See Paris, *from which the scene above is taken. Will winces from impending embrace by a titled Russian.*

Herbert Hoover was elected President of the United States in 1928, but the editors of *Life* concluded that Will Rogers was the unanimous, if unofficial, choice of what they called the Great Silent Vote. The newspapers, they wired Will on election night, might say that the other candidates had piled up millions of votes, but that had little to do with the true sentiments of the country. "You're in," the message read, and, in a sense, they were right. By now he was one of the most popular and best loved of all Americans.

This was in some respects a reflection of his total public personality—the folksy humorist, the old country boy who remained a country boy, the homespun columnist who seemed able to put his finger so accurately on what was troubling people and put things into perspective for them. But there was something else, too—a quality Will had of giving himself wholeheartedly and unstintingly to causes in which he believed deeply. There had been the Red Cross, notably, various public benefits, and small personal acts of kindness without number. And in the summer of 1928 he came to the aid of an old friend in his typically generous way, which everyone admired.

That spring the actor Fred Stone had learned to fly, and in April Will had flown with him from New York to Hagerstown, Maryland. On August 4 Stone was critically injured when his plane crashed, and the next day Will's daily telegram asked his readers to pray for the actor's return to the stage. In the meantime, he had taken matters into his own hands. Stone was to open on Broadway that fall with his daughter, Dorothy, in a musical called *Three Cheers*. The show was already in rehearsal, the opening date was set, costumes and sets were made, but there was no chance whatever that Stone could appear. When Will heard about the accident he immediately wired his friend to say that he would go into the show in Fred's place, "just to sort of plug along till you are able to rejoin, and I will do the best I can with the part." Dorothy could tell him how Fred would have played it, and she would of course be the star—Will didn't even want any billing. Beyond the fact that this offer meant a considerable extra drain on his time and energy, it also meant that he would have to cancel his lecture tour at some financial sacrifice and give up other plans as well in order to stay with the show.

According to Betty, Will had only two weeks of rehearsals before the opening, and that in itself was a new experience for him; he said he had been twenty-three years on the stage and never rehearsed his lines before. But it didn't seem to matter. The musical opened on October 25 and was an immediate smash hit. Will, of course, was playing himself—not the part written for Fred Stone. Although he sang the songs ("I feel that is as far as any man has ever gone for a friend," he remarked) and was dressed as King Pompanola of Itza, wearing a crown and red leggings, he kept the script in his hip pocket, consulted it shamelessly, and simply used the part as a vehicle for the kind of routine he had done in the Follies for years—commenting on the news in the latest editions of the papers.

"I am afraid Will Rogers disorganized the show," one reviewer said, "but so far as I am concerned, he can continue to disorganize shows for the rest of his and my life." He added that he had "learned more about American politics from Mr. Rogers in one evening than I have learnt from all the editorials and textbooks I have read. . . ." Another critic suggested that "all other inferior comedians" should make a study of his technique. Rogers' material, he said, was his own and inimitable, but he had a way of putting it over that no one else quite matched. Analyzing it, he thought it was a matter of progression and timing—first one statement, then another, then a third, all making perfectly good sense and often funny enough so that the listener began to smile. Then would come a sudden final thrust, followed by an explosion of laughter. "Will Rogers," he said, "is master of this slow-fuse business." What was unique about Will was a public platform manner that made it possible for him to talk to an audience privately and confidentially: "Even before he opens his mouth to speak, the barrier of the footlights is down and we are in the same room with him." Without that, and without what the critic called his "drawling tact," some of the things he said about prominent people would have sounded fresh or in poor taste.

Robert Sherwood of *Life* offered another view of *Three Cheers*. What he liked best about it was the fact that Will put on a different performance every night. A person could see the show at a matinee and return that evening and not know it was the same musical. This unpredictability, Sherwood noticed, did not please the theatre doorman, who was responsible for letting chauffeurs know what time they should call for their parties after the show. Some nights the curtain would ring down a little after eleven; but other times, if Will was in an especially talka-

In top hat, white tie, tails, and bare feet, Andy Tombes and Will run through a number from Three Cheers *for the recuperating Fred Stone, daughter Dorothy, and wife.*

WILL ROGERS MEMORIAL, CLAREMORE, OKLA.

tive mood and the audience was especially receptive, he might keep going until midnight.

This was to be Will's final Broadway performance. After a successful New York run, *Three Cheers* went on the road in April, 1929, and closed in Pittsburgh on June 1. The following day Will flew to California to launch another career: playing in talking pictures.

As noted, Thomas Edison had originally planned to combine his Kinetoscope with a phonograph to produce a moving picture with sound accompaniment, and although he lost interest in the scheme, other inventors had not. Lee de Forest, originator of the audion tube that had made long-distance broadcasting feasible, synchronized sound and moving images on film,

A hit: Connecticut Yankee *(1931) with Myrna Loy*
BOTH: CULVER PICTURES, 20th CENTURY FOX FILM CORP.

and his first "phonofilms" were shown in New York in 1923, but without causing much of a stir. Nor had Hollywood displayed any particular enthusiasm for talking pictures until 1926, when William Fox brought out something called a Movietone, and the nearly bankrupt Warner Brothers company agreed to take on the Vitaphone produced by a subsidiary of the Western Electric Company. The first sound films were shorts, but in 1927 the Warners produced *The Jazz Singer*, starring Al Jolson, which was the first feature film with sound dialogue and music. It was an immediate and stunning success, and the rest of Hollywood realized that the old silent days were gone for good (only Charlie Chaplin held out into the thirties).

Like all revolutions, this one left a cluster of pathetic derelicts in its wake—those once-popular stars whose voices were not suited to the new medium. Pola Negri and Clara Bow, the "It Girl," disappeared, and John Gilbert, the great lover of the silent screen whose high-pitched voice was incongruous for the roles he played, committed suicide rather than face the oblivion to which the talkies doomed him.

But to a Will Rogers, talkies were quite another matter. The fact was that he had never been as successful in silent pictures as he had been on the stage or the lecture platform, simply because his act was so dependent on what he had to say and the way he said it. When he went into talking pictures he had something else going for him, too—a considerable reputation as a hu-

Listening to Stepin Fetchit in Judge Priest *(1934)*

morist and commentator, a personality already familiar to millions of Americans.

From the beginning Will took a relaxed, amused view of what he called the "noisies." As the Hollywood studios moved full tilt into production of sound films, he commented that "Everybody that can't sing has a double that can, and everybody that can't talk is going right on and proving it." Everyone he met was chattering like a parrot, just practicing talking, "so busy ennunciating that they pay no attention to what they are saying." He had been on the stage for twenty-three years, he added, and never heard the word "annunciation" or knew what it was. In the old days, everybody "was practicing to make signs. Now they are practicing noises."

Yet when Will's first talkie, *They Had to See Paris*, opened in September, 1929, he refused to attend the preview. The excuse he gave readers of his daily telegram was that the producers were charging $5 for a ticket, "and I just couldn't stand by and be a party to such brigandage"; but Homer Croy, who wrote the script for the film, had a rather different version of why Will didn't show up. It was the old nervousness and lack of assurance that accompanied each new venture he attempted. As the time approached for the picture to be shown, Will became increasingly apprehensive, and finally announced to the startled studio executives that he had to go to Oklahoma and would not attend the preview. He was not himself, Croy said, and even

With Zasu Pitts and unruly bear in Mr. Skitch *(1933)*
MUSEUM OF MODERN ART, 20th CENTURY FOX FILM CORP.

refused to have his picture taken as he climbed into a plane bound for Tulsa. Not until the day after he arrived in Oklahoma was his mind set at ease; he received a telegram from Betty reporting that the picture had opened and he could come home now.

Not surprisingly, the talkies he made ran to a pattern. In them he usually played a thinly disguised version of himself: a rustic, somewhat seedy common man, an underdog speaking out against wealthier, unscrupulous characters. He was the kindly, impractical philosopher, a sort of deputy of the American conscience, reflecting the innate honesty and idealism of the plain folks of the land.

256

Unlike most Hollywood movies of the period in which romantic love was revealed to be the single most important objective in life, in Will's pictures the love interest was subdued and secondary. To see any of the talkies he made—*A Connecticut Yankee in King Arthur's Court, David Harum, The County Chairman, State Fair, Life Begins at Forty, Steamboat 'Round the Bend,* and others—is to be transported suddenly into another world, a world that was gentle, kind, and thoroughly predictable. The simple virtues and homely truths were always opposed by easily discernible villainy, and while the vicissitudes appeared to be insurmountable, there was never any doubt that good would triumph at the end. They were not only pictures that children wanted to see; they were pictures the children's parents *wanted*

With Mickey Rooney in The County Chairman *(1935)*
CULVER PICTURES, 20TH CENTURY FOX FILM CORP.

them to see, and in some towns school was dismissed so that students could attend special matinee performances of a Will Rogers film. Will Hays, president of the Motion Picture Producers and Distributors of America (who had also established a production code governing the morals of movies), explained why Will's pictures were never censored. "Will never would make a movie that parents didn't want their children to see," he said. "I talked with him about a story a friend of his wanted him to do. 'I know it is a fine play by a great writer,' he said, 'but it's for grownups. Most of the story is great but there is a scene in it that people wouldn't want their children to see. You can't omit that scene without spoiling the story. It should not be left out, but I just don't want to play in any picture where folks may think they shouldn't have brought their children.' "

Will was a thoroughly untypical Hollywood star. Although a considerable portion of his income came from making movies, he never quite took it seriously, and it never became more than a sideline as far as he was concerned. He was simply not a part of Hollywood. Every tourist who visited the movie capital wanted to see him, and he was continually badgered at the studio by people who dropped by to meet him and hear him talk. They came to his office in Beverly Hills, they appeared at the Santa Monica ranch, and on most occasions he obliged by interrupting what he was doing to say a few words to them. Then one evening when he and Betty were returning home they saw a sightseeing bus in the drive to the ranch, with a guide telling tourists all about the Rogers home and its occupants. It was too much for Betty, and despite Will's protests that it wouldn't be neighborly, she insisted on putting a gate at the entrance, three-quarters of a mile from the house.

Despite his growing fame, his dress remained as casual as his personality—as often as not he wore blue jeans and boots and the small cowboy Stetson or a well-traveled felt hat. He drove his own car to the studio, the back seat filled with the paraphernalia of his trade: portable typewriter, a stack of newspapers, telegraph blanks, ropes, some old clothes, and an extra pair of boots. When he arrived, it was evident that he was the most popular person on the lot; everyone said good morning to Will Rogers.

What never failed to astound old hands in the business was Will's approach to making a picture. The night before shooting was to begin he would take the script home and read it through, just to get the gist of it, and the next morning would appear on the set with no idea whatsoever of what his lines were. Oblivious to all the hectic activity around him, he would slouch in a canvas chair, eyeglasses down on his nose, reading the morning papers. He never bothered to memorize lines; when he was called to play a scene he would ask the script girl to read what he was supposed to say and that, as often as not, would remind him of a story he would tell while the director and other players waited. This could lead to one digression after another until the director announced that the day was getting on and they had to complete a certain amount of shooting.

At last they would begin, and those actors who were newcomers to the business of playing opposite Will Rogers sud-

Young Shirley Temple succeeded Will as top box-office attraction the year of his death.
CULVER PICTURES
20th CENTURY FOX FILM CORP.

denly realized what it meant. Most of them, Joel McCrea remembers, were scared to death, because no one knew for certain what he would say or how long he might talk. As one of Will's cameramen described an actor's dilemma, "He waits for a certain cue in a speech. The cue doesn't come. For Will ad-libs his lines. Furthermore, he improvises them differently every time he plays the scene. . . . It isn't because he's too lazy to learn them; it's because each time he rehearses a scene he thinks of a better way of delivering a speech. Something spontaneous that fits the situation far better than the lines the author has written." When Will and the humorist Irvin Cobb were performing in *Steamboat 'Round the Bend* the director, John Ford, finally asked if either of them had the faintest idea of what the story was about, or whether they had had time to glance at the script.

"Been too busy roping calves, John," Will replied. "Tell you what, you sort of generally break the news to us what this sequence is about, and I'll think up a line for Irvin to speak, and then he'll think up a line for me to speak and that way there won't be no ill feelings or heart-burnings."

It was Will's idea that Cobb, who was no actor, should play opposite him in that film just because they were old friends and Will enjoyed his company. Cobb had been a newspaperman before he began writing humorous books and short stories (the movie *Judge Priest*, in which Will starred, was based on them) and was one of the few men ever to get the best of Will in an exchange of wit. Both were speakers at a dinner in New York, and Will Hays introduced Will Rogers, saying that "when this Oklahoma cowboy first strolled in here from the open spaces, it did not take New York long to discover that Will Rogers had something under the old ten-gallon hat besides hair."

Without a second's hesitation Cobb jumped to his feet. "Ladies and gentlemen," he said, "I want to endorse from a full heart the glowing words that have just been spoken, and I want to add that it was high time somebody in this broad land of ours said a good word for dandruff."

At the end of the morning's shooting when it was time to break for lunch, Will would call out "Lunchee! Lunchee!" and head for the studio cafeteria trailed by the cast and crew, who knew they would be entertained by a running barrage of jokes throughout the meal. Afterward he would walk out to his car, climb in, and thumb through the newspapers again, marking items that interested him with the stub of an old pencil. When

Released in 1932, Too Busy to Work *was the ninth talkie in which Will played the lead.*
CULVER PICTURES
20th CENTURY FOX FILM CORP.

he had what he wanted, he would put the typewriter on his lap and sit with his feet on the running board—a picture of utter concentration—pecking away at the daily article. Frequently, he took the finished copy and read it to the studio crew to get their reaction, and if they didn't get what he was trying to say he would change it, send for a messenger, and ask him to take it to the telegraph office. Then, to the director's dismay, he might disappear to the car again for a nap.

One quality he had that was virtually unheard of in the acting profession was to help other members of the cast by making suggestions as to how they could improve their lines or their timing. (Louise Dresser, who played opposite Will in a number of films, wished that "every newcomer to the screen could play

In Life Begins at 40 (*1935*), *with Slim Summerville*
BOTH: CULVER PICTURES, 20th CENTURY FOX FILM CORP.

his first picture with Will Rogers, for with him to help, that camera panic from which we have all suffered would be nothing at all.") Another was to see that minor or bit players got more of a part than the director had planned for them. Bill Robinson, the great Negro dancer whom Will had known on the stage, recalled that Will "put me in fifteen or sixteen scenes in [a] picture that I wasn't written in for. . . . He wouldn't let them hide my face." Will seemed to have none of the usual professional jealousy about scene-stealing. He was the star, he was getting star billing, and if someone else got a break, that was fine with him.

Romantic parts were not for Will. As he once told a script

writer, "Hollywood park benches are filled with ex-actors who didn't know they were too old to make love." But something else—an innate modesty and sense of propriety—kept him from playing love scenes. In one film the script called for him to kiss his wife, played by Irene Rich, but Will kept putting off the scene until the director said they couldn't wait any longer. Still no sign of acquiescence from Will. Then the director took Miss Rich aside and told her to give Will a kiss when the time came, and she did, taking him completely by surprise. Embarrassed and flustered, he rubbed his chin, grinned sheepishly, and said, "I feel as if I'd been unfaithful to my wife."

Although he was completely natural on the movie set, outgoing and affable, never using makeup, never seeming to act

Ever the roper, in Steamboat 'Round the Bend *(1935)*

when he was before the camera, there was something about him that baffled those who thought they were close to him and knew him well. Whenever people were around he was the Will Rogers of the stage—easygoing, wisecracking, friendly with everybody, seemingly a wholly uncomplicated person. But beneath the surface, Homer Croy said, the private man was "vastly reserved; there was a wall that no one went beyond; and there were dark chambers and hidden recesses that he opened to no one." The actor Spencer Tracy thought he was "at the same time, one of the best-known, and one of the least-known, men in the world. By inclination, he is a grand mixer; by instinct, he is as retiring as a hermit." Whenever he talked about someone else he was witty and brilliant, but when he was asked about himself he was "shy, incurably, painfully shy, ill at ease, embarrassed, eager to escape."

The public personality craved an audience, and when Will collected one he tried out his material on them, bringing out jokes and ideas that had been running through his mind. If people were around he wanted to be the center of attention, but if someone else took over the conversation he often turned and walked away. But as both Croy and Tracy suggested, the private personality was something else again. He would discuss serious matters with another individual, asking questions, sounding out opinions, probing for information on topics about which the other person was knowledgeable. Joseph "Jocko" Clark—a former Oklahoman and naval aviator who became an admiral in World War II—often saw Will in California and recalled that whenever they were alone together "he asked me questions and our conversation went more on a serious vein. He was interested in everything, in the Navy and in aviation, and it was only when a crowd came around or somebody else came around that he was funny."

Frank Borzage, a director who worked with Will on several movies, claimed that it was his ability to make audiences forget that he was a comedian from time to time that made him such a popular film comedian. He was capable of portraying simple, human emotions with sincerity and conviction, so that there was always pace to his films, and people seeing them realized that he was more than a comic who cracked jokes. It is impossible to read all his columns without appreciating that he was basically a man of many causes and that the humor which came so naturally to him was the most effective means of getting a message across to people, whether he was putting ideas on paper or acting them out in motion pictures.

He was aware, it appears, that the talkies, far more than silent films, were a medium by which posterity would remember him. According to a biographer, Donald Day, he was discussing the comedienne Marie Dressler with a director not long after she had died and remarked that "there is a permanent record of her on these talking pictures, and she'll always be with us. Don't worry, old Will himself will always be there, too, unless they get tired of me."

In the early thirties there did not seem any likelihood that American audiences would weary of seeing Will Rogers on the screen. According to a chart of the top ten box-office stars compiled by *Motion Picture Herald*, Will was in ninth place in 1932. In 1933 he was second (behind Marie Dressler); in 1934 he reached the top of the ratings; and in 1935—the year of his death—he was in second place behind the sensationally popular child star, Shirley Temple. At the outset he received $110,000 for each picture he made, and he averaged three a year. In 1930 he signed a new contract with the Fox Film Corporation calling for payment of a total of $1,125,000 for six pictures, or nearly $200,000 each.

For all his success, however, he never quite fit the conventional image of a movie star. The Fox studio provided him with an ornate Spanish bungalow for his dressing room; in it were a large reception room with a fireplace, an office, a dressing room, huge closets, a couch, and a bathroom, but Will regarded the place as somewhere to throw his clothes. He preferred using his car for relaxation at the studio. That was where he wrote his articles, and there he would curl up on the seat or stretch out on the running board to read or nap.

He thoroughly enjoyed making a picture, and there were few dull moments when he was around. During the filming of *State Fair*, the plot of which centered around a prize boar, the film company bought Iowa's grand champion boar to use in the movie. Known as Blue Boy, it was a mountainous creature with huge tusks and a vile disposition, and when it arrived the director, Henry King, cautioned Will to be careful of the animal and keep away from it. "I've always been on friendly terms with hogs," Will said. "Me and him'll get along all right." But King pleaded with him to be wary—certainly, this was no animal to fool with.

A docile Blue Boy, his co-star in State Fair, *found a home via Will, in California's agricultural schools.*
UPI

The first time a scene was to be shot with Blue Boy, King sent for Will, but he was nowhere to be found. King and the other actors went over to the pen where the boar was kept and there they saw the animal, asleep, with Will stretched out on the ground beside him, his head pillowed on the hog's side and his hat over his eyes, apparently sleeping. What Will knew and King did not was that as long as he didn't disturb the animal he was quite safe, and as soon as he saw King's horrified reaction to the gag and had his laugh he got to his feet and climbed out of the pen.

When the picture was finished, a studio official asked Will if he would like to buy Blue Boy; there was a lot of meat there for the Rogers family. After a momentary pause, Will said "no," he just couldn't do it. "I wouldn't feel right eatin' a fellow actor."

Moonlighting
on the Movie Set

*The one thing Will Rogers seems never
to have done while on a movie set was
study his lines. When he wasn't working before the cameras he was reading
a clutch of daily newspapers, pecking
at a typewriter, revising his daily
article, napping, or twirling a lasso.
Unperturbed and undistracted by all
the confusion that swirled about him,
he could concentrate on reading or writing, and many of his daily and weekly
columns were written while he patiently awaited the director's call.*

A break in the shooting of Down to Earth *(above) and* A
Connecticut Yankee *(below) finds Will devouring the papers.*

BOTH: CULVER PICTURES

"If Will took himself at all seriously as a writer," said Betty Rogers, *"it was as a reporter."* Above, he diligently types out a weekly column while on location in 1927; below, he reads on the set in the early thirties.

CULVER PICTURES

WILL ROGERS MEMORIAL, CLAREMORE, OKLA., GIFT OF PROJECT 20

BOTH: UPI

"We are continually buying something that we never get, from a man that never had it."

In September, 1929, the eyes of Will and Henry Ford (left) and the nation were on the World Series. Next month nothing mattered but the Stock Exchange (above), where lights burned all night while margin calls went out.

Except for an occasional swipe at politicians and some observations on stock market speculation and the international scene, Will's columns during the first half of 1929 were mostly concerned with inconsequential matters—the automobile show, Coolidge's departure from the White House, Prohibition, a Shriners' convention, aviation endurance records, sports events, and visitors from abroad. It was also the year of the St. Valentine's Day massacre in Chicago, when seven men were lined up against the wall of a garage and gunned down by a rival mob; the year when a telephone was installed on the desk of a U.S. President for the first time ("Mr. Coolidge had been going down to the corner drug store to phone," Will surmised —or "maybe he had one in, and took it out with him when he left"). More Americans were visiting Europe than ever before, and not much was going on in Washington during the summer, he reported; Congress was not in session, so the capital was in the doldrums and comedy was "mighty slack."

Will had intended to visit China during the summer, but his commitment to Fred Stone and *Three Cheers* prevented that, and perhaps it was just as well—it was beginning to look as if war between China and Russia would break out momentarily. Noting that both countries had recalled their diplomats, Will commented, "If they had both done that before the argument started there would have been no argument. That's why diplomats don't mind starting a war, because it's a custom that they are to be brought safely home before the trouble starts. There ought to be a new rule saying: 'You start a war while you are your country's official handicap to some other country, you have to stay with any war you start.' " Already, England had recognized Russia's Communist government, and the United States would undoubtedly follow suit; and that, he suggested, means "they are getting all set for the old war contracts. . . . All our highly civilized nations are great humanitarians but if two countries are going to kill each other off, neutrals at least would like the privilege of furnishing the ammunition. When Judgment Day comes, civilization will have an alibi, 'I never took a human life, I only sold the fellow the gun to take it with.' "

In the fall of 1929 Will was invited to Detroit for a celebration honoring the inventor Thomas Edison, who was nearing the end of his long, productive life. Henry Ford had built a museum of the history of industry and invention—about a third of it memorializing the achievements of Thomas Alva Edison—and decided to combine the dedication of his Dearborn Village with a commemoration of the fiftieth anniversary of the lighting of Edison's first electric lamp. To this grand occasion he summoned the nation's most eminent figures, including President Hoover, Owen D. Young, Thomas Lamont, J.P. Morgan,

Will said that Henry Ford (left) "has run over more people in one month" than were killed in the Revolution and the Civil War.
WILL ROGERS MEMORIAL, CLAREMORE, OKLA.

When Ford (left) moved Edison's New Jersey laboratory to Dearborn, Michigan, he even brought along some New Jersey red clay to put alongside it. "God damn, Henry," said the old man (right), "where'd you get this?"

EDISON LABORATORY NATIONAL MONUMENT

Charles M. Schwab, Otto Kahn, Orville Wright, and—almost as a matter of course—his friend Will Rogers.

When Will arrived in Chicago he learned that his flight to Detroit had been canceled because of bad weather. Impatient to get there, he located a pilot who was willing to fly, and reached the Detroit airfield only to find that there were no lights on. The pilot told Will they would have to go back to Chicago; but, as they were circling over that city, the aviator passed a note to Will in the rear cockpit saying they were out of gas and that he should brace himself for an emergency landing. Going down through the darkness Will could see the lights of the city twinkling everywhere and was certain they were going to hit something; but the pilot released some flares that almost miraculously lit up a vacant lot, and the little plane headed for it. When the wheels touched down Will breathed a sigh of relief and relaxed, but his reaction was premature: as the plane roared across the lot it flipped over, throwing him against the side of the craft and stunning him. This was his third plane crash. The pilot helped him out of the plane and into a cruising taxicab, but when the driver asked where he wanted to go Will didn't know where he was. Then it came to him: "Chicago."

"Well, buddy," the cabbie said, "you're in Chicago now."

He spent the night in a hotel, where a doctor strapped up his side, and the next day he was off to Detroit. (Not until he went to New York after the Edison dinner was he x-rayed, and it was discovered that he had fractured all his ribs. When he returned to California he was bound up with adhesive tape and complaining that he couldn't even ride a horse. The Rogers' chauffeur had an answer: he took an old inner tube, split it, and wrapped it around Will's middle, and for several weeks Will wore the odd girdle around his torso. Each night when he came home from the studio he said he was comfortable, because the inner tube had gradually slid downhill, and at the day's close it lay like a loose doughnut around his waist.)

Despite considerable pain, Will had a good time at the Edison affair in Detroit. He was one of the speakers, and, as usual, enjoyed teasing his subject. The inventor, he remarked, "had no idea when he invented that all-day lantern that it would lead to so much glory and confusion. He just invented it because he needed it to work by," and Ford had honored him because another of Edison's inventions had enabled people to start a Model T car without breaking an arm cranking it. There were so many wealthy industrialists present, Will said, that every time he spilled some coffee out of his saucer, it landed on a millionaire. John D. Rockefeller, Jr., numerous railroad presidents and automobile executives, Julius Rosenwald, the head of Sears, Roebuck, and others were all just "bumming around" in Ford's Dearborn Village, admiring the buildings the automobile executive had transplanted there from all parts of the country. The museum pieces brought back memories, "for after all pretty near all of our big men are country or small town boys."

Those big men had something rather more pressing than the good old days on their minds in the autumn of 1929, however, for the economic storm cloud was directly overhead now and threatening to burst. Since the Armistice, unprecedented changes had shaken the nation's economic structure, but without any corrective adjustment in the political and financial machinery which might have maintained some sort of order.

". . . there wasn't any Republicans in Washington's day. No Republicans, no Boll Weevil, no income tax, no cover charge, no disarmament conferences, no luncheon clubs, no stop lights, no static, no headwinds. "Liquor was a companion, not a problem; no margins, no ticket speculators, no golf pants or Scotch jokes . . . My Lord, living in those times, who wouldn't be great?"

from Daily Telegram
Feb. 21, 1929

Merger after merger had taken place during the decade. The holding company, which Will described as "a thing where you hand an accomplice the goods while the policeman searches you," was now the accepted means of assembling and binding up a complex pyramid of stock holdings. By 1929 there were only half as many banks as there had been ten years earlier; fifteen companies controlled 90 per cent of all the power produced in the country; four tobacco concerns and three automobile manufacturers completely dominated their fields; U.S. Steel owned more than half of the nation's iron ore deposits; the Aluminum Company of America was a virtual monopoly.

Yet statistics and statements by men in the know assured Americans that this was for the nation's good and that all would be well. Between 1923 and 1926 trading on the New York Stock Exchange had doubled, while the average price of twenty-five representative stocks was up 54 per cent. (Anyone who doubted what the big boys were making out of all this could read that Pittsburgh's Mellon family had increased its net worth by $300 million on the value of Aluminum Company and Gulf Oil holdings alone.) Even when the Federal Reserve Board in Washington had attempted to discourage stock speculation in 1927, President Coolidge calmly predicted that the year would be "one of continued healthy business activity and prosperity"; and Secretary Mellon, interviewed before he sailed for Europe, commented that "the stock market seems to be going along in an orderly fashion, and I see no evidence of over-speculation."

Stock trading increased spectacularly. There seemed no limit to the money that could be made in the right stocks. The radio industry, for one, was clearly here to stay, and in a big way: only six years after its commercial beginnings, the sale of sets accounted for nearly two-thirds of a billion dollars, and Radio Corporation of America rode the heady tide. The stock's low in 1928 was 85 ½ ; the following year it reached 549. Everyone in New York talked stock prices. Bootblacks and barbers, shoe clerks and cabbies—all had a tip to pass on to anyone who cared to listen. As Will put it, "There had never been a time in our history when as many fools are making money as now."

Inauguration day—March 4, 1929—produced a confident message from the new President, Herbert Hoover: "I have no fears about the future of our country. It is bright with hope." Like Coolidge, he opposed government controls and meddling in the stock market, and the speculative spiral went on unabated. Optimism about the future was such that investors hardly

"There is two things that can disrupt business in this country. One is war and the other is a meeting of the Federal Reserve Bank."

from Daily Telegram
Apr. 2, 1929

needed the *Wall Street Journal*'s assurance that the outlook for earning was "extremely promising." In August there was a momentary pause in the upward trend when the Federal Reserve Board increased the interest rate from 5 to 6 per cent, sending a shudder through financial circles and causing Will to observe that "Any business that can't survive a 1 per cent raise must be skating on mighty thin ice." Just let Wall Street have a nightmare, he said, "and the whole country has to help get them back in bed again." Despite such temporary lapses, the listed value of stocks more than doubled during the six-month period between March 3 and September 3, 1929. But what no one at the time realized was that that final day, Tuesday, September 3, was the dying effort of the great bull market.

On September 5 came unwelcome news. The economist Roger Babson, speaking to a National Business Conference, stated flatly: "Sooner or later a crash is coming, and it may be terrific." This was the signal for the so-called Babson break in the market, and from then on the trend was down.

Babson was by no means the only prophet of doom. A year earlier, in August, 1928, Sinclair Lewis, the author who had put "Babbitt" and "Main Street" into the language as symbols of boosterism out there in middle America, gazed from a window overlooking Madison Avenue and observed dourly, "Within a year this country will have a terrible financial panic." He didn't just think it, he said—he could smell it: "I can see people jumping out of windows on this very street." According to a biographer of Calvin Coolidge, when someone pressed Grace Coolidge to explain her husband's reason for not "choosing" to run for re-election, she replied simply, "Poppa says there's a depression coming." Others saw portents in the agricultural woes that had begun in 1920 and were continuing, with farm surpluses growing while prices went steadily down. There were waves of labor unrest, an increasing number of bank failures, exposures of cruelly low wages (Congressional investigators heard in 1929 from a fourteen-year-old girl who received $4.95 a week for 60 hours' work in a Southern textile mill). The thing was there, if anyone cared to heed the warning signs.

Yet on October 17, while the industrialists were on their way to Dearborn to honor Edison, there were some optimists; the political economist Irving Fisher of Yale asserted that the market was on a permanent high plateau and would be a good deal higher within a few months. Less than a week later the president of New York's National City Bank said there was "nothing fundamentally wrong with the stock market or with the underlying business and credit structure" of the country. That remark preceded by just two days the landmark known forever after as Black Thursday, when the whole house of cards collapsed. Despite efforts of New York's most highly placed bankers and the vice president of the Exchange, Richard Whitney, to stem the tide, an angry, half-hysterical crowd on the floor of the Exchange fought to unload their stock before it was too late. On that day 13,000,000 shares were sold, and the ticker was four hours late at closing time. The following Tuesday was even worse: trading volume exceeded 16,400,000 shares—a record that would stand for more than thirty years. In a single day the value of stocks listed on the New York Exchange plummeted $14 billion, and no bottom was in sight.

President Hoover was understandably bitter about the debacle that ruined his first autumn in the White House. Some of New York's financiers, he said, were not bankers at all—merely

The economic boom's death knell was sounded on "Black Thursday," October 24, but five days later came the final convulsion (announced below).

k Times.

THE WEATHER

Rain today and probably tomorrow; somewhat colder tomorrow.

Temperatures Yesterday—Max. 51. Min. 47.
U. S. Weather Forecast—For details see Page 63.

mpany.

29, 1929.

TWO CENTS In Greater | **THREE CENTS** | **FOUR CENTS** Elsewhere
New York | Within 200 Miles | Except 7th and 8th Postal Zone

DISTURBED
AN ACTION
TION DEBT

---

an Explanation
irect Payments
ermany.

--- ----

TIGE INVOLVED

---

ntinent Feel That
Have Faith in
n Institution.

AID TO HOOVER

---

d to Wish to Avoid

STOCK PRICES SLUMP $14,000,000,000 IN NATION-WIDE STAMPEDE TO UNLOAD; BANKERS TO SUPPORT MARKET TODAY

Sixteen Leading Issues Down $2,893,520,108;
Tel. & Tel. and Steel Among Heaviest Losers

A shrinkage of $2,893,520,108 in the open market value of the shares of sixteen representative companies resulted from yesterday's sweeping decline on the New York Stock Exchange.

American Telephone and Telegraph was the heaviest loser, $448,905,162 having been lopped off of its total value. United States Steel common, traditional bellwether of the stock market, made its greatest nose-dive in recent years by falling from a high of 202½ to a low of 185. In a feeble last-minute rally it snapped back to 186, at which it closed, showing a net loss of 17½ points. This represented for the 8,131,955 shares of common stock outstanding a total loss in value of $142,293,446.

In the following table are shown the day's net depreciation in the outstanding shares of the sixteen companies referred to:

Losses in

PREMIER ISSUES HARD HIT

Unexpected Torrent of Liquidation Again Rocks Markets.

--- - ---

DAY'S SALES 9,212,800

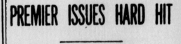

Nearly 3,000,000 Shares Are
Traded In Final Hour—The

This was the chaotic scene in the financial district on October 29, 1929.

stock promoters. After Andrew Mellon was dispatched to England as ambassador, Hoover recalled some of the former Treasury Secretary's views on economic conditions. Mellon, he said, felt that a panic "was not altogether a bad thing." In its wake the high cost of living would come down and people would work harder and lead "more moral" lives. "Values would be adjusted, and enterprising people will pick up the wrecks from less competent people." Thus Mr. Mellon, according to Mr. Hoover. Or to put it differently, the fit, the bold, and the fortunate would survive.

Amid the welter of statistics and conflicting high-level opinions, the American newspaper reader could still find a wry, no-nonsense view of the nation's tangled economic picture in Will's columns. Will was in New York City on Black Thursday, or "wailing day," as he called it, when "you had to stand in line to get a window to jump out of, and speculators were selling space for bodies in the East River." As he said later of the nation's financial center, "I don't believe New York has got the nerve to stand it like lots of folks all over the country . . . this place's nerves are more jumpy." The following Saturday he was in Oklahoma, musing about the contrast between the canyons of Wall Street and the lovely, pastoral countryside he had just flown over. "Why, if the cows of this country failed to come up and get milked one night," he thought, "it would be more of a panic than if Morgan and Lamont had never hald a meeting . . . an old sow and a litter of pigs make more people a living than all the steel and General Motors stock combined." A few days later, back in California, he was more rueful: "Sure must be a great consolation to the poor people who lost their stock in the late crash to know that it has fallen in the hands of Mr. Rockefeller, who will take care of it and see that it has a good home and never be allowed to wander around unprotected again. There is one rule that works in every calamity," he added: "Be it pestilence, war or famine, the rich get richer and the poor get poorer." Do not gamble, he urged his readers: "Take all your savings and buy some good stock, and hold it till it goes up, then sell it. If it don't go up, don't buy it."

What irked him was the talk about how Rockefeller and other financiers were "stabilizing" the market. What was really needed, he suggested, was "another bunch of men that will stabilize it during its next 100-point drop." He had never had much use for bankers or for Wall Street. Anyone ought to know that Wall Street was "located in the sharp end of New York, that not only the traders but the Street itself is short, that neither end don't lead anywhere."

Toward the close of the year, thinking about the harrowing events of the past few months, he tried to sum up what had gone wrong. People had been so carried away by the fever of speculation that if the president of a company was "a good after-dinner speaker and made a good appearance, why his stock would go up to two or three hundred." Nothing solid was behind the price of a stock—only the fact that it was going up. "Oh, it was great while it lasted. All you had to do was to buy and wait till the next morning and just pick up the paper and see how much you made, in print. But all that has changed." People had to get over the idea that they could live by gambling: "Somebody has to do some work."

While the repercussions of the crash sent tremors all over the world, another economic development on the American scene made it almost certain that European nations, in particular, would be disastrously affected. During the summer of 1929 the House of Representatives had begun discussing the tariff, and the bill that finally emerged from Congress, drawn by two extreme protectionists—Senator Reed Smoot of Utah and Congressman Willis Hawley of Oregon—just about finished off a European economy that was already staggering from the effects of the market panic. By forcing the price of Europe's goods so high that Americans stopped buying them altogether, it sent foreign markets into a decline, from which they would not recover for years. As Will described the intricacies of the tariff to his readers, it was a little like the weather—"What suits you don't feel so good to me." The tariff, he said, "is an instrument invented for the benefit of those who make to be used against those who buy. As there is more buys than there is makes, it is a document of the minority, but what a minority!" Or, to put it another way, "Twenty men can enter a room as friends and someone can bring up the tariff and you will find nineteen bodies on the floor with only one living that escaped."

Another episode that involved Europe was the visit, in October, 1929, of Britain's Socialist Prime Minister Ramsay MacDonald to the United States. MacDonald was greeted in New York with a ticker-tape parade and went on to visit Hoover to discuss certain unfinished matters relating to naval disarmament. ("Watch him, Herbert," Will warned. "Englishmen are the only race of people that never travel for just fun." An Englishman, he continued, "can insult you, but he can do it so slick and polite that he will have you guessing till away after he leaves you just whether he was friend or foe.") Evidently Mr. Hoover wasn't listening. The upshot of the MacDonald visit was the London Disarmament Conference in January of 1930.

Thanksgiving came, and Will's thoughts turned to the nation's farmers, who had been having an increasingly hard time since the boom days of the World War. Signs of their dilemma could have been observed as early as 1920–23 when, in Missouri, 10 per cent of the farmers either lost their farms or were permitted to hang onto them only through the leniency of creditors. And what happened in Missouri was typical of the farm belt as a whole. Now, Will said, the farmers could be thankful: "Didn't the farm board decide in Washington last week that they could have cheaper interest? All the farmers have to do now is to find something new to put up as security." They could also take courage from the announcement that the next session of Congress was going to "relieve the farmer again —relieve him of any encouragement that he might have received during the last one."

"There is only one form of employment in our country that I can think of, but what has its bright spots, and that's coal mining. There is generally an overproduction and they are out of work; if not that, it's a strike. Then when they do go to work, the mine blows up. Then if none of these three things happen, they still have the worst job in the world."

from Daily Telegram
Dec. 19, 1929

In the meantime, the President was seeking the assistance of responsible Americans on his overriding domestic problem. The question was how to restore confidence among millions of citizens who had lost it as a consequence of the market crash. Will said he would like to help, but was puzzled as to how he could do so. He had, he said, restored a lot of things in his time, such as cattle to the home range, Follies girls to the stage door at curtain time, interest in national political conventions, and he had helped the Democrats and other worthy charities. But this dilemma of the President's was one of the toughest he had ever tackled, and he described in a homely lecture the madness the country had gone through in recent days.

The dumb ones like himself couldn't quite understand what had happened on Wall Street; all they knew was that if somebody had lost money, then someone else must have made it, and he used a personal anecdote to illustrate the point. Every time he signed a contract for stage or screen work, he and Betty would try to figure out what they would have left by the end of the season, but when that time came "we had the figures but we couldent find the money." When it came to stocks, he simply couldn't understand what the price of a security had to do with keeping the company that issued it operating. If a company's stock had all been sold, he asked, what difference did it make to the company whether their stock was selling at a thousand dollars a share or if people were kindling fires with it? About all he could think to tell people was that the country as a whole was "sound." The United States "is bigger than Wall Street, and if they don't believe it, I show 'em the map." What he neglected to say was that Wall Street was not so much a cause as a symptom of a far more serious and widespread disorder. A relatively small percentage of the total population was directly affected by the crash, after all. What was not so clear at the time was that America's problems went far beyond the money market, affecting nearly all levels of society, and it is doubtful whether Will Rogers was fully aware just then how grave conditions in the country really were.

This is not to suggest that he was insensitive to the plight of most Americans—far from it, as his tireless efforts to help the unfortunate during the next few years were to demonstrate. But as 1929 drew to a close it must have been almost impossible for a man of his circumstances to comprehend the difficulties facing millions of his fellow countrymen. In 1929 the average family income was about $2,300; three years later it would fall to

"I could have told [Mr. Hoover] before sundown what's changed our lives, buying on credit, waiting for relief, Ford cars, too many Republicans, Notre Dame coaching methods and two-thirds of the Americans, both old and young, thinking they possessed 'it.'"

from Daily Telegram
Dec. 20, 1929

$1,600 or less. At the same period Will's annual income from movies, radio and other appearances, and daily and weekly columns exceeded $500,000. He had never invested in the stock market. He had substantial capital in land, endowment policies totaling $200,000, nearly half a million dollars in life insurance, plus annuities and U.S. bonds.

In 1930, when he signed a contract for fourteen radio talks for the sum of $72,000, there was criticism over the fact that he was being paid the unprecedented fee of $350 a minute to tell jokes. What was not generally known was that he donated the money to charity; but there were those who came to his defense on other grounds altogether. As an editorial in *World's Work* put it, he told Americans "the hard, blunt truths about ourselves— truths about our politics, our civic standards, and our social habits. They are the sort of truths we do not always like to hear, but we will take them with a contagious chuckle and a piece of chewing gum—Confession is good for the soul, and he supplies it."

"Never blame a legislative body for not doing something. When they do nothing, that don't hurt anybody. When they do something is when they become dangerous."

from Daily Telegram
Nov. 22, 1929

What Will may have thought about this is not known. He was between pictures, a disarmament conference was about to meet in London, and in January, 1930, fearful that the American delegation might get "the disarming done" before he got there, he booked passage for England on the *Bremen*. As a small boy in Indian Territory, he recalled, he had once seen a sheriff disarm a party of men and it had fascinated him; "when I arrived in New York and they told me they were going to disarm whole nations over in London next week, I grabbed the first boat."

As usual, he was in a hurry. Since the decision to go was made on the spur of the moment he had neither passport nor a dark suit for dinner on board the ship (he did not wear a tuxedo). As his wife told the story, one of the studio executives managed to get him a passport, but by the time he went in search of a suit all the stores were closed. He cruised around the city in a taxi, finally found a cut-rate shop on Broadway that was open, and dashed in to purchase shirts, socks, ties, and the one blue serge suit that came close to fitting. The pants were too long, so Will waited while the suit was sent down the street to a cleaning establishment for alterations, paid $19.85 for it, and stuffing the purchases under his arm, headed for the *Bremen*.

In mid-January, after another seasick voyage, he was in London listening to the king open the conference, hobnobbing with George Bernard Shaw and Lloyd George, visiting with the U.S.

delegates, and concluding—when it was all over—that he could "print the history of the present results of this disarmament conference on the head of a pin and have room enough left for the chorus of 'Yes, We have no Bananas.' " The trouble, he decided, was the way the conferees decided to establish ratios that would determine the number of ships each nation was to have. "The minute you rate a nation they naturally think you are establishing their importance in comparison to everybody else. Nations don't mind being small, but they don't want it advertised to the world."

For months after his return to the States, Will kept an eye on the conference through the newspapers, and reached several conclusions. The U.S. had gone to London in the first place seeking parity, but was short-changed. "That's the characteristic of our country," he said. "We can get all lathering at the time over some political campaign promise, or some conference pledge, but if the thing just drags along long enough we forget what it was that was originally promised. The short memories of the American voter is what keeps our politicians in office." In the late spring of 1930, when the Senate began looking askance at the terms brought back by the American delegates (Japan, it seemed, had come away with the best of it, and U.S. legislators were both angry and anxious), Will remarked that "it looks like our boys went after a treaty and Japan's gang went after ships. Well, they both got 'em. So now in case of trouble . . . why, for every ship they send out to attack us, we shoot 'em down with a treaty." We had a unique record: "We never lost a boat in battle, but we have had many a one shot from under us at a conference." When at last the Senate confirmed the treaty, he labeled the whole matter asinine. The idea sounded good, but in practice it was ridiculous. "You can no more tell a nation what inch gun he is to shoot you with than you can tell him what to wear while shooting you." What we ought to do is agree with other nations to quit holding conferences, stop conferring, and just be friends again. Otherwise, the various countries would settle down to serious shipbuilding between conferences; if they didn't they would have nothing to sink when they met again. Most of the ships they promised to destroy were "vessels that would sink themselves if the conference was postponed for another year. England is to sink three battleships that competed against the Spanish Armada. Japan is raising two that the Russians sunk, and will re-sink them for the treaty and the weeklies. We are building two to sink."

Will Rogers says:
"A politician is not as narrow-

It sure did kick up some excitement in the Senate when Senator Moses called the other Senators "sons of wild jackasses." Well, if you think it made the Senators hot, you wait till you see what happens when the jackasses hear how they have been slandered.

Never blame a legislative body for not doing something. When they do nothing, that don't hurt anybody. When they do something is when they become dangerous.

You know, [Congressmen] are the nicest fellows in the world to meet. I sometimes really wonder if they realize the harm they do.

On account of us being a democracy and run by the people, we are the only nation in the world that has to keep a government four years, no matter what it does.

If you can start arguing over something, and get enough publicity, and keep the argument going, you can divide our nation overnight as to whether spinach or broccoli is the most nutritious. We can get hot and bothered over nothing and cool off faster than any nation in the world.

Things in our country run in spite of government. Not by aid of it.

Lord, the money we do spend on Government and it's not one bit better than the government we got for one third the money twenty years ago.

What they need in all these Latin countries is a party that compares with our Democrats, one who loses and don't do nothing about it but talk.

They have an unwritten law [in the Senate] that a new member is not allowed to say anything when he first gets in, and another unwritten law that whatever he says afterwards is not to amount to anything.

Did anybody ever see a United States Senator in his home state after the night he is elected? I have met 'em all over the world when Congress was not in session, but never saw one at home. They are always making speeches about "My fine people back home," but they never want to go see 'em.

So I hereby start a movement to create another week, like Apple week and Prune week. It's "Meet your Own Senator week," and make him come home, no matter what happens to him.

You remember . . . I wanted to have the home folks meet their Senator? You would be surprised at the amount of resentment that has come to my roll top desk. . . . They all claim they don't want to see their Senator. That's why they elected him—was to get rid of him.

If they had wanted him at home, they would have kept him at home.

If all politicians fished instead of spoke publicly, we would be at peace with the world.

Once a man holds a public office he is absolutely no good for honest work.

Every time we have an election, we get in worse men and the country keeps right on going. Times have proven only one thing and that is you can't ruin this country ever, with politics.

It's just got so that 90 percent of the people in this country don't give a damn. Politics ain't worrying this country one tenth as much as parking space.

280

minded as he forces himself to be."

I guess the truth can hurt you worse in an election than about anything that could happen to you.

———

The trouble with Senators is the ones that ought to get out don't.

———

It's pitiful when you think how ignorant the founders of our Constitution must have been. Just think what a Country we would have if men in those days had the Brains and forethought of our men today!

———

Congress meets tomorrow morning. Let us all pray to the Lord to give us strength to bear that which is about to be inflicted upon us.

———

We have been staggering along now about 155 years under every conceivable horse-thief that could get into office and yet here we are, still going strong.

———

Come pretty near having two holidays of equal importance in the same week—Halloween and election. And of the two, election provides us the most fun. On Halloween they put pumpkins on their heads and on election they don't have to.

———

Our municipal election run true to political form. The sewer was defeated but the councilmen got in.

———

The Democrats are having a lot of fun exposing the Republican campaign corruptions, but they would have a lot more fun if they knew where they could lay their hands on some of it themselves for next November.

———

Did you ever figure it out? [Senators] are the only people in the world that are paid to do one job and do every other one there is but that.

Sometimes it makes you think we don't need a different man as bad as we need different advisers for the same man.

———

Washington, D.C. papers say, "Congress is deadlocked and can't act." I think that is the greatest blessing that could befall this Country.

———

You can't make the Republican Party pure by more contributions, because contributions are what got it where it is today.

———

Congress has promised the country that it will adjourn next Tuesday. Let's hope we can depend on it. If they do it will be the first promise they have kept this session.

———

We shouldn't elect a President; we should elect a magician.

———

If we got one-tenth of what was promised to us in these acceptance speeches there wouldn't be any inducement to go to Heaven.

———

Elect 'em for a six-year term; not allow 'em to succeed themselves. That would keep their mind off politics.

———

Corruption and golf is two things we might just as well make up our minds to take up, for they are both going to be with us.

———

Outside of traffic, there is nothing that has held this country back as much as committees.

———

To the Senate and the House, a Merry Xmas. May the literacy test never be applied to your constituents.

———

If we could just send the same bunch of men to Washington for the good of the nation and not for political reasons, we could have the most perfect government in the world.

PHOTOWORLD

"... the unemployed here ain't eating regular, but we will get round to them soon as we get everybody else fixed up O.K."

On a visit to England, Arkansas, in 1931 Will and Red Cross workers greet school children outside a local soup kitchen. The cartoon expresses public mystification over the Depression.
ST. LOUIS *Post Dispatch*, JAN. 11, 1931

In 1930 Depression gnawed at the vitals of American society. That year nearly four and one half million people were unemployed as compared with one and one half million in 1929 (the figure would rise to eight million in 1931, twelve million in 1932, and thirteen million in 1933). No one seemed to know what to do. Calvin Coolidge, writing articles in his retirement, had only absurd platitudes to offer: "When more and more people are thrown out of work, unemployment results," or, "The final solution of unemployment is work." Although the government in Washington was neither unaware nor indifferent, it did not fully comprehend the extent or the nature of the disaster. Hoover had no answers for the jobless, who were lining up outside soup kitchens waiting for something to eat, and it was somehow indicative of his response to the situation that he approved an appropriation of $45 million to feed cattle affected by the 1930 drought while opposing the expenditure of $25 million to feed farm families. The latter, he believed, were the responsibilities of local governments or the Red Cross.

The blight could be seen everywhere—on farms, in factories, small enterprises, and enormous industrial concerns. In a curious way those who appeared to suffer most were the ones least accustomed to adversity: members of the middle class—white-collar workers from banks, insurance agencies, architects' offices, and department stores—who suddenly found themselves without work, without status, without hope. Washington's initial reaction to the deepening crisis was to recommend charity—"neighbor to neighbor, community to community," as Mr. Hoover said. He was convinced that the economy was fundamentally sound, that the Depression was merely a passing interlude in the nation's life, and that the most

By 1933 thirteen million Americans were unemployed, and that spring thousands of hungry men queued up to get handouts of bread and soup and coffee. This was a scene in New York City.
NEW YORK PUBLIC LIBRARY

critical need was to support the banks—many of which were closed—in order to make credit available to individuals and to businesses. After reading one of the President's speeches on the subject, Will remarked, "He said if we could afford to live through it, things would get better. . . . He read a lot of statistics. . . . They told how poor some fifteen or twenty other countries were doing. I had no idea that Ecuador was as bad off as Oklahoma, but it is. So before you complain, think of Peru."

Drought seared the farm country, where the price of wheat had already dropped from $1.35 to 76 cents a bushel in a year's time. In a bountiful land bread lines were everywhere. As Will described the paradox, "We are going through a unique experience. We are the first nation to starve to death in a store house that's overfilled with everything we want." The jobless who were not standing in line were on the move—thousands of migrants roaming the country seeking work, hoping to wash dishes or harvest wheat or do anything else that would produce a day's work or a dollar or two.

During the second winter of the Depression, isolated groups of people began taking matters into their own hands. Five hundred farmers marched up to a country store in the little town of England, Arkansas, and demanded food for their wives and children; and Will, reading the news, compared them with Paul Revere: "These birds woke up America. I don't want to discourage Mr. Mellon and his carefully balanced budget but you let this country get hungry and they are going to eat no matter what happens to budgets, income taxes or Wall Street values." When the Senate appropriated $15 million for food and the House turned it down he wrote, "They seem to think that's a bad precedent, to appropriate money for food. It's too much like the 'dole.' They think it will encourage hunger. The way things look, hunger don't need much encouragement. It's just coming around naturally." A week later the same legislators voted the same amount of money to improve entrances to the National Parks, and he regarded it as a clear indication that "You can get a road anywhere you want to out of the government, but you can't get a sandwich." In two years, he supposed, there wouldn't be a poor farm that didn't have a concrete highway leading to it.

In mid-January of 1931 Will was in Washington, conferring with the President, exploring his proposal that the Red Cross should meet the crisis. But Hoover told him that it would set a bad precedent for the government to appropriate money for the Red Cross. Once the people received relief, Mr. Hoover said, "they will always expect it," and that would disrupt the program of voluntary giving, which the Red Cross had worked so many years to develop. With some misgivings about the wisdom of Hoover's approach ("I don't think we have anybody in Washington that don't want to feed 'em, but they all want to feed 'em their way"), Will nevertheless determined to do what he could to raise funds for the Red Cross.

He set out on a trip across the country to see at firsthand the farm communities most seriously affected by drought and to publicize the private relief efforts. After visiting a Red Cross soup kitchen in England, Arkansas—which he called the neediest section in America, where the people had absolutely nothing, despite the fact that it was "the most fertile land you ever saw"—he wrote, "You don't know what hard times are till you go into some of these houses." Later in the month he embarked on a charity tour for the benefit of the Red Cross, flying in a Navy plane piloted by Frank Hawks, giving performances in several towns each day, paying all the expenses for himself and whatever additional talent he could scrape up, and adding his personal check to the contributions received in each place. In Wichita Falls, Texas, he raised over $9,000; in Abilene at breakfast the next morning he got $6,500. In between those two stops he sandwiched three performances in Fort Worth, and when a group of Negroes said they wished they could hear him, he took time out to visit a Baptist church where he was introduced by a blind preacher. Altogether he raised $18,000 in Fort Worth.

The more he saw of people's need, the angrier he became over what was going on in Washington. Amid all the turmoil, at a time when "seven million people's minds are on their next cup of coffee," the Wickersham report on Prohibition was published, and Will was boiling mad. "The only possible thing you could think of that we don't need right now, outside the Einstein theory, is the Prohibition theory." If someone could just butter the report and put it between two loaves of bread, it might be worth something, he suggested, and he sensed the irony of it all. "Poor Hoover! When somebody does do something for him, they do it at the wrong time." When the Senate turned to a debate on Prohibition, Will supposed "There must have been some pretty important business before them. They never argue over it only in the busiest times." Reading that Hoover had sent a flier to Arkansas to see how bad conditions really were, he snapped, "He could have sent a blind man and found out." Meantime, he had raised $90,000 in Oklahoma and had flown to Arkansas, where he discovered a little circus stranded in Forest City. The town was feeding the circus people, he reported, but the lone elephant and the lions and tigers were eating a lot more than the humans, and no one seemed anxious to buy the elephant. Pleading with his readers to send money to Arkansas, he commented, "Lots of folks can't seem to get excited over humans being hungry; maybe they can over wild animals. This elephant hasn't seen a peanut since last summer."

In eighteen days he had visited fifty cities or small towns in Texas, Oklahoma, and Arkansas, raising $225,000 in cash, plus an additional amount in pledges. His only requests were that every cent of the proceeds go to the needy, to be divided equally between those in urban and rural areas, and that a portion of the Oklahoma funds be set aside specifically for the relief of Cherokee Indians. Whenever possible he traveled by plane, but on at least one occasion in Texas rain and fog kept him from flying, so he rented an automobile, wired ahead to ask "the folks to

There was always a final wisecrack before Will's plane took off for the next stop.
WILL ROGERS MEMORIAL, CLAREMORE, OKLA.

286

Typical of the scenes of desti-
tution observed by Will on his
charity missions was this
glimpse of an Arkansas share-
cropper's house, visited by a
member of the Red Cross.
LIBRARY OF CONGRESS

sit up and wait" for them, and drove through the muddy roads
to his destination. With a sure instinct for what was likely to
produce the desired results, he did what he could to prepare the
way for his entry into each town: just before he was to appear in
Tulsa, for example, he let it be known that he expected to raise
at least $25,000 there. "I know that bunch," he said. "They'll
do more broke than Oklahoma City will rich."

The effects of Will's whirlwind tour went far beyond the
money he raised. Suddenly, people who had known nothing
but unending discouragement and neglect became aware that
there was at least one prominent man in the nation who cared
deeply enough about them and their troubles to try to help. His
one-man missions of mercy came like a breath of fresh air to
thousands of heartsick Americans, and their reaction was an
outpouring of affection and love the likes of which few men are
privileged to receive.

The most vivid record of it is in newsreel films from the time.

On the edge of a desolate prairie landing strip outside a tiny Texas or Oklahoma town a crowd of people stands, looking off into the distance. Then the camera pans around to catch a small aircraft approaching, its wings wobbling in the wind as it comes in for the landing. Before the wheels touch the ground the crowd surges away from the edge of the field and begins to move—men, women, and children running, overcoats flapping behind them—and as the camera picks up the blurred faces in the headlong rush it is suddenly apparent that they are laughing and cheering out of sheer joy, oblivious of everything but getting to that airplane as fast as their legs will carry them. And then there is Will Rogers, climbing out of the plane, somewhat startled to see the size of the crowd, grinning, waving, shaking hands with hundreds of strangers who are his friends and who will remember to their dying day the moment he brought laughter and a ray of hope into their lonely lives.

When he had to return to California in February to make a picture, he read that the government had finally appropriated $20 million for drought-stricken farmers. But there was a string attached: the money was to be loaned against security put up by the farmers. "Now the man and his family that are hungry down there have no security," he explained. "If he had any security he wouldn't be hungry." Given the prevailing mood in Washington, there appeared to be no alternative to private assistance through the Red Cross, and in an unusually bitter column Will suggested that there were certain people the Red Cross couldn't reach—people so far back in the woods that the rest of the world had almost forgotten them: "I am speaking of the Senate and Congress of these United States." And he proposed a relief program for "this little known but patriotic group." On February 22 his mood turned even more sour. "Here is what George Washington missed by not living to his 199th birthday," he wrote. "He would have seen our great political system of 'equal rights to all and privileges to none' working so smoothly that seven million are without a chance to earn their living. He would see 'em handing out rations in peace time, that would have reminded him of Valley Forge. . . . I bet after seeing us, he would sue us for calling him 'Father.' "

Noting that the stock market had picked up a bit, which would make the rich boys feel better, he observed that U.S. Steel might go to a thousand, "but that don't bring one biscuit to a poor old Negro family of fifteen in Arkansas who haven't got a chance to get a single penny in money till their few little

". . . that's the tough part about a Hero. He has to eat. We take care of them with too much newspaper space and not enough permanent endowment. We have great fellows back from the war that can show you two medals for every sack of flour they have in the house. They got a Foreign Decoration for every American dollar they have. "Heroing is one of the shortest lifed professions there is."

from Weekly Article
Feb. 15, 1925

288

bales of cotton are sold away next fall." He was sick at heart over the attitude of the Republicans in general and Andrew Mellon in particular, who was dead set against increasing the income tax on those in high brackets. The G.O.P. spoke of such an increase "almost like a national calamity," he remarked; "I really believe if it come to a vote whether to go to war with England, France, and Germany combined, or raise the rate on incomes over $100,000 they would vote war." Republicans were claiming that business was getting better "because there is fewer apples being sold on the street. Lord that only means it's getting worse."

While Congress debated the possibility of paying veterans of World War I the bonus they had been promised, important men in the financial community advised against it, arguing that it was "bad economy" to do so at this time. "When," Will asked, was "anything connected with the war good economy? Even entering it wasn't a stroke of financial genius." A debt was a debt—just as difficult for a government to repay as for an individual—and none ever came due at a convenient time. About the only note of cheer he could find in the papers was that Congress planned to adjourn. "Then watch things hum," he promised, "if we can only prevent another drouth and disarmament conference."

In the fall his active help was sought by the President—a remarkable request, all things considered, indicating the extent of Will's hold on the American public. On October 31, in a nationwide hookup, Herbert Hoover and Will Rogers spoke over the radio on the subject of unemployment, and in his introductory remarks, Will described the circumstances behind his unusual appearance. Owen D. Young, the industrialist, had called to ask if he would make the talk, and "I told him I was very particular who I appeared with, and who would be the other speaker," Will replied. "He said would Mr. Hoover be all right [and] I told him I would think it over, so I did, I looked everything up about him, and inquired, and found that after discounting about two thirds that the Democrats said about him, found I had nothing much to lose by appearing with him, so I took the chance. So if we do all right today, there's liable to be a new team on the radio."

It says something for Will's loyalty and determination to do anything he could to lend a hand at this critical hour that, despite personal misgivings about the efficacy of the President's approach, his talk was basically an appeal for the type of public-spirited generosity and private support on which Hoover counted so heavily. What effect it may have had on the unemployment situation is difficult to ascertain—the situation having gone well beyond the thumb-in-the-dike measures Hoover was requesting. But it did cast Will Rogers in his most important role by far (excerpts from the talk appear on the facing page) and produced the memorable line: "We are the first nation in the history of the world to go to the poorhouse in an automobile."

Beyond America, the world at large was suffering other acute problems. Germany's senile president Paul von Hindenburg reported that his country was rife with "internal and external tensions caused by distress and despair"; off in the wings, Adolf Hitler was preparing to seize power. As Will sized up the situation, "China is in a mess, not only again, but yet. Russia is starving her own people in order to feed propaganda to the rest of the world; a guy named Hitler has Germany like Capone has Chicago; France has plenty of gold, but is short on friendship; England has her fine diplomats, but no work; Spain is trying to get a republic. They think one is great, that shows their ignorance. Italy has black shirts, but no pants to go with 'em; Brazil has coffee, but no president. So before you think of giving up your citizenship here, you better think it over." He didn't like the smell of events in Europe. War, he feared, "is nearer around the corner than prosperity is."

About six months after making that statement, Will decided to visit Central America and the Caribbean, which now had regular air service. He completed a movie, *Young As You Feel*, in the spring of 1931 and prepared to leave (as Betty had long since realized, "finishing a picture usually meant a trip"). His first stop was Managua, Nicaragua, where, eight days earlier, an earthquake had reduced the city to rubble, and he was there to report on the scene and to do what he could to help. The Nicaraguans had lost everything but the clothes on their backs (he said he had finally found someone "poorer than a southern cotton renter"), and at once Will appealed to Americans to send aid through the Red Cross; he contributed $5,000 himself and put on several benefits during his stay. Then he continued south, stopping in Costa Rica, Panama, Colombia, and Venezuela—and came away with the feeling that every one of them should be under a Mussolini. Venezuela already had a dictator —"the only ones that seem to get anything done in these times" —but wherever he went he heard rumors of threatened revolutions and plots against the government. "What they need in all these latin countries is a party that compares with our Democrats, one who loses and don't do nothing about it but talk."

On reaching the Virgin Islands he became aware of the animosity aroused by President Hoover's slighting reference, on a recent visit, to the islands as a "poorhouse." "These virgins are up in arms against him," Will reported. In the days before Prohibition the islanders had manufactured rum and prospered; now they were virtually bankrupt. Will advised the natives he met to go ahead and make it again. There was no reason, he felt, for them to take the Prohibition law seriously just because they belonged to the United States. Certainly few Americans did.

In two weeks' time he had visited fifteen countries and traveled eight thousand miles—all, he noted, for $600 air fare. When he landed in Miami he knew he was on American territory; "I don't see any Marines."

The big international news of 1931 centered on Europe's continuing economic woes and what the United States could do, if anything, to help solve them. Hoover at last responded to the pleas by declaring a one-year moratorium on international payments due the United States as a result of World War I debts. At first Will took a philosophical attitude toward the move. He had had the same idea earlier, he claimed, but his solution was that *all* debts should be canceled—personal as well as international ones—but the only people who fell for it were two men who owed him money. It wasn't government debts that worried people, in any case, "It's individual debts that's got the 119 million by the nape of the neck." When he learned that Andrew Mellon had been sent to Paris to explain to the French why Germany should be permitted to default on its debts for a year, he could imagine the French reply: "That's fine, Mr. Mellon, from a Pittsburgh angle, but we happen to live right across the river from 'em and we know what's going to happen to us soon as they are able again. What are you trying to do, shorten our lives one year?" As far as Germany was concerned, he believed that one portion of its debt ought to be wiped out entirely—the money owed as payment for the armies of occupation after the war. "That was just like sitting over the grave of a dead man for a year to see if he was coming to life and then charging his family the price of the sitting." In the final analysis, he could not imagine how the affairs of the world were going to be set right by any such program: "It's fellows with schemes that got us into this mess. Plans get you into things but you got to work your way out." As negotiations between the United States and the European nations dragged on, his attitude hardened, and a year later he took a position similar to that of Calvin Coolidge, who had asked, "They hired the money, didn't they?" But before that time, conditions in the United States were to grow increasingly worse.

In 1931 twenty-three hundred U.S. banks went under. In 1932 the industrial empire of public utilities magnate Samuel Insull collapsed; Ivar Kreuger, the Swedish match king, committed suicide as the chaos created by his financial maneuvering became known; Detroit's unemployed auto workers, who had stood in line for days on end hoping for a few hours' work, confronted Henry Ford's factory guards in an ugly battle, leaving behind four dead and a number of wounded. And in the Pacific Northwest a band of World War veterans, determined to collect the bonus Congress had voted but had not appropriated, began moving eastward in May, 1932, picking up supporters in every city along the way.

These men were angry, they were desperate, but they were remarkably peaceable in their intentions; they were led by a veteran who had been out of a job for eighteen months, and who imposed on the Bonus Expeditionary Force the rules of "no panhandling, no drinking, no radicalism." When they arrived in Washington they were permitted to camp on the flats along the Anacostia River, where they waited patiently for Congress to deliver their bonus. Time dragged on, the administration did little beyond threatening to disperse them, the bill for immediate payment was voted down, and the thousands of increasingly restive men threatened to remain until they had seen Hoover and received their money. Toward the end of June they got another kind of answer: the chief of staff of the Army, Douglas MacArthur, assisted by Dwight Eisenhower, George Patton, and other officers, led tanks, machine gunners, and a column of infantry with fixed bayonets along Pennsylvania Avenue and scattered the veterans and burned their camp in what was called the battle of Anacostia Flats.

While Will did not approve of the bonus march, he conceded that they had as much right to put pressure on Congress as any other lobbyists, particularly since they were acting only in their own behalf, "which placed 'em right away about 90 percent higher in public estimation than the thousands of lobbyists that are there all the time." But what he admired especially about the veterans was their conduct throughout the long, sordid mess. "They hold the record for being the best behaved of any 15,000 hungry men ever assembled anywhere in the world. They were hungry, and they were seeing our government wasting thousands and millions before their eyes, and yet they remained fair and sensible. Would 15 thousand hungry bankers have done it? 15 thousand farmers? 15 thousand preachers? And just think what 15 thousand club women would have done to Washington even if they wasn't hungry. . . . It's easy to be a gentleman when you are well fed, but these boys did it on an empty stomach."

In the meantime trouble was mounting in the farm belt. In the Plains states, where land that should never have been plowed had been worked for years, drought and erosion had turned thousands of acres to hardpan or dust, and the topsoil blew away on the summer winds or ran off in spring floods. In the early thirties the dust storms began—thick brown clouds sometimes five miles high that forced men and women and children to huddle indoors or tie handkerchiefs around their noses and mouths when they went outside. When the winds did not blow, the dust lay like a thick fog, piling up on houses and fenceposts, smothering the few plants that survived. (On Armistice Day of 1933 the sky was dark with dust as far east as Albany, New York.) Thousands of debt-ridden tenant farmers, unable to work their fields or find work in nearby towns, packed up their pitiful belongings and drove away. In Iowa striking farmers, armed with clubs and pitchforks, blocked the roads, barring the movement of milk into the cities (dairymen were then receiving two cents a quart for their milk). Once again, violence broke out before the strike was called off, but nothing was accomplished; it only dramatized the critical situation in America's breadbasket.

Will observed, in August, 1932, that farm machinery shares had gone up on the stock market, but where, he wanted to know, was the farmer who could pay his taxes or purchase groceries? And "how is he going to buy any farm machinery? He has no more credit if he wanted to, he couldn't get a garden hoe much less a threshing machine. He can plow with a forked stick and raise more than he can sell." He sympathized with the striking farmers in Iowa, who were "stopping the trucks and eating what the other farmers send to town. In that way the farmer only has to haul it half as far." It impressed him as a pretty good scheme; if farmers would eat all they raised, not

TEXT CONTINUED ON PAGE 296

In July, 1932, Hoover summoned troops to oppose the Bonus Expeditionary Force.

SHERMAN GRINBERG FILM LIBRARIES, INC.

293

This veterans' march along Pennsylvania Avenue was unlike any parade the nation's capital had witnessed.

SHERMAN GRINBERG FILM LIBRARIES, INC.

On July 28, 1932, cavalry and tanks moved up Pennsylvania Avenue to evict any lingering bonus marchers.

UNDERWOOD & UNDERWOOD

A makeshift city of tents and shacks arose on Anacostia Flats, within sight of the U.S. Capitol (right).

NATIONAL ARCHIVES

UPI

The Battle of Anacostia Flats

During the spring of 1932 World War veterans marched on Washington, determined to stay until Congress authorized payment of a bonus they had been promised. Camping on Anacostia Flats at the edge of the city, their numbers swelled to 17,000. Finally the government agreed to pay their way home, but 2,000 remained, and an attempt by police to evict them led to bloodshed. President Hoover called on the Army to maintain law and order, and Chief of Staff Douglas MacArthur (right, with aide Dwight D. Eisenhower) ousted the veterans.

only would they get fat but the price of farm products would undoubtedly rise. "Course," he added, "on account of this not being an economist's idea it might not work."

Hoover, still intent on relieving the banks, had pushed a bill through Congress establishing the Reconstruction Finance Corporation in February, 1932—a sort of banker's bank capitalized at $2 billion to make credit available. To run it Hoover named Charles G. Dawes, Coolidge's Vice President and a former ambassador to Great Britain. Will opposed the idea of loans just on general principle. "Our only solution of relief," he said, "seems to be to fix it so people who are in a hole through borrowing can borrow some more." But he was especially suspicious of the motivation behind the RFC, much as he liked Dawes personally. He viewed the agency as a device created "to relieve bankers' mistakes and lend to new industries. You can always count on us helping those who have lost part of

Throughout the farm belt, members of the Farmers' Holiday Association, armed with pitchforks and clubs, blocked roads. In Council Bluffs, Ia. (below), sixty strikers were arrested.

UPI

296

their fortune," he commented, "but our whole history records nary a case where the loan was for the man who had absolutely nothing."

Not long afterward Dawes' role in the RFC proved a public embarrassment to Hoover. Six months after taking the job Dawes resigned to attend to the troubled affairs of his Central Bank and Trust Company in Chicago, and there was widespread dismay—a few weeks after his departure—when the RFC loaned his bank $90 million. Try as Hoover might to justify the loan by emphasizing the importance of Dawes' institution, this—on top of all the other failures for which his administration was blamed—was the kind of action that made Americans lose faith in his ability to solve the crisis. "Democracy," Hoover said later, "is not a polite employer," and the tragedy of this able, dedicated man was that he clung throughout his term of office to a faith and a course of action which might have served an earlier generation but which was inadequate when sweeping innovations were required. It was his misfortune to be struck down by a catastrophe not of his making, and although he did all he could by his own lights, his name became a prefix of contempt throughout the nation he had tried to serve.

As often as Will criticized Hoover and his method of dealing with the Depression, he had considerable sympathy for and understanding of him. Comparing his administration with that of his predecessor, he once remarked that "Nobody ever asked Coolidge to fix a thing. We just let everything go, and everybody grabbed off what he could. . . . Now Mr. Hoover is elected and we want him to fix everything. Farm relief—we want him to fix the farmer. Now, the farmer never had relief. . . . He never had it even under Lincoln . . . but he wants it under Hoover. Prohibition—they think Mr. Hoover ought to fix prohibition. . . . Prosperity—millions of people never had it under nobody and never will have it under anybody, but they all want it under Mr. Hoover. Women—women in this country, they think that Mr. Hoover ought to come in and wash the dishes . . . and help take care of the baby or something. If the weather is wrong, we blame it on Hoover."

Luck, he thought, had simply been against Hoover all the way. "He arrived at the picnic when even the last hard-boiled egg had been consumed. Somebody slipped some limburger cheese into his pocket and he got credit for breaking up the dance."

Will Rogers says: "We are the first nation in the history of the world to go to the poorhouse in an automobile."

We used to be told that depression was just a state of mind, but starvation has changed that impression, depression is a state of health, its moved from the mind to the stomach, and it ain't really depression either, its just a return to normalcy, we are just getting back to earth and it don't look natural to us anymore, we are back to two bit meals and cotton underwear, and off the $1.50 steaks and silk underrompers. The trouble with us in America is we are just muscle bound from holding a steering wheel, the only place we are callused from work is the bottom of our driving toe.

Now everybody has got a scheme to relieve unemployment,—there is just one way to do it and that's for everybody to go to work. *"Where"* why right where you are, look around you will see a lot of things to do, weeds to cut, fences to be fixed, lawns to be mowed, filling stations to be robbed, gangsters to be catered to. There is a million little odds and ends right under your eye that an idle man can turn his hand to every day. Course he won't get paid for it, but he won't get paid for not doing it. My theory is that it will keep him in practice in case something does show, you can lay off so long that you can lose the habit, so keep practicing so work won't be a novelty when it does come. You eat just as much loafing as you do working, in fact more, you got more time.

The trouble with us is today we are in such bad shape that it takes us all day to tell about it, we just keep yawning and yapping for the good old days of '26, '27 and '28. Well we just as well wake up, for those "Cuckoo" times are not coming back anymore. How we all escaped a lunatic asylum during that time is

BOTH: WILL ROGERS MEMORIAL, CLAREMORE, OKLA., COURTESY SHERMAN GRINBERG FILM LIBRARIES, INC.

The pictures above and opposite were taken while Will was making the broadcast on unemployment.

more than we know now. We paid a dollar down on everything under the sun that anybody had to sell. I had a fifty cent equity in every lot in America.

Now here we are worrying and reading in the papers about a hundred different problems that they got us all excited and making us believe they amount to something. This country has got just one problem . . . to so arrange it so that a man that wants work can get work, and give him a more equal division of the wealth the country produces. Now if our big men in the next year can't fix that, well they just ain't big men, that's all. What does all this yapping about disarmament amount to, compared to your own people that haven't worked in two years?

What does prohibition amount to, if your neighbors children are not eating? Its food, not drink is our problem now. We were so afraid the poor people might drink, now we fixed it so they can't eat. Is Japan's and China's troubles more to us than our bread lines? We got more wheat, more corn, more food, more cotton, more money in the banks, more everything in the world than any nation that ever lived ever had, yet we are starving to death, we are the first nation in the history of the world to go to the poorhouse in an automobile. We been so busy in the last few years getting radios and bathtubs and facial creams, and straight eights, that we forgot to see if we had any bacon and beans.

Now don't wait for the Government to feed these people. I have seen lots of audiences and heard lots of appeals, but I have yet to see one where the people knew the need . . . that they didn't come through. I don't know anything about "America" being fundamentally sound and all that after dinner "Hooey," but I do know that America is "Fundamentally Generous."

WILL ROGERS MEMORIAL, CLAREMORE, OKLA.

"A Man that don't love a Horse, there is something the matter with him."

Patiently waiting for a rider, Soapsuds stands at the end of the shaded arbor in front of the Santa Monica ranch house (left). Above is Will, posing in informal polo attire.
UPI

Something so untypical of Will Rogers' normal behavior occurred during 1931 that his wife Betty went out of her way to record it: after his return from the tour of Central America and the Caribbean he spent six months at home.

Home, by this time, was the Santa Monica ranch—and the move, Betty explained, had been prompted initially by their daughter Mary's lack of a bathroom. In the Beverly Hills house she shared a bath with her parents, who decided in 1928 that she ought to have one of her own. An architect was consulted, and remodeling began; termites were discovered in the structure, the remodeling got completely out of hand, and Will, in disgust, finally had the workmen tear down the home in which they had lived for more than ten years and which he called "the house that jokes built." By then the Santa Monica place was finished and that, in any case, was where he wanted to live. He liked a lot of room to move around in, and he wanted more space for the horses.

While not by nature an acquisitive man, Will had a special fondness for owning land, and in the early twenties when he learned that a highway was to be built between Beverly Hills and Santa Monica he purchased the property, assuming that it would only increase in value. The entrance was off to the right of the road (eventually named Sunset Boulevard), and a long curving drive—dotted with hundreds of eucalyptus trees set out by Will—wound up along the hill to a broad plateau, with brush-covered mountains and canyons in the distance. At the top of the drive was the long green sweep of a polo field. Beyond were the house, a garage and other outbuildings, a large horse barn, corrals, a cage for practicing polo, an oval-shaped roping ring, and a tennis court. That court, Will Jr. said, "was typical

While Betty was abroad, Will had the roof at the extreme left end of the house raised. Opposite is the remodeled living room, filled with souvenirs of the Old West and Will's career. The swinging couch is suspended on chains from the rafters.

of the way Dad operated. He decided one day that we ought to have one and told some workmen, 'Put it there.' The trouble was that there wasn't room enough for a standard-size court, so you really couldn't play tennis. We used it for basketball.'' Off to one side of the house were several golf holes for the use of friends. Will never had cared for the game (he couldn't understand why anyone would walk when he could ride), and when visitors were playing he would ride around on a horse and with a polo mallet hit the balls back to the unnerved golfers.

The house, which Anne Lindbergh described after a visit as "so quiet and far away and protected" that she and her husband felt "completely private and free," looked as if it had always been lived in and loved—relaxed and comfortable, with a casual beauty and no airs or architectural pretensions about it. The original building included three small bedrooms, a large living room, and a patio built around two live oaks; later this structure was enlarged piecemeal to suit the needs of the family —becoming, at last, a long, rambling house. There was no dining room, since Will had an aversion to eating indoors, hated formal dinners, and preferred to eat or entertain on the patio, where he often did the cooking himself at a barbecue grill. Everything about the house and grounds was arranged under

BOTH: WILL ROGERS MEMORIAL, CLAREMORE, OKLA.

his direction; he would appear in the car followed by a truck loaded with roses, bougainvillea, and pots of flowers for the patio, or shrubs to be planted around the ranch, and would see to the placement of each one.

The big living room overflowed with the mementos he loved: over the stone fireplace was the head of a Texas steer with an awesome pair of horns; a light fixture in the ceiling was made from an old wagon wheel he had found on the ranch; there were spurs, riding quirts, and beautifully worked saddles from all over the world; Navaho blankets and rugs; Western paintings by his friends Charlie Russell and Ed Borein; skins of a tiger and a black leopard sent him by the Sultan of Johore; the model of a covered wagon; a hurdy-gurdy and musical instruments he played when the mood struck him; a barrel full of his ropes; and, for a couch, a porch swing that hung from the exposed beams. Under the stairway, available for use at any time, was a stuffed calf on casters on which he practiced roping.

With all his nervous energy Will found it almost impossible to sit still throughout an entire meal, and between courses he would get up from the table and throw a rope—keeping up a steady flow of conversation all the while. If Fred Stone was there for dinner the two men would leave the table together and

303

begin swinging lassos while they talked and joked—sometimes aiming at a chair, sometimes throwing a loop over another dinner guest. Ed Borein finally tired of being roped and presented Will with the stuffed calf, which led to his remark that he was "without a doubt the best dead-calf roper in the world."

The room originally had a ceiling of conventional height, but that interfered with Will's indoor roping, so when Betty was absent on a trip to the Holy Land he hired workmen and had them raise the ceiling at one end of the room, adding a second story with two guest rooms and a bath, off a balcony. While Betty was away he mentioned in his daily article that he was "raising the roof," but whether she got the message is not clear. When she returned she discovered that one side of the house had been entirely altered.

At the opposite end of the living room was a big picture window which Florenz Ziegfeld had given them, and it also came as a surprise. The producer had always admired the view from the house but didn't like having to go outside to see it, so one day when Will was not home he sent his chauffeur to take measurements, and the next thing the Rogers family knew, workmen were tearing out the wall and installing the window. At a table in front of it, Will ate breakfast, read the morning papers, and planned his daily article. If he didn't have to go to the studio he banged out his column there or in his study on the second floor, at the east end of the house. Above his desk in the study were rolls of maps and a pointer he used, teacher-fashion. Adjacent to the study was a specially built shower compartment with a seat, a shower head in the ceiling, and several horizontal rings, which sprayed water from all directions and at various levels. The study had an outside door and an exterior staircase so that he could enter that way after an afternoon's roping.

Now in his early fifties, Will had begun to experience some difficulty in reading; the old "Injun eyes" weren't quite as good as they once were. One day in the Lambs' Club in New York an actor friend saw him holding the newspaper at arm's length, offered his glasses, and Will put them on and left the club with them in his pocket. He never bothered to have his eyes tested; Betty simply had the friend's prescription duplicated and ordered them by the dozen, since Will was so hard on them. When reading, he wore them down on the end of his nose, but when he was talking to someone he would take them off and twirl them around in his hand or chew on the ear pieces until they were twisted and gnawed out of shape.

When he was at home Will was outdoors constantly. If he was not roping calves or riding or playing polo, he was having new fences built, new roads or bridle paths cut into the hills, alterations made to one building or another, or a new corral constructed. Several Mexicans were employed full-time for this type of work, and to help around the house there was a butler named Emil Sandmeier and a former cowboy-turned-chauffeur, whose principal qualification in Will's eyes was that he could teach the children how to rope. Of all the activities, he most enjoyed going out in the roping ring to work with the calves. There was always a small bunch of them on the place, kept for just this purpose; but Will discovered that they became too tame after he had roped them again and again, so he would ship them off and replace them with another lot that provided more sport.

The two boys, Bill and Jim—and, for a time, Mary—played polo with Will, and since each rider needed five or six mounts

Will spent some of his happiest, most relaxed hours in this roping ring at the ranch.

WILL ROGERS MEMORIAL, CLAREMORE, OKLA.

*"Thoroughbreds are a very
nervous, nutty lot. I like an old
gentle, kind of dopey horse,
that is I mean, to ride around
and mess about on. I want one
you kinder got to work your
passage on and kinder nudge him
in the stomach at every step.
We have a lot of pretty steep
mountain trails out here and they
are plenty narrow and steep
sometimes, and there is a lot
of difference in the way different
horses negotiate 'em."*

from Weekly Article
May 12, 1935

for an afternoon's game, the stables and corrals were usually full. Naturally, Will had his favorites. There was Dopey, the little pony he had bought for the children when they were living on Long Island; Bootlegger, a roping horse that became one of his best polo ponies; and Soapsuds, his pet for roping. (Betty said she couldn't recall a single day when Will was at home that he didn't rope or ride on Soapsuds.) Bootlegger was smaller than the normal polo horse, but made up for lack of weight by extraordinary speed and quickness in turning. Customarily, polo ponies' manes were roached and the tails cropped or tied up to give the player more freedom in swinging his mallet, but Bootlegger was such a handsome animal that Will wouldn't have this done. People who had seen him always asked Betty about Bootlegger—they remembered "the little black pony and what a beautiful sight he was, with his long mane and tail standing out stiff in the wind, as he and Will came flying down the field."

All this exercise—none of it for any purpose except fun and diversion—kept Will in superb physical condition (he still did the Texas skip, jumping back and forth through a vertically spinning loop, every morning). And the result, his son Jim remembers, was that "he was *tough*, physically." Active as he was, he also had the ability to relax completely. Coming into the house after roping or riding, he could sit down and be sound asleep within minutes; then he would wake up revived and start on another project. He was, Jim says, an extremely nervous person who simply could not sit still—he always had to keep moving—"and like so many creative people, he had days when he was riding high, on the crest of the wave, and the next day he would hit bottom. Mother always knew when to jolly him along and how to play to his moods." She was also the calming influence, "the balance wheel" as Will himself called her, the one who maintained some semblance of tranquillity in the wake of the activity and confusion that trailed her husband wherever he was. And he was fully aware of it. As he wrote on their twenty-fifth wedding anniversary, "The day I roped Betty, I did the star performance of my life."

Disciplining the children was evidently another of Betty's jobs; she once told an interviewer that Will had never spanked them—she took care of that. Even so, Jim retains a vivid recollection of his father's quick temper—his "short fuse." Will had a one-eyed steer he used to rope in exhibitions, and one day Jim and a cousin climbed into the chute with the steer and tied a string of Chinese firecrackers to its tail. When the gate opened

306

and the steer charged out into the ring where Will was waiting to rope it the firecrackers went off, scaring the steer and Will's horse half to death. "Dad never did catch that steer," Jim says, "and I didn't go near the house for days, as long as he was home."

Whatever tension may have flared up occasionally between parents and children, Will's feelings on the matter were expressed in a letter he wrote his daughter Mary on her nineteenth birthday: "Sometimes we old ones dont see eye to eye with you Kids. But its *us* that dont stop to see your modern viewpoint. Times change. But Human Nature dont." The same letter, with which Will enclosed a check for Mary, who was about to leave on a trip to Europe, included a typically male observation on what she was going to do with the money. "You will want to get you some things in Paris," he surmised, even though "you can get better ones at home. But you are nineteen now, and Daddy cant argue with you. You being a Woman will think Paris is the Clothes Place so this is just for a little of that."

The pattern of the Rogers home life—simple and almost untouched by the veneer of Hollywood—was directly traceable to Betty and Will's upbringing and background. "Our parents were wholesome country people," Betty once said, "and that's the kind of life we like. And the kind we want our children to like."

All three children were given music and dancing lessons, but Will didn't want them in show business. He was content to have Mary play in summer stock, but he didn't want her career to go further than that. Hollywood hopefuls were constantly besieging him to get them a break in the movies, and on one occasion a woman brought her child to the Santa Monica ranch and had her go into a tap-dance routine for Will. Couldn't he get her daughter into the movies, the mother inquired. No, he couldn't, Will replied; he wouldn't know how. He walked into the house, grinned, and told his children, "I'm glad you don't have any talent."

Nearly four decades after a man's death it is difficult to judge what he was like as a private person, as distinct from the familiar public personality, or to put a finger on the relationships he enjoyed with his family and close friends. On certain points his two sons' recollections agree; on others they diverge. Both recall that their parents were away from home continually; there never seemed a time when they were growing up when their father, in particular, was not involved in

The coach gives son Jim advice from the sidelines before the polo match begins.

UPI

307

something that took him away. While the children were still young Betty Rogers had had to make a choice: to be with her husband as much as possible or to stay at home with them, and she chose the former, after arranging for her unmarried sister, Theda Blake, or "Aunt Dick" as the children called her, to be with Bill, Mary, and Jim. For several years, while the family was in Beverly Hills, Will's niece Paula McSpadden also lived at the house, helping the youngsters with their lessons, riding with them, and taking them to plays, ball games, picnics, and Mary on her first date.

Even when his father was at home, Bill recalls, the demands of his career were considerable—the movies, lectures, columns and other writing made enormous inroads on his time. During the last years of his father's life Bill, the oldest child, was away at preparatory school and college, with the result that he feels he hardly knew him. And at the time he sensed that his father and his brother were more congenial than he and his father could ever be. "Jim liked horses," he remarked, "and I could either take them or leave them alone." At times he was bothered by the pressure his father put on him to look after the horses or to play polo when he had something else he wanted to do. Jim never felt pushed in quite the same way: "I suppose that was because I was more cowboy than Bill was. I probably never felt I was being made to do it because I was always hanging around the barn anyway. I always did like horses."

In the fall of 1931 both boys were away at school, and there must have been some discussions between their mother and father about their failure to write home, because Will took the unusual step of bringing the matter to his readers' attention. His column on October 29 brightened the day for many an American parent: "Early in the autumn," he wrote "Mrs. Rogers and I sent two sons away supposedly to schools (we got tired trying to get 'em up in the morning). One went north here in this state, another to New Mexico. Since then we have received no word or letter. We have looked in every football team all over the country. Guess they couldn't make the teams, knew their education was a failure and kept right on going. Any news from any source will be welcome. I am flying to Mexico City today. The big one spoke Spanish so maybe he is there. The little one didn't even speak English but he loved chili and hot tamales so he may be there too."

The two sons agree that Will, for his thousands of acquaintances, had few intimate friends. "He was a loner," Jim says.

But the men he saw most frequently, who could be considered his closest personal friends, were Fred Stone, his lawyer Oscar Lawler, Ed Borein the artist, Irvin S. Cobb, Leo Carillo the actor, Joe Schenck the film producer, and Big Boy Williams, who played in numerous movies with Will. Because of his schedule he wasn't able to see any of them regularly or over extended periods; yet even after long absences they were the kind of friends with whom he could pick up a relationship where they had left off.

Will had always had an itch to seek out prominent people, and he usually had someone important in tow at Santa Monica. One man for whom he had a high regard was Will Durant, the philosopher, and on one of his visits to the ranch Bill, who was then a freshman at Stanford University, visibly upset his father by arguing with their guest on his own subject. The professors at the university, the young man informed Durant, did not think highly of *The Story of Philosophy* because it was a popularization.

In 1932 Bill accompanied his father to the Democratic convention and shared a hotel room with him in Chicago. He never got any sleep at night because Will was constantly on the telephone (most of the time talking to someone about the imminent failure of Charles Dawes' bank), and during the day it was his job to keep people away from his father as much as possible, since everyone seemed to want to meet him. At one point a man dressed in an old sailor suit approached, and Bill dutifully began to fend him off; the sailor called out to Will, who

TEXT CONTINUED ON PAGE 312

Will with two of his old cronies—the actor Fred Stone and the artist Ed Borein
WIDE WORLD

Will Rogers says: "He is the only Painter of Western Pictures . . . that a Cowboy can't Criticise."

From the moment he first saw his work, Will recognized the genius of the painter Charlie Russell in capturing the feel of the Old West. As he wrote to Betty from Butte, Montana, in 1908, "I just found a lot of great post cards, lots of them marked C.M.R. are by a man I know, a cowboy C.M. Russell (The Cowboy Artist), he is the greatest artist of this kind in the world. Remington is not in it with him. . . ."

By 1924—two years before Russell's death—his oils and water colors were included in many important private collections, and Will realized that the credit for this achievement was due not only to the quality and authenticity of the pictures but to the untiring efforts of Russell's wife in gaining recognition for his work. (Will personally owned a number of paintings and pieces of sculpture by Russell.)

In his weekly article of April 13, 1924, he had this to say about his friend Charlie:

If, as the saying goes, "It's the things that we have done that are Remembered after we are gone that really amounts to Anything," well, I have a Cowboy friend who is doing Things today that will live longer with People who know and appreciate Art and Beauty and Genius, than anything any Cowpuncher ever did.

Think of a 40 dollar a month Cowhand, who never had a Lesson in his life, taking a little Paint Brush, a few daubs of Paint and producing Scenes of our West, which are fast passing, that have sold (not only one, but three of them) to England's Future King. . . .

I don't need to mention his name to any Art Conniseur. . . . Now they all, as I say, know who I am talking about already, but the trouble is that there is so little percentage of Artistic people who read my Articles that I

will have to tell you his name.

It is Charles M. Russell of Great Falls, Montana. He went west from his home in St. Louis at the age of 15, and landed by Stage Coach in Montana in 1880, and has lived there Ever Since.

He gained his first local fame in Montana, in the winter of '86 and '87. It was a Terrible Cold Winter. He was working for a Cow Outfit and they had been snowed in all winter and the cattle had about all died. The Owner finally got word through to ask the Boss how Everything was. The Boss wrote him a letter telling him the bad News. Then Charlie, who was just one of the Hands, drew a Picture of one old lone Cow in a Blizzard. She was surrounded by a pack of Wolves, and he had under it "The last of the 10 Thousand, or Waiting for a Chinook." A Chinook, by the way, is one of those Warm Winds which come in that Country which melt the Snow and it feels warm like Summer, and the stock has a Chance to get something to Eat.

Well, when the Boss saw that Picture, just painted on the back of an old Envelope, He said, "Why write him a letter? Just send him this! It will tell him more than I can write." And that is held in Montana today as one of the most famous of Russell's Paintings.

He used to paint a Picture, bring it in and Sell it if he could for a few Dollars and, if not, give it over the Bar for a round of Drinks for himself and Friends. For in those days Charlie was a pretty Wild kind of a Hand. So, as a consequence, the Silver Dollar Saloon housed many a Russell Masterpiece, and it became Noted.

Then Charlie got to riding up to Cascade, a

little mining Town near and it was Noised Around that there was a School Teacher up there that must be Sitting for a Portrait. They were not Sure until they Heard that he had given her his favorite Horse. Then "Old Yank," a Character, Miner, Stage Coach Driver, and all around Town Philosopher, said, "Charlie sure is going to marry that Gal. Now, I hear he give her his Horse and he will have to Marry her to get him Back."

He got not only the Horse back but a Wife, and not only a Wife but a Manager. The last Russell Painting had gone over the Bar. She said: "You paint these things. I will attend to the Distribution end of this Enterprize." She enlarged his Market from what had been purely local Consumption to one which embraced two Continents.

Now for another side of this Remarkable Woman. Lots of People forgot when they were celebrating over the Remarkable Good that Prohibition would bring, that it was also putting out of Business a few good men among Saloon Keepers, who had always paid their license and were conducting as Legitimate a Business as any other, and did not just Switch to a Bootleggery. Well, the Silver Dollar Saloon happened to be one of them,

and the owners had Misfortune and they had their Home Mortgaged and would have lost it, when in steps Mrs. Charlie Russell, sold just part of The Pictures, paid off the Home, and left the Owner comfortably fixed, and still able to enjoy Art such as few have. . . .

The first one of his Pictures which Brought a big Price naturally attracted a lot of News in the Home Paper. One of the Cowpunchers on reading it went to Charlie and said, "Charlie, what is it that makes them Pictures cost so much? Is it the Brush or the Paint?"

He is the only Painter of Western Pictures in the World that a Cowboy can't Criticise. Every little piece of Leather or Rope is just where it would be. Eddie Borein, the greatest Etcher of Western Subjects we have, is also a great Painter himself, and a Real Ex Cowpuncher. He says Russell is "The Master."

Now every Story should point a Moral and this one is: If you are going to Paint (or do anything else) know what you are Painting about and if you are going to Marry, marry somebody that can manage you RIGHT.

So here is to an Old 40-Dollar-A-Month Cowpuncher, whose work will live for centuries. Maybe longer than that. Maybe as long as the Republican Party is under Suspicion.

MONTANA STOCKGROWERS ASSOCIATION

While a lady photographer prepares to take a shot, Will confers with columnist Arthur Brisbane, who was also covering the Republican convention in the year 1932.

UPI

hurried over, greeted him with open arms, and introduced him to his son as Carl Sandburg. One of Bill's colorful recollections of that convention was a late night in the hotel room when Will, Sandburg, and Groucho Marx sat together playing guitars and singing. Will had a high regard for Groucho, who "can play as good on the guitar as Harpo can on the harp, or Chico on the piano, but he never does. He is really what I call an ideal musician. He can play but don't."

Despite considerable evidence to the contrary, by his own and Betty's account, Will was not much of a reader of books, although the library at the ranch was filled with autographed volumes written by acquaintances. ("Busy men that you would think would have something important to do," he observed, were all writing books.) The old impatience showed through his comments on books: "It takes 'em so long to describe the color of the eyes of all the characters." As he put it on another occasion:

I am fifty-two years old, sound of body, but weak of mind, and I never did read hardly any books. I like to read but I don't have the time. If I got any spare time I like to get on a horse and ride around, or sit and blather with somebody. But I do a lot of newspaper reading. I try to get all breeds, creeds, and every single different political one. If they would just quit printing newspapers for about a year, I could get some books read, but by the time I go through the daily papers, I am sound asleep. I am kind of a slow reader anyhow, and a lot of the stuff I have to read is not delivered in what you would call a straightforward or lucid vein, so I have to go back over it a few times to catch the meaning.

I just got started in wrong. All educated people started in reading good books. Well I didn't. I seem to have gone from Frank Merriwell and Nick Carter, at Kemper Military Academy, right to the Congressional Record, just one set of low fiction to another.

There are occasional glimpses of his pride in having succeeded without benefit of college or degree, but he regretted not having taken advantage of the opportunities to acquire a good education. In May, 1931, hearing that a group of Oklahomans planned to give him an honorary degree, he fired off a telegram to the editor of an Oklahoma City paper:

WHATS ALL THIS MESS OVER SOME DEGREE, BILL ESTES AND HIS OKLAHOMA CHAMBER OF COMMERCE BEEN WIRING ME ABOUT IT, THEY ARE AS BAD AS I AM, A DEGREE WOULD READ AS FOREIGN TO ANY OF THEM AS A PRESCRIPTION. WHAT ARE YOU TRYING TO DO, MAKE A JOKE OUT OF COLLEGE DEGREES? THEY ARE IN BAD ENOUGH REPUTE AS IT IS, WITHOUT HANDING 'EM AROUND TO COMEDIANS. THE WHOLE HONORARY DEGREE THING IS THE "HOOEY." I SAW SOME COLLEGE GIVE MELLON ONE, AND HE IS A BILLION BUCKS SHORT. I GOT TOO MUCH RESPECT FOR PEOPLE THAT WORK AND EARN 'EM TO SEE 'EM HANDED AROUND TO EVERY NOTORIOUS CHARACTER. I WILL LET OOLOGAH KINDERGARTEN GIVE ME ONE—D.A. (DOCTOR OF APPLESAUCE).

The following month, when Mary graduated from preparatory school in Los Angeles, Betty and Will were on hand for the ceremonies, as were the actors Douglas Fairbanks and Wallace Beery and the director Frank Lloyd—all of whom had young relatives graduating. As Will said, he and the other Hollywood elders sat and purred like "old tomcats basking in a little reflected sunshine and secretly congratulating ourselves on choosing a profession where education played no part."

Although he belonged to no church and rarely attended services, he was a deeply religious man on his own terms. Before there was a church in Beverly Hills the Rogers children attended Sunday-school classes at the local school, and Will was indignant about that; he and a group of citizens donated the money to build a small community church. But his general attitude toward religion was not unlike that of a growing number of Americans; it was not the lack of religious inclination that kept people out of church on Sunday mornings, "just that you can't beat Sunday morning to get the old car out and ramble.

"In London five years ago, old Lord Dewar, a great humorist and character and the biggest whiskey man in the world, gave the children a little white dog (Sealyham), saying, 'If this dog knew how well he was bred he wouldn't speak to any of us.'

"We have petted him, complained at him, called him a nuisance, but when we buried him yesterday, we couldn't think of a wrong thing he had ever done.

"His bravery was his undoing. He lost to a rattlesnake, but his face was toward him."

from Daily Telegram
Mar. 24, 1931

. . . Folks are just as good as they ever were, and they mean well, but no minister can move 'em like a second hand car.'' Perhaps the time would come, he thought, when they would hold services "on rainy days, and days when they are fixing the roads, and they will pack 'em in.''

After visiting the Soviet Union in the twenties he had said, "There never was a nation founded and maintained without some kind of belief in something.'' The Communist government, he remarked, had chosen to suppress the one thing that was "absolutely necessary to run a Country on, and that is Religion. Never mind what kind; but it's got to be something or you will fail at the finish.'' He had been raised a Methodist, he once told a clergyman, but having traveled so widely and seen so many different types of people, "I don't know now just what I am. I know I have never been a non-believer. But I can honestly tell you that I don't think that any one religion is *the* religion. Which way you serve your God will never get one word of argument or condemnation out of me.''

If his whole outlook on living was relaxed and casual, the trait was reflected nowhere so much as in his lack of plans for the future and his manner of living each day as it came. He disliked plans intensely, Betty said, and "would not make an engagement two weeks ahead of time if he could possibly help it.'' His idea of heaven was to have a free day so that he and Betty could get in the car and drive without any preconceived notion of where they were going, and she recalled those trips as some of the happiest times they had together, when she had him all to herself. "Come on, Blake, let's get going,'' he would say, and they would drive until it was time to file his daily article. He would pull off the road and sit on the running board with the typewriter on his knees while she worked at her knitting, and then they would drive to the nearest telegraph office. If they had no sandwiches with them, Will liked to stop at a small town grocery store and wander from shelf to shelf, collecting cans and boxes of food for lunch; then he would chat for a while with the storekeeper before they went on.

Driving with Will could be an experience. He handled a car the same way he rode a horse "and could usually make it do what he wanted,'' Betty said, but that was all he knew about automobiles—she wasn't entirely sure he even knew how to change a tire.

He had a rule about clothes. "He dressed only once a day,'' Betty said. "After his bath in the morning he put on a clean shirt, and that bath and that shirt had to last him through the evening, no matter what came up." On the ranch he wore work clothes—blue jeans, boots, a cowboy shirt and sometimes a handkerchief around his neck, and a small, light-colored Stetson; for more formal occasions he had a reliable double-breasted blue serge suit which, with a white shirt and black bow tie, had to do also for evening wear. He did not dress up for anyone. (There is some reason to suppose that to a certain degree this habit was deliberate. As a boy he had been something of a dude where clothes were concerned, but in his mature years he was, after all, a "character" in the eyes of the public and did little to distort the image—to the joy of the studio's publicity department.)

Formal wear was not in Will's line; he just put on the old blue serge and appended a black bow tie.
WILL ROGERS MEMORIAL, CLAREMORE, OKLA.

At times the Rogers boys were uncomfortably aware of their father's double standard on the subject of clothing. He insisted that they have their shirt collars buttoned at all times, no matter how hot it was, and when they traveled on board ship he expected them to dress for dinner. "*We* had to wear a tuxedo to dinner every night," Jim recalls, "but he never did. He was a stickler for us doing the right thing."

It occurred to Betty now and again that she had four children not three, "and that Will was the greatest child of all." (He was not unaware of this himself: speaking to a radio audience he alluded to "the mother of our little group," saying that she "has been for twenty-two years trying to raise to maturity four children, three by birth and one by marriage. While she hasn't done a good job, the poor soul has done all that mortal human could do with the material she has had to work with.") When they celebrated Christmas, the children took turns playing Santa Claus, but Will was the ringleader in charge of plans. He was never comfortable in large department stores or smart shops, but he liked to do his own Christmas shopping. Putting it off until the last possible moment, he would hurry off alone, buy a staggering number of presents for everyone—including all those who worked for or with him—wandering from store to store, spending hours over the counters selecting clothing and toys. He never asked the price of anything, and when he had finished he would carry his bundles to the car, drive home, and spend the remaining hours of Christmas Eve wrapping his packages.

Despite the Depression, there was little concern about the family fortunes in the Rogers household while Will was alive. (If ever his father did feel the need of ready cash, Bill remem-

315

bers, he used to say he could always make another lecture tour; there was more money in that than in anything else.) Will's own attitude toward money was simple: he liked making it, he wanted to make a lot of it, but once he had it he disposed of it prodigally. The family had all it needed, but Will had little use for material possessions beyond his horses, plus a rather modest list of creature comforts. He regarded money more in terms of what it would do for him and others than what it would buy. Money was for the constant trips, and he liked to travel in style; it was also something to be given away, and he was extraordinarily generous to relations less fortunate than he, to charities, and to friends.

The country's economic plight had brought to an end the golden days of Florenz Ziegfeld. He was faced, in the early thirties, with failing health and mounting debts, but still he would come over to Will's ranch, immaculately attired in riding habit, looking for all the world as if nothing had changed, and the two oddly matched companions (Will was still calling him Mr. Ziegfeld) would ride out across the hills, talking of the old days when life had been so good to the showman. In 1932 Ziegfeld died, a bankrupt, and Will—after delivering a moving tribute to his old boss in his newspaper articles—quietly paid his medical and funeral expenses.

Will considered the Santa Monica property (which could easily be subdivided) a hedge against potential reverses. After buying the ranch he began investing in beach property, and his first purchase was a stretch of ocean frontage in Santa Monica for which he paid $20,000. It happened to be near some land that William Randolph Hearst was acquiring for his mistress, Marion Davies, and Hearst sent a real estate agent to make Will an offer. What did he want for it?

"$40,000," was the reply.

"Ridiculous," said the agent as he walked away. But soon he was back to announce that Mr. Hearst would pay $40,000. Will told him that the price had gone to $80,000.

Again the man walked out; again he came back; and eventually Will sold the land to Hearst for $100,000.

"Gee, how long has this been going on?" Will asked. "I got to get me some more of that beach." And this prompted his later purchase of two miles of beach front at the foot of Santa Monica canyon—an investment worth millions of dollars today. Despite his confidence that it would be like money in the bank for the family, about ten years after he acquired it the state of

California condemned and bought the beach from Will's heirs for less than Will had originally paid for it.

In spite of the immense amount of time he devoted to his career, that aspect of his life was rarely discussed within the family circle. He regarded it quite simply as a job, and he did not want to bring his work home with him any more than he had to. He treated what he was doing casually, suspecting that the public "would catch onto" him sooner or later. And when people did, he figured, he and Betty might go back to Claremore, Oklahoma, where he had purchased about thirty acres on a hillside at the edge of town. That would be the site of their house.

What success he had achieved he viewed largely as the result of luck or accident, and he never considered himself a public figure. He was an entertainer—"watching the Government and reporting the facts"—and when some people began giving serious thought to the possibility that he might run for office he was both annoyed and embarrassed. He got a kick out of having his name put in nomination at the 1924 Democratic convention; he rejoiced in the Anti-Bunk candidacy of the 1928 Presidential election. However, in 1931 matters took a different turn. A committee called on him to urge that he run for Senator from California, and that overture was followed by talk of his running for President.

He had dealt with this matter once before, and his feelings about it remained unchanged. When someone proposed him as a candidate in 1928, he had observed, "Now when that was done as a joke it was alright, but when it's done seriously it's just pathetic. We are used to having everything named as Presidential candidates, but the country hasn't quite got to the professional comedian stage."

Now, in 1931, the language was considerably stronger. "Will you do me one favor," he wrote, "if you see or hear of anybody proposing my name for any political office, will you maim said party and send me the bill? . . . I hereby and hereon want to go on record as being the first Presidential, Vice-Presidential, Senator, or Justice of Peace candidate to withdraw. I not only 'Don't choose to run,' I won't run. Now I hope in doing this that I have started something that will have far reaching effect. Who will be the next to do the public a favor and withdraw? It's one year away but the candidates will be Hoover and Curtis versus Franklin D. Roosevelt and some Western or Southern Democratic Governor."

The Santa Monica Ranch

No matter where the family lived, they had horses, but not until he bought the ranch in Santa Monica did Will have access to the kind of space that appealed so much to him. Here, when he was not roping or playing polo, he would supervise the cutting of new trails through the mountains or launch some new building project. By most standards, the previous home in Beverly Hills (below)—"the house that jokes built"—was an exceptionally comfortable place; but the Santa Monica establishment was an approximation (in an area soon to become urbanized) of the ranch life he had known so well back in Oklahoma.

Above, the house in Beverly Hills. At right, an aerial photograph shows the ranch's developed areas. The drive winds up to the polo field, beyond which (at left) is the house. At rear are the stables—hub of all the mountain trails.

ALL: WILL ROGERS MEMORIAL, CLAREMORE, OKLA.

Above is the Rogers family in a rare moment of inactivity. At the time the two pictures were taken, Jim was thirteen years old, Bill seventeen, and Mary fifteen. The solemn character on the grass is Jock, a Sealyham given them by Lord Dewar. Below, Jim prepares to feed Sarah, pet calf from the King Ranch.

BOTH: WILL ROGERS MEMORIAL, CLAREMORE, OKLA.

WILL ROGERS MEMORIAL, CLAREMORE, OKLA., GIFT OF PROJECT 20

Will could be as informal as he liked at the ranch—and usually was. Above, he and Betty entertain a group of visitors (including actress Billie Burke, turning to face camera) on the shaded terrace. The extensive stables are shown below; wings on each side of the central section contained box stalls for the family's horses.

WILL ROGERS MEMORIAL, CLAREMORE, OKLA.

BOTH: UPI

"If he burned down the capitol we would cheer and say, "'Well, we at least got a fire started, anyhow.'"

One of Will's most successful public appearances was at the Democratic convention of 1932 (left). In September he introduced candidate Roosevelt at Hollywood Bowl, with the result shown above.

Will's prediction was wrong on one count. Roosevelt's running mate was a Southerner *and* a Westerner, but not a governor—he was the Speaker of the House of Representatives, John Nance Garner of Texas. As anyone else could have guessed, the campaign—which came at the bottom of the Depression—was as bitterly contested as that of 1928.

Fifteen million people were out of work. In New York City alone, a hundred thousand meals were served each day to destitute souls waiting in bread lines; seventeen thousand New York families were being evicted, with their furniture, from their homes every month. Huey Long, a vulgar, rough-talking Louisianan, the self-styled "Kingfish," had stomped onto the national political scene, echoing the protests of the poor, promising the confiscation and redistribution of wealth to make "Every man a king, every girl a queen." A radio priest named Charles Coughlin was preaching about social justice to thousands of rapt listeners; Dr. Francis E. Townsend was giving elderly Americans on the West Coast a vision of a society in which anyone over sixty would receive $200 a month; across the land other politicians were taking up Huey's cry: "Share the Wealth!"

By no means everyone took seriously the candidacy of Franklin Roosevelt when it was announced in January, 1932. The best that columnist Walter Lippmann could say of the New York governor was, "He is a pleasant man who, without any important qualifications for the office, would very much like to be President." Al Smith, whom Roosevelt had nominated for the Presidency in 1924 and 1928 and whom he had succeeded in the Albany state house in 1929, was now leading a movement to stop his former protégé, criticizing him for his effort "to delude

From the Shrine of the Little Flower near Detroit, Mich., Father Coughlin broadcast to huge radio audiences.
UPI

the poor people of this country," reminding him that "oratory puts nobody to work." That, in rebuttal to Roosevelt's radio speech calling for aid for "the forgotten man at the bottom of the economic pyramid."

Will had regarded Roosevelt as the Democrat's likeliest candidate since 1930, when he wrote of his re-election as governor, "The Democrats nominated their President yesterday, Franklin D. Roosevelt." But his nomination was by no means a sure thing. Not only was the Democratic party split into factions supporting one candidate or another; it was divided along religious and sectional lines, by disparate views on Prohibition, and by a host of other ideological disputes. When Will arrived in Chicago late in June he was astonished to see so many smiling delegates; certainly, he thought, they were not going to "degenerate into a party of agreement and mutual admiration." He was not disappointed. The next day "They fought, they fit, they split and adjourned in a dandy wave of dissension." That was the old party spirit he was accustomed to: "The Democrats are the only known race of people that give a dinner and fight over it. No job is ever too small for them to split over. But you would a loved 'em today. They was real Democrats."

During those dead hours while the platform committee was meeting, Will was called upon to address the convention delegates—to kill time and "act the fool," he said, until the committee members sobered up and brought in the Prohibition plank. For a quarter of an hour he kept them laughing as he joked about the delegates and complimented the Republicans on nominating Hoover ("They did the best they could with what little they had"). Then he came to his point: "Now, you rascals, I want you to promise me one thing. No matter who is nominated, don't go home and act like Democrats. Go home and act like he was the man you came to see nominated. Don't say he is the weakest man you could have nominated. Don't say he can't win. You don't know what he can do or how weak he is until next November. I don't see how he could be weak enough not to win. If he lives until November, he is in!" As he left the rostrum to an enormous ovation, with the crowd standing and whooping in the aisles, begging for more, it was enough, wrote the newspaperman Damon Runyon, to make Roosevelt's backers uneasy. "They fear it will wind up with Will being nominated for President, but they may calm their fears. Will wouldn't accept. He makes more money at his own racket." Heywood Broun, commenting on Will's appearance, remarked: "It seems a little ironical that the same Convention which thinks Will Rogers is a clown accepts Huey Long as a Statesman."

When the nominations began, Will received Oklahoma's 22 votes as a "favorite son" on the first ballot, but it was an ephemeral thing. As he said, "Politics ain't on the level. I was only in 'em for an hour but in that short space of time somebody stole 22 votes from me. I was sitting there in the press stand asleep and wasn't bothering a soul when they woke me up and said Oklahoma had started me on the way to the White House with 22 votes. I thought to myself, well, there is no use going there this late in the morning, so I dropped off to sleep again, and that's when somebody touched me for my whole roll, took the whole 22 votes, didn't even leave me a vote to get breakfast on." It was a shame, he thought: he might have traded those votes to Roosevelt for a job as Secretary of State, or Al Smith might have made him mayor of New York.

By the time the convention settled down to more serious business, Roosevelt had an almost certain majority, but the coalition Smith had organized still had the potential of stopping him. On the first ballot Roosevelt lacked 100 votes of the two-thirds majority required, although he led Smith and Garner by a comfortable margin. There was little change on the second or third ballots, which saw Roosevelt gaining only slightly, and as the possibility of a deadlock increased, the tension mounted perceptibly. Something had to give, and it was not yet clear what that would be. Then the break came. Garner released his Texas delegates; William Gibbs McAdoo, who had a score to settle with Al Smith dating back to 1924, announced that California cast its votes for Roosevelt; and it was all over. As Smith left the hall in anger the band struck up the tune that was to become the perennial anthem of the "Squire of Hyde Park"—"Happy Days Are Here Again."

Symbolic of FDR's intention to change the old ways dramatically was his sudden flight to Chicago to accept the nomination, which, Will said, "gave aviation the biggest boost it ever had." In his acceptance speech the nominee pledged a "new deal" for the American people and promised a fresh approach to the nation's problems: "Let it be from now on the task of our party to break foolish traditions."

What Will called "the same old vaudeville team of Hoover and Curtis" had been renominated without opposition earlier in June at a "convention held for no reason at all," and Hoover

Bombastic Huey Long, the "Kingfish," delivers an address to Des Moines farmers, advocating share-the-wealth.
UPI

"That's what makes us a great country. The little things are serious and the big ones are not."

from Daily Telegram
Oct. 18, 1933

was quick to announce that he perceived in Roosevelt's philosophy elements of the poison that had already spread through Europe and "the fume of the witch's caldron which boiled in Russia." That was an early indication of the lines along which the campaign would be fought, with each side predicting calamitous results if the other were elected. At the outset Will took a fairly relaxed view of things: "This is not an election of parties or policies," he wrote. "It's an election where both sides really need the work"; and he suggested that all opposing candidates agree to split the salary of the office for which they were contending so that the country could call off the election. The two Presidential rivals did not see it quite that way. Hoover foresaw that grass would grow in the streets of a hundred cities and a thousand towns if Roosevelt's tariff proposals were adopted; weeds would overrun millions of farms; and the election would determine the direction the nation would take for a century to come.

Midway into September Roosevelt was scheduled to make a campaign speech in Los Angeles when he learned that the city's Republican mayor would not welcome him. FDR's managers got in touch with Will, who plunged into the breach and assured them he would greet their candidate. (As a former mayor of Beverly Hills, he thought he was entitled to welcome the man to southern California.) On Saturday night, September 23, he introduced the Democratic challenger to a huge crowd at the Hollywood Bowl while Roosevelt led the laughter at a series of jokes about him. "Now, I don't want you to think that I am overawed by being asked to introduce you," Will told him. "I'm not. I'm broadminded that way and will introduce anybody. This introduction may have lacked logic, and particularly floweriness, but you must remember you're only a candidate yet. Come back when you are President and I will do better. I am wasting no oratory on a mere prospect."

The following Monday Will commented on Roosevelt's obvious cheerfulness. "That is one thing about Democrats," he said, "they never are as serious as the Republicans. They been out of work so long they got used to it. The Democrats take the whole thing as a joke, and the Republicans take it serious but run it like a joke. There's not much difference."

Autumn came, and with it the World Series, which Will followed with his customary interest. Then, deciding he had had all he wanted of politics for a while, he departed in October for South America to escape the barrage of newspaper and radio comments about the coming election—he was tired of reading "Hoover said this" and "Roosevelt says that." He flew down the west coast of the continent to Chile, whence he would travel to Argentina and Brazil, returning to the States just before the election.

Chile, he reported, had had five presidents already that fall: "One inaugural parade started out with one President and wound up at the White House with another," and "the man that's in now is afraid to send out his laundry." He visited an Argentine estancia and watched the gauchos perform, attended a football game in Montevideo (the casualties nearly equaled those in a revolution), and in Brazil found that they were just sweeping up the streets after a political upheaval of their own.

For some reason he had miscalculated the date of the U.S. elections, arriving in New York earlier than he had planned— "in the midst of the most colossal rodeo of applesauce in the history of our national pastime." He was also in time to stir up a first-class rhubarb with his daily article of November 1, in which he advocated a moratorium on speeches by the candidates, who had already "called each other everything in the world they can think of." Stating that these two ordinarily fine men had been goaded by their political advisers to say things that

Sick of politics, Will traveled to South America in 1932 and picked up this memento of an evening spent with five hundred Americans at a dinner in Buenos Aires.

*To Ambassador Bill
from Ambassador Bob*

*Buenos Aires
October 19 1932.*

WILL ROGERS MEMORIAL, CLAREMORE, OKLA.

327

On Father's Day:
*"There is nothing outside of an
economist that's been any more
overestimated than a father.
He is a necessity, and that
about lets him out."*
from Daily Telegram
June 18, 1933

"if they were in their right minds they wouldn't think of saying," he pointed to Hoover's remark that any change of policies would bring disaster to every fireside in America. That was ridiculous: "This country is a thousand times bigger than any two men in it. . . . This country has gotten where it is in spite of politics, not by the aid of it," and the people's ability to survive so much political bunk proved how superior they were. "If by some divine act of providence we could get rid of both these parties and hire some good men, like any other big business does, why that would be sitting pretty."

In conclusion, he advised both candidates to go fishing until the election on Tuesday instead of calling each other names. "You will be surprised," he told them, "but the old United States will keep right on running while you boys are sitting on the bank." When you come back on Wednesday, he added, "we will let you know which one is the lesser of the two evils."

A few days later found him in a more philosophical mood. Even though the candidates had lost their tempers, he advised voters not to be too critical. Neither man was going to save the country, neither would ruin it. If Hoover lost, people ought to feel sorry for him, because he had done the best he could; if Roosevelt lost, it would not be long before everyone could feel sorry for him, too. For if the Depression continued, the loser was going to be the winner: "This President business is a pretty thankless job. Washington or Lincoln, either one, didn't get a statue until everybody was sure they was dead." As far as he was concerned, the one redeeming aspect of the election was that it would be over soon, and everybody ought to pray that it would not end in a tie—"We couldn't go through with this thing again." He advised Americans to cheer up and be friends again. "One of the evils of democracy is, you have to put up with the man you elect whether you want him or not. That's why we call it democracy."

For his remarks of November 1 Will was attacked by partisans of both sides, but he decided to bide his time and allow the controversy to simmer down before replying. When he did, it took the form of a letter to the editor of the Los Angeles *Times*, which had been one of his severest critics. He regarded that particular article as one of his best—"a change from the usual bunk I had been dishing out"—and was surprised that people were so exercised over his suggestion that the candidates go fishing. There was not a man in public life he didn't like; most of them were his good friends—"but that's not going to keep me from taking a dig at him when he does something or says something foolish." Hoover knew better than to say grass was going to grow in the streets—"You can't get it to grow on your lawns." And it was foolish for Roosevelt to blame the Depression on Hoover because he knew it was not so. Will meant what he said about the United States being bigger than any two men or any two parties.

In the wake of the election he offered solace to Mr. Hoover. The people, he wrote, had simply lost their taste for the Republican party, which only proved "There is something about a Republican that you can only stand for him just so long. And on the other hand, there is something about a Democrat that you can't stand him for quite that long." Hoover had been "handed a balloon that was blowed up to its utmost"; he had held onto it "as carefully as anyone could, but the thing busted right in [his] hands. . . . It wasn't you, Mr. President. The people just wanted to buy something new, and they didn't have any money to buy it with. But they could go out and vote free and get something new for nothing. So cheer up. You don't know how lucky you are."

Then he had some advice for the incoming Chief Executive, which he sent in the form of a personal telegram. "Your health," he told Roosevelt, "is the main thing. Don't worry too much." A smile in the White House again would "look like a meal to us." As for handling Congressmen and Senators, "don't scold 'em. They are just children that's never grown up. Don't send messages to 'em, send candy."

There was counsel on every front: in foreign affairs, the President-elect should send Nicaragua "wishes but not Marines" and should agree to "disarm with the rest of the world, but not without it"; he ought to keep off the radio until he had something to say, treat the newspapermen right but "stay off that back lawn with those photographers." And Will saw no reason why he could not move into the White House "and have a good time. We want our President to have some Fun. Too many of our Presidents mistake the appointment as being to the Vatican and not to just another American home. Just don't get panicky. All you have to do is manage 120 million 'hoodlums.' " The better educated they are, the harder it is to deal with them: "The illiterate ones will all work, and you will have no trouble with them. But watch the ones that are smart, for they have been taught in school they are to live off the others. In fact, this . . . is about all that is the matter with our country."

"I love a dog. He does nothing for political reasons."
from Daily Telegram
Dec. 3, 1933

In the month following the election a number of daily telegrams voiced his thoughts on Europe's war debts to the United States—an old and favorite topic. "Don't ever lay the fault on Europe for not paying us," he advised. "They would start tomorrow if we would just loan 'em the money to do it on." He urged that the United States give European governments a four-word message: "Pay up or default." The latter choice was one they could never accept since it would spoil their credit rating and "they couldn't borrow any money any more."

Perhaps the mood of the country was changing; perhaps Will's comments were slightly more acerb. Whatever the reason, he received an increasing amount of criticism from readers and newspaper editorial writers—notably in the *New York Times*. The *Times* published a spate of letters from readers who were irritated by Will's pronouncements on the war debts, including one from a young Harvard graduate named Charlton Ogburn, who called Will "the most vociferous expositor of the 'hick' or 'dirty foreigner' viewpoint in the country." Others took him to task for his destructive criticism, lack of taste, and general mischief-making on this crucial issue, while several called him a "dangerous influence" and urged the *Times* to cancel his column. There were letters in his defense, too, but the newspaper in an editorial blandly assumed a hands-off posture, while harrumphing about the importance of publishing views that differed from its own.

Will's response to that was to dish out some of the same medicine: "I would like to state to the readers of the *New York Times* that I am in no way responsible for the editorial or political policy of this paper. I allow them free rein as to their opinion, so long as it is within the bounds of good subscription gathering. . . . Every paper must have its various entertaining features, and their editorials are not always to be taken seriously, and never to be construed as policy."

In the meantime, he was also under fire for a suggestion he gave Roosevelt in another column. Hoover had invited the President-elect to the White House to discuss the foreign debt problem, and Will urged him not to accept, on the grounds that two Presidents could not run the country. He advised FDR to tell Hoover that the issue of the debt moratorium "is your onion, you will have to peel it"—raising an immediate hue and cry from readers about the cowboy humorist who did not have sense enough to leave affairs of state to the people who understood them. Predictably, Roosevelt stayed away from Hoover,

". . . it's always been a question whether it made any difference whether you did or didn't understand what any Senator was saying. Most people have just become reconciled to 'em."

from Daily Telegram
Jan. 17, 1933

and Will had the last word: "Say, lot of you birds sure take the hide off me when I am wrong . . . but give me credit when I do guess right."

There were signs that incessant travel and the demands of his complicated life were beginning to tell on Will. Increasingly sensitive to criticism, he grew petulant or indignant over unfavorable comments that appeared in newspapers and was now defending his opinions by replying to letters that he might have ignored in earlier years. In 1933 he wrote a column praising Mussolini, whose success in governing Italy had always impressed him. "Say, Mussolini could run this country with his eyes shut. In fact, that's the way our Congress has been running it. Mussolini, with no money, no natural resources, no nothing, has kept his country going, while us with a surplus of everything under the sun, are mangy with representatives and liberty. But we cant digest either one of 'em."

That statement provoked an editorial response from the San Diego *Union*, calling Will's attention to the fact that Italy had no elections, no independent newspapers, no political opposition, and a policy of repression and terror. Will's impulsive reply was the sort of remark that caused a Socialist journal, *American Freeman*, to complain that "many of his wisecracks reveal a hidden sympathy for the Fascist type of Demagogue." In a letter to the editor of the San Diego paper Will stated that "Mussolini is an amateur compared to Mr. Roosevelt's power and the whole country is tickled to death. Dictatorship is the best government in the world provided you have the right dictatorship."

One tragic occurrence in 1932 had had a profound effect on Will. On March 1 the nineteen-month-old son of Charles and Anne Morrow Lindbergh was kidnapped from their home in Englewood, New Jersey. Only two weeks earlier Will had visited them and watched in delight as the aviator played with the child, and in the days following the crime his columns reflected the nationwide feeling of horror and outrage. "Why don't lynching parties widen their scope and take in kidnappings?" he suggested. Deeply troubled by his friends' tragedy, he lashed out at the society that had somehow permitted it to occur. "120 million people cry one minute and swear vengeance the next. A Father who never did a thing that didn't make us proud of him. A Mother who though only the wife of a hero, has proven one herself. At home or abroad they have always been a credit to their country. They have never fallen

On the inauguration of Franklin D. Roosevelt: *"America hasn't been as happy in three years as they are today, no money, no banks, no work, no nothing. But they know they got a man in there who is wise to Congress, wise to our so-called big men. The whole country is with him. Even if what he does is wrong they are with him, just so he does something. If he burned down the capitol we would cheer and say, 'Well, we at least got a fire started, anyhow.' We have had years of 'Don't rock the boat.' Go on and sink it if you want to, we just as well be swimming as like we are."*

from Daily Telegram Mar. 5, 1933

Three years after the kidnap-murder of his son, Lindbergh took the witness stand in the trial of Bruno Hauptmann, the man convicted of the crime.
WIDE WORLD

down. Is their country going to be a credit to them? Will it make him still proud that he did it for them? Or in his loneliness will . . . a thought creep into his mind that it might have been different if he had flown the ocean under somebody's colors with a real obligation to law and order? America goes further into debt, and the debt is to the Lindberghs."

In January of 1933 he bade farewell to an old friend. "Mr. Coolidge," he wrote, "you didn't have to die for me to throw flowers on your grave. I have told a million jokes about you, but every one was based on some of your splendid qualities. . . . History generally records a place for a man that is ahead of his time. But we that lived with you will always remember you because you was 'with' your times. By golly, you little red-headed New Englander, I liked you." After a ceremony was held in the House of Representatives to honor the memory of the former President, Will's comment had a bite to it: "The lawmakers . . . can pay more homage to a President in death and deal him more misery in life than happens in any civilized nation."

As winter and the Depression deepened, America's banks faced a new crisis. Over the past three years, despite Hoover's reassurances that the credit system was sound, five thousand banks had closed, and despite the President's efforts to resuscitate them with aid from the RFC, in mid-February Michigan's banks began closing their doors, compelling the governor to declare a "bank holiday." In the waning days of office the agitated Hoover wrote a personal note to Roosevelt (misspelling his name on the envelope), proposing that he commit himself in advance to the economic policies of the Hoover administration and repudiate his proposed New Deal in order to restore confidence in the government. Roosevelt dismissed the letter as "cheeky" and would have none of Hoover's scheme; as inauguration day approached, the panic spread to other banks in other states.

Will likened the bank closing to the moratorium on Europe's war debts ("Funny we thought of it in Europe, but not for ourselves") and suggested that the country "take it on the chin and grin." The Rogers family, he reported, had laid in no supplies against the emergency and would be living on horse meat, their ranch's sole product. "I love horses and I only ask, don't let me know which one we are eating today."

When Roosevelt proclaimed in his inaugural address that "the only thing we have to fear is fear itself" and almost immediately declared a national bank holiday, there was a feeling on the part of many Americans that the bottom had somehow been reached, that there might now be an end to the uncertainty that had plagued the country. In an almost springtime mood, people made the most of a common plight, accepted scrip and joked about it, adjusting to a bankless economy. According to Will, "America hasn't been as happy in three years as they are today—no money, no banks, no work, no nothing." He was confident that the entire nation was behind the new President. "Even if what he does is wrong they are with him, just so he does something. If he burned down the capitol we would cheer and say, 'Well, we at least got a fire started, anyhow.'"

He dismissed the bank holiday and the government's proposed use of scrip on the grounds that Americans had for years been seeking a substitute for money. The Republicans had never voluntarily closed a bank—"Their theory was to leave

"Ten million people have gone without work for three years just listening to 'big men' solve their problem. I don't know what will be the first commission Mr. Roosevelt will appoint, but millions hope that it won't be the 'President of this concern' or 'the head of that corporation,' but ten men who have been without work; we will at least get an original view point. If the non worker has to go to the dogs, he at least should have a voice on the commission that sends him."

from Daily Telegram
Jan. 1, 1933

*Two of America's most peripatetic citizens—Will Rogers and the First
Lady, Eleanor Roosevelt—meet, appropriately, on the steps of an airplane.*

WILL ROGERS MEMORIAL, CLAREMORE, OKLA., GIFT OF PROJECT 20

'em open till they shut. We can think of the most things that
would benefit the patient, but we never think of 'em till we see
the hearse going by." It was astonishing, he thought, how little
money people really needed to get by on; even if the banks
never reopened, "it's such a novelty to find that somebody will
trust you that it's changed our whole feeling toward human nature." He couldn't recall when the country had seemed more
united, and explained it by suggesting that "The worse off we
get the louder we laugh, which is a great thing. And every
American international banker ought to have printed on his office door, 'Alive today by the grace of a nation that has a sense of

humor.'"

He was full of praise for Roosevelt, whose "fireside chats" on the radio "pointed a lesson to all radio announcers and public speakers what to do with a big vocabulary—leave it at home in the dictionary." Whatever additional authority the President might request, the country ought to give it to him, "even if it's to drown all the boy babies, for the way the grown up ones have acted, he will be perfectly justified in drowning any new ones." Above all, he admired the way the new occupant of the White House was dealing with Congress, making them act for the first time in their lives like U.S. citizens and not like Senators or Representatives. "Roosevelt just makes out a little list of things every morning that he wants them to do that day (kinder like a housewife's menu list)," and they were doing it. And Eleanor Roosevelt immediately endeared herself to Will by making it plain that she was air-minded—"no maid, no secretary, just the first lady of the land on a paid ticket on a regular passenger plane."

At the outset of Roosevelt's first term Will asked people to have patience and see what the New Deal might accomplish. "We are all on a drunk for the time being," he said, "and the durn thing might accidentally work permanently." As program after program was launched in bewildering succession, he couldn't help wondering where the money to pay for them would come from, but as he contemplated the FERA, the AAA and the PWA, the NRA and the CCC, he observed that "Never was a country in the throes of more capital letters than the old USA, but still we haven't sent out the SOS." What pleased him most was the sense of optimism he began to detect in trips around the country. "Actual knowledge of the future was never lower," he suspected, "but hope was never higher. Hope will beat predictions any time." As the year drew to a close he wrote a Christmas message to readers, telling them that the best cheer he perceived was "in the heart, the confidence, and in the renewed hope of everybody." It was true that huge numbers of Americans were still unemployed, but he found it remarkable that those people had rarely complained. "I doubt if a parallel will be found where millions hung on with such continued hope and patience as in this country"—and now, although many of them would not see a turkey on Christmas Day, they were able to imagine one in the future. No one would mourn the passing of the year 1933, but future historians would see it as "the year of the big switch—from worse to better."

Will Rogers says:

"Diplomats are nothing but high-class

You often hear it said we need Diplomats. We don't need Diplomats; we need a Keeper or a Warden.

A Diplomat's job is to make something appear what it ain't.

A diplomat is one that says something that is equally misunderstood by both sides, and never clear to either.

. . . diplomats don't mind starting a war, because it's a custom that they are to be brought safely home before the trouble starts. There should be a new rule saying: "You start a war while you are your country's official handicap to some other country, you have to stay with any war you start."

It always helps out in your recruiting and your patriotism if you can make your own people believe you was the one pounced on. I think the only real diplomacy ever performed by a diplomat is in deceiving his own people after their dumbness has got them into a war.

The way we got in the last war was through notes. We send so many that nations can't tell which one we mean. Our wars ought to be labeled "entered on account of too much penmanship."

It takes a strong man to remember what country he is representing when the wine and the flattery start flowing.

Diplomats have a thing they call diplomatic language. It's just lots of words, and when they are all added up, they don't mean anything. . . . A diplomat has a hundred ways of saying nothing, but no way of saying something, because he has never had anything to say. That's why they call 'em diplomats.

When you really figure it out, there is no individual that is as funny as a nation. . . . An Argentine president visited Brazil (the first time in generations). He went there in an Argentine battleship, was met by Brazilian cruisers and seventy-five fighting planes. (Now all this, mind you, is on a good-will trip.)

Imagine individuals doing that. I go to visit you, take along a rifle and belt full of cartridges, you meet me at your gate with your best polished machine gun, and two forty-fives.

But at the Brazilian banquet that night there were wonderful speeches of good will. Then next morning both of 'em started building more guns.

Viva Diplomacy. Nobody is fooled, nobody is hurt.

Did you read all the New Year's optimism and apple sauce in the papers today by all our leading men and bankers? Every one either a millionaire or an office-holder. Now, there is 30,000 millionaires in the country and 110,000,000 that are not. Yet, you never see a New Year's prediction by one of the 110,000,000. Looks like just for the novelty one paper would print just what some poor man saw in store for the coming year.

See where Congress passed a 2 billion-dollar bill to relieve bankers' mistakes and lend to new industries. You can always count on us helping those who have lost part of their fortune, but our whole history records nary a case where the loan was for the man who had absolutely nothing.

Our only solution of relief seems to be to fix it so people who are in a hole through borrowing can borrow some more. Borrowing, that's what's the matter with the world today. If no

awyers—some ain't even high class."

individual or country could borrow a dime for five years that would be the greatest five-year plan ever invented.

———

[Bankers] are likeable rascals, and now that we are all wise to 'em, and it's been shown that they don't know any more about finances than the rest of us know about our businesses (which has proven to be nothing), why they are getting just as human as the groceryman, the druggist or the filling station man. This panic has been a great equalizer, it's done away entirely with the smart man.

———

You see there is a lot of things these old boys have done that are within the law, but it's so near the edge that you couldn't slip a safety razor blade between their acts and a prosecution.

———

America has one hundred and ten million population, 90 per cent of which are lawyers, yet we can't find two of them who have not worked at some time or another for an oil company. There has been at least one lawyer engaged for every barrel of oil that ever come out of the ground.

———

You might wonder if they pay so much to lawyers how do they ever make anything out of the oil. Foolish question! They don't make anything out of the oil. They only make money out of the stock they sell. You buy a share of oil stock and for every dollar you pay, 60 per cent goes for lawyers' fees, 30 per cent to cover capitalization, and 10 per cent goes to the boring of a dry hole.

———

. . . [lawyers] are so well fortified against every emergency. They are just like a Baseball Team. Now if it should happen to be a Dark Rainy Day when they argue the Case, why they have

Dark Day Lawyers—men who are better in the Dark than other Lawyers. Then they have Expert Technicality Lawyers. That is, a Lawyer that don't know or have to know Anything at all about the Case, but who, if it goes against his side, why he can point out that Witness So and So had on the Wrong color Tie when he Testified, and that in signing his Name he had failed to dot one of his I's, and that Therefore that rendered the whole of his testimony Null and Void.

———

Then they have one Car load of just Postponement Lawyers. Men who can have the Falls of Niagara put back on account of the water not being ready to come over. Men who on the last Judgment Day will be arguing that it should be postponed on account of Lack of Evidence.

———

Then there is just the plain every day Long Winded Lawyer who argues so long and loud that they decide in his favor just to get him to stop. So you see, when you have every Species of Lawyer there is, you are a hard man to beat.

———

It it wasn't for Wills, lawyers would have to go to work at an essential employment.

———

The minute you read something and you can't understand it you can almost be sure that it was drawn up by a lawyer. Then if you give it to another lawyer to read and he don't know just what it means, why then you can be sure it was drawn up by a lawyer. If it's in a few words and is plain and understandable only one way, it was written by a non-lawyer.

———

Every time a lawyer writes something, he is not writing for posterity, he is writing so that endless others of his craft can make a living out of trying to figure out what he said, course perhaps he hadent really said anything, thats what makes it hard to explain.

BOTH: WILL ROGERS MEMORIAL, CLAREMORE, OKLA.

"I never met a man I didn't like."

The President and Mrs. Roosevelt
request the pleasure of the company of
Mr and Mrs Rogers
at a reception to be held, at
The White House
Thursday evening, February the first
nineteen hundred and thirty-four
at nine o'clock

For several seasons, Will's Sunday evening broadcasts (left) attracted millions of loyal listeners. As the invitation above suggests, it was not only the ordinary folk who enjoyed his talk.

Whatever critics of his columns might have said, the public's regard for Will Rogers was never higher than in the spring of 1933. Admired and loved as a human being, he had made a special place for himself that was never more evident than during the Great Depression—one of the darkest hours in American memory. One reason for it was his humor: his irreverence for the sacred cows of the world; his way of puncturing balloons without malice and with such good nature that even the target of his remarks could join in the general laughter. Yet more was behind it than that. The twenties and thirties had seen a succession of heroes flash like meteors across the national scene—Byrd, Amundsen, Lindbergh, Amelia Earhart, Wiley Post, Tilden, Dempsey, Babe Ruth, Red Grange, and a host of others—but none managed to retain such constant, unwavering affection. Will Rogers was the one man, people seemed to believe, who was above fame and success. The world's great might be on his visiting list, but he never lost touch with the ordinary man.

His consuming interest and involvement in the nation's affairs were such that no man's importance was quite confirmed until he had been kidded by Will Rogers—no event complete unless it drew the gentle barb of his wit.

His brief commentary was the first item to which millions of Americans turned in their daily newspaper. His motion pictures were so successful that he now ranked as the number two box-office attraction in Hollywood. (*State Fair*, starring Will and Blue Boy, the hog, appeared in 1933 along with *Dr. Bull* and *Mr. Skitch;* the following year *David Harum, Handy Andy,* and *Judge Priest* were scheduled for release.) And now another string was added to the bow.

In May it was announced that Will had signed a contract to make seven nationwide broadcasts for the Gulf Oil Company. He would be paid $50,000 for the series, and immediately said he would donate all the money to unemployment relief—half to be distributed by the American Red Cross, half by the Salvation Army. As he described the arrangement, he had wanted to make a contribution through these two organizations and Betty suggested the means of doing so. " 'You got the wind to do it,' " he quoted her as saying. "She figured out how I could do it with just talk, which I would be doin' for nothin' anyhow to anybody I could make listen to me, so I am to preach for seven Sundays. . . . I got nothin' to lose in the transaction but my voice and I never lost it yet."

Four decades later it is difficult to suggest the powerful hold radio had on Americans, when the voices of Amos 'n' Andy, Rudy Vallee, Kate Smith, Jack Benny, Fred Allen, Eddie Cantor, George Burns and Gracie Allen, Edgar Bergen and Charlie McCarthy, were as familiar as those of old friends in the nation's living rooms. During the Depression years listening to radio became the public's greatest diversion—one of the few free mediums of entertainment. For many it was a ticket to laughter and excitement, a momentary release from the woes of a world gone wrong. On weekdays between 7 and 7:15 P.M., when thirty million people were listening to Amos 'n' Andy, the use of telephones regularly fell off by 50 per cent. And for two years after Will's initial series of Gulf broadcasts, listening to Will Rogers on Sunday nights at 9 P.M. was a ritual that people still remember with a smile.

Will's success in show business, as he readily admitted, was the result of a happy coincidence of talent and timing. He had appeared on the scene with a highly original act when vaudeville and the Ziegfeld Follies were at the height of their popularity; his arrival in Hollywood coincided with the heyday of the silent films; his personality and manner were precisely right for the advent of talking pictures; and although he was never as comfortable in the medium of radio, his style was superbly suited to the format of the variety show, which offered a half-hour of humorous comment sprinkled with light music.

His first broadcast for Gulf, on April 30, 1933, established the pattern for those that followed. After a medley by Al Goodman's orchestra and a song from the Revelers (the quartet that had accompanied him on so many benefit performances), Will came on to deliver a monologue that ran about fifteen minutes. Once again, it was a variation on the familiar Follies routine, of which audiences never seemed to tire. He drew on the headlines and news of the day for his commentary, so it was no accident that Franklin D. Roosevelt dominated the programs. In the opening broadcast Will proclaimed it to be President's Day: "We generally recognize anything by a week. . . . We have apple week, and potato week, and don't murder your wife week. . . . So somebody hit the bright idea, if prunes are worth a week, the President ought to be worth something anyhow. And so they figured they couldn't give him a week, but they could compromise on a day."

Roosevelt had been in office for seven weeks, and "That bird has done more for us in seven weeks than we've done for ourselves in seven years. We elected him because he was a Democrat, and now we honor him because he is a magician. He's the Houdini of Hyde Park. . . . He was inaugurated at noon in Washington, and they started the inaugural parade down Pennsylvania Avenue, and before it got halfway down there, he closed every bank in the United States." Jokes followed about Republicans, Mahatma Gandhi, Al Smith, the Wickersham Report, repeal of Prohibition, and Presidential commissions. He contrasted Roosevelt with Hoover and Coolidge: Hoover's mistake, he said, was in *asking* Congress to do something; Coolidge never paid any attention to them at all; while Roosevelt — as if following the advice Will had given him before he took office — never scolded Congressmen, since they were "really just children that's never grown up."

Some of Will's initial malaise on radio was attributable to the nature of the act he had perfected over the years — saying whatever happened to come into his head, rambling from one anecdote to another, gauging his remarks to the response of an audience, with no real concern for the length of time he talked. But radio, he discovered, was geared to split-second timing; if a program was scheduled to end at 9:30, that was when it ended, even if the star performer was in mid-sentence. His free-wheeling style in that opening broadcast must have caused the producer and sponsors some consternation, because in succeeding weeks he was much more conscious of the time allowed him. Characteristically, he took advantage of the situation to extract a few additional laughs from the audience by bringing an alarm clock to the studio. "The hardest thing over this radio is to get me stopped," he announced. "So tonight, I got me a clock here. . . . When that alarm goes off, I am going to stop, that is all there is to it. I don't care whether I am in the middle of reciting Gunga Din or the Declaration of Independence, I am going to stop right when that rings." And every Sunday night thereafter the alarm would ring when his time was up (producing another guffaw); he would quickly tell the listeners what was in store for them in his next appearance, and sign off.

During that series of broadcasts he must have given considerable thought to his feelings about working on radio, because on the final program of the spring he discussed its pros and cons. He admitted he did not like the microphone, which put him in mind of an automobile radiator cap, but by now he was reconciled to that; he had feared that the listeners weren't much interested in politics, but had discovered that they knew more about it than a Congressman; and he had thought he might have to speak as well as an announcer did, but found that "you don't have to speak correctly at all, and you are understood by everybody." Having relieved his mind of those worries, he concluded that the only trouble with radio was that "you never know how good you are." The studio audience might applaud; but the real test was whether Gulf sold more gasoline. It reminded him of the movies: you could make a wonderful picture and receive fine notices, but the acid test came at the end of the year when the box-office receipts were in. He still preferred the stage: "Boy, when you walk on and off they tell you whether you are any good that night or not. You don't have to wait until anything is sold. You only get one crack at 'em on the stage."

When the Chicago World's Fair opened in 1933, Will asked his listeners if they agreed with its theme — "A Century of Progress." One hundred years earlier, he reminded them, we only had 36 Senators, "and the evil has grown now until we have 96." In 1833 there was no such thing as a stenographer ("every Congressman could write then"), and there had been only two bank failures. As for unemployment, in those days "If a man was not working, he sat in front of the grocery store and whittled. Also, if one man was idle in one part of the country, you didn't hear about it in the other parts of the country. This thing called statistics was the worst thing that was ever invented. . . . We wouldn't know how bad the others were doing if we didn't have statistics." We were on the gold standard in 1833; there was no golf except in Scotland; there were no chamber of commerce luncheon speakers; and you lived until you died and not until you were run over by an automobile.

In one program, broadcast from the Mayflower Hotel in Washington, he presided over an imaginary session of the United States Senate; and when it was rumored in the late spring that he was considering not returning to the air in the fall, a telegram signed by Vice President Garner and members of the Senate asked for assurance that he would be back soon to preside over that body again. Actually, there was little risk that Will would give up radio once he had made a success of it. As with so many enterprises he embarked upon, he was filled with doubts at the beginning, and only after he realized that he was good at it and that audiences were responding satisfactorily did he regain his self-confidence. He signed up to make six additional broadcasts for Gulf in the fall of 1933; the next year he was on the radio every Sunday night for twenty-four weeks; and in 1935 he gave sixteen more weekly performances.

The Chicago World's Fair of 1933 (below) was, according to Will, "exactly what everybody needs. People been sitting at home grouching at each other for three years."

WIDE WORLD

Visiting John Garner (left) at his Texas ranch, Will noted that where other Vice Presidents made speeches, "Garner just fishes. If all politicians fished instead of spoke publicly, we would be at peace with the world."
WILL ROGERS MEMORIAL, CLAREMORE, OKLA.

Nor did this perceptibly tax his phenomenal store of energy. In the spring of 1934, while making three motion pictures and writing his daily and weekly articles, he sandwiched in a role in Eugene O'Neill's stage hit, *Ah, Wilderness!* in California, and in July he and his family sailed from San Francisco for a trip around the world. Will had made a similar trip alone in the fall of 1931, intending, as he set out for the Far East, to observe what was happening in Manchuria, where war between China and Japan had broken out. He had sailed that year to Japan and flown to Korea with Floyd Gibbons, the war correspondent, who had been with him on shipboard. In many respects it was a sad and depressing trip. In the struggle for Manchuria, he reported, "China is trying to save its country, Japan is trying to save its investments, the League of Nations is trying to save its face. Now somebody has got to lose." It was 32 degrees below zero when he reached Harbin (he claimed that the horses were wearing snowshoes), and he was shocked by what he saw of the Russians. The lot of the women, especially, bothered him. In order to eat they "had to live under the most degrading circumstances," and the suicide rate was the highest in the world. He found the Reds "a mighty hard looking lot—when you get everybody alike, that should be the height of Communism."

In Mukden he discovered that the League of Nations was sending a mission to observe the situation, which was "like the sheriff examining the stall after the horse has disappeared." The Manchurian problem would not be settled for a long time, he predicted, and urged the United States to keep hands off: "America could hunt all over the world and not find a better fight to keep out of." In Peiping (now Peking) he observed that the American missionaries had "taught the Chinese not to fight but to rely on the Lord, and the Chinese diplomats have taught the people to rely on the League, but now they feel they have both fallen down on 'em." On December 25 he was in Shanghai, lonely and homesick, away from his wife and children for the first time on Christmas.

From there he traveled to Hong Kong, Singapore, Malaya, India, Pakistan, and then on to Cairo, Athens, Rome, Paris, and London, where Betty met him. Will had hoped to arrange an interview with Adolf Hitler, but bad weather kept him from flying to Munich, and he went to the Disarmament Conference in Geneva instead, where he summed up the proceedings by noting that "There is nothing to prevent their succeeding now but human nature."

The 1934 trip, however, was an altogether different sort of occasion; this was in the nature of a second honeymoon, with the boys, Bill and Jim, accompanying them. (Will had tried to interest Mary, who was playing in a summer theatre in Maine, in going with them, but she turned him down.) The preliminaries to a family expedition, Will realized, were far more complicated than they were when he was traveling alone and carrying only the "old soft, flat red grip that packed itself." Betty had gone on a clothes-buying spree, and the Santa Monica house was a mess, filled with "dress makers, cutters and fitters" who were constantly under foot while Betty packed and repacked. Since the boys would not be home until just before they left, she "felt that she had to dress them by remote control to get them ready." Will wanted to be outside roping calves, but Betty and the butler, Emil Sandmeier, insisted that he try on some white shoes and new Palm Beach suits—a type of garb that wasn't supposed to fit, "if it does, it's uncomfortable." Emil proposed that he solve the problem of what to take by packing a dozen of

*On their twenty-fifth wed-
ding anniversary Betty and
Will made a trip around the
world, and posed for a picture in Tokyo with the son
of Prince Fumimaro Konoye.*
UPI

everything, which reminded him that the last time he had been
so well outfitted was when he was sent off to Kemper Military
Academy in 1896. The last straw was to find that someone had
packed his bathrobe: "You only wear them when you are getting well from an operation." By the time they were ready to
leave they had so much luggage that Will told Betty and Emil
he was going to charge them for the excess baggage fees he
would have to pay on plane flights. He planned to dispose sur-
reptitiously of all the personal items he didn't need along the
way and expected to arrive in New York harbor at the end of
the trip with his traditional gear, "the little red bag, the old
blue serge, and the typewriter."

En route to Hawaii on the S.S. *Malolo* the radio operator
woke Will in the middle of the night to tell him that John
Dillinger, the FBI's most wanted criminal, had been shot and

killed after leaving a movie theatre. The next day his daily article carried the suggestion that Dillinger had met his end by not following advice: anyone could have told him to stay away from the movies' bad influence, and Will wondered "What picture it was [that] got him. Hope it was mine."

Their arrival in Honolulu coincided with Roosevelt's visit to the islands, and the President and the comedian were honored at a dinner at which Will was kept speaking by an enthusiastic crowd for two hours. After visiting Scofield army barracks and the naval installation at Pearl Harbor, Will decided that "if war was declared with some Pacific nation we would lose the Philippines before lunch but if we lost these it would be our own fault." He and the President had an opportunity to chat about something that was very much on FDR's mind; when he learned that the Rogers were going to Japan, he said, "Will, don't jump on Japan, just keep them from jumping on us." (Will took the counsel to heart; when he reached Tokyo he reported, "They want a bigger navy and I think I will let 'em have it for they are going to build it anyway.") Traveling around, he concluded that that country would not hold its supremacy in business for long. "I saw a lot of golf courses being put in—that's the beginning of a nation's commercial decline."

From Japan they retraced Will's 1931 route to Korea and then went to Siberia, where they boarded the trans-Siberian train after laying in a supply of food for the long trip, including a big basket of oranges, a canned-heat cooker, and plenty of beans for Will and the boys. Outfitted, Will said, "like we was going over the Chilkoot pass," they were cooped up in a tiny compartment, with their luggage and supplies stacked around them, for nearly eight days. In Tokyo Will had been advised at the Soviet embassy that they would be met at Novosibirsk by an airplane that would take them the rest of the way to Moscow, but at Novosibirsk neither plane nor message could be found, and they stayed aboard the train. The unspoiled, wild country appealed to Will, Betty said, but he disliked sightseeing from a railroad car. "He wanted to get out and into it. He wanted to see it in the only way one can really see such a vast country—from the sky." Even so, it made a deep impression, reminding him of his youth in Oklahoma. "It's exactly like the Indian Territory was when I grew up in it as a boy. And if you can find a finer one that that was before they plowed and ruined it, I don't know where." Siberia was ideal cow country, he believed: "Not a fence, all you would need would be one drift line between you

Although Will fussed about the time it took to cross Siberia by train, he held onto this souvenir of the trip.
WILL ROGERS MEMORIAL, CLAREMORE, OKLA.

and the Arctic Ocean.''

Moscow, when they arrived at last, was something else—''a town on a boom,'' with buildings going up everywhere, women constructing the new subway, the excitement of a horse race, and some stimulating talk with Russian experts Maurice Hindus, Walter Duranty, and Louis Fischer. From Moscow Will and Betty went to Leningrad, leaving Bill to go to Germany and Jim to Paris. Before leaving the States Will had announced his intention of ''finding Finland.'' If Finland could go to the trouble of repaying its war debts, he said, ''I can certainly take the time to try and find them,'' and he was happy to arrive in the land of ''integrity's last stand.'' Then he and his wife toured the Scandinavian countries, Austria, and the Balkans before going to the British Isles.

He found Europe unnaturally quiet—''don't hear much war talk so I guess that means one will break out. That's when they have 'em when there ain't any reason.'' In London he saw a report about the dilemma facing America's wealthy men: the Depression had dried up all the good investment opportunities, it was said, and they didn't know what to put their money into. Will used this as a springboard for his first radio talk in the fall—broadcast while he was still in England—in which he gave listeners a report on what he had seen on his travels.

'' 'What I can do with my money?' '' he said, ''is a unique problem. Every nation in the world would give a right leg to have that same thing wrong with 'em.'' He had learned that England, which he described as the first country to recover from the Depression, had ''the highest income tax rate of anybody in the world, that they are the nation that first give the dole to unemployed,'' and that the reason they were now sitting on top of the heap was that ''all their big men never lost confidence in England. They bet on England to win. And ours are betting on our country to lose.''

Russia, ''the poorest country in the world for a Communist to go to,'' was getting along better than he had expected because ''there is no Communists or Reds there''—no agitators, no one trying to start a strike. Each country, he concluded, had its own form of government peculiar to it—''Russia has her Soviet, Italy her dictator, England her king, Japan her Son of Heaven, China her various bandits, and us, we don't know what form of government it is. But whatever it is, it's ours. . . . And as bad off as we are we are better than anybody else I have seen.''

Probably the statement most frequently associated with Will

Reporters inevitably met the Rogers when they returned from their trips. Will was always good copy and was never at a loss for words.
UNDERWOOD & UNDERWOOD

Rogers, and the one that endeared him most to the American public, was his remark, "I never met a man I didn't like." This was the attitude that characterized all his trips abroad; in Moscow, Dublin, Hong Kong, or Mexico City, he talked to everyone with whom he could strike up a conversation—in the streets, in restaurants, wherever he went—and his inclination was to see the positive side of human nature and to believe that the world was basically a family in which all would be well if man's native instincts were allowed to prevail instead of being gummed up by the politicians. This old-fashioned confidence in the virtues of the common man, seasoned with a benevolent tolerance for the human condition and mankind's frailties, was suspected as a pose by some critics of his day. They refused to believe that anyone as successful or as wealthy as Will Rogers

349

could possibly remain the eternal homespun cowboy; after all, he traveled in circles not customarily open to the ordinary mortal, spending much of his time in the company of presidents and prime ministers and notable figures in every segment of society. It had to be a pose, they said, or incredible naiveté.

Will had become something of a folk hero, and his success as a humorist was constructed, as are all such successes, upon a formula. But the formula was concocted out of real elements and was an extension of a personality that had not altered substantially since he was a boy in Indian Territory. What had changed was not Will Rogers but the world, and something of what audiences responded to was the aura of nostalgia he and his manner suggested—a trace of the days when life had seemed far less complex, confused, and phony. In a curious way, his radio broadcasts came closer to suggesting what Will was all about than did his stage or movie appearances, because what he said to an audience that could not see him was not obscured by gestures or mannerisms. No shuffling about, no pulling the forelock, no sheepish grins or sly winks or glances from under his eyebrows intruded on the talk—and the talk itself was largely extemporaneous, a potpourri of thoughts that popped into his mind as he turned from subject to subject.

Speaking in his self-deprecatory way about the differences between the stage, the movies, and radio, he suggested that in the first two "they never take you serious. They could look at you and tell when you're kidding. . . . But the radio bunch—there's just a few of them [who] take it serious. They don't realize that us comedians is just up here trying to fill in fifteen minutes. That's all we're up here for. We have no mission or no message for the world whatever. What we say is to be taken no more serious than a speech delivered in the halls of Congress. We're just killing time up here, just like a preacher stallin' while the deacon passes the hat."

More original than what he said was the peculiar twist he gave it, with the result that the listener—hearing pretty much what he thought or knew all along, but put in an entirely different context, suddenly found himself thinking that Will had put his finger on the matter and uttered something approximating eternal truth. For example, in 1934 everyone knew about Austria's troubles with Hitler's Germany, but it was left to Will to say that "If ever a nation lived in the wrong place it seems to be them." The moral of Austria's experience in World War I was, "Never enter a war on the wrong side. You know, on the losing side. If you want to go in, go in on the right side." Nearly everyone had seen pictures of Engelbert Dollfuss, the pint-sized dictator who had seized power in 1933, but it was Will who described him as being so small "they can't assassinate him because if they miss him they'll shoot themselves in the foot."

In so much of what he said there was a strong element of compassion, as when he remarked that "we are the last civilized nation, if you can call us that, to do anything for old people. All we do is just watch them get older." Or, on the subject of government relief programs, "Now is this thing of havin' millions of people—you know, everybody workin' for the government—is that a good thing? Well, no, it's not a good thing, but it's better than starvin.'" When Calvin Coolidge died at the age of sixty-one, Will criticized the system that ignored former Presidents, "retiring 'em into total unusefulness, just when they had learned and wished to be of public service. Oh, if our government would only do something to utilize the talents and the brains and the experience of these ex-Presidents. . . . They spend from four to eight years learning our government and . . . there must be somewhere in our great country's government that politics would not conflict—some consulting or advisory board. . . . It's the thought of being ignored that kills these men. It's not over-work; it's under-work. Their illness is of the heart—not of the body." Returning to the same theme in a broadcast several weeks later, he said he had taken up the ex-Presidents' cause since "they was the only class or industry that I could find that didn't have a lobby in Washington tryin' to get somethin' out of the government. So I appointed myself lobbyist for the ex-Presidents' association. But you folks mustn't take that serious because I doubt if it goes through. It's got too much merit to ever be adopted."

When not discussing politics or the international scene, he frequently dealt with the homely, unexceptionable virtues—God, family, mother, honesty, common sense, the underdog, just plain folks—contriving to do so in a way that was neither maudlin nor cloying. On Mother's Day in 1935 he reminded the audience that "it's a beautiful thought, but it's somebody with a hurting conscience that thought of the idea. It was someone who had neglected their mother for years and they figured out, I got to do something about mama, and then they says, 'Well, we'll give mama a day.' . . . You give her a day and then in return mother gives you the other 364. . . . They could have given mother a week, but that would have been giving

In Europe in 1934 Will observed the rise of Nazi power. Austrian Chancellor Engelbert Dollfuss (above) was one of the early victims.

351

mother a little the best of it, so they said, we'll give mother a day."

Before Will and the family left on their round-the-world trip he said he had hit on a formula for avoiding wars. Most friction between countries, he stated, was caused by proximity. "Now Germany and France, they fight every forty years, you know — just as true as history. Every forty years they just come around, and they look at the calendar and start fighting. Well, it isn't anyone's particular fault, but it just seems to be habit." So he had devised a scheme to move neighbors away from each other if they couldn't get along. "Take Germany, for instance, and place it where Mexico is." And once Mexico was transplanted to Germany's place, "France and Mexico would get along fine." Since England and Ireland were always fighting, he would swap Ireland and Canada, being careful not to let England know where the Irish were going.

The trip somehow convinced him, despite the ominous rumblings from Europe, that there would be no war. In his travels, he said, he had found one sure-fire thing to say when he arrived in a country: " 'Folks, I bring you no good will.' The whole world is fed up on somebody bringing good will in. . . . Nations don't want to have any good will, and all that. They want to be let alone, the same as we do. Let 'em alone and let 'em work out their own plans and their own salvation. . . . Us and England, we're always horning into everything. We're fixing up the world. There's not a nation in the world today that wants war. . . . Nobody's got any money. They can't fight till they borrow something, and there ain't nobody to borrow it from."

Unhappily, events were getting out of hand, beyond the control of the ordinary man in whom Will had such faith. In March, 1935, Hitler tore up the Versailles treaty, which, as Will said, "wasn't a good treaty, but it was the only one they had." Mussolini had pounced on Ethiopia, civil war was about to erupt in Spain, and Will, saddened by the course of events, could only mourn, "England's got a gun, France has got a gun, Italy's got a gun, Germany wants a gun, Austria wants a gun. All God's children want guns . . . going to buckle on the guns and smear up all of God's heaven."

The state of the world was not the only thing on his mind that spring, fortunately. He had three pictures to make, and when they were finished, he thought he might take another trip — maybe fly someplace he had never been before. It was the sort of prospect he never tired of dangling in front of himself.

Will Rogers says: "Peace is kinder like prosperity. There is mighty few nations that can stand it."

Asking Europe to disarm is like asking a man in Chicago to give up his life insurance.

A sure certainty about our Memorial Days is as fast as the ranks from one war thin out the ranks from another take their place. Prominent men run out of Decoration Day speeches, but the world never runs out of wars. People talk peace, but men give their life's work to war. It won't stop till there is as much brains and scientific study put to aid peace as there is to promote war.

That's one good thing about wars. It takes smarter men to figure out who loses 'em than it does to start 'em. . . . The more ignorant you are the quicker you fight.

You can't say civilization don't advance . . . for in every war they kill you in a new way.

Southern Methodist Conference passed a resolution asking Congress to exempt them from war. Don't know what claim they had over other denominations unless it's that they are always fighting so much among themselves that two wars at once would be a hardship on 'em.

If you want to know when a war is coming, just watch the U.S. and see when it starts cutting down on its defense. Its the surest barometer in the world.

Speeches is what starts the next war. It's not armament, it's oratory that's wrong with this country.

I would like to stay in Europe long enough to find some country that don't blame America for everything in the world that's happened to 'em in the last fifteen years—debts, depression, disarmament, disease, fog, famine, or frostbite.

The way we got in the last war was through notes. We send so many that nations can't tell which one we mean.

Our wars ought to be labeled, "Entered on account of too much penmanship."

Bands playing, soldiers marching, orators orating, telling you it's your duty to "Buy Liberty Bonds."

Fifteen years later no bands, no marching, no orators, just a patriotic girl or a broken piece of human frame trying to sell a poppy for a few cents, made by even a more unfortunate brother in one of our hospitals. Given fifteen years to think it over, war has degenerated from the price of a Liberty Bond to the price of a poppy.

There is only one sure way of stopping war, that is to see that every "statesman" has the same chance to reflect after its over that these boys making the poppies have had.

. . . our slogan will be now: Have your civil wars wherever and as far away as you want, but on the opening day we will be there.

We will stop these Chinese from fighting among themselves if we have to kill them to do it.

When American diplomacy gets through messing us around over in China, I can tell them what has caused this hate of us over there. It's our missionaries who have been trying to introduce "chop suey" into China. China didn't mind them eating it there, but when they tried to call it a Chinese dish that's what made them start shooting at us.

All we ask of the Chinese is that they settle down and let us and England keep collecting and running their customs for them. I don't see why they should refuse a little thing like that. China owes us four million and we take over their customs revenue. France owes us four billion and we are afraid to send them a bill for it. What a great difference in diplomatic relations an army and navy make!

It takes quite a sense of humor for these people to understand us shaking hands with one hand and shooting with the other.

China is having a new war and we are having trouble getting into it. We always have gunboats there, so if there is any shooting why one of our boats will get shot at and that gives us the usual alibi. But this time it seems we only had one gunboat and it had to maneuver around for days before it could get in the line of fire.

We get into more things for less reason than any nation in the world. Not long ago China wanted to have a war. Now China is an awful peaceful nation, they don't bother nobody; China goes along, attends to their own business and they don't mess with nobody else's. We learned an awful lot of useful things from China, you know, and they are poor people and they don't get much pleasure and they wanted to have a civil war, just have a nice little war among themselves to kinda break the monotony of being a Chinaman. Do you think they could have that war alone? No, they couldn't have it; we was there the day it opened, we was right there, we was the first one there; we got there before the Chinamen did, us and England—there's another old busybody nation; they have to horn into everything, too.

Mr. Hoover just got back from Porta Rica after a call with our little dark brown cousins. He told 'em he would see that they had the same opportunities we enjoy here, so I guess he is having . . . stock brokers put in a branch down there. That will give them a leisure class, and the rest of 'em employment working for 'em. . . .

I guess I am all wet, but I never have seen any reason why we or any other nation should hold in subjection any islands or country outside of our own. We say we have to have [Honolulu] to protect the Pacific. Why don't we have to have the Azores to protect the Atlantic? We are going to get into a war some day, either over Honolulu or the Philippines. Let's all come home and let every nation ride its own surf board, play its own ukeleles and commit its devilment on its own race.

The U.S. Senate sentenced the Philippines to twelve more years of American receivership. Will you tell me one thing? How can one nation tell when another nation is ready for independence? But our government can do it. Yes, sir, there is not a dozen of 'em that's ever been west of the Golden Gate, but they could just tell you to a day twelve years from now, just when the "Little Brown Brothers" would be able to mess up their affairs as bad as ours.

Certainly lucky for us we got our liberty when we did. Suppose the House of Commons in England was holding clinic over us to decide if we were ready for "self-determination."

We never had a greater example of why there will always be war than we are having right now. 21 nations of the league denounce Japan's Chinese invasion. Also the U.S. while not a member, also agrees with them. Now all in the world they got to do to stop it instantly is to agree to not trade with an aggressor nation, meaning Japan, but they won't sacrifice their trade just to save bloodshed. . . . What's a few thousand dead Chinamen compared to Japan as a cash customer?

China has been awful nice to us; they let us use their home grounds to send our Marines when we didn't have any other war on for them at the time. They have let us mingle in every private war they have had. Why, there has been times that if it hadn't been for China allowing us to go in and shoot at them, why we wouldn't have had a soul in the world to shoot at. . . .

They are the most self-sustained country in the world, and would like to live and exist all off to themselves. But, of course, countries like us and England and Germany and France, we can see right away that wouldn't really be the thing for them to do, so we have to go in and help them out. Sometimes we have to shoot 'em, they are so hard headed and won't see it our way.

We send many missionaries there. Missionaries teach 'em not only how to serve the Lord, but run a Ford car. Then the American agent sells 'em one. You take religion backed up by commerce and it's awful hard for a heathern to overcome.

I don't care how little your country is, you got a right to run it like you want to. When the big nations quit meddling, then the world will have peace.

Must seem like the old Republican days to the Marines, to be loading on a boat and going to somebody else's country to help 'em run it. I see where . . . they are supposed to pick out Cuba's next week's President. . . . Cuba don't care so much for a new President as it does just to see how quick the last one can leave town.

Well, I guess I am all wet as usual, but a headline like this don't particularly add to my patriotism: "Cuba picks new president as battleship Mississippi steams into port". Any more than the following would: "United States of America having internal trouble, and His Majesty King George has dispatched his dreadnaughts to stand by in New York harbor to protect British investments in America, and to see that the right man is elected."

But that couldn't happen for they are both big nations, and it would mean war. . . . The whole thing as I see it all over the world today, is that the little nation has got no business being little.

Take the sugar out of Cuba and we would no more be interested in their trouble than we would a revolution among the Zulus.

Looks like my single-handed crusade to keep us out of Cuba hasn't been very successful. Now we got to go in to protect Americans— who would have needed no protection, had we had no diplomacy or battleships to get us in wrong in the first place.

WILL ROGERS MEMORIAL, CLAREMORE, OKLA.

"This Alaska is a great country."

SMITHSONIAN INSTITUTION, COURTESY L. E. GRAY

A smiling Will emerges from the plane in which he flew to Alaska with Wiley Post (in the cockpit). Post, an enthusiastic hunter, bagged the Kodiak bear, above, on an earlier journey to Alaska.

To what extent chance plays a part in human affairs is beyond all knowing. It may be, as Voltaire suggested, that there is no such thing as chance, that nothing can happen or exist without some cause. Certain actions are taken on the basis of sudden whim; others result from a chain of interrelated factors that, on examination, appear to resemble the intricate pieces of a Chinese puzzle that fall into place, one by one. Something like the latter was responsible for the trip Will made to Alaska in 1935.

Two years earlier he had received a letter from a big-game hunter in the territory, urging him to visit, but Will had no intention of going there for the purpose of hunting. "Here is a queer streak in me," he admitted. "I am no hunting man (or fishing either). . . . I just don't want to be shooting at any animal and even a fish I haven't got the heart to pull the hook out of him. But I do want to make that Alaska." What appealed to him was the lure of a vast, unspoiled country and the opportunity to talk with some of the old-timers who had gone north at the time of the Klondike gold rush in 1896. All the prospectors who had returned to the States, he thought, "were such liars, I would like to go up and meet the old boys that had the nerve to stick."

Apart from the desire to go, he had the time, which came about in an odd way as a result of his playing the lead in a stage production of Eugene O'Neill's *Ah, Wilderness!* in 1934. When the show was in Pasadena—Will enjoying himself immensely, although suffering a from having to commit someone's else's lines to memory for the first time (he had "quite a bit of trouble reading 'em, much less learning 'em," he said)—he received a letter from a clergyman. The man had taken his fourteen-year-old daughter to the show, assuming that it, like all of Will's performances, was something suitable for a young person to see. But after watching a scene in which Will lectured his "son" on the subject of immoral relations with a woman, the minister left the theatre, taking his daughter with him, and in his letter told Will that he had not been able to look her in the face since.

Will was stunned. He had regarded the play as just an "old family affair," but decided that if it struck even one person as improper, he wanted nothing further to do with it. "I am through," he stated. "I could never again say those lines—even to myself in the dark." He not only quit the play but decided he would not accept the role he had been offered in the screen version, for which he was to be loaned by Fox to MGM the following year. Because of a letter from an indignant clergyman, he would have the summer of 1935 open and would be free to travel.

Another factor in the equation was the state of Will's mind in the spring of 1935. As Betty Rogers described it, for the first

Because of his decision not to make the movie version of Ah Wilderness!, *in which he had played the lead in a stage production (below), Will was free to go to Alaska in the summer of 1935.*

WILL ROGERS MEMORIAL, CLAREMORE, OKLA.

time in his life he was showing signs of weariness. At the age of fifty-five his incredibly demanding schedule was beginning to take its toll. In addition to the radio broadcasts, he had recently given speeches or played benefits all over the country—in Pennsylvania, Indiana, Washington, D.C., Texas, Louisiana, and New York. The daily and weekly articles consumed their usual share of his time. Under the terms of his contract with Fox, he was obligated to make three movies annually, and he had worked it out so that he crowded all three into the first half of the year in order to have the remaining six months to himself. The plain fact was that he was worn out, and the steady pressure of his commitments, Bill Rogers remembers, had made him increasingly nervous, restless, and tense.

He longed to be on the wing. After a long siege of movie-making, he knew, "I sorter begin to looking up in the air and see what is flying over, and Mrs. Rogers in her wise way will say, 'Well, I think you better get on one. You are getting sorter nervous.' " So on the July 4 weekend he flew to Texas for a cowboy reunion—"not a professional rodeo like you see everywhere else, but a real celebration in a real cowtown by real old timers." These quick trips made Will envy those Americans who could simply pile into an automobile and leisurely tour the countryside; they must have a better time than anyone, and he longed for the opportunity "to prowl slow through this country." He never seemed to have time for that; "I go too fast to see much—only the tops of everything." He seized any opportunity he could to relax with Betty at a little log cabin he was building in the Santa Monica hills, away from the ranch house and its steady stream of visitors. He wanted to have a little fun "without some director hollering at me" and spend a few days "messing around doing this and that and not much of either. Get on old 'Soapsuds' and ride off up a little canyon I got here."

Alert as always to what was happening in the world, Will wrote in June, 1935, "We are living in great times. A fellow can't afford to die now with all this excitement going." But more and more during these past few years his mind turned to the old days, and his weekly articles were filled with talk about those glowing moments of the past and the friends of his youth. On one visit to Stillwater, Oklahoma, he had run into his former boss, Colonel Zach Mulhall, at the airport. Walter Harrison of the *Daily Oklahoman*, who witnessed the meeting, wrote that Mulhall "was crying like a baby as he put his arms around Will, and the tears in Rogers' eyes were not caused by the bit-

In January Will entertained Indiana legislators and had them rolling in the aisles.
WIDE WORLD

359

In Will's last movie he and humorist Irvin S. Cobb played rival riverboat captains.
WIDE WORLD

ing wind that was blowing." The crowd was too thick for Will to catch more than a moment with the older man, but when they reached the hall where he was scheduled to perform he asked Harrison to find a place where he could talk to Zach alone. A meeting was arranged on a fire escape, and the newspaperman saw the two men hug each other and talk for a minute or so. Then Will pulled out a roll of bills, thrust it into the old man's hand, and said goodby. Someone, it seems, had told him that Mrs. Mulhall was sick and that the Colonel could not pay her hospital bills.

On location outside Sacramento, California, for the filming of *Steamboat 'Round the Bend* with Irvin S. Cobb, Will heard that Buck McKee, his old vaudeville partner, was in the vicinity. It was a Sunday, and after working until four in the afternoon under a broiling sun (with Will taking his usual break to thump out the daily article) he and Cobb drove into town for his evening broadcast—an unrehearsed program that consisted of the two men exchanging ad libs. By the time it ended, Cobb said, he was "dead beat," while Will's fatigue showed in the deep lines in his jaws. Cobb wanted to get back to "The Pride of Paducah," the riverboat on which they were living, where it would be quiet and cool, but Will said he had something else in mind. "I just found out that the old boy who worked with me in vaudeville thirty years ago when I first broke in is livin' in a little ranch about nine miles from town. I guess he's too shy to come to see me, but by gum, I ain't too shy to go call on him." And off he drove.

When he caught sight of Buck, the two men just stared at each other while all the wonderful moments they had shared came flooding over Will. During the four or five years Buck had worked with him, riding the horse Teddy, they had played all over the United States and even made two trips to Europe, delighting audiences as Will roped a running horse for the first time on any stage. After Will and Betty were married in 1908, there were times when "the salary wasent any too big to ship Buck and his wife and Teddy, my wife and self, to the next town. In fact I think Buck rode some of the short jumps." Seeing Buck now made him realize how sad the demise of vaudeville was. "Nothing in the world ever give the satisfaction of a good vaudeville show. We was mighty proud to be playing in it. It had class in those days."

Earlier that year he and Betty had been in New York for one of his broadcasts and two benefit performances, and had met a number of old friends—Charles Winninger, who had been with the Follies; Charley Aldrich, a bucking-horse rider; Lillian Shaw, a vaudeville singer; Blanche Ring, Elsie Janis, and many others—and at the Amsterdam Theatre, where Will had spent so many years in the Follies, he found that some of the old stagehands were still around. The experience set him to wondering about the effects of radio and motion pictures on all those people whose trade was "a profession and not an accident —people who have spent a lifetime perfecting the art of entertaining people, then to have the whole stage profession snatched from under them, and ship your entertainment to you in a can." He had been one of the fortunate ones to survive and succeed in both worlds, but he couldn't avoid the thought that "those were great old days (but darn it any old days are great old days. Even the tough ones, after they are over, you can look back on with great memorys)."

He reminisced about the silent pictures he had made—in particular, three films in which he had acted with Irene Rich, who was just coming into her own as a leading lady, thanks to Will's help. Recalling that he had played "one of the love interests" then, Will realized that there were no such parts for him nowadays: he had to "fix it for some young ones. They won't let me have anything to do with it personally." Not that he had been any great shakes as a screen lover, "but in those days your age never mattered. Audiences figured that old people fell in love too, but now that's all out. Modern audiences think that old folks are just to be the fathers and mothers of the young ones."

On the last day of shooting for *Steamboat 'Round the Bend* Cobb looked for Will to say goodby and found him hunched up in his car outside the sound stage, saying, "Come on out to the ranch. We'll get a couple of bronks and ride up the trail to the top of the canyon." Cobb's physique was not designed for riding, and Will added with a grin, "I love to see you in a saddle—you do such humorous things on a horse and ain't deliberately tryin' to be funny neither." Cobb wanted to go; he prized the long, leisurely afternoons they had shared, but he knew that Will really preferred to be by himself, roping calves. So he said he had something else to do.

"Better change your mind, old timer," Will called after him. "This picture's done and I'm fixin' to go 'way and we may not get together again for quite a spell."

The navy flier Jocko Clark, who visited Will at the time he was finishing the movie, remembered his saying that it was the last one he would make for a while. "I want to fly to places I've never been before, I want to go everywhere," Will announced, indicating that he hoped to find a pilot who would be at his beck and call to take him anywhere his fancy dictated. Clark, who knew something of the hazards involved in flying "everywhere" in a small plane, wondered where Will would have it serviced or overhauled in remote places. "I had the feeling that night that he was overconfident in the capabilities of the aircraft of that time. . . . But he seemed to have boundless enthusiasm, and a complete misplaced confidence in aviation."

In July, the movie done, Will was considering making a long trip and contemplated flying to Rio de Janeiro to pick up the

Graf Zeppelin, which was making regularly scheduled flights from there up the coast of Africa to Europe. Nothing had quite jelled, however, and his plans were still vague when another piece of the puzzle dropped quietly into place. It took the form of a visit from a famous aviator, who possessed in abundance the qualities that appealed to Will. He was a cool, courageous, glamorous figure—a fellow Oklahoman who had started life with nothing and had gained a worldwide reputation entirely on his own.

Wiley Post was born in Texas, the son of an itinerant farmer, and had spent much of his boyhood in Oklahoma. Quite early he decided that farming was not for him, and in 1913, when he first saw an airplane, he realized what he wanted to do: from that day on he was determined to become a pilot. He worked as a roughneck in the oil fields, took a job with a flying circus as a parachute jumper, acquired some flight training, and was back working on an oil rig when an accident occurred that made it possible for him to purchase his first plane. An iron chip from a sledgehammer lodged in his left eye, which became infected and had to be removed, and Wiley was awarded $1,700 in compensation, with which he immediately bought a damaged Canuck aircraft. Having exchanged an eye for wings, he had to prove that he was capable of flying, and for months he worked on training his vision, learning how to calculate distances by guessing how far it was to a tree or building, then pacing it off to see how near right he was.

He married a Texas girl, became a barnstormer, took passengers on rides for $2.50, and gave flight instructions for $3 an hour. He was a natural pilot, one of his students said: "He didn't just fly an airplane, he put it on." When barnstorming failed to provide enough income he landed a job as personal pilot for two Oklahoma oil men, Powell Briscoe and F.C. Hall. What Briscoe remembered vividly was that Wiley didn't have a nerve in his body: "When other people were scared, Wiley just grinned"—an impression borne out by another friend, who described Wiley as a "nerveless, all-steel farm boy [who] came as near to being a mechanical flying machine as any human who ever held a stick."

After some months of braving the wind in an open cockpit, Hall was ready for a novel craft developed by Lockheed that became available in 1928. It was a cabin ship called the Vega, with plywood fuselage and no exposed struts or braces, and Hall bought one, named it the *Winnie Mae* for his daughter, and

TEXT CONTINUED ON PAGE 366

COURTESY PHILLIPS PETROLEUM

Above, Post stands beside the **Winnie Mae** *in Bartlesville, Oklahoma. In the photograph below, a triumphant and weary Post is greeted by a jubilant crowd after his unprecedented solo flight around the world in 1933.*

Wiley Post, Aviation Pioneer

Although he had lost one eye in an oil-field accident, Wiley Post overcame the disability and became a superb and fearless pilot. He broke the round-the-world speed record twice (the first time with Harold Gatty, and the second alone) in his Lockheed Vega, the Winnie Mae, *and pioneered the flying of jet streams and developed a practical pressure suit (right) for high-altitude flights. In 1935 he was said to be studying the practicability of a trans-Pacific route via Alaska and Russia.*

SMITHSONIAN INSTITUTION, COURTESY EDWIN O. COOPER

SMITHSONIAN INSTITUTION

For the Alaska trip with Will, Post had a different plane, on which he installed a pair of oversize pontoons. Here he tests the ship in the bay at Seattle.

UPI

had Wiley fly it, until the stock market crash of 1929 forced him to sell the plane.

For a year Wiley worked as a Lockheed test pilot; then Hall bought another Vega, to which he gave the same name, and in 1931 he decided to sponsor Post and an Australian navigator named Harold Gatty in a round-the-world flight. In one of those dramatic air exploits of which the twenties and thirties were so full, Post and Gatty flew around the globe in 8 days, 15 hours, 51 minutes, arriving in New York to a wild heroes' welcome. "No news today," Will commented at the time, "as big as this Post and Gatty that are making this world of ours look like the size of a watermelon." (One result of the flight was the construction of an airport in Claremore, which Will described as "the best landing field in the world"—created in four days so that Post and Gatty could pay a triumphal visit to Will's home town. Will flew to Tulsa to participate in the celebration for the Oklahoma boy, and rode with them in the *Winnie Mae* to Claremore.)

In California, Post visited Will on the movie set, where he was introduced to Will Jr. (at left), actress Billie Burke, and Fred Stone.

CULVER PICTURES

Two years later Wiley became the first man to circumnavigate the earth twice in an aircraft when he made a solo trip in a little under eight days—a record that Howard Hughes (who made the same trip in 1938 in less time, but with a crew of five) called "the most remarkable flight in history"—one that could never be duplicated because Post had done it alone. "What did I tell you about that little one-eyed Oklahoma boy?" Will crowed. "He is a hawk, isn't he? He holds the doubles and singles championship now."

Meantime, Post—an innovator as well as a superb pilot— had become interested in high-altitude flying. Convinced that airplanes "can travel at terrific speeds above 30,000 feet by getting into the prevailing wind channel," he was the first man to ride the jet streams and pioneered in developing the first practical high-pressure suit—a forerunner of the equipment worn to the moon. In 1935, having decided that the *Winnie Mae* should be retired (he had promised it to the Smithsonian Institution in Washington), Wiley acquired a new airplane.

Because he was short of funds he had to settle for a compromise—a hybrid aircraft assembled from the parts of two previously damaged ships. The basic plane was a Lockheed Orion with a Pratt & Whitney Wasp engine that had been operated by TWA for two years until it was disabled in a crash. To this had been added the wings taken from a Lockheed Explorer (a plane originally designed for an abortive New York to Paris attempt in 1930) that had crashed in the Canal Zone and turned over. The Lockheed Company did not encourage this amalgamation of parts, but Post applied for a restricted license to operate the ship for experimental cross-country flights and other special tests. (It was not certifiable under Bureau of Air Commerce regulations, which controlled regular commercial licenses, but was restricted to operations involving a pilot and up to two qualified crew members.) Some flight instruments from the *Winnie Mae* were installed in the racy-looking plane, which was painted bright red with a horizontal silver stripe, but Post discovered that he was going to have difficulties with the unconventional craft. When the plane was operated at low air speeds and low power, there was a definite heaviness in the front end and a tendency for it to pitch forward that was almost impossible to control.

At the time Post visited Will in California a flood of rumors was circulating about what the aviator was going to do next. According to one story, he and his wife and a young woman pilot named Fay Gillis had applied for permission to fly to Siberia. Wiley, it was said, wanted to study the feasibility of an air route between Alaska and Russia that would avoid the long haul across the Pacific, and Pan American Airways had reputedly agreed to finance the trip. Will, in a daily article, denied a rumor that he and Post were thinking of flying to Siberia; they were only going to New Mexico, he said—which they did, visiting the Waite Phillips ranch, where Wiley fished and Will looked at cattle. On July 29 both men were back in California, and in August Wiley and Mae Post flew from San Francisco to Seattle. Will had not yet made up his mind about going, and suggested that Wiley telephone him from Seattle, where he was going to have a set of pontoons installed in place of landing wheels, at which time Will would let him know definitely whether he was coming.

"There was nothing unusual about his vagueness," Betty recalled. "Our trips were nearly always made that way, and after we had our tickets we didn't plan beyond the first stop." She had not fully reconciled herself to Will's departure—not because of the Alaska leg of the flight, but because she dreaded his flying across Siberia. Yet she could tell that "Will wanted me to want him to go. He was always happier about anything he did if he felt that I wanted him to do it. And so I tried to be happy about this."

By August 3 Will was fairly certain he would make the trip. The day before he had made out a check for $7,540 to the Bank of America to cover a $5,000 letter of credit, $2,000 worth of traveler's checks, and $500 in cash. That Sunday morning he and Betty went for a long ride over the ranch, discussing what he wanted done on the place while he was away, and stopping to see the log cabin that had just been completed in a canyon back in the hills. Will was disappointed that he had not been able to spend the night there yet, but when Betty suggested that he put off his trip for a few days so they could camp out, he said, "No, let's wait till I get back." There were dozens of matters Betty wanted him to attend to before he flew to Seattle (pictures and books to autograph, letters to sign), but Will seemed to be superstitious about doing them and said that all those things could wait until he returned. On one point he gave in: she asked him to write a will, and since their friends Eddie Vail, a California rancher, and Ewing Halsell of Vinita, Oklahoma, were visiting the ranch that day, they served as witnesses to the document, which left all of his property to Betty, with the provision that if she did not survive him it would go to his three children in equal shares.

Early in the afternoon he packed two bags—discarding, in the process, about nine-tenths of what Betty and Emil had laid out for him to take. While he was packing Betty came into the room several times, and once he called her back, gave her a sheepish look, and said, "Say, Blake, you know what I just did? I flipped a coin."

Betty said she hoped it came out tails.

Will laughed, held out his hand, and replied, "No, it didn't. It's heads. See, I win."

Late in the afternoon they visited a nearby ranch to watch the end of a polo game, then Will roped calves until suppertime. Their son Bill had dinner with them, and that evening they went to a rodeo at Gilmore Stadium in Los Angeles. It was a cool night, and Betty was conscious of the incongruity of seeing a rodeo after dark from a grandstand; she missed the hot sunshine and the smell of cattle. As usual, Will knew most of the performers and waved to them from his box, and a number rode over to shake hands. During the evening someone gave him a small wood-and-paper puzzle, and Betty watched him toy with it unconsciously while he watched the riders in the arena. "It was a mannerism I knew so well," she said, "and which was so much a part of him. His restless hands could never stay still. Then, when the show was over, I saw him stuff the puzzle in the pocket of his coat." In with it went the rodeo program. His pockets, Betty said, were always filled with trinkets like those of a little boy, and he never went to a banquet or theatre without bringing home a souvenir menu or program.

Will had a reservation on the 11 P.M. flight to San Francisco, and after stopping at an open-air restaurant for a sandwich, they drove to the airport. It was crowded, so he and Betty and Bill waited outside until it was time to say goodby. Then Will, with an overcoat slung over a shoulder and a stack of late newspaper editions clutched under an arm, climbed the steps and boarded the plane. Betty caught a last glimpse of him in the window, smiling, and she and Bill watched until the green and red wing lights of the plane vanished in the night sky.

In Seattle Wiley Post was having his problems. He had ordered a set of Edo pontoons, similar to those used by Alaskan bush pilots, but they had not arrived by the time Will got there, and since Will was financing the trip and was impatient to be off, Wiley settled for what he could find. (In addition to the obvious advantages of enabling them to land on water in the rugged Alaska countryside, there is some reason to suppose that the pontoons gave Will a sense of security. Years before he had written, "If a flier was going from New York to San Francisco, where it is all overland—you never see them do it with a hydroplane where they can land only on water—then why is it they take a land plane across the ocean? No one has disappeared yet over water in a hydroplane.")

What Wiley found was a pair of pontoons from a Fokker trimotor—much heavier than what was required for his Orion Explorer. After they were installed, he took the plane up and discovered that the big pontoons accentuated the nose-heaviness he had detected earlier, which meant that the landing or the takeoff would be quite hazardous unless the plane was operated under a good deal of power. Will asked about the pontoons, thinking they were "awful big looking things," but Wiley replied laconically, "None too big." The pilot, Will was learning, was "kinder a Calvin Coolidge on answers; none of 'em are going to bother you with being too long."

Post decided that if Will rode as far aft in the plane as possible, his weight would compensate slightly for the heaviness of the nose. Evidently, it would have been possible to correct the condition more scientifically by installing a new stabilizer-elevator on the plane, but Wiley was fearful that he could not obtain approval from the Commerce Department for his hybrid ship. Since an attempt to do so would delay their departure further, the change was not made.

In the front of the plane was a single seat; Wiley had removed the other to provide as much room as possible for their baggage, a rubber boat and canoe paddle, some life vests, several coils of rope, sleeping bags, and Post's rifle and fishing tackle. Will wasn't sure he looked forward to spending much time in a sleeping bag; he had never used one and suspected that if his usual luck with zippers held, he might have to walk around in the bag all day.

Mae Post had decided not to accompany them; Will thought it was going to be a rugged trip with a lot of camping out, and had discouraged her from coming. (After debating the possibility of traveling north by ship to join them in Alaska, she finally decided against it and returned to Oklahoma by way of California.) At 9:20 A.M. on August 6, after loading two precious cases of chili aboard the plane and dodging a reporter's question as to whether they planned to fly around the world,

Wiley taxied out onto the waters of Lake Washington, made a short run; and "took off like a bird," in Will's phrase, pointing the ship's nose in the direction of Juneau, Alaska.

En route Will's enthusiasm for the beauty of the scenery was equaled only by his admiration of Post's skill at navigating: the maze of channels and islands along the coast all looked alike to him, "but this old boy turns up the right alley all the time." Musing about conditions back home, the thought occurred to him that the person who would really enjoy making this trip with them was President Roosevelt. In Juneau, where they were grounded for several days because of bad flying conditions, Will met the governor of the territory and spent a nostalgic evening with Rex Beach, who had written his first silent movie, *Laughing Bill Hyde*. Will still considered it the best picture he had made, "for I hadent learned to try to act. There aint nothing worse than an actor when we act."

Will and Beach stayed up until midnight talking of old times while Post fell asleep with his head in his arms, and before they left, Beach asked, "What are your plans?" Will grinned and said nothing, but Post—suddenly loquacious—replied, "We haven't any. We're just on a vacation. We want to see Dawson and Fairbanks and those farmer colonists at Matanuska, of course, and we'd like to see the MacKenzie River, too. We might even hop across to Siberia and go home that way. We have the maps, and it would make a swell trip to go home by

On their arrival in Juneau, Wiley and Will were greeted by Mayor Goldstein (left), Will's old friend, novelist Rex Beach (center), and Joe Crosson, noted Alaska pilot.
INTERNATIONAL NEWS

way of Iceland and Greenland. The longest water jump is only a thousand miles."

Before taking off the next morning Will bought a red fox fur, took it to the post office in Juneau, and mailed it to Betty. As the plane made its way north he sat in the rear seat, typewriter in his lap, pounding out his daily and weekly columns, which were chatty, newsy travelogues, filled with accounts of the scenery and people he saw, observations on the vastness of Alaska and the isolation of little towns and fishing villages, comments on the Eskimos and their way of life. He was fascinated with some of the animal stories he had heard: a near-legendary, two-thousand-mile drive of a herd of reindeer that had taken five years; the enormous size of the caribou herds, which reminded him of the buffalo on the Plains; how several huskies had made possible the delivery of some infantile paralysis serum to Nome.

Flying east into Canada, they traveled over the Yukon and the Klondike region, then headed north along the MacKenzie River to the Arctic Ocean, and landed at Fairbanks, having drifted wherever the spirit took them. "Was you ever driving around in a car and not knowing or caring where you went?" Will wrote on August 12. "Well, that's what Wiley and I are doing. We sure are having a great time. If we hear of whales or polar bears in the Arctic, or a big herd of caribou or reindeer, we fly over and see it."

The next day, with nothing pressing to do, they went down to Anchorage in a different plane, piloted by two local fliers—Joe Crosson, who was known as Alaska's best bush pilot, and Joe Barrows—flying over Mt. McKinley on a brilliant sunny day, which Will said was the most beautiful sight he had ever seen. They also visited the Matanuska Valley, the scene of a recent pioneering experiment. Some seven or eight hundred people from the States had migrated to the area, hoping to find good farm country, but the venture was in a state of chaos when Will dropped by. Their plane rolled to a stop on the rough landing strip and was immediately surrounded by the transients who swarmed out for a glimpse of Will. "How do you feel, Mr. Rogers?" one asked.

"Why, uh, why—wait'll I get out, will you?" Will replied. "I came to look around, not to report on my health. Where you boys from?" he asked, surveying the group. "Anybody here from Claremore?"

At the end of an hour and a half inspection trip, during which Will had the crowd laughing most of the time, they were climbing into the plane when a construction crew cook rushed up with half a dozen fat cookies. "They're good!" Will called, taking a bite. "But I'll toss 'em out if we can't get off the ground." And on a wave of laughter Post taxied down the strip.

Reporting on their stop in his daily article of August 15, Will —with his habitual compassion for the plight of human beings caught in a situation beyond their control—made a plea for workmen to assist these people to get some adequate housing before winter set in. It was only a matter of weeks before the first snowfall, the immigrants were living in tents, and he reminded his readers that "there is a lot of difference in pioneering for gold and pioneering for spinach."

One man Will wanted to see while he was in Alaska was Charles Brower, an old-timer known as the "King of the Arctic," who had spent nearly half a century in the territory as a trader and whaler and who was now U.S. Commissioner in Barrow, a little settlement three hundred miles north of the Arctic Circle. When Will spoke to Crosson about going there, the flier, who had observed the excessive nose-heaviness of Wiley's aircraft, advised against it until some alterations could be made to correct the problem. As an experienced bush pilot, he was concerned about the possibility of engine failure and realized that if Post had to make a forced landing somewhere without power, he might be in grave trouble. In a powerless glide, the flow of air over the horizontal stabilizer would be sharply reduced, affecting the efficiency of the elevators, and Crosson doubted if Post would be able to prevent the plane from nosing over into a forward dive.

From Fairbanks Post radioed the government weather station in Barrow for a report on conditions and was told that snow, sleet, and zero visibility made a landing impossible; but after waiting a day Wiley decided they could make it. Crosson, who knew what the weather could be like five hundred miles to the north, after they crossed the glowering peaks of the Brooks Range, didn't like the sound of this. But when he realized that Post was determined to leave, he advised him to head for Anaktuvuk Pass and fly directly north until he sighted the Arctic Ocean; then he should turn west, hugging the coast until he reached Point Barrow, an easily identifiable peninsula that was the northernmost reach of the North American mainland.

Ten miles south of Point Barrow lay the village of Barrow, a fishing community inhabited by about three hundred Eskimos and nine whites. Dr. Henry W. Greist and his wife, a nurse, were in charge of a Presbyterian mission and hospital there, ministering to the needs of the local people and anyone else who required help within a radius of five hundred miles; the Army Signal Corps operated the weather station; and Charles Brower, the U.S. Commissioner, described his own work as recording births and deaths, performing marriages, and trying to play Solomon in settling disputes. The surrounding region was bleak, treeless, Arctic tundra, one of the most desolate places imaginable. When the ice broke up, an occasional boat brought news of the outside world (mail was delivered only four times a year); and the natives lived by catching fish, seals, whales, walrus, and reindeer.

Before leaving Fairbanks about 11 A.M. on August 15, Will handed his daily article to Joe Crosson and asked him to take it, with a telegram he had written to his daughter Mary, to the telegraph office. He wired her:

GREAT TRIP. WISH YOU WERE ALL ALONG. HOW'S YOUR ACTING? YOU AND MAMA WIRE ME ALL THE NEWS TO NOME. GOING TO POINT BARROW TODAY. FURTHEST POINT OF LAND ON WHOLE AMERICAN CONTINENT. LOTS OF LOVE. DON'T WORRY.

DAD

Mary was in Skowhegan, Maine, performing in summer stock in a company that included Keenan Wynn, the son of another great comedian. That week she had the lead in *Ceiling Zero*, a play in which her stage father was killed in an airplane crash.

Post wisely decided not to take off with a full load of fuel from the narrow, winding Chena River in Fairbanks. He arranged for a supply of gasoline for the hop to Barrow, and headed north. After passing over the small village of Wiseman, the little red plane made its way through the notch in the mountain barrier, and somewhere beyond the north face ran into a storm described by Charles Brower as one of the worst he had ever experienced in Barrow. There, at times, it was impossible to see more than fifty yards.

Ninety miles from the settlement some natives tending a herd of reindeer heard the sound of a plane overhead and once caught a fleeting glimpse of it. A trader named Gus Masik heard it while he was crossing Smith's Bay; so did an Eskimo at Point Tangent; and from these reports it appeared that Post, flying blind after losing his way in the storm, had skirted the coastline for a while, moving northwest, but at some point turned due west. Providentially, about three o'clock in the afternoon he spotted a break in the dense cloud cover and caught sight of land and a stream. Flying low along the stream, he came to a lagoon big enough to set the plane down on, and went in for a landing.

The body of water was known as the Walakpa lagoon, and as luck would have it, there was an Eskimo camp on the shore, where some men were fishing. Wiley taxied over, cut the engine, and he and Will climbed out onto the pontoons and spoke to two of the natives—Claire Okpeaha and his wife, who taught in Dr. Greist's Sunday school and knew English fairly well. There was a brief conversation: Wiley asked how far and in which direction Barrow was (it was no more than a ten-minute flight); Will inquired what the Eskimos were fishing for and was told that they were after seals; and after the two Americans held a brief consultation they climbed back into the plane, waved, and taxied to one end of the lagoon to begin their takeoff. The small, landlocked waterway was too short for Post to make a preliminary run to warm up the engine. His first pass at it had to be the only one.

Watching from the lonely shoreline, the Eskimos heard the motor rev up to a deafening pitch and saw the plane begin moving faster and faster across the water—the pontoons throwing twin sprays behind as the plane came up on the steps of the floats. Then it lifted off, started to climb and banked to the right, making the turn toward Barrow, and suddenly there was a different sound. The engine misfired, sputtered, and went dead. The red plane turned nose down, hurtling like a stone into the shallow lagoon, spewing a geyser of sand and gravel and water into the air as the fuselage split open on impact. One wing broke off, the plane flipped over on its back, and at the same instant there was a dull explosion and a quick flash of fire, which went out immediately. Then silence. As a film of oil slowly spread over the surface of the water there was only the soft lapping of waves on the shore as ripples from the shattered plane broke, ebbed, and finally died.

The terrified Eskimos' first instinct was to run away; then Claire Okpeaha took courage and went as close to the plane as he could and shouted, again and again. There was no answer.

He told his wife that he must get word to the Americans in Barrow, and leaving the others behind to stare in disbelief at the spectral, broken hulk in the water, he started running toward Barrow and help.

"A Little Sightseeing Trip with Wiley Post"

Unlike most American tourists, Will could not be bothered with a camera. "No," he wrote as he and Wiley Post took off from Seattle, Washington, "that's what we are going on this trip for, to get away from cameras, then too I don't know nothing about 'em and can't work 'em. We may see some fine sights but you can always lie about a thing better than you can prove it. Then you always have to explain that 'This picture don't near do the scene justice.'" As the photographs on these pages indicate, however, wherever Will Rogers went, someone wanted to record his visit with a camera, while others collected autographs (right).

Will, luggage, and typewriter, at Matanuska Valley

WILL ROGERS MEMORIAL, CLAREMORE, OKLA.

He had flown so much that catching some sleep in a plane was no problem, as this earlier photograph suggests.

WILL ROGERS MEMORIAL, CLAREMORE, OKLA., GIFT OF PROJECT 20

UPI

At Fairbanks, Alaska, Wiley Post learned that Barrow—which Will wanted to visit— was socked in, and they waited for a day in hopes the weather would clear. Three of these pictures were taken there on the morn- ing of August 15, 1935, when Post decided they could safely depart. In Barrow, mean- time, no one imagined that Post and Rogers would even attempt the flight until a more favorable weather report was forthcoming.

Below, Will seems to be in charge of loading the plane.

WIDE WORLD

Will talks with reporters (above, left). Here he poses with pilots Seppala, Post, and Crosson at Fairbanks.

WILL ROGERS MEMORIAL, CLAREMORE, OKLA.

Above, and overleaf, are Eskimos at the scene of the crash of Post's plane in the bleak Arctic wasteland near Barrow.

WILL ROGERS MEMORIAL, CLAREMORE, OKLA.
WIDE WORLD

New York World Telegram

WILL ROGERS AND
WILEY POST KILLED
IN AIR CRASH

EXTRA!

CULVER PICTURES

"A smile has disappeared from the lips of America...."

John McCormack

The headline that appeared over Rollin Kirby's drawing (left) was "All I Know Is What I Read in the Papers." Will's typewriter (above), with an unfinished column still in it, was salvaged from the wreckage of the airplane.
WILL ROGERS MEMORIAL, CLAREMORE, OKLA.

Five hours after the crash Claire Okpeaha, having run for sixteen miles through the tundra grass, skirting dozens of lakes and bogs, finally staggered into the store in Barrow, almost too exhausted to speak. Gasping for breath, he told the owner, a man named Bert Panigeo, about the crash he had seen, and Panigeo called Frank Dougherty, the local schoolteacher, on the telephone. No one seemed to have much idea about the plane's identity, but there was some immediate speculation that it might be a party of American hunters or possibly a Russian plane that had gone off course. As Charles Brower said, it occurred to nobody that it might be Will Rogers and Wiley Post; since they had been warned about local weather conditions, they were not expected for several days.

Dougherty's first reaction was to send Okpeaha to find Brower and tell him what had happened, while he phoned Sergeant Stanley Morgan, the Signal Corps man in charge of the weather station, got a launch into the water, and rounded up a rescue party. Dougherty, Morgan, and a group of Eskimos headed out at once; Brower, who had a faster launch, loaded it with blankets, sleeping bags, and medicine, and sent it after them, with his son David in charge. Dave's boat also towed an oomiak, a large, light open boat made of hides stretched over a wooden frame, which could be portaged across the sandbar surrounding the lagoon.

In the launch with Dougherty and Morgan, Okpeaha recovered his composure and his tongue, and on the long voyage through the fog and ice gave Sergeant Morgan some additional details about the catastrophe. "One mans big, have tall boots," he said, "Other mans short, have sore eye, rag over eye." And, suddenly, it dawned on Morgan who must be in the plane.

At the lagoon they found that the Eskimos from the sealing camp had removed Will's broken body from an opening in the side of the fuselage but had been unable to extricate the pilot, who was wedged between the engine and one of the big pontoons. After Dave Brower arrived with a block and tackle, they pulled off the pontoon and one wing, and with great difficulty got Post's body out. They placed the two corpses in sleeping bags they found in the plane, loaded them into the oomiak, and headed for open water and the long trip to Barrow.

It was three o'clock in the morning when Charles Brower and Dr. Greist heard the launches returning. (Greist had been performing an operation at the hospital and was unable to accompany the search party.) From the sounds they knew at once that the worst had happened: the motors were throttled down to normal speed, and the doctor could hear the voices of the Eskimos, chanting the "plaintive song they sing when the headman in a village dies. . . . Once heard it is never forgotten," he said. "The sight of the boats coming in, the little oomiak bobbing along, and the song floating to us—I'll never forget it."

A group of Eskimos from the sealing camp assisted the three Americans from Barrow in extricating the bodies of Wiley and Will from the smashed Orion Explorer.

Dave Brower came ashore, saw his father, and told him, "Dad, it's Will Rogers and Wiley Post."

"How do you know?" asked Charlie, who couldn't believe

WIDE WORLD

that they would have flown in the face of the weather report they had received. Morgan then told him what he had learned from Claire Okpeaha on the way to the lagoon.

The two bodies were carried to the hospital, where the badly shaken Greist, his wife, and Brower removed the men's clothing and began to prepare the corpses for burial. For more than three hours they worked, while outside in the hospital some fifteen Eskimos waited quietly, knowing nothing about the tragedy except that it had profoundly affected all the Americans in the remote outpost.

When the contents of the pockets were examined, it was noted that Wiley Post's gold watch had stopped at 8:18 P.M., the time of the crash (he was still carrying Oklahoma time, which meant that it was 3:18 at Barrow). In Will's clothing Dr. Greist found cash and traveler's checks, a newspaper clipping with a picture of his daughter, a stub of a pencil, a pocket knife, a pair of eyeglasses, a magnifying glass, and a pocket watch that was still running. Thinking how much these items resembled those a small boy might carry, the doctor also noticed that there was a program from a rodeo in Los Angeles and a curious little puzzle made of cardboard and wood. To Charlie Brower the watch somehow symbolized "all that made Will the simple, beloved man of the people he was. It couldn't have cost over a dollar and a half. He wore it tied to the end of an old string."

In Will's badly smashed portable typewriter was a sheet of paper on which he had been typing the third page of his latest weekly article. There was a description of their departure from Fairbanks only hours before and of their glimpse of Wiseman on the way north, and several stories about Alaskan dog teams. He had started to tell of their visit with Joe Crosson and a yarn he heard about Joe's partner, a Swede, and a wire-haired terrier who had the unfortunate habit of barking at bears, but he had not finished the article. It ended abruptly in the middle of a sentence, and the last word he had typed was "death."

Precisely what happened between the time the Orion Explorer lifted off the lagoon and the moment, a few seconds later, when it banked and crashed will never be known for certain, but there was enough information about the plane and its characteristics to permit fairly accurate speculation about what must have occurred. Several weeks after the accident Eugene L. Vidal, the director of the Bureau of Air Commerce, released a report, which was supplemented two months later by officials investigating the tragedy. In essence, these reports indicated

Behind Claire Okpeaha the plane's pontoons are visible above the lagoon's surface.
WIDE WORLD

385

that the various alterations to the plane—the combination of the wings from one craft with the fuselage from another, the addition of the oversize pontoons—had created a serious imbalance, making the ship "decidedly nose-heavy." The investigators concluded that it would have been difficult, if not impossible, to control the plane without the aid of the engine—something Post himself had discovered—but why the engine had failed at takeoff was not answered. It was noted that the temperature near Barrow was 40 degrees Fahrenheit, suggesting that the motor might have cooled off while Post and Rogers were talking with the Eskimos at the edge of the lagoon. Or, the investigators thought, ice or water may have condensed in the carburetor. The official conclusion was that "the probable cause of this accident was loss of control of the aircraft at a low altitude, after sudden engine failure, due to the extreme nose-heaviness of the aircraft."

Because Will's life was heavily insured, his insurance companies requested official copies of the license issued to Post for the plane, questioning if the craft had been properly certified after the pontoons were added. The aeronautical inspector in Seattle indicated that the airplane had not been checked by him after their installation—there had not been time; Post flew to Alaska the morning after they were put in place. Subsequently, the Department of Commerce issued a statement: "With respect to the restricted form of aircraft license here under consideration . . . the substitution of pontoons for wheel type landing gear on said airplane would not constitute grounds for revocation or suspension of said license because of the purpose for which it was issued." (That is, for permission for up to three persons to be carried aboard the airplane while in flight.)

No one was certain what caused the crash. Dr. Greist, who talked with Joe Crosson and others, had his own ideas about what had caused the engine to fail. Some years later he told Homer Croy that the plane was equipped with two gas tanks, one in each wing, which meant that when gasoline in one tank ran low, the pilot had to turn a hand control to open the other. Perhaps, the doctor thought, since Post had been circling for some time trying to find a clearing in the fog, the tank on which he had been operating was almost out of fuel. Then, when the airplane was airborne and he banked to the right, he heard the engine misfire, realized that the tank was empty, and quickly turned the hand control. But he was too late; the plane was only about fifty feet off the ground, and before the gasoline could reach the engine the nose-heavy plane plunged into the lagoon. The position of Will's body in the rear of the cabin, behind the baggage, indicated that Post was taking no chances on the weight distribution at the time of takeoff, but as he had known all along, they were in real danger if ever they lost power.

Charles Brower was more positive than anyone about what had occurred. In a book describing his fifty years in Alaska, published in 1963, he told what his son Dave had found that night on Walatka lagoon after the bodies had been removed from the wreckage. "Before leaving, Dave examined the plane carefully to try and discover why it had crashed. That was easy. Not only did none of the tanks contain so much as a drop of gas but there was no sign of any on the surface of the landlocked lagoon. Add to this evidence the sudden sputtering and dying of the motor which Okpeaha had mentioned, and it seems certain that the men were entirely out of gas when they landed on the lagoon for the first time. Perhaps they thought they had enough for a bare twelve miles or more. Perhaps they didn't even check their gauge. We shall never know."

As soon as the bodies were brought to Barrow and positively identified, a radio message from Sergeant Morgan went out to Seattle. Communications between the northern outpost and the outside world were so tenuous that it had to be relayed twice en route, taking nearly two hours to reach the continental United States. The message read:

Ten p.m. native runner reported plane crash fifteen miles south of Barrow. Immediately hired fast launch, proceeded to scene. Found plane complete wreck, partly submerged, two feet of water. Recovered body of Rogers, then necessary tear plane apart extract body of Post from water. Brought bodies Barrow. Turned over Dr. Greist. Also salvaged personal effects, which are holding. Advise relatives and instruct this station fully as to procedure. Natives camping small river fifteen miles south here claim Post, Rogers landed and asked way to Barrow. Taking off, engine misfired on right bank while only fifty feet off water. Plane, out of control, crashed nose on, tearing right wing off and nosing over, forcing engine back through body of plane. Both apparently killed instantly. Both bodies bruised. Post's wrist watch broken, stopped 8:18 P.M.

Betty Rogers was in Skowhegan, Maine, visiting Mary, and the last word she had had from Will was the telegram sent by Joe Crosson on August 15 from Fairbanks, the day of the crash.

What disturbed her was Will's reference to Nome, the point from which Wiley intended to fly to Siberia. She was still hoping that Will, after flying around Alaska for a week or two, would have had enough and would leave Post, return to the States, and join her in Maine. If Will made the trip it meant considerable inconvenience for her: before he left, they had agreed that if he accompanied Post to Russia, Betty would return to California to pack, cross the country again, sail to Europe, and meet him. There had been some talk of meeting friends, the Winfield Sheehans, who would be honeymooning in Europe about that time, and in fact Sheehan, a Fox Film executive, had received a telegram from Juneau saying that Will was definitely continuing with Post and hoped they could meet in Paris.

Bill Rogers was working that summer as a wiper in the engine room of a tanker, and his brother Jim and a cousin were driving east from California. On August 16 Betty, her sister Theda Blake, and Mary planned to fly to Bar Harbor for the day, and Betty was talking with a friend outside her cottage when she saw a car coming up the road and recognized the driver as the manager of the theatre where Mary was working. When he got out of the automobile and spoke to her sister, something about his manner alarmed Betty, whose first thought was that something had gone wrong on Jim's trip.

She ran to speak to him.

"Has something happened to Jimmy? Tell me," she pleaded.

There was no answer from the theatre manager, but her sister told her, "No, Betty, it's Will. Will has had an accident."

For an instant, Betty remembered, she felt only relief, knowing that nothing could possibly happen to Will—nothing more serious than mechanical trouble or a forced landing. Then she was told of Sergeant Morgan's message from Barrow.

Perhaps not since the death of Abraham Lincoln had a tragedy touched so many Americans as did the loss of Will Rogers and Wiley Post. When the story appeared in newspapers it overshadowed everything that was going on in the world. Four full pages of the *New York Times* were devoted to the event on Saturday, August 17; Sunday's edition was nearly the same; and for a week the newspaper and radio coverage continued. There were full accounts of the lives of both men, side by side with expressions of grief from President Roosevelt, members of the Senate and House, Cabinet members, leaders of the entertainment world and the aviation frater-

It was a black day for Oklahoma, as this extra edition of the Claremore newspaper indicates. (It included Will's column about his visit to the colony of emigrants living in the Matanuska Valley.)
WIDE WORLD

nity. Messages of sympathy came from all over the globe, and the most poignant were those from countries Will had visited and helped in one way or another—from Ireland, where he had put on a benefit performance in 1926 for victims of a theatre disaster; from Puerto Rico, where he had aided victims of the 1932 hurricane; from Nicaragua, whose President recalled how Will "made me cry one minute and laugh the next during the bitter days following the 1931 earthquake."

The *Times* printed a separate editorial on each man. Post, it

One of five Will Rogers commemorative stamps issued by Nicaragua, recalling his visit to the country in 1931.
WILL ROGERS MEMORIAL, CLAREMORE, OKLA.

was said, "belonged to the long line of pioneers that began by strapping futile wings to their backs and ended by soaring over oceans and continents. . . . He ran risks not to make money—his world flights gained him virtually nothing—or to break a record, although that almost inevitably happened, but to advance aviation technically."

It was extraordinarily difficult then, as now, to describe the hold Will Rogers had on so many millions of Americans. "A peculiar sense of national loss will be stirred by the tragic death of Mr. Rogers," the editorial read. "He had a unique career, which we all like to think could have been run only in America. He came to hold such a place in the public mind that, of his passing from the stage it might be said, as it was by Dr. Johnson of Garrick's, that it will 'eclipse the gayety of nations.' For Mr. Rogers had an inimitable and genial wit which endeared him to all sorts and conditions of men. His rise to fame was much like the slow emerging of a star above our horizon. . . . It is certain that we shall not look upon Will Rogers' like again. Let us hope, however, that in the mysterious evolution and constant surprises of our native talent, some one may arise to help us as he did to keep our mental poise, to avoid taking all our national geese for swans, and by wholesome laughter make this world seem a better place to live in."

It was left for John McCormack, whom Betty and Will had heard sing at the St. Louis Exposition so many years earlier and who had become their friend over the years, to sum it up. "A smile has disappeared from the lips of America," he wrote, "and her eyes are now suffused with tears. He was a man, take this for all in all, we shall not look upon his like again."

From every city and hamlet across the land came stories of people shocked and heartbroken, knowing—as the *Times* and McCormack had said—that there would never be another Will. A letter to Betty described the scene in a grocery store in a small New Hampshire town; customers were waiting to be served when a little boy came in and told them that Will Rogers was dead. No one spoke. Then three or four people walked out silently, their errand forgotten, the clerks stopped what they were doing, and one woman, "as though she were not able to stand, looked down helplessly and found a box or something and just sat down." In Locust Grove, Oklahoma, half a dozen Cherokees were building a fence when an old man drove along the road to tell them the news. Again, there was only stunned silence—people could find no words to express themselves in

the face of this. After a time some of the Indians spoke of how
they had known Will or remembered a favor he had done for
someone. Then one said, "I can't work any more today," and
all of them stacked their tools and quietly walked away.

Shortly after Betty Rogers learned of Will's death, Charles
Lindbergh called to say that he would take charge of bringing
the bodies home and that Pan American Airways, for which he
worked as a consultant, would make its facilities available for
this purpose. Joe Crosson, who had delivered Will's final daily
article and the telegram to Mary to the telegraph office on
August 15, flew to Barrow to pick up the linen-wrapped bodies,
and on August 17 Will and Wiley began their journey home. In
Fairbanks the next morning hundreds of Alaskans saw Crosson
off when he left for Vancouver. In Seattle people had waited all
night for a glimpse of his airplane, the flags were at half-mast,
planes overhead dipped their wings in salute, and there Crosson
was joined by a Pan American official and Will's close friend
Amon Carter, who wanted to travel with him on his last flight.

On the nineteenth Crosson landed in Burbank, California,
just as darkness was falling, and as the plane moved slowly
through the twilight into the hangar, the throb of its idling motors reminded thousands of onlookers of muffled funeral drums.

While arrangements were being made for Will's funeral,
Post's body was put aboard another plane bound for Oklahoma
City. His parents wanted his remains to be brought to Mays-
ville, where they lived, but other members of the family per-
suaded them to hold the service in Oklahoma City; so many

*The family—Theda Blake,
Jim, Mary, Betty, and Will
Jr.—was photographed just
before they boarded the train
for the long, sad journey home
to Santa Monica, California.*

INTERNATIONAL NEWS

In Burbank, California, the special plane bearing the bodies (piloted by Joe Crosson) is met by a silent crowd.
INTERNATIONAL NEWS

people wanted to be there. Without telling anyone, the elderly couple drove to the Oklahoma City airport, parked their car among the thousands of others, and waited, unrecognized by anyone, to see their son's body arrive. "We didn't want to create a stir," Wiley's father said, "so we drove up to the edge of the crowd where we could get a view and sat there and waited." They saw the plane appear out of the west, land, and taxi across the field and into the hangar, and when it was safely inside Mrs. Post said, "it was just the way Wiley would have wished—coming home in an airplane."

On the day before Betty, her three children, and Theda Blake were due to arrive on the coast by train, Betty's brother James Blake received a parcel addressed in a familiar, rambling scrawl to Mrs. Will Rogers, in care of J.K. Blake. It was postmarked Juneau, Alaska, and inside was Will's final gift to his wife—a small, red fox fur.

On August 22 the last rites for Will Rogers were held in Los Angeles. Prior to a simple service at the Wee Kirk o' the Heather, his casket lay in state in Forest Lawn Memorial Park, where fifty thousand people—many of whom had been standing in line since the previous night—filed by in silence under a scorching sun. Other memorial services were held in the Hollywood Bowl, in Beverly Hills, and in Claremore; in many towns the flags were at half-mast; the nation's motion picture theatres were darkened; the CBS and NBC networks observed a half-hour of silence; and in New York a squadron of planes, each towing a long black streamer, flew over the city in final tribute to the hero and the friend of aviation.

More than any event of an individual's life, his death causes people to stop and make a reckoning; in the words of the woodsman's proverb, the tree is best measured when it is down. Across the nation Americans were pausing to take Will Rogers' measure and to think what a different place their world would be now that he was gone. None of the descriptive labels—cowboy-philosopher, humorist, star of stage, screen, and radio— suggested what was in the hearts of most Americans when they learned of his death.

Whether they had encountered him personally, or knew him as a voice from the radio, an image on the screen, or the man who wrote the words they read in their newspapers, they knew him as a friend. In a world where there was little enough neighborliness or caring, he had brought them both, in a way they could understand and cherish, and now that the smile and the voice were gone, and men tried to define the unique quality that had made him the most beloved figure of his time, they sensed that they had witnessed a phenomenon seldom duplicated before or since. Damon Runyon hinted at something of the sort when he called Will Rogers "the closest approach to what we call the true American." Perhaps it was quite a simple thing, after all—no more than an ancient tribal dream. What people saw in him was only what they wanted to be themselves.

In 1938, when the Will Rogers Memorial in Claremore, Oklahoma, was dedicated, Franklin D. Roosevelt wrote to Will's friend Walter Harrison:

We remember Will Rogers with gratitude and affection because he knew how to revive the spirit of laughter in hearts that had known too much of the distractions and anxieties of a busy world. His mission in life was to cheer, to comfort and to console.

There was something infectious about his humor. His appeal went straight to the heart of the nation. Above all things, in a time grown too solemn and somber he brought his countrymen back to a sense of proportion.

Will Rogers knew out of the fullness of a blithe heart that few things in life are to be taken seriously and that our troubles multiply if we take them tragically. And so he showed us all how to laugh. From him we can learn anew the homely lesson that the way to make progress is to build on what we have, to believe that today is better than yesterday and that tomorrow will be better than either.

In the years following his death, many memorials to Will Rogers were established. The Santa Monica ranch was given in 1944 by Will's children to California for a state park. On a high cliff above the Walatka lagoon, facing the Arctic Ocean, is a marker of Oklahoma stone in which these words are cut: "Will Rogers and Wiley Post ended life's flight here, August 15, 1935." Clem Rogers' old ranch in the Verdigris valley was flooded when the Oologah Dam and Reservoir were built by the Army Engineers; but not before the ranch house where Will was born was moved to high ground about a mile west of its original location. In 1959 the family donated a 100-acre tract to the state, with the understanding that the house be relocated.

In 1938 Betty Rogers gave 20 acres of land in Claremore to Oklahoma for a memorial to her husband. It was a hillside Will had purchased in 1911, with the thought that he would come back there to live one day. Here, in 1944, his remains were brought from California, and a month later, when Betty died, she and their infant son Fred were buried at his side. In the rambling limestone building are all his letters, his newspaper articles, films, broadcast transcriptions, and the personal memorabilia of fifty-five restless, energetic years.

This is the place to which more than half a million Americans journey each year to pay tribute to the man they have never forgotten. In the center of the towering hall, facing the windows that overlook a sunken garden and the simple marble tomb, is a bronze statue of Will that bears the epitaph he wrote for himself: "I never met a man I didn't like."

The statue by Jo Davidson is a deep brown color, except for two gleaming bright spots on the toes of the shoes. Nearly every one of those millions of Americans who have come here since 1938 has paused before the statue, looked up at the face, and then, before moving away, silently reached out to touch the tip of one shoe in a gesture of love. As it did in life, a little of Will Rogers has rubbed off on each of them.

In the gathering darkness the hearse carrying Will's body is escorted from the airport by motorcycle policemen. Overleaf, a still from a newsreel film shows the squadron of planes, each trailing long black streamers, that flew over New York on the day the last rites were held for Will Rogers in California.

WILL ROGERS MEMORIAL, CLAREMORE, OKLA., COURTESY SHERMAN GRINBERG FILM LIBRARIES, INC.
WILL ROGERS MEMORIAL, CLAREMORE, OKLA., COURTESY JOHN E. ALLEN, INC.

At the entrance to the Will Rogers Memorial in Claremore stands an equestrian statue of Oklahoma's beloved native son. Below is the tomb in the garden, where Will, Betty, and their infant son are buried; and at right is Jo Davidson's bronze statue of Will, a duplicate of which is in the Capitol in Washington.

ALL: WILL ROGERS MEMORIAL, CLAREMORE, OKLA.

"There's no other country with as much air, and not knowing where it's going as this country."   "Now if there is one thing that we do worse than any other nation, it is try and manage somebody else's affairs."   "Nobody wants to be called common people, especially common people."

"Americans are getting like a Ford car. They all have the same parts, the same upholstering and make exactly the same noises."   "I am no fisherman, and hope I never get lazy enough to take it up."   "Lord, the money we do spend on Government and it's not one bit better than the government we got for one third the money twenty years ago."   "Liberty dont work as good in practice as it does in speeches."   "Party politics is the most narrow minded occupation in the World. . . . All you would have to do to make some men Atheists is just to tell them the Lord belonged to the opposition Political Party."   "The Income Tax has made more Liars out of the American people than

Golf has." "Every time we have an election, we get in worse men and the country keeps right on going. Times have proven only one thing and that is you cant ruin this country ever, with politics." "Most all new Senators are earnest and mean well. Then the air of Washington gets into their bones and they are just as bad as the rest." "There's one thing no nation can ever accuse us of and that's Secret diplomacy. Our foreign dealings are an open book . . . generally a check book." "The higher up our officials get, the less they seem to know about human nature or how to deal square with nations the same as they would with individuals." "It's not what you pay a man but what he costs you that counts." "I'll bet you the time ain't far off when a woman won't know any more than a man." "There is nothing as stupid as an educated man if you get him off the thing he was educated in." "Everybody is ignorant, only on different subjects."

Index

NOTE: References to illustrations and marginal quotations are in *italics*.

A

Ruth, Babe, 194, 339

S